Get the ebook FREE!

To get a free PDF copy of this book (sold separately for $51.99) purchase the print book and register it at the Manning website following the instructions inside this insert.

That's it!

Thanks from Manning!

CW385322

SQL Server
DMVs in Action

BETTER QUERIES WITH
DYNAMIC MANAGEMENT VIEWS

IAN W. STIRK

MANNING

Shelter Island

For online information and ordering of this and other Manning books, please visit
www.manning.com. The publisher offers discounts on this book when ordered in quantity.
For more information, please contact

>Special Sales Department
>Manning Publications Co.
>20 Baldwin Road
>PO Box 261
>Shelter Island, NY 11964
>Email: orders@manning.com

♾ Recognizing the importance of preserving what has been written, it is Manning's policy to have
the books we publish printed on acid-free paper, and we exert our best efforts to that end.
Recognizing also our responsibility to conserve the resources of our planet, Manning books
are printed on paper that is at least 15 percent recycled and processed without the use of
elemental chlorine.

Manning Publications Co.   Development editor: Katharine Osborne
20 Baldwin Road   Copyeditor: Linda Recktenwald
PO Box 261   Proofreader: Katie Tennant
Shelter Island, NY 11964   Typesetter: Dennis Dalinnik
                                   Cover designer: Marija Tudor

ISBN: 9781935182733
Printed in the United States of America
1 2 3 4 5 6 7 8 9 10 – MAL – 17 16 15 14 13 12 11

To Joan, Karen, and Catherine,
for yesterday, today, and tomorrow

brief contents

contents

preface

When I first discovered DMVs, I was enthralled because they made many difficult things so easy. It was simple to identify, typically within seconds, the core performance problems that affect SQL Server databases. For example, I could quickly discover which queries were taking the longest time to run, which indexes were missing, and why queries were being blocked. This was only the tip of the iceberg; the deeper I dug into DMVs, the more information they provided to help me fix performance problems.

Although I was captivated by the power of DMVs, I was frustrated because there was very little awareness, even among experienced DBAs, of their existence. In response to this I wrote an article for Microsoft's *MSDN* magazine that was published in January 2008, which showed how useful DMVs could be. I then waited, expecting someone to write a book about the subject.

Time passed, and although several articles about DMVs were subsequently published, the book I wanted to read was not forthcoming. So late in 2009 I contacted Manning Publications to discuss the possibility of writing such a book. You're now holding the fruit of that conversation.

I'm confident this book will help you successfully identify and target your performance problems as well as suggest solutions to these problems, giving you better-performing SQL Server databases.

It's heartening to hear comments from people when they first discover the power of DMVs; they too are amazed at how easily DMVs can help identify problems and propose possible solutions to these problems. Like me, they're probably mystified why DMVs aren't more widely used. I hope this book will help correct this situation.

acknowledgements

I'd like to start off by thanking the whole Manning team, in particular Katharine Osborne, Michael Stephens, Marjan Bace, Mary Piergies, Janet Vail, Linda Recktenwald, Katie Tennant, and Dennis Dalinnik. Thank you, Katharine, for your professionalism and steering me in the right direction, and thank you Michael and Marjan for believing the subject of DMVs could make an important contribution to improving SQL performance. I'm indebted to the Manning production team, Mary, Janet, Linda, Katie, and Dennis, for guiding me through the production process and helping make this a better book.

I'd like to express my thanks to Elvira Chierkoet, for checking and reading every sentence and helping ensure my ideas were sensible.

To the technical reviewers, I want to thank you for your feedback and for making this a more accurate book: Tariq Ahmed, Christian Siegers, Nikander Bruggeman, Margriet Bruggeman, Amos Bannister, Richard Siddaway, Sumit Pal, Dave Corun, and Sanchet Dighe, and special thanks to the main technical reviewer, Deepak Vohra.

I want to give a special thank-you to Karen Stirk, Catherine Stirk, and Charlie for their support and encouragement. A special thank-you is owed to my grandparents, Joan and Bill Bridgewater, and the rest of the Bridgewater family (Karen, Timmy, Brenda, Caroline, Kenny, Patty, Jenny, Mary, Jacky, David, and Diane). And thanks also to my old chemistry teacher, Jim Galbraith. Without these people, I would have turned out a lesser person.

I've been lucky enough to know some interesting and helpful people, both as friends and colleagues, and I'd like to thank you all: Tim Noakes, Dave Starkey,

Mark Hadley, Gerald Hemming, Albert Morris, Martin Gunning, Chris Conn, Roy Carter, Mark Woodward, Kevin Bowen, Lee Humphries, Steven Hines, Gus Oliver, Jason Hales, Marina Barbosa, Mark Barrett, Chris Ambrose, John Dillon, Jeremy Braithwaite, Ken Piddlesden, Steve Forrester, Maria Lynch, Ernie French, Chris Cuddy, Sean Farmer, Michael O'Boyle, Ione Farias, Suresh Konduru, Francis Spencer, Iain Roy, Paul Williams, Doug Victor, Paul Weeks, John Cousins, Dale Rainsford, Scott Eggert, Julie Mathews, Pierre Bressollette, Manuel Dambrine, Alexander Godschalk, Lars Grønkjær, Raimond Bakkes, Yan Huang, Chris Homer, Lasse Lundby Franck, Andy van Dongen, Shobha Mittal, Jeroen Ameling, Alek Kudic, Ruud Lemmers, Henk Leppers, Patricia Pena Torres, David Fanning, Mike Diment, Livia Raele, Raj Kissan, Alex Rougge, David Barker, Ron Finch, Tina Simon, John Predgen, Dave Fisher, Phil Fielding, Brian Wright, Maria Iturburu, Jerome Farnon, Harbans Heer, David Randall, Bruce Pitman, Lawrence Moore, Manal Koujan, Mike Bowler, Angela Dedeng, Russell Case, Cornelius van Berkel, Sarah Hamed, and Michael Hipkin.

about this book

This book captures a wealth of experience that can be used along with code snippets to immediately improve the performance of your databases. SQL Server is finding its way into an increasing number of businesses. Although most servers are conspicuous, some appear almost hidden, for example, SharePoint servers and Customer Relationship Management (CRM) servers. In addition, increasing amounts of data are getting stored within SQL Server. Both of these trends have a bearing on the performance of your SQL Server databases and queries. You can use the advice and code snippets given in this book to fight back and reclaim your high-performing SQL Server.

Who should read this book?

If you want to improve the performance of your SQL Server databases and the queries that run on them, you should buy this book.

Anyone who wants to ensure their SQL Server databases are running as efficiently as possible will find this book very useful. The following groups of people in particular will find this book valuable: database administrators (DBAs), developers working with SQL Server, and administrators of SharePoint servers, CRM systems, and similar servers.

When a new version of a software product appears, for example, Microsoft Word or SQL Server, new features are typically added to the existing core. Microsoft Word is still primarily used to enter and store text; this core functionality hasn't changed, despite the numerous version releases. Similarly, although this book is written primarily for SQL Server 2005 and 2008, the core functionality of the DMVs is unlikely to change in future versions (for example, SQL Server 2011), and so it should be applicable to future versions too.

DBAs need to ensure the databases under their command are running as efficiently as possible. Running the code snippets provided in this book will identify any problem areas and help provide solutions to these problems.

Developers need to ensure their applications can retrieve and store data efficiently. Using the supplied code snippets, developers will be able to ensure appropriate indexes are being used, the data is being retrieved efficiently, and any changes are tested for defined improvement.

Increasingly, SharePoint servers, CRM servers, and similar servers that have SQL Server as their underlying database are being installed in organizations with little thought for ongoing maintenance. With time, the performance of these unattended servers can degrade. Applying the code snippets included in this book will identify areas where performance can be improved.

One final point: Often organizations install third-party applications on their SQL Servers. Although it's usually not possible to change the code in these applications, it is possible to run the code snippets in this book against these databases, with a view to either applying any missing indexes (if this is allowed) or providing feedback to the third party to make the required changes.

Roadmap

This book contains 100-plus code snippets to help you investigate your SQL Server databases. In addition to identifying the problem areas, potential solutions are discussed.

The book is divided into two sections. The first section provides an overview of what DMVs are and how they can identify and solve problems easily and quickly. In addition, this section contains details of common patterns that are used throughout the rest of the book. The second section contains scripts and discussions for improving performance relating to indexes, queries, the operating system, the Common Language Runtime (CLR), transactions, space usage, and much more. Using the code snippets and advice given in this section will provide you with a more optimally performing SQL Server.

Chapter 1 provides an overview of the power of DMVs. It shows you what DMVs are and why they're important. Various examples are given to get you investigating your performance problems in seconds. Structures such as indexes and statistics are discussed in the context of DMVs. Finally, DMVs are discussed in the context of other performance tools.

Chapter 2 discusses common patterns that are used throughout the book. Rather than describing these patterns everywhere, they are discussed once in this chapter and referenced in the rest of the book.

Chapter 3 looks at index-based DMVs. Indexes are a great tool for improving the performance of your SQL queries. However, unused or little-used indexes can have a detrimental effect on performance. The code snippets included in this chapter will help you improve your index usage, resulting in improved SQL queries.

Chapter 4 takes a look at DMVs that relate to your queries. Code snippets are provided to identify your slowest-running queries, queries that are blocked the most, queries that use the most CPU, and queries that use the most I/O. All these snippets allow you to investigate performance problems from differing viewpoints.

Chapter 5 is an extension of chapter 4, discussing further aspects of how to improve the performance of your queries.

Chapter 6 relates to operating system DMVs. It discusses why your queries, as a whole, are not able to run, what resources they're waiting for, and how these resources can be improved to give faster queries. Windows performance counters are also examined in relation to these collective queries.

Chapter 7 focuses on the Common Language Runtime DMVs. The use of the CLR within SQL Server is illustrated with a CLR class that provides regular expression functionality for use within your own SQL queries.

Chapter 8 opens with a look at transactions, locking, blocking, and deadlocks. A small case study is provided to illustrate the transaction-based DMV code snippets. Ways of reducing both blocking and deadlocking are explored.

Chapter 9 discusses database-related DMVs. The first section discusses the importance of tempdb and shows how to examine its usage when space problems arise. The second section examines various aspects of index usage that can help you diagnose and improve your queries.

Chapter 10 contains code snippets that can be used to automatically improve the performance of your SQL Server databases. Snippets include intelligently updating statistics, recompiling slow routines, and implementing missing indexes.

Chapter 11 has useful snippets that don't fit into any of the other chapters. The snippets include a generic test harness, estimating the finishing time of jobs, how memory is used by your database, and a simple lightweight DMV trace utility.

Code conventions and downloads

All source code in listings or set off from the text is in a fixed-width font like this to separate it from ordinary text. Code annotations accompany many of the listings, highlighting important concepts. In some cases, numbered bullets link to explanations that follow the listing.

The source code for all of the examples in the book is available from the publisher's website at www.manning.com/SQLServerDMVsinAction.

Author Online

The purchase of *SQL Server DMVs in Action* includes free access to a private forum run by Manning Publications where you can make comments about the book, ask technical questions, and receive help from the author and other users. You can access and subscribe to the forum at www.manning.com/SQLServerDMVsinAction. This page provides information on how to get on the forum once you're registered, what kind of help is available, and the rules of conduct in the forum.

Manning's commitment to our readers is to provide a venue where a meaningful dialogue between individual readers and between readers and the author can take place. It isn't a commitment to any specific amount of participation on the part of the author, whose contributions to the book's forum remain voluntary (and unpaid). We suggest you try asking the author some challenging questions, lest his interest stray!

The Author Online forum and the archives of previous discussions will be accessible from the publisher's website as long as the book is in print.

About the author

I love to investigate and discover new things, play around with ideas, and just spend time in thought. The mind can be a wonderful playground. I'm lucky enough that my inquisitive nature has found a natural home among the problems in the software industry. As Churchill commented, "If you find a job you really love, you'll never work again." With this in mind, the boundary between work and play often dissolves.

As an example of my curiosity, I remember as a child examining a droplet of water on my fingertip and noticing that the droplet magnified the detail of my fingerprints. It made me wonder if an earlier civilization (such as the Romans, who had used glass) had also noticed this, and if they did, why they didn't develop experiments that would have led to the earlier introduction of the study of optics and the advancement of science and civilization.

I've worked in the software industry since 1987, using a variety of platforms and programming languages. I've worked in a variety of business areas, including banking, insurance, health, telecoms, travel, finance, software, and consultancies. Since 1995 I've worked freelance.

My core competencies are primarily Microsoft-based technologies, with an emphasis on software performance, which naturally extends into database performance. I'm also interested in the developing mobile technologies.

In the course of my work I often create software utilities; when possible I author articles on these utilities to share with other developers. I feel it's important to give something back to the industry that provides me with a living.

On a final note, I'm a freelance consultant, and I'm available to help improve the performance of your SQL Servers. You can contact me for availability and cost at ian_stirk@yahoo.com.

About the cover illustration

The figure on the cover of *SQL Server DMVs in Action* is captioned "Habit of Aureng-zeeb" and is taken from the four-volume *Collection of the Dresses of Different Nations* by Thomas Jefferys, published in London between 1757 and 1772. The collection, which includes beautifully hand-colored copperplate engravings of costumes from around the world, has influenced theatrical costume design ever since it was published. Aurengzeb was the name given to the sixth Mughal Emperor of India, whose reign lasted from 1658 until his death in 1707. The name means "ornament of the throne." He was a warrior and conqueror, greatly expanding the reach of his empire during his lifetime. His exploits were the topic of many poems, legends, and dramas.

The diversity of the drawings in the *Collection of the Dresses of Different Nations* speaks vividly of the richness of the costumes presented on the London stage over 200 years ago. The costumes, both historical and contemporaneous, offered a glimpse into the dress customs of people living in different times and in different countries, bringing them to life for London theater audiences.

Dress codes have changed in the last century and the diversity by region, so rich in the past, has faded away. It's now often hard to tell the inhabitant of one continent from another. Perhaps, trying to view it optimistically, we've traded a cultural and visual diversity for a more varied personal life. Or a more varied and interesting intellectual and technical life.

We at Manning celebrate the inventiveness, the initiative, and the fun of the computer business with book covers based on the rich diversity of regional and historical costumes brought back to life by pictures from collections such as this one.

Part 1

Starting the journey

You're lucky. You're about to embark on a rewarding journey with the goal of improving your SQL Server performance problems using DMVs. This part provides an overview of what DMVs are and the range of problems they can solve. You'll be able to use the basic examples provided to immediately begin identifying and fixing your performance problems. Various common patterns that are used repeatedly throughout the book are detailed here. This section provides a solid foundation for the rest of the book.

The Dynamic Management Views gold mine

1

This chapter covers

- What Dynamic Management Views are
- Why they're important
- Ready-to-run practical examples

Welcome to the world of Dynamic Management Views (DMVs). How would you like to fix problems on your SQL Servers with little effort? Or fix problems before they become noticeable by irate users? Would you like to quickly discover the slowest SQL queries on your servers? Or get details of missing indexes that could significantly improve the performance of your queries? All these things and more are easily possible, typically in a matter of seconds, using DMVs.

In a nutshell, DMVs are views on internal SQL Server metadata, and they can be used to significantly improve the performance of your SQL queries, often by an order of magnitude. A more thorough definition of DMVs follows in the next section.

The first part of fixing any problem is knowing what the underlying problem is. DMVs can give you precisely this information. DMVs will pinpoint where many of your problems are, often before they become painfully apparent.

3

DMVs are an integral part of Microsoft's flagship database SQL Server. Although they have existed since SQL Server 2005, their benefits are still relatively unknown, even by experienced software developers and database administrators (DBAs). Hopefully this book will help correct this deficit.

The aim of this book is to present and explain, in short snippets of prepackaged SQL that can be used immediately, DMV queries that will give you a valuable insight into how your SQL Server and the queries running on it can be improved, often dramatically, quickly and easily.

In this chapter you'll learn what DMVs are, the kinds of data they contain, and the types of problems DMVs can solve. I'll outline the major groups the DMVs are divided into and the ones we'll be concentrating on. I'll provide several example code snippets that you'll find immediately useful. DMVs will be discussed briefly in the context of other problem-solving tools and related structures (for example, indexes and statistics).

I'm sure that after reading this chapter you'll be pleasantly surprised when you discover the wealth of information that's available for free within SQL Server that can be accessed via DMVs and the impressive impact using this information can have. The DMV data is already out there waiting to be harvested; in so many ways it's a gold mine!

1.1   *What are Dynamic Management Views?*

As queries run on a SQL Server database, SQL Server automatically records information about the activity that's taking place, internally into structures in memory; you can access this information via DMVs. DMVs are basically SQL views on some pretty important internal memory structures.

Lots of different types of information are recorded that can be used for subsequent analysis, with the aim of improving performance, troubleshooting problems, or gaining a better insight into how SQL Server works.

DMV information is stored on a per–SQL Server instance level. You can, however, provide filtering to extract DMV data at varying levels of granularity, including for a given database, table, or query.

DMV information includes metrics that relate to indexes, query execution, the operating system, Common Language Runtime (CLR), transactions, security, extended events, Resource Governor, Service Broker, replication, query notification, objects, input/output (I/O), full-text search, databases, database mirroring, change data capture (CDC), and much more. In addition, many corollary areas enhance and extend the DMV output. I'll discuss these a little later, in the section titled "DMV companions."

Don't worry if you're not familiar with all these terms; the purpose of this book is to help explain them and present examples of how you can use them to improve the performance and your understanding of your SQL queries and SQL Server itself.

Most sources categorize DMVs in the same manner that Microsoft has adopted, based on their area of functionality. This book takes a similar approach. A brief outline of each of the DMV categories follows in table 1.1.

Table 1.1   The major DMV groups

DMV group	Description
Change data capture	Change data capture relates to how SQL Server captures change activity (inserts, updates, and deletes) across one or more tables, providing centralized processing. It can be thought of as a combination of trigger and auditing processing in a central area. These DMVs contain information relating to various aspects of change data capture, including transactions, logging, and errors. This group of DMVs occurs in SQL Server 2008 and higher.
Common Language Runtime	The Common Language Runtime allows code that runs on the database to be written in one of the .NET languages, offering a richer environment and language and often providing a magnitude increase in performance. These DMVs contain information relating to various aspects of the .NET Common Language Runtime, including application domains (these are wider in scope than a thread and smaller than a session), loaded assemblies, properties, and running tasks.
Database	These DMVs contain information relating to various aspects of databases, including space usage, partition statistics, and session and task space information.
Database mirroring	The aim of database mirroring is to increase database availability. Transaction logs are moved quickly between servers, allowing fast failover to the standby server. These DMVs contain information relating to various aspects of database mirroring, including connection information and page-repair details.
Execution	These DMVs contain information relating to various aspects of query execution, including cached plans, connections, cursors, plan attributes, stored procedure statistics, memory grants, query optimizer information, query statistics, active requests and sessions, SQL text, and trigger statistics.
Extended events	Extended events allow SQL Server to integrate into Microsoft's wider event-handling processes, allowing integration of SQL Server events with logging and monitoring tools. This group of DMVs occurs in SQL Server 2008 and higher.
Full-text search	Full-text search relates to the ability to search character-based data using linguistic searches. This can be thought of as a higher-level wildcard search. These DMVs contain information relating to various aspects of full-text search, including existing full-text catalogs, index populations currently occurring, and memory buffers/pools.
Index	These DMVs contain information relating to various aspects of indexes, including missing indexes, index usage (number of seeks, scans, and lookups, by system or application, and when they last occurred), operational statistics (I/O, locking, latches, and access method), and physical statistics (size and fragmentation information).

Table 1.1   The major DMV groups *(continued)*

DMV group	Description
Input/Output (I/O)	These DMVs contain information relating to various aspects of I/O, including virtual file statistics (by database and file, number of reads/writes, amount of data read/written, and I/O stall time), backup tape devices, and any pending I/O requests.
Object	These DMVs contain information relating to various aspects of dynamic management objects; these relate to object dependencies.
Query notification	These DMVs contain information relating to various aspects of query notification subscriptions in the server.
Replication	These DMVs contain information relating to various aspects of replication, including articles (type and status), transactions, and schemas (table columns).
Resource Governor	In the past, running inappropriate ad hoc queries on the database sometimes caused timeout and blocking problems. SQL Server 2008 implements a resource governor that controls the amount of resources different groups can have, allowing more controlled access to resources. These DMVs contain information relating to various aspects of Resource Governor, including resource pools, governor configuration, and workload groups. This group of DMVs occurs in SQL Server 2008 and higher.
Service Broker	Service Broker is concerned with providing both transactional and disconnected processing, allowing a wider range of architectural solutions to be created. These DMVs contain information relating to various aspects of Service Broker, including activated tasks, forwarded messages, connections, and queue monitors.
SQL Server Operating System	These DMVs contain information relating to various aspects of the SQL Server Operating System (SQLOS), including performance counters, memory pools, schedulers, system information, tasks, threads, wait statistics, waiting tasks, and memory objects.
Transaction	These DMVs contain information relating to various aspects of transactions, including snapshot, database, session, and locks.
Security	These DMVs contain information relating to various aspects of security, including audit actions, cryptographic algorithms supported, open cryptographic sessions, and database encryption state (and keys).

Because this book takes a look at DMVs from a practical, everyday troubleshooting and maintenance perspective, it concentrates on those DMVs that the DBA and database developer will use to help solve their everyday problems. With this in mind, it concentrates on the following categories of DMV:

- Index
- Execution
- SQL Server Operating System

- Common Language Runtime
- Transaction
- Input/Output
- Database

If there's sufficient subsequent interest, perhaps another book could be written about the other DMV groups.

1.1.1 A glimpse into SQL Server's internal data

As an example of what DMV information is captured, consider what happens when you run a query. An immense range of information is recorded, including the following:

- The query's cached plan (this describes at a low level how the query is executed)
- What indexes were used
- What indexes the query would like to use but can't, because they're missing
- How much I/O occurred (both physical and logical)
- How much time was spent executing the query
- How much time was spent waiting on other resources
- What resources the query was waiting on

Being able to retrieve and analyze this information will not only give you a better understanding of how your query works but will also allow you to produce better queries that take advantage of the available resources.

In addition to DMVs, several related functions work in conjunction with DMVs, named *Dynamic Management Functions* (DMFs). In many ways DMFs are similar to standard SQL functions, being called repeatedly with a DMV-supplied parameter. For example, the DMV sys.dm_exec_query_stats records details of the SQL being processed via a variable named sql_handle. If this sql_handle is passed as a parameter to the DMF sys.dm_exec_sql_text, the DMF will return the SQL text of the stored procedure or batch associated with this sql_handle.

All DMVs and DMFs belong to the sys schema, and when you reference them you must supply this schema name. The DMVs start with the signature of sys.dm_*, where the asterisk represents a particular subsystem. For example, to determine what requests are currently executing, run the following:

```
SELECT * FROM sys.dm_exec_requests
```

Note that this query will give you raw details of the various requests that are currently running on your SQL Server; again, don't worry if the output doesn't make much sense at the moment. I'll provide much more useful and understandable queries that use sys.dm_exec_requests later in the book, in the chapter related to execution DMVs (chapter 5).

1.1.2   Aggregated results

The data shown via DMVs is cumulative since the last SQL Server reboot or restart. Often this is useful, because you want to know the sum total effect for each of the queries that have run on the server instance or a given database.

But if you're interested only in the actions of a given run of a query or batch, you can determine the effect of the query by taking a snapshot of the relevant DMV data, run your query, and then take another snapshot of the DMV data. Getting the delta between the two snapshots will provide you with details of the effect of the query that was run. An example of this approach is shown later, in the chapter concerning common patterns, section 2.10, "Calculating DMV changes."

1.1.3   Impact of running DMVs

Typically, when you query the DMVs to extract important diagnostic information, this querying has a minimal effect on the server and its resources. This is because the data is in memory and already calculated; you just need to retrieve it. To further reduce the impact of querying the DMVs, the sample code is typically prefixed with a statement that ignores locks and doesn't acquire any locks.

There are cases where the information isn't initially or readily available in the DMVs. In these cases, the impact of running the query may be significant. Luckily these DMVs are few in number, and I'll highlight them in the relevant section. One such DMV is used when calculating the degree of index fragmentation (sys.dm_db_index_physical_stats).

In summary, compared with other methods of obtaining similar information, for example by using the Database Tuning Advisor or SQL Server Profiler, using DMVs is relatively unobtrusive and has little impact on the system performance.

1.1.4   Part of SQL Server 2005 onward

DMVs and DMFs have been an integral part of SQL Server since version 2005. In SQL Server 2005 there are 89 DMVs (and DMFs), and in SQL Server 2008 there are 136 DMVs. With this in mind, this book will concentrate on versions of SQL Server 2005 and higher. It's possible to discover the range of these DMVs by examining their names, by using the following query:

```
SELECT name, type_desc FROM sys.system_objects WHERE name LIKE
➡ 'dm_%' ORDER BY name
```

In versions of SQL Server prior to 2005, getting the level of detailed information given by DMVs is difficult or impossible. For example, to obtain details of the slowest queries, you'd typically have to run SQL Trace (this is the precursor of SQL Server Profiler) for a given duration and then spend a considerable amount of time analyzing and aggregating the results. This was made more difficult because the parameters for the same queries would often differ. The corresponding work using DMVs can usually be done in seconds.

1.2 The problems DMVs can solve

In the section titled "What are Dynamic Management Views?" I briefly mentioned the different types of data that DMVs record. I can assure you that this range is matched by depth too. DMVs allow you to view a great deal of internal SQL Server information that's a great starting point for determining the cause of a problem and provide potential solutions to fix many problems or give you a much better understanding of SQL Server and your queries.

> **NOTE** DMVs aren't the sole method of targeting the source of a problem or improving subsequent performance, but they can be used with other tools to identify and correct concerns.

The problems DMVs can solve can be grouped into diagnosing, performance tuning, and monitoring. In the following sections I'll discuss each of these in turn.

1.2.1 Diagnosing problems

Diagnosing problems is concerned with identifying the underlying cause of a problem. This is perhaps the most common use of DMVs. It's possible to query the DMVs to diagnose many common problems, including your slowest queries, the most common causes of waiting/blocking, unused indexes, files having the most I/O, and lowest reuse of cached plans. Each of these areas of concern and more could be a starting point to improving the performance of your SQL Server, whether you're a DBA maintaining a mature server environment or a developer working on a new project.

It's possible to view problem diagnosis at various levels, including from a server perspective, a database perspective, or investigating a particular known troublesome query. Applying the correct filtering will allow you to use the DMVs at each of these levels.

Sometimes, identified problems aren't real problems. For example, there may be queries that run slowly but they run at a time when it doesn't cause anyone any concern. So although you could fix them, it would be more appropriate to focus your problem-solving skills on issues that are deemed more important.

No one ever says their queries are running too fast; instead, users typically report how slow their queries seem to be running. Taking the slow-running query as an example of a performance problem, you can use the DMVs to inspect the query's cached plan to determine how the query is accessing its data, how resources are being used (for example, if indexes are being used or table scans), or if the statistics are out of date, as well as to identify any missing indexes and to target the particular statement or access path that's causing the slowness. Later we'll look at interpreting the cached plan with a view to identifying performance bottlenecks.

Knowing the areas of the query that are slow allows you to try other techniques (for example, adding a new index) to see its effect on subsequent performance. Applying these new features leads us into the area of performance tuning. We'll investigate a great many ways of identifying problems in the rest of the book.

One final point: sometimes if a query is too complicated and contains lots of functionality, you should try breaking it down into smaller steps. Not only might this highlight the problem area with finer granularity, but it might also solve it! Maybe the optimizer has more choices available to it with simpler queries and generates a better plan. You can see if this is the case by examining the relevant execution DMVs, as will become clear in chapter 5.

1.2.2   *Performance tuning*

Performance tuning is concerned with applying suggested remedies to problems identified by problem diagnosis with a view to improving performance. Examination of the information shown by the DMVs should highlight areas where improvement can be made, for example, applying a missing index, removing contention/blocking, determining the degree of fragmentation, and so on. Again, the query's cached plan is a primary source of ideas for improvement.

Measurement of any improvement is typically reflected in time or I/O counts and can be made with traditional tools such as turning on STATISTICS IO or STATISTICS TIME SQL commands or using a simple stopwatch. But for more comprehensive results, you can look at the time recording provided by the DMVs. This includes, for each individual SQL statement, time spent on the CPU (worker_time) and total time (elapsed_time). A large difference between these two times indicates a high degree of waiting/blocking may be occurring. Similarly, DMVs also record the amount of I/O (reads/writes at both the physical and logical level) that can be used to measure the effectiveness of a query, because less I/O typically reflects a faster query.

Again, you can examine the cached plan after the improvements have been made to determine if a more optimal access method has been chosen. Performance tuning is an iterative process. This new cached plan and DMV metrics could be used for further improvements, but again you need to ask if any remaining problem is worth solving, because you should always aim to fix what is deemed to be the most important problems first.

You need to be careful of the impact performance-based changes can have on the maintainability of systems; often these two needs are diametrically opposed because complexity is often increased. Rather than guess where optimization is needed, you should undertake appropriate testing first to determine where it's needed. As the renowned computer scientist Donald Knuth said, "We should forget about small efficiencies, say about 97% of the time: premature optimization is the root of all evil."[1] I'll discuss this in more detail in chapter 5.

1.2.3   *Monitoring*

A large group of DMVs (those starting with sys.dm_exec_) relates to what's currently executing on the server. By repeatedly querying the relevant DMVs, you get a view of

---

[1]   Donald Knuth, "Structured Programming with go to Statements," *ACM Journal Computing Surveys* 6, no. 4 (December 1974): 268.

the status of the server instance and also its history. Often this transient information is lost, but it's possible to store it for later analysis (for example, into temporary or semi-permanent tables). An example of this is given in chapter 11, section 11.7, titled "Who's doing what and when?"

Sometimes you have problems with the overnight batch process, reported as a timeout or slow-running queries, and it would be nice to know what SQL is running during the time of this problem, giving you a starting point for further analysis.

Although you might know what stored procedure is currently running on your server (from your overnight batch scheduler or sp_who2), do you know what specific lines of SQL are executing? How are the SQL queries interacting? Is blocking occurring? You can get this information by using DMVs combined with a simple monitoring script. I've used such a script often to examine problems that occur during an overnight batch run.

> **NOTE** This example uses routines I've created and fully documented in the web links given in the following code sample (so you see, not only is code reuse good but article reuse too). Rather than talk in detail about the contents of these two utilities, I'll talk about them as black boxes (if you do want to find out more about them, look here for the routine named dba_Block-Tracer: mng.bz/V5E3; and look here for the routine named dba_WhatSQLIs-Executing: mng.bz/uVs3). The code for both of these stored procedures is also available on the webpage for this book on the Manning website. This way you'll be able to adapt this simple monitor pattern and possibly replace the two utilities with your own favorite utilities. Later in this chapter I'll go through the code that forms the basis of one of the stored procedures (dba_WhatSQLIsExecuting).

The following listing shows the code for a simple monitor.

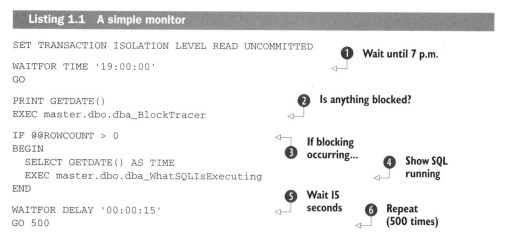

Listing 1.1   A simple monitor

```
SET TRANSACTION ISOLATION LEVEL READ UNCOMMITTED
                                                    ❶ Wait until 7 p.m.
WAITFOR TIME '19:00:00'
GO

PRINT GETDATE()                                     ❷ Is anything blocked?
EXEC master.dbo.dba_BlockTracer

IF @@ROWCOUNT > 0                                   ❸ If blocking
BEGIN                                                  occurring...
  SELECT GETDATE() AS TIME                                        ❹ Show SQL
  EXEC master.dbo.dba_WhatSQLIsExecuting                            running
END
                                                    ❺ Wait 15
WAITFOR DELAY '00:00:15'                                seconds    ❻ Repeat
GO 500                                                               (500 times)
```

This code snippet waits until a specified time (7 p.m. in this example ❶) and then prints the date/time and runs a routine named dbo.dba_BlockTracer ❷. If anything is blocked, dbo.dba_BlockTracer displays information about both the blockers and the blocked items. Additionally, if anything is blocked (and output produced) the variable @@ROWCOUNT will have a nonzero value ❸. This causes it to output the date and time and list all the SQL that's running ❹ (including the batch/stored procedure and the individual SQL statement within it that's running). The utility then waits a specified time (15 seconds in this example ❺) and repeats. All this is repeated (except waiting until 7 p.m.) a number of times, as specified by the last GO statement (500 in this example ❻).

The routines show not only what's being blocked but also details of what SQL is running when any blocking occurs. When a SQL query runs, SQL Server assigns it a unique identifier, named the *session id* or the *SQL Server process id* (spid). You'll notice that the output in the various grids contain spids that can be used to link the output from the two utilities together. An example of the type of output for this query is given in figure 1.1.

The first two grids show the root-blocking spid (this is the cause of the blocking) and the blocked spid. This is followed by a grid showing the date and time the blocking occurred. Finally, details of everything that's currently running are shown; these include the individual line of SQL that's running together with the parent query (stored procedure or batch).

A special mention should be made about the humble GO command. The GO command will execute the batch of SQL statements that occurs after the last GO statements. If GO is followed by a number, then it will execute that number of times. This is useful in many circumstances; for example, after an INSERT statement if you put GO 50, the insert will occur 50 times.

This GO *number* pattern can be extended to provide a simple concurrency/blocking/deadlock test harness. If you enter a similar batch of SQL statements into two or more distinct windows within SQL Server Management Studio (SSMS), and the statements are followed with a GO 5000 and the SQL in all windows run at the same time, you can discover the effect of repeatedly running the SQL at the same time.

Figure 1.1 Output showing if anything is blocked and what individual SQL queries are running

It's possible to determine what's running irrespective of any blocking by using an even simpler monitoring query, given in the following snippet:

```
SET TRANSACTION ISOLATION LEVEL READ UNCOMMITTED

WAITFOR TIME '19:00:00'
GO

SELECT GETDATE() AS TIME
EXEC master.dbo.dba_WhatSQLIsExecuting

WAITFOR DELAY '00:00:15'
GO 500
```

❶ **Wait until 7 p.m.**

❷ **Show running SQL**

❸ **Wait 15 seconds**

❹ **Repeat (500 times)**

The query waits for a given time (7 p.m. ❶) and then displays the date and time together with details of what SQL queries are running ❷. It then waits for a specified period (15 seconds ❸) and repeats ❹ (but doesn't wait until 7 p.m. again!).

Queries often compete for resources, for example, exclusive access to a given set of rows in a table. This competition causes related queries to wait until the resource is free. This waiting affects performance. You can query the DMVs to determine what queries are waiting (being blocked) the most and aim to improve them. We'll identify the most-blocked queries later, in chapter 4, section 4.5, "Queries that spend a long time being blocked."

You can use the simple monitor utility discussed previously to determine why these identified queries are being blocked; the DMVs will tell you what is blocked, but they don't identify what's blocking them. The monitoring utility can do this. The monitor utility can be a powerful tool in identifying why and how the most-blocked queries are being blocked.

Having looked at what kind of problems DMVs can help solve, let's now dive into some simple but useful DMV example code that can be helpful in solving real-life production problems.

1.3 DMV examples

The purpose of this section is to illustrate how easy it is to retrieve some valuable information from SQL Server by querying the DMVs.

Don't worry if you don't understand all the details given in these queries immediately. I won't explain in detail here how the query performs its magic; after all, this is meant to be a sample of what DMVs are capable of. I will, however, explain these queries fully later in the book.

> **NOTE** All the examples are prefixed with a statement concerning isolation level. This determines how the subsequent SQL statements in the batch interact with other running SQL statements. The statement sets the isolation level to read uncommitted. This ensures you can read data without waiting for locks to be released or acquiring locks yourself, resulting in the query running more quickly with minimal impact on other running SQL queries. The statement used is
>
> ```
> SET TRANSACTION ISOLATION LEVEL READ UNCOMMITTED
> ```

It's often the case that you have several different databases running on the same server. A consequence of this is that no matter how optimal your individual database may be, another database on the server, running suboptimally, may affect the server's resources, and this may impact the performance of your database. Because of this, we offer scripts that inspect the DMVs across all the databases on the server. It's possible to target the queries to a specific database on the server instance by supplying a relevant WHERE clause (many other filters can be applied).

Bear in mind the purpose of these samples is to illustrate quickly how much useful information is freely and easily available within the DMVs. Richer versions of these routines will be provided later in the book.

1.3.1　*Find your slowest queries*

Does anyone ever complain, "My queries are running too fast!"? Almost without exception, the opposite is the case, because queries are often reported as running too slowly. If you run the SQL query given in the following listing, you'll identify the 20 slowest queries on your server.

> **Listing 1.2　Find your slowest queries**

```
SET TRANSACTION ISOLATION LEVEL READ UNCOMMITTED

SELECT TOP 20                                                      ❶ Get query
  CAST(qs.total_elapsed_time / 1000000.0 AS DECIMAL(28, 2))          duration
                            AS [Total Elapsed Duration (s)]
  , qs.execution_count
  , SUBSTRING (qt.text,(qs.statement_start_offset/2) + 1,          ❷ Extract SQL
    ((CASE WHEN qs.statement_end_offset = -1                         statement
    THEN LEN(CONVERT(NVARCHAR(MAX), qt.text)) * 2
    ELSE
      qs.statement_end_offset
    END - qs.statement_start_offset)/2) + 1) AS [Individual Query]
  , qt.text AS [Parent Query]
  , DB_NAME(qt.dbid) AS DatabaseName
  , qp.query_plan
FROM sys.dm_exec_query_stats qs
CROSS APPLY sys.dm_exec_sql_text(qs.sql_handle) qt
CROSS APPLY sys.dm_exec_query_plan(qs.plan_handle) qp             ❸ Sort by slowest
ORDER BY total_elapsed_time DESC                                    queries
```

The DMV sys.dm_exec_query_stats contains details of various metrics that relate to an individual SQL statement (within a batch). These metrics include query duration ❶ (total_elapsed_time) and the number of times the query has executed (execution_count). Additionally, it records details of the offsets of the individual query within the parent query. To get details of the parent query and the individual query ❷, the offset parameters are passed to the DMF sys.dm_exec_sql_text. The CROSS APPLY statement can be thought of as a join to a table function that in this case takes a parameter. Here, the first CROSS APPLY takes a parameter (sql_handle) and retrieves the text of the query. The second CROSS APPLY takes another parameter (plan_handle) and retrieves

	Total Elapsed Duration (s)	execution_count	Individual Query	Parent Query	DatabaseName	query_plan
1	1938.76	1	SELECT req.[RequestD...	SELECT req.[Request...	NULL	<ShowPlan>
2	1401.30	2	SELECT req.[RequestD...	SELECT req.[Request...	NULL	<ShowPlan>
3	1380.77	1	SELECT req.[RequestD...	SELECT req.[Request...	NULL	<ShowPlan>
4	710.39	2	update #AllPNL set /*D...	CREATE PROCEDUR...	PARISBAU	<ShowPlan>
5	698.82	1	select @COB as 'COB...	CREATE PROCEDUR...	PARISBAU	<ShowPlan>
6	629.58	1	INSERT INTO dbo.bgpt...	INSERT INTO dbo.bgp...	NULL	<ShowPlan>
7	620.99	2	SELECT req.[RequestD...	SELECT req.[Request...	NULL	<ShowPlan>
8	522.10	1	SELECT req.[RequestD...	SELECT req.[Request...	NULL	<ShowPlan>
9	411.12	1	SELECT req.[RequestD...	SELECT req.[Request...	NULL	<ShowPlan>
10	397.86	1	SELECT req.[RequestD...	SELECT req.[Request...	NULL	<ShowPlan>

Figure 1.2   Identify the slowest SQL queries on your server, sorted by duration.

the cached plan associated with the query The cached plan is a primary resource for discovering why the query is running slowly, and often it will give an insight into how the query can be improved. The query's cached plan is output as XML. The results are sorted by the total_elapsed_time ❸. To limit the amount of output, only the slowest 20 queries are reported. Running the slowest-queries query on my server gives the results shown in figure 1.2.

The results show the cumulative impact of individual queries, within a batch or stored procedure. Knowing the slowest queries will allow you to make targeted improvements, confident in the knowledge that any improvement to these queries will have the biggest impact on performance improvement.

It's possible to determine which queries are the slowest over a given time period by creating a snapshot of the relevant DMV data at the start and end of the time period and calculating the delta. An example of this is shown later, in the chapter concerning common patterns, in section 2.10, "Calculating DMV changes."

The NULL values in the DatabaseName column mean the query was run either ad hoc or using prepared SQL (that is, not as a stored procedure). This in itself can be interesting because it indicates areas where stored procedures aren't being reused and possible areas of security concern. Later, an improved version of this query will get the underlying database name for the ad hoc or prepared SQL queries from another DMV source.

Slow queries can be a result of having incorrect or missing indexes; our next example will show how to discover these missing indexes.

1.3.2   *Find those missing indexes*

Indexes are a primary means of improving SQL performance. But for various reasons, for example, inexperienced developers or changing systems, useful indexes may not always have been created. Running the SQL query given in the next listing will identify the top 20 indexes, ordered by impact (Total Cost), that are missing from your system.

Listing 1.3   Find those missing indexes

```
SET TRANSACTION ISOLATION LEVEL READ UNCOMMITTED

SELECT TOP 20                                            ❶ Calculate cost
  ROUND(s.avg_total_user_cost * s.avg_user_impact *
    (s.user_seeks + s.user_scans),0) AS [Total Cost]
  , s.avg_user_impact
  , d.statement AS TableName
  , d.equality_columns
  , d.inequality_columns
  , d.included_columns
FROM sys.dm_db_missing_index_groups g
INNER JOIN sys.dm_db_missing_index_group_stats s
    ON s.group_handle = g.index_group_handle
INNER JOIN sys.dm_db_missing_index_details d
    ON d.index_handle = g.index_handle          ❷ Sort by cost
ORDER BY [Total Cost] DESC
```

The DMV sys.dm_db_missing_index_group_stats contains metrics for missing indexes, including how it would have been used (seek or scan), if it would have been used by an application or system (for example, DBCC), and various measures of cost saving by using this missing index. The DMV sys.dm_db_missing_index_details contains textual details of the missing index (what database/schema/table it applies to, what columns the index would include). These two DMVs (metrics and names) are linked together via another DMV, sys.dm_db_missing_index_groups, which returns information about missing indexes in a specific missing index group.

You should note how the Total Cost field of the missing index is calculated ❶. Total Cost should reflect the number of times the index would have been accessed (as a seek or scan), together with the impact of the index on its queries. The results are sorted by the calculated Total Cost ❷.

Applying these indexes to your systems may have a significant impact on the performance of your queries.

Running the missing indexes query on my server displays the results shown in figure 1.3.

	Total Cost	avg_user_impact	TableName	EqualityUsage	InequalityUsage	Include Clourns
1	3846455	93.17	[Paris].[dbo].[RiskValue]	[RequestId]	NULL	[PositionGridCellId], [Co...
2	921788	34.19	[ParisDev].[dbo].[PNLValue]	[BaseValue]	[LocalValue]	[PNLValueId], [Position...
3	887350	99.76	[ParisDev].[dbo].[RequestPNL...	[BatchNbr]	NULL	NULL
4	620383	79	[ParisDev].[dbo].[PNLAdjustme...	[Status]	NULL	[PNLAdjustmentQueueI...
5	282331	20.41	[ParisDev].[dbo].[PNLAdjustme...	NULL	[Status]	[PNLAdjustmentQueueI...
6	249135	53.88	[ParisDev].[dbo].[Component]	[ComponentCode]	[BookCode]	[DealId]
7	231713	98.69	[ParisDev].[dbo].[RequestDeal...	[BatchNbr]	NULL	NULL
8	171123	14.43	[Paris].[dbo].[Deal]	[DealTypeId]	NULL	[DealId], [DealCode], [...
9	150870	41.97	[ParisDev].[dbo].[PNLAdjustme...	NULL	[Status]	[PNLAdjustmentQueueI...
10	73727	12.98	[ParisDev].[dbo].[PNLAdjustme...	NULL	[LocalValue], [...	[PNLAdjustmentQueueI...

Figure 1.3   Output from the missing indexes SQL

The results show the most important missing indexes as determined by this particular method of calculating their Total Cost. You can see the database/schema/table that the missing index should be applied to. The other output columns relate to how the columns that would form the missing index would have been used by various queries, such as if the columns have been used in equality or inequality clauses on the SQL WHERE statement. The last column lists any additional columns the missing index would like included at the leaf level for quicker access.

Given the importance of indexes to query performance, I'll discuss many aspects of index usage throughout this book, and especially in chapter 3, "Index DMVs."

1.3.3 *Identify what SQL statements are running now*

Often you may know that a particular batch of SQL (or stored procedure) is running, but do you know how far it has gotten within the batch of SQL? This is particularly troublesome when the query seems to be running slowly or you want to ensure a particular point within the batch has safely passed.

Inspecting the relevant DMVs will allow you to see the individual SQL statements within a batch that are currently executing on your server.

To identify the SQL statements currently running now on your SQL Server, run the query given in listing 1.4. If a stored procedure or batch of SQL is running, the column Parent Query will contain the text of the stored procedure or batch, and the column Individual Query will contain the current SQL statement within the batch that's being executed (this can be used to monitor progress of a batch of SQL). Note that if the batch contains only a single SQL statement, then this value is reported in both the Individual Query and Parent Query columns. Looking at the WHERE clause, you'll see that we ignore any system processes (having a spid of 50 or less), and we also ignore this actual script.

Listing 1.4 Identify what SQL is running now

```
SET TRANSACTION ISOLATION LEVEL READ UNCOMMITTED
SELECT
  er.session_Id AS [Spid]
  , sp.ecid
  , DB_NAME(sp.dbid) AS [Database]
  , sp.nt_username
  , er.status
  , er.wait_type
  , SUBSTRING (qt.text, (er.statement_start_offset/2) + 1,        ❶ Extract SQL
    ((CASE WHEN er.statement_end_offset = -1                         statement
      THEN LEN(CONVERT(NVARCHAR(MAX), qt.text)) * 2
        ELSE er.statement_end_offset
      END - er.statement_start_offset)/2) + 1) AS [Individual Query]
  , qt.text AS [Parent Query]
  , sp.program_name
  , sp.Hostname
  , sp.nt_domain
  , er.start_time
```

```
FROM sys.dm_exec_requests er
INNER JOIN sys.sysprocesses sp ON er.session_id = sp.spid
CROSS APPLY sys.dm_exec_sql_text(er.sql_handle)as qt
WHERE session_Id > 50
AND session_Id NOT IN (@@SPID)
ORDER BY session_Id, ecid
```

❷ Join request to sysprocesses

The DMV sys.dm_exec_requests contains details of each request, the SQL query ❶, executing on SQL Server. This DMV is joined to the catalog view sys.sysprocesses ❷ based on its session id. Catalog views are similar to DMVs but contain static data; I will talk more about them shortly, in the section "DMV companions." The catalog view sys.sysprocesses contains information about the environment from which the request originated and includes such details as user name and the name of the host it's running from. Combining the DMV and catalog view gives you a great deal of useful information about the queries that are currently running.

As discussed previously, in the section "Find your slowest queries," we get the running query's SQL text by passing the request's sql_handle to the DMF sys.dm_exec_sql_text and apply string manipulation to that SQL text to obtain the exact SQL statement that's currently running. Running the "what SQL is running now" query on my server gives the results shown in figure 1.4.

	Spid	ecid	Database	User	Status	Wait	Individual Query	Parent Query	Program	Hostname	nt_domain	start_time
1	55	0	ParisDev		background	WAITFOR	waitfor delay '00:00:01'	– use of alter going f...				2009-11-18 17:48:43.283

Figure 1.4   Output identifies which SQL queries are currently running on the server.

The output shows the spid (process identifier), the ecid (this is similar to a thread within the same spid and is useful for identifying queries running in parallel), the database name, the user running the SQL, the status (whether the SQL is running or waiting), the wait status (why it's waiting), the hostname, the domain name, and the start time (useful for determining how long the batch has been running). I'll explain these columns and their relevance in detail later in the book, in chapter 5, section 5.9, "Current running queries."

You can see the route a SQL query takes in answering a query by examining the query's cached plan; this can provide several clues as to why a query is performing as it is. Next we'll look at how these plans can be found quickly.

1.3.4   *Quickly find a cached plan*

The cached plan (execution plan) is a great tool for determining why something is happening, such as why a query is running slowly or if an index is being used. When a SQL query is run, it's first analyzed to determine what features, for example, indexes, should be used to satisfy the query. Caching this access plan enables other similar queries (with different parameter values) to save time by reusing this plan.

It's possible to obtain the estimated or actual execution plan for a batch of SQL by clicking the relevant icon in SQL Server Management Studio. Typically the estimated plan differs from the actual plan in that the former isn't actually run. The latter will provide details of actual row counts as opposed to estimated row counts (the discrepancy between the two row counts can be useful in determining if the statistics need to be updated).

But there are problems with this approach. It may not be viable to run the query because it may be difficult to obtain (for example, the query takes too long to execute; after all, that's often the reason we're looking at it!).

Luckily, if the query has been executed at least once already, it should exist as a cached plan, so we just need the relevant SQL to retrieve it using the DMVs. If you run the SQL query given in listing 1.5, you can retrieve any existing cached plans that contain the text given by the WHERE statement. In this case, the query will retrieve any cached plans that contain the text 'CREATE PROCEDURE' ❶, of which there should be many. Note that you'll need to enter some text that uniquely identifies your SQL, for example, the stored procedure name, to retrieve the specific cached plans you'd like to see.

Listing 1.5   Quickly find a cached plan

```
SET TRANSACTION ISOLATION LEVEL READ UNCOMMITTED
SELECT TOP 20
    st.text AS [SQL]
    , cp.cacheobjtype
    , cp.objtype
    , COALESCE(DB_NAME(st.dbid),
        DB_NAME(CAST(pa.value AS INT))+'*',
        'Resource') AS [DatabaseName]
    , cp.usecounts AS [Plan usage]
    , qp.query_plan
FROM sys.dm_exec_cached_plans cp                              ← Join cached plan and
CROSS APPLY sys.dm_exec_sql_text(cp.plan_handle) st             SQL text DMVs
CROSS APPLY sys.dm_exec_query_plan(cp.plan_handle) qp
OUTER APPLY sys.dm_exec_plan_attributes(cp.plan_handle) pa
WHERE pa.attribute = 'dbid'                                  ❶ Text to search
AND st.text LIKE '%CREATE PROCEDURE%'                        ← plan for
```

Running the query from listing 1.5 on my server gives the results shown in figure 1.5.

	SQL	cacheobjtype	objtype	DatabaseName	Plan usage	query_plan
1	/*---------------...	Compiled Plan	Proc	Paris	2	<ShowPlanXML xmlns="http://schemas.microsoft.com...
2	CREATE PROCEDURE [List].[PickLis...	Compiled Plan	Proc	Paris	3	<ShowPlanXML xmlns="http://schemas.microsoft.com...
3	/*---------------...	Compiled Plan	Proc	Paris	1	<ShowPlanXML xmlns="http://schemas.microsoft.com...
4	/*---------------...	Compiled Plan	Proc	Paris	1	<ShowPlanXML xmlns="http://schemas.microsoft.com...
5	/*---------------...	Compiled Plan	Proc	Paris	1	<ShowPlanXML xmlns="http://schemas.microsoft.com...
6	CREATE PROCEDURE [PNLAdjustm...	Compiled Plan	Proc	Paris	6	<ShowPlanXML xmlns="http://schemas.microsoft.com...
7	CREATE PROCEDURE [PNLAdjustm...	Compiled Plan	Proc	Paris	1	<ShowPlanXML xmlns="http://schemas.microsoft.com...
8	/*---------------...	Compiled Plan	Proc	Paris	1	<ShowPlanXML xmlns="http://schemas.microsoft.com...
9	/*---------------...	Compiled Plan	Proc	Paris	1	<ShowPlanXML xmlns="http://schemas.microsoft.com...
10	/*---------------...	Compiled Plan	Proc	Paris	1	<ShowPlanXML xmlns="http://schemas.microsoft.com...

Figure 1.5   Output showing searched-for cached plans

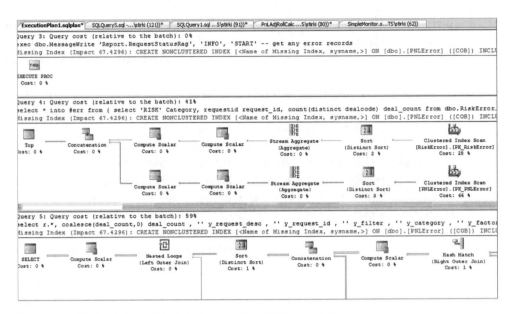

Figure 1.6   Missing indexes details included with a 2008 cached plan

When you identify the relevant query you want the cached plan for (the previous query is quite generic, looking for plans that contain the text 'CREATE PROCEDURE'), clicking the relevant row under the column named query_plan will display the query plan. How it does this differs depending on whether you're using SQL Server version 2005 or 2008. If you're using version 2005, clicking the column will open a new window showing the cached plan in XML format; if you save this XML with an extension of .sqlplan and then open it separately (double-click it in Windows Explorer), it will open showing a full graphical version of the plan in SSMS. If you're using SQL Server 2008, clicking the query_plan column will open the cached plan as a full graphical version; this is shown in figure 1.6.

As a side note, if you're using SQL Server 2008, when you see the graphical version of the cached plan, if there are any missing indexes, they'll be given at the top of each section in green, with text starting "Missing Index" (again see figure 1.6). If you right-click the diagram, you can select Missing Index Details. Clicking this will open a new window with a definition of the missing index ready to add; you just need to add an appropriate index name. An example of this is shown here.

Listing 1.6   Missing index details

```
/*
Missing Index Details from ExecutionPlan1.sqlplan
The Query Processor estimates that implementing the following index could
improve the query cost by 67.4296%.
*/
```

```
/*
USE [YourDatabaseName]
GO
CREATE NONCLUSTERED INDEX [<Name of Missing Index, sysname,>]
ON [dbo].[PNLError] ([COB])
INCLUDE ([RequestId],[DealCode])
GO
*/
```

If I search for the cached plan of a routine that contains a reference to something named SwapsDiaryFile, I can quickly get its cached plan, part of which is shown in figure 1.7.

Looking at figure 1.7, you can see that each statement within a batch or stored procedure has a query cost associated with it (here you'll notice that the first two queries have a 0% cost, followed by another query that has a 100% cost). Once you find the section of code that has a high query cost, you should then inspect the components (shown as icons) that make up that cost. They too are numbered (in our example, Query 3 is divided into three parts, with cost values of 0%, 62%, and 38%. You can

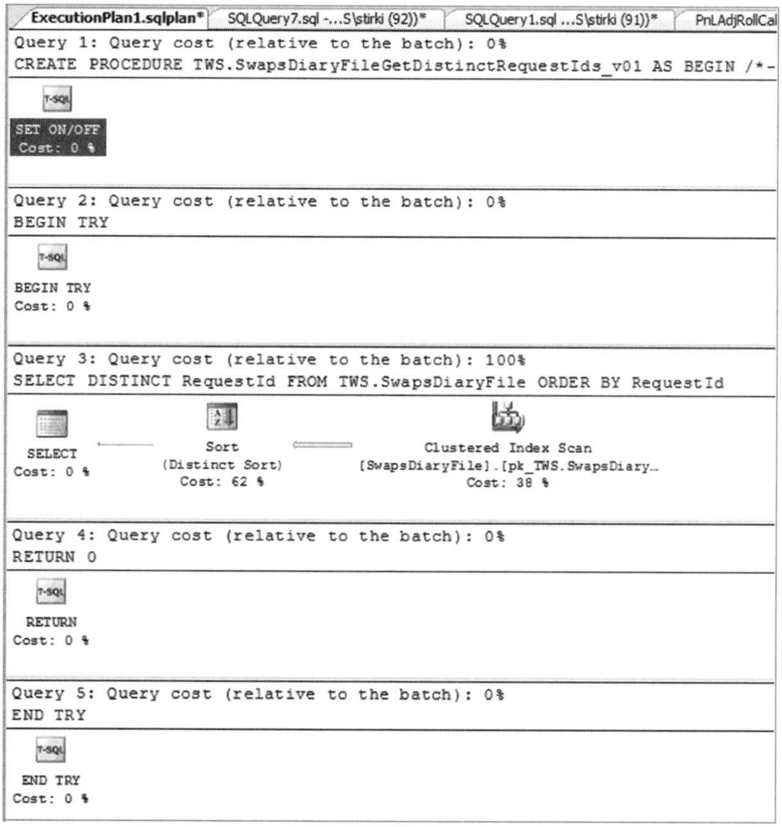

Figure 1.7 Cached plan showing cost by statement and within each statement

thus identify the section within the batch that should be targeted for improvement; in our case it's the operation that cost 62%.

Before DMVs can be used, you need to ensure that the appropriate permissions have been assigned and that you're aware of the accumulative nature of DMVs; we discuss these next.

1.4   Preparing to use DMVs

A great many exciting DMV insights into our SQL queries await us. But before you can dive into using DMVs, you need to ensure that you're aware of certain prerequisites. The first of these relates to permissions to the DMVs/DMFs, and the second relates to circumstances under which you might want to clear the DMVs.

1.4.1   Permissions

There are two levels of DMV and DMF usage, namely, *server-scoped* and *database-scoped*. Server-scoped requires VIEW SERVER STATE permission on the server, and database-scoped requires VIEW DATABASE STATE permission on the database. Granting VIEW SERVER STATE permission infers VIEW DATABASE STATE permission on all the databases on the server.

Note that if a user has been granted VIEW SERVER STATE permission but has been denied VIEW DATABASE STATE permission, the user can see server-level information but not database-level information for the denied database.

Rather than assign these permissions to existing groups or users, it's often preferable to create a specific login (named, for example, DMV_Viewer) and assign appropriate permissions to that login.

If you're undertaking testing, you may want to be able to clear various DMVs; to do this you'll need ALTER SERVER STATE permission on the server. Details of the various methods used to clear the DMVs are given in the following section.

1.4.2   Clearing DMVs

Often when you want to find the effect of a given query or system action, you'll want to clear the relevant DMVs to give you a clean starting point from which to make measurements. Various DMVs can be cleared in different ways.

Before we discuss how the DMVs can be cleared, it's worth noting that another approach exists to allow you to determine the effect of a given query or system action. DMV data is cumulative, so to determine the effect of a query, you can to take a snapshot of the relevant DMVs, run the query under investigation, and then take a second

> **Clearing DMVs**
> Please note that you should clear DMVs on production machines only after careful consideration, because this will result in queries taking longer to run because they need to be compiled again.

snapshot. You can determine the effect of the query by comparing the two snapshots and calculating the differences (delta). Several examples of this approach are given subsequent chapters; for example, see section 6.8 titled "Effect of running SQL queries on the performance counters."

Another possible way of using the DMVs without clearing them is to retrieve SQL query data from a given time period (best if it has run recently), because several DMVs record when the query was last run.

The simplest way to clear the DMVs is to stop and restart the SQL Server service or alternatively reboot the SQL Server box. While this may be the easiest method, it's probably also the most drastic in terms of impact on users, so you should use it with caution.

Alternatively, it's possible to clear some specific DMVs, in particular, those that relate to cached plans and query performance. These DMVs start with a signature of sys.dm_exec_.

To clear the DMVs that relate to cached plans, at the server level use the following command: DBCC FREEPROCCACHE. This clears all the cached plans on all databases on the server. In SQL Server 2008 this command can also be supplied with a parameter to remove a specific cached plan from the pool of cached plans.

The parameter supplied to DBCC FREEPROCCACHE, on SQL Server 2008 and higher, is either a plan_handle, sql_handle, or pool_name. The plan_handle and sql_handle are 64-bit identifiers of a query plan and batch of SQL statements, respectively, that are found in various DMVs. The pool_name is the name of a Resource Governor workload group within a resource pool.

You can also clear the cached plans for a specific database only, using the following commands:

```
DECLARE @DB_ID INT
SET @DB_ID = DB_ID('NameOfDatabaseToClear') -- Change this to your DB
DBCC FLUSHPROCINDB(@DB_ID)
```

When SQL Server is closed down or the SQL Server service is stopped, the DMV data is lost. There are methods of creating a more permanent version of this transient information for later analysis. An example of this is given in section 11.7, "Who is doing what, and when?"

> **NOTE** It should be noted that not all queries are cached; these include DBCC commands and index reorganizations. In addition, queries can be removed from the cache when there are memory pressures.

The power of DMVs can be enhanced considerably if you link to various other database objects including indexes, statistics, and cataloged views. These are discussed next.

1.5 DMV companions

Although this book is primarily concerned with the usage of DMVs, to get the most out of the DMVs it's necessary to know more about some peripheral but related areas, including catalog views, cached plans, indexes, and database statistics. Knowing about these other areas should give you a better understanding of what the DMVs provide and what you can do to improve performance.

1.5.1 Catalog views

DMVs and catalog views together provide a more complete view of your internal SQL Server data, where DMVs contain dynamic data and catalog views contain static data. To take full advantage of the various DMVs, you'll need to join the DMVs with various catalog views to produce more meaningful output. For example, when you're processing DMVs that relate to indexes, you'll often join with the catalog view sys.indexes, which contains information about indexes, such as index type or its uniqueness, created on tables in the current database.

Earlier versions of SQL Server held this internal metadata in system tables; these tables are still present in later versions. But it's not recommended to query these system tables directly, because future internal changes that Microsoft makes may break your code. These system tables have been replaced by the following:

- *Catalog views*—Tables that describe objects, for example, sys.columns
- *Compatibility views*—Backward compatible with older tables, for example, syscolumns

Where possible, you should use catalog views, which like DMVs are part of the sys schema. Catalog views contain both server- and database-level objects and tend to be more user friendly (for example, better-named columns) than the older system tables.

1.5.2 Cached plans

When a query is run, a cached plan for it is created. This details what tables are accessed, what indexes are used, what types of joins are performed, and so on. Storing this information in a cached plan allows subsequent similar queries (where the parameters differ) to reuse this plan, saving time.

When using the DMVs that relate to SQL queries, you'll often look at the query's cached plan to get a greater insight into how the query is fulfilling its requirements (for example, getting or updating data). This will allow you to target many problems and get ideas of any possible improvements.

Examining a query's cached plan can give you a great deal of insight into why a query is running slowly. Maybe the query isn't using an index. Maybe the query is

> **Understanding the cached plan**
> In many ways, a cached plan is analogous to the well-trodden tourist excursion many of us have undertaken when we take a vacation. The experienced tour guide knows the most efficient routes to use to fulfill the expectations of the group of tourists. Similarly, the SQL Server optimizer knows the most efficient routes to access different tables for its SQL queries.

using the wrong index. Maybe the data's statistics are out of date. All this information and more can be gleaned by examining the cached plan.

The output from your sample SQL snippets will often contain the cached plan associated with the SQL; understanding it will give insight into how a query currently works and how you might want to change it to improve its performance, for example, adding a missing index or updating any stale statistics. You'll hear more about reading cached plans later.

Luckily, you can use DMVs to access the cached plans, allowing you to investigate further why the query is having problems and potentially provide solutions. You saw earlier, in the section titled "Quickly find a cached plan," how you can use a cached plan to target the area costing the most in terms of performance.

1.5.3 Indexes

Perhaps the main tool for improving the performance of your queries is the index. Indexes are used for fast retrieval of data (imagine looking for something specific in this book without the index at the back!). Additionally, indexes are also useful for sorting and providing unique constraints.

The DMVs record many index-related details, including how often an index is used, how it's used (as part of a scan, as a lookup, by the application, or by system routines), whether it isn't used at all, any concurrency problems accessing the indexes, and details of any missing indexes.

Knowing about how the different types of indexes are used will give you a greater pool of knowledge from which you can propose solutions. In essence, for retrieving a small number of relatively unique rows you want an index that can quickly identify the subset of rows. These are typically nonclustered indexes. For longer reporting-like queries, you typically want a range of rows that are hopefully physically next to each other (so you can get them with fewer reads). This typically means a clustered index. We'll discuss indexes in more detail in chapter 3.

1.5.4 Statistics

When a query is run, the optimizer inspects the relevant tables, row counts, constraints, indexes, and data statistics to determine a cost-effective way of fulfilling the query. Statistics describe the range and density of the data values for a given column. These are used to help determine the optimal path to the data. This information is used to create a plan that's cached for reuse. In essence, statistics can greatly influence how the underlying data is queried.

When the data in the table changes, the statistics may become stale, and this may result in a less-efficient plan for the available data. To get around this, the statistics are typically updated automatically, and any necessary plans are recompiled and recached.

For tables with more than 500 rows, a 20% change in the underlying data is required before the statistics are automatically updated. For large tables, containing, for example, 10 million rows, 2 million changes would be necessary before the statistics are recalculated automatically. If you were to add 100,000 rows to this table on a daily basis, it would require 20 days before the statistics are updated; until that time you may be working with stale statistics and a suboptimal plan. Because of this, it's often advisable to update the statistics more regularly using a scheduled job. I've experienced many occasions when queries have been running slowly, but they run almost instantaneously when the table's statistics are updated.

In many ways, especially for larger tables on mature systems, I feel statistics are a critical element in the efficiency of database systems. When you run a query, the optimizer looks at the columns you join on, together with the columns involved with your WHERE clause. It looks at the column data's statistics to determine the probabilities involved in retrieving data based on those column values. It then uses these statistical probabilities to determine whether an index should be used and how it should be used (for example, seek, lookup, or scan). As you can see, having up-to-date statistics is important. Later in the book (chapter 3, section 3.10, "Your statistics"), I'll show you a SQL script to determine whether your statistics need to be refreshed.

1.6   Working with DMVs

You can tackle problems from several angles, using a variety of tools. The point to note is some tools are more appropriate than others for given tasks. For example, you could use a screwdriver or a blunt knife to undo a screw; both could probably do the job, but you'll find one is easier than the other. Similarly, if you want to determine which queries are running slowly, you could use SQL Server Profiler, but a quicker, smarter way would be to use DMVs.

This isn't to say that DMVs are better than other tools. The point I want to make is that sometimes, depending on the problem you're trying to investigate, using DMVs may provide a quicker and easier method of investigation. The different tools should be seen as complementary rather than mutually exclusive.

Part of the problem of using DMVs is that they tend to be little known and untried compared with the more established tools. Hopefully the code samples given in this book will help form the basis of an additional approach to problem solving.

1.6.1   In context with other tools

Developers and DBAs who lack knowledge of DMVs typically turn to the traditional problem-solving database tools, including tracing, cached plan inspection, Database Tuning Advisor, and Performance Monitor. These are discussed briefly in comparison with using DMVs.

SQL SERVER PROFILER

SQL Server comes with a SQL Server Profiler utility that allows you to record what SQL is running on your SQL Server boxes. It's possible to record a wide range of information (for example, number of reads/writes or query duration) and filter the range of data you want to record (for example, for a given database or spid).

SQL Server Profiler is a well-known and much-used utility, typically allowing you to target the cause of a problem. But it does use system resources, and because of this running it on production systems is usually not recommended.

There are various reasons for using SQL Server Profiler, including discovering what SQL queries are being run, determining why a query is taking so long to run, and creating a suite of SQL that can be replayed later for regression testing. You've already seen in the DMV examples section how you can discover both what is running and the slowest queries easily and simply by using the DMVs. With this in mind, it may be questionable whether you need to use SQL Server Profiler to capture information that's already caught by the DMVs (remember that you can get the delta between two DMV snapshots to determine the effect of a given batch of SQL queries).

Looking further at using SQL Server Profiler to discover why a batch of SQL is running slowly, you have the additional task of summing the results of the queries, some of which may run quickly but are run often (so their accumulative effect is large). This problem is compounded by the fact that the same SQL may be called many times but with different parameters. Creating a utility to sum these queries can be time consuming. This summation is done automatically with the DMVs.

In chapter 11, section 11.12, I'll present a simple and lightweight DMV alternative to SQL Server Profiler.

DATABASE TUNING ADVISOR

The Database Tuning Advisor (DTA) is a great tool for evaluating your index requirements. It takes a given batch of SQL statements as its input (for example, taken from a SQL Server Profiler trace), and based on this input it determines the optimal set of indexes to fulfill those queries.

The SQL statements used as input into the DTA should be representative of the input you typically process. This should include any special processing, such as month-end or quarterly processing. The DTA can also be used to tune a given query precisely to your processing needs.

The DTA amalgamates the sum total effect of the SQL batch and determines whether the indexes are worthwhile. In essence, it evaluates whether the cost of having a given index for retrieval is better than the drawbacks of having to update the index when data modifications are made.

Where possible, you should correlate the indexes the DTA would like to add or remove with those proposed by the DMVs, for example, missing indexes or unused or high-maintenance indexes. This shows how the different tools can be used to complement each other rather than being mutually exclusive.

PERFORMANCE MONITOR

Performance Monitor is a Windows tool that can be used to measure SQL Server performance via various counters. These counters relate to objects such as processors, memory, cache, and threads. Each object in turn has various counters associated with it to measure such things as usage, delays, and queue lengths. These counters can be useful in determining whether a resource bottleneck exists and where further investigation should be targeted.

In SQL Server 2008 it's possible to merge the Performance Monitor trace into the SQL Server Profiler trace, enabling you to discover what's happening in the wider world of Windows when given queries are run.

These counters measure various components that run on Windows. A subset of them that relates to SQL Server in particular can be accessed via the DMV sys.dm_os_performance_counters; I'll discuss these in chapter 6 ("Operating system DMVs"). If you query this DMV at regular intervals and store the results, you can use this information in diagnosing various hardware and software problems.

CACHED PLAN INSPECTION

We've already discussed how you can get the cached plan for a given query and also its importance in relation to DMVs. Having a cached plan is a great starting point for diagnosing problems, because it can provide more granular details of how the query is executed.

Each SQL statement within a batch is assigned a percentage cost in relation to the whole of the batch. This allows you to quickly target the query that's taking most of the query cost. For each query, the cached plan contains details of how that individual query is executed, for example, what indexes are used and the index access method. Again, a percentage is applied to each component. This allows you to quickly discover the troublesome area within a query that's the bottleneck.

In addition to investigating the area identified as being the mostly costly, you can also check the cached plan for indicators of potential performance problems. These indicators include table scans, missing indexes, columns without statistics, implicit data type conversions, unnecessary sorting, and unnecessary complexity. We'll provide a SQL query later in the book that will allow you to search for these items that may be the cause of poor performance.

DMVs are typically easier to extract results from, when compared with other more traditional methods. But these different methods aren't mutually exclusive, and where possible, you should combine the different methods to give greater support and insight into the problem being investigated.

1.6.2   Self-healing database

Typically we get notified of a problem via an irate user, for example, "My query's taking too long; what's happening?" Although identifying and solving the problem using a reactive approach fixes the immediate difficulty, a better, more stress-free and professional approach would be preemptive, to identify and prevent problems before they become noticeable.

A preemptive approach involves monitoring the state of your databases and automatically fixing any potential problems before they have a noticeable effect. Ultimately, if you can automatically fix enough of these potential problems before they occur, you'll have a self-healing database.

If you adopt a preemptive approach to problems, with a view to fixing potential problems before they become painfully apparent, you can implement a suite of SQL Server jobs that run periodically, which can not only report potential problems but also attempt to fix them. With the spread and growth of SQL Server within the enterprise via tools such as SharePoint and Customer Relationship Management (CRM) systems, as well as various ad hoc developments (that have typically been outside the realms of database developers or DBAs), there should be an increasing need for self-healing databases and a corresponding increase in knowledge of DMVs.

If you take as your goal the premise that you want your queries to run as quickly as possible, then you should be able to identify and fix issues that counteract this aim. Such issues include missing indexes, stale statistics, index fragmentation, and inconsistent data types.

Later in this book I'll provide SQL queries that run as regular SQL Server jobs that will at least attempt to automate the fixing of these issues with a view toward creating a self-healing database. These queries will report on the self-healing changes and, if necessary, implement the self-healing changes. These queries will be provided in chapter 10, "The self-healing database."

1.6.3   *Reporting and transactional databases*

Using DMVs you could present a case for separating out the reporting aspects of the database from the transactional aspects. This is important because they have different uses and they result in different optimal database structures. Having them together often produces conflicts.

A reporting database is one primarily concerned with retrieving data. Some aggregation may have already been done or else is done dynamically as it's required. The emphasis is on reading and processing lots of data, often resulting in a few, but long-running, queries. To optimize for this, we tend to have lots of indexes (and associated statistics), with a high degree of page fullness (so we can access more rows per read). Typically, data doesn't have to appear in the reporting database immediately. Often we're reporting on how yesterday's data compares with previous data, so potentially it can be up to 24 hours late. Additionally, reporting databases have more data (indexes are often very large), resulting in greater storage and longer backups and restores.

By comparison, a transactional database is one where the queries typically retrieve and update a small number of rows and run relatively quickly. To optimize for this, we tend to have few indexes, with a medium degree of page fullness (so we can insert data in the correct place without causing too much fragmentation).

Now that I've outlined the differing needs of both the reporting and transactional databases, I think you can see how their needs compete and interfere with each other's optimal design. If your database has both reporting and transactional requirements, then when you update a row, if there are additional indexes, these too will need to be updated, resulting in a transactional query that takes longer to run, leading to a greater risk of blocking, timeout (in .NET clients, for example), and deadlock.

Additionally, the transactional query, although it would run quickly, might be blocked from running by a long-running reporting query.

You can look at the DMVs to give you information about the split of reporting versus transactional requirements. This data includes the following:

- Number of reads versus the number of writes per database or table
- Number of missing indexes
- Number and duration of long-running queries
- Number and duration of blocked queries
- Space taken (also reflects time for backup/restore)

Usually, the missing indexes need to be treated with caution. Although adding indexes is great for data selection (reporting database), it may be detrimental to updates (transactional database). If the databases are separated, you can easily implement these extra indexes on the reporting database.

With a reporting database, you can create the indexes such that there's no redundant space on the pages, ensuring that you optimize data retrieval per database read. Additionally, you could mark the database (or specific file groups) as read-only, eliminating the need for locking and providing a further increase in performance.

Using this data can help you determine whether separating out at least some of the tables into another database might lead to a better database strategy (for example, tables that require lots of I/O could be placed on different drives, allowing improved concurrent access). There are many ways of separating out the data, including replication and mirroring.

1.7   *Summary*

This chapter's short introduction to Dynamic Management Views has illustrated the range and depth of information that's available quickly, easily, and freely, just for the asking.

You've discovered what DMVs are and the type of problems they can solve. DMVs are primarily used for diagnosing problems and also assist in the proposal of potential solutions to these problems.

Various example SQL snippets have been provided and discussed. These should prove immediately useful in determining your slowest SQL queries, identifying your mostly costly missing indexes, identifying what SQL statements are running on your server now, and retrieving the cached plan for an already executed query. In addition, a useful simple monitor has been provided.

The rest of the book will provide many useful example code snippets, which cover specific categories of DMVs but always with a focus on the developer's/DBA's needs. Because we tend to use similar patterns for many of the SQL snippets, it makes sense to discuss these common patterns first, which I'll do in the next chapter.

Common patterns

The core of this book will supply many ready-to-run code snippets that will give you useful information about the cause of your performance problems, show how to improve your SQL queries, and also give you a better understanding of your SQL Server.

Many of the code snippets in this book have approaches (patterns) that are used over and over again. Rather than explain the patterns repeatedly for each of the code snippets that use them, the purpose of this chapter is to explain these patterns once, in detail. Please feel free to refer back to this section if you're unsure of some of the common code that you'll see repeatedly in the snippets throughout this book.

We'll kick off with a look at how you can reduce any blocking the DMV code snippets might cause or encounter.

2.1   *Reducing blocking*

When SQL queries run concurrently, locks are necessary to ensure the integrity of any changes. For example, a SELECT statement will issue locks that may prevent an UPDATE statement from running, because the latter will want exclusive access to the relevant rows. These locks can result in blocking, which causes queries to run more slowly, and potentially locks can lead to client timeouts or, at its extreme, deadlocks.

To minimize the effect of our code snippets on other running routines, the scripts given in this book will typically start with the following statement:

```
SET TRANSACTION ISOLATION LEVEL READ UNCOMMITTED
```

This statement ensures that no locks are taken by the subsequent statements; in addition, it doesn't honor most existing locks. Both of these aspects will improve the performance of this book's code snippets and other queries that are running on the server.

2.2   *Using CROSS APPLY*

The CROSS APPLY function is used to join many DMVs with their associated DMFs. The APPLY clause lets you join a table with a table value function (TVF). Table value functions are similar to other SQL functions, but instead of returning simple data, they can return tables. This can provide a powerful alternative to using views. They can be used anywhere a view or table can be used.

In essence, CROSS APPLY returns a row, if the right table source returns a row when it accepts a parameter from the left table source. A CROSS APPLY can be viewed as similar to an INNER JOIN. The related OUTER APPLY returns a row from the left table source irrespective of whether the parameter passed to the right table source returns a row; in this respect it acts like an OUTER JOIN.

The following example illustrates how CROSS APPLY is used. The query reports on the first 20 SQL queries on the server, together with when they were last executed. Detailed metrics of each query are recorded in the sys.dm_exec_query_stats DMV; these include the sql_handle used to identify the underlying query text. To obtain this SQL text, the sql_handle is passed as a parameter to the sys.dm_exec_sql_text DMF, and the DMV and DMF are joined via CROSS APPLY.

```
SELECT TOP 20 qt.text, qs.last_execution_time
FROM sys.dm_exec_query_stats qs
CROSS APPLY sys.dm_exec_sql_text(qs.sql_handle) as qt
```

2.3   *Restricting output to a given database*

Some of the DMVs collect data at the server instance level. Luckily, many also record a database identifier that can be translated into a database name. This allows you to target a specific database or indeed to compare the different databases on the server to determine which databases are interesting and worthy of further investigation.

For example, you can get the number of reads and writes that have taken place on a specified database by running the query given in listing 2.1. The number of reads and writes (input/output, or I/O) reflects the number of retrievals and modifications occurring on the server. This is useful for determining the effectiveness of I/O subsystems, indexes, and transactional/reporting contention.

Listing 2.1   Restricting output to a given database

```
SET TRANSACTION ISOLATION LEVEL READ UNCOMMITTED

SELECT SUM(qs.total_logical_reads) AS [Total Reads]
      , SUM(qs.total_logical_writes) AS [Total Writes]
      , DB_NAME(qt.dbid) AS DatabaseName
FROM sys.dm_exec_query_stats qs
CROSS APPLY sys.dm_exec_sql_text(qs.sql_handle) as qt          Specify
WHERE DB_NAME(qt.dbid) = 'ParisDev'                 ◁┘        database here
GROUP BY DB_NAME(qt.dbid)
```

The built-in Transact-SQL (T-SQL) function DB_NAME takes as its input a database identifier and returns the related database name. We use this in our query to restrict the query so it returns only data for the database we're interested in (ParisDev in our example).

As well as restricting output to a given database, you can further restrict output in many scripts by specifying the database schema or even a subset of detailed objects (for example, indexes that belong to a given table).

2.4   *Restricting output by using the TOP command*

Sometimes you're interested in only the extreme examples of problems, because this allows you to target your efforts on areas that you know will have the most significant impact. For example, if you're interested in the longest-running queries, you could get a list of 100 or more of them. But it's probably true that the most expensive 10 or 20 will account for most of the slow performance seen on the server.

T-SQL has the TOP keyword to limit the number of rows output. If you order the query output by the item you're interested in (for example, query duration), and if you then apply a TOP 10 to the query, you'll get the top 10 queries, as defined by the ORDER BY clause.

For example, to find the top 10 longest-running queries, you can run the query given in the following listing. Here the results are ordered by the Total Time column, and the top 10 ❶ are retrieved.

Listing 2.2   Top 10 longest-running queries on server

```
SET TRANSACTION ISOLATION LEVEL READ UNCOMMITTED

SELECT TOP 10                                       ◁┐   Number of rows
  qs.total_elapsed_time AS [Total Time]             ❶   to report on
  , qs.execution_count AS [Execution count]
  , SUBSTRING (qt.text,(qs.statement_start_offset/2) + 1,
    ((CASE WHEN qs.statement_end_offset = -1
      THEN LEN(CONVERT(NVARCHAR(MAX), qt.text)) * 2
        ELSE
```

```
            qs.statement_end_offset
      END - qs.statement_start_offset)/2) + 1) AS [Individual Query]
  , qt.text AS [Parent Query]
  , DB_NAME(qt.dbid) AS DatabaseName
  , qp.query_plan
FROM sys.dm_exec_query_stats qs
CROSS APPLY sys.dm_exec_sql_text(qs.sql_handle) as qt
CROSS APPLY sys.dm_exec_query_plan(qs.plan_handle) qp
ORDER BY [Total Time] DESC;
```

You can hardcode the number of rows you want returned by the TOP expression, but this hardcoded value can be replaced by a variable value. This can be useful in giving you a single point of change, in a batch of SQL scripts, for specifying the number of rows you want returned by the TOP command.

2.5   *Creating an empty temporary table structure*

Often you want to create a temporary table to hold the results of any transient data, especially if you're collecting data from various sources/databases for comparison purposes. The easiest way for you to do this, so that you automatically get the correct column names and data types, is to use a query that joins the relevant tables but has a WHERE condition of $1 = 2$ **❶**. Clearly this condition means no rows will be retrieved; however, the temporary table will be created with all the relevant metadata. An example of this is shown here.

Listing 2.3   Creating a temporary table WHERE 1 = 2

```
SELECT f.FactorId, f.FactorName, pf.PositionId
INTO #Temp01
FROM dbo.Factor f
INNER JOIN dbo.PositionFactor pf ON pf.FactorId = f.FactorId      ❶  This creates
WHERE 1 = 2                                                          empty table
```

The query plan for this query is shown in figure 2.1

Note that this method is fast because the query itself isn't executed. You can see this from the query plan shown in figure 2.1. Instead, the table's metadata is queried to obtain the data types and data names.

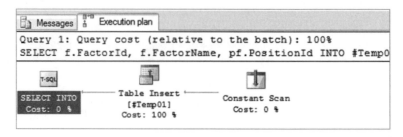

Figure 2.1   Execution plan for WHERE 1 = 2

2.6   *Looping over the databases on a server*

Often servers contain many databases, and the server's resources are shared among these databases. This means that no matter how optimized a given database is, its queries could still perform suboptimally because another database on the server is running poorly and hogging the server's shared resources. These shared resources include CPU, memory, and tempdb. Because of this, where possible, you should consider all the databases on the server when you inspect the DMVs, with a view to improving performance.

DMVs report data at a server or database-level of detail. For example, the DMV sys.dm_os_wait_stats reports at the server level the causes of all the waits on the server irrespective of individual databases. But sometimes you need to obtain data at the database-level of detail, for example, joining DMV data with database-level data contained in the catalog views. This typically provides richer data. For example, you may want to retrieve index information from the catalog view sys.indexes; such information includes index name and type of index.

The data held by the sys.indexes view is held in each database on the server. In order to extract this index data, so you can compare the data across all databases on the server, you need to loop around all the databases on the server. Luckily, Microsoft provides a stored procedure for doing this, the relatively little-documented sp_MSForEachDB.

As an example of its use, you can print out the name of each of the databases on the server using the following command:

```
EXEC sp_MSForEachDB 'PRINT ''?'';'
```

Now back to our specific DMV use. We need to loop around the databases and join to the relevant database-specific sys.indexes catalog view, so we can obtain some useful information about the index, including the index name and type of index. In the following case we'll use the example of finding the most-used indexes to demonstrate the looping-over-the-databases pattern.

> **Looping over the tables in a database**
>
> As an interesting side note, Microsoft also provides another, related stored procedure, which loops over the tables within a given database. For example, to discover the names of each of the tables in a given database, together with the number of rows they contain, you can run the following SQL query:
>
> ```
> EXEC sp_MSForEachTable 'PRINT ''?''; SELECT ''?'' as [TableName],
> COUNT(*) AS [RowCount] FROM ?;'
> ```
>
> This pattern can be used for various maintenance tasks, such as marking the tables for recompilation (this effectively recompiles any stored procedures that use the tables) or updating a table's statistics.

Knowing about the most-commonly used indexes is important, because it suggests they're the primary means of accessing data. Knowing this, you should ensure that everything about these indexes is optimal. For example, make sure the statistics are up to date and have a good sampling percentage and the fill factor is such that you retrieve as much data as possible for every read (taking into account any updates/ inserts that may occur). You should also ensure that the level of index fragmentation is low. Alternatively, a highly used index may indicate that a more optimized index is required but isn't available, so SQL Server is forced to use whatever index is available, resulting in the apparent heavy index usage. Cross-checking this against the missing indexes DMV will help determine if this is true. Don't worry if you're not familiar with all the index terms I've just mentioned; they'll be explained fully in chapter 3, "Index DMVs."

Running the code snippet given in the following listing will loop over each database on the current server and report on the 10 most-used indexes across all the databases.

Listing 2.4   Looping over all databases on a server pattern

```
SET TRANSACTION ISOLATION LEVEL READ UNCOMMITTED
SELECT
    DB_NAME() AS DatabaseName
    , SCHEMA_NAME(o.Schema_ID) AS SchemaName
    , OBJECT_NAME(s.[object_id]) AS TableName
    , i.name AS IndexName
    , (s.user_seeks + s.user_scans + s.user_lookups) AS [Usage]
    , s.user_updates
    , i.fill_factor                                              ❶ Temp table to
INTO #TempUsage                                                    hold results
FROM sys.dm_db_index_usage_stats s
INNER JOIN sys.indexes i ON s.[object_id] = i.[object_id]
    AND s.index_id = i.index_id
INNER JOIN sys.objects o ON i.object_id = O.object_id
WHERE 1=2
                                                                 ❷ Loop around
EXEC sp_MSForEachDB 'USE [?];                                       all databases
INSERT INTO #TempUsage
SELECT TOP 10
    DB_NAME() AS DatabaseName
    , SCHEMA_NAME(o.Schema_ID) AS SchemaName
    , OBJECT_NAME(s.[object_id]) AS TableName
    , i.name AS IndexName
    , (s.user_seeks + s.user_scans + s.user_lookups) AS [Usage]
    , s.user_updates
    , i.fill_factor
FROM   sys.dm_db_index_usage_stats s
INNER JOIN sys.indexes i ON s.[object_id] = i.[object_id]
              AND s.index_id = i.index_id
INNER JOIN sys.objects o ON i.object_id = O.object_id
WHERE s.database_id = DB_ID()
```

```
    AND i.name IS NOT NULL
    AND OBJECTPROPERTY(s.[object_id], ''IsMsShipped'') = 0
ORDER BY [Usage] DESC'
```
❸ **Identify most-used indexes**

```
SELECT TOP 10 * FROM #TempUsage ORDER BY [Usage] DESC

DROP TABLE #TempUsage
```

The code snippet in listing 2.4 first creates a temporary table using the WHERE 1 = 2 pattern described earlier ❶. This creates a data structure with the correct names and data types. Next, we call the stored procedure sp_MSForEachDB ❷, with two parameters. The first parameter specifies the database to use (this is enumerated and is represented by a question mark); the second parameter is the query we want to run on that database. You'll notice that we select the 10 most-used indexes on each database, as defined by their usage ❸, and store their details (name and various counters) into the temporary table. Finally, we select the 10 most-used indexes from the temporary table (remember that this reflects all the databases).

> **NOTE** For the results to make sense, the number of rows associated with the TOP command given with the sp_MSForEachDB command must match the number used for the final retrieval from the temporary table.

Remember, here we're explaining the pattern, not the specifics. The details will be explained later in the appropriate DMV section, for example, in examining the most-costly unused indexes (section 3.3.1).

2.7 Retrieving a query's cached plan and SQL text

When a query executes, a cached plan is created for it. A cached plan describes, at a granular level, how the query will be executed, for example, how indexes will be used. In many of our snippets we'll retrieve the cached plan associated with a query. A cached plan is a great starting point in determining why a query is behaving as it is, for example, why it's running slowly. Often it also offers clues on how performance can be improved.

One of the examples given in chapter 1 showed how to quickly find a cached plan. Although the query was immediately usable, I didn't explain how it performed its magic. I'll do that now. The following listing shows a simplified version of the "Quickly find a cached plan" example given in chapter 1.

Listing 2.5 Quickly find the most-used cached plans—simple version

```
SET TRANSACTION ISOLATION LEVEL READ UNCOMMITTED

SELECT TOP 10
    st.text AS [SQL]                                   ❶ Show SQL query
    , DB_NAME(st.dbid) AS DatabaseName
    , cp.usecounts AS [Plan usage]
    , qp.query_plan                                    ❷ Show cached plan
FROM sys.dm_exec_cached_plans cp
CROSS APPLY sys.dm_exec_sql_text(cp.plan_handle) st    ◁ Join relevant DMVs
```

```
CROSS APPLY sys.dm_exec_query_plan(cp.plan_handle) qp
WHERE st.text LIKE '%CREATE PROCEDURE%'                    ◁──┐  Search for plans
ORDER BY cp.usecounts DESC                                 ❸   with this text
```

Listing 2.5 explains how to extract the text of the SQL query ❶ and cached plans ❷. The DMV sys.dm_exec_cached_plans contains various metrics about the cached plan (for example, the number of times it has executed) but not the cached plan itself. Instead, it contains the identifier of the cached plan, named plan_handle, which can be used to retrieve the cached plan. To retrieve the cached plan, we pass the plan handle, via the CROSS APPLY function, to the DMF sys.dm_exec_query_plan. The cached plan is retrieved as XML and is shown in the output under the column named query_plan. In this example, we search for cached plans that contain the text "CREATE PROCEDURE" ❸.

> **NOTE** We've also included a join to the DMF sys.dm_exec_sql_text, to obtain the text of the query, because we typically want to filter the results to find a specific query. Obtaining the text of a query works in a similar way to obtaining the cached plan. We pass the cached plan's plan_handle, via the CROSS APPLY function, to the DMF sys.dm_exec_sql_text. This is discussed in more detail next.

An example of the type of output for this query is shown in figure 2.2.

Often you'll want to determine information about a given SQL statement within a SQL query. I'll discuss how to achieve this next.

2.8   *Extracting the Individual Query from the Parent Query*

In many cases you'll show details that relate to a given SQL statement (the Individual Query), within a stored procedure or batch (the Parent Query). The details of the specific SQL statement are obtained by applying start and end offsets to the Parent Query. The start and end offsets are given in the DMV sys.dm_exec_query_stats and are applied to the text of the SQL query that's obtained from the DMF sys.dm_exec_sql_text. Running the SQL query in the following listing will retrieve the 20 most-executed individual lines of SQL on the server.

	SQL	DatabaseName	Plan usage	query_plan
1	CREATE procedure [dbo].[...	Paris	34446	<ShowPlanXML xmlns="http://schemas.microsoft.com...
2	CREATE procedure [dbo].[M...	Paris	12644	<ShowPlanXML xmlns="http://schemas.microsoft.com...
3	CREATE PROCEDURE [PN...	Paris	5525	<ShowPlanXML xmlns="http://schemas.microsoft.com...
4	CREATE PROCEDURE [db...	Paris	4476	<ShowPlanXML xmlns="http://schemas.microsoft.com...
5	CREATE PROCEDURE [db...	Paris	4476	<ShowPlanXML xmlns="http://schemas.microsoft.com...

Figure 2.2   Output showing the most-used cached plans that contain the text "CREATE PROCEDURE"

Listing 2.6 Extracting the Individual Query from the Parent Query

```
SET TRANSACTION ISOLATION LEVEL READ UNCOMMITTED

SELECT TOP 20
      qs.execution_count
    , SUBSTRING (qt.text, (qs.statement_start_offset/2) + 1
    , ((CASE WHEN qs.statement_end_offset = -1
        THEN LEN(CONVERT(NVARCHAR(MAX), qt.text)) * 2
          ELSE qs.statement_end_offset
        END - qs.statement_start_offset)/2) + 1) AS [Individual Query]
    , qt.text AS [Parent Query]
    , DB_NAME(qt.dbid) AS DatabaseName
FROM sys.dm_exec_query_stats qs
CROSS APPLY sys.dm_exec_sql_text(qs.sql_handle) as qt
ORDER BY execution_count DESC;
```

The SQL text (qt.text) is stored using the NVARCHAR data type. This uses Unicode storage and takes twice the space of the corresponding International Organization for Standardization (ISO) VARCHAR storage. The offsets are zero-based and are applied to the SQL text as if it were ISO format (hence the need to divide the offset difference by 2). The SUBSTRING function is one-based, hence the need to add 1 to the offset differences.

With these conditions in mind, to extract the Individual Query from the Parent Query we use the SUBSTRING function. This takes three parameters: the first is the text involved (our SQL text), the next is the start offset, and the last is the length (calculated as the difference between the end and start offsets). In this particular case, we set the start of the SQL text to extract as the adjusted offset start, for a length defined as the difference between the adjusted start and the adjusted end, all modified to take into account the change from zero-based offset to one-based offset of the SUBSTRING function.

It's possible to create a SQL function that accepts as parameters the Parent Query text together with the start and end offsets and use these to return the Individual Query. I haven't done this in the scripts given in this book, because I wanted the scripts to be understood as standalone utilities.

2.9 *Identifying the database used by ad hoc queries*

When a stored procedure is run, information about the database it runs on is stored internally and accessed via the DMF sys.dm_exec_sql_text. When ad hoc SQL is run (a SQL query not in a stored procedure), the database it runs against is shown as NULL in the DMF sys.dm_exec_sql_text. This can be problematic when you're trying to investigate all the queries (both stored procedures and ad hoc) that run on a database.

Luckily, you can obtain the database information from another DMF named sys.dm_exec_plan_attributes. This DMF takes as its input parameter the plan_handle identifier from the cached plans DMV sys.dm_exec_cached_plans. The DMV sys.dm_exec_plan_attributes contains many values for the various attributes associated with a database (many relate to connection variables). You can select the one that relates to the database identifier (dbid) using the following condition:

```
WHERE pa.attribute = 'dbid'
```

You can find the top 20 most-used cached plans, for both stored procedures and ad hoc queries, with the database shown, by running the SQL query given in the following listing.

Listing 2.7   Identify the database of ad hoc queries and stored procedures

```
SET TRANSACTION ISOLATION LEVEL READ UNCOMMITTED

SELECT TOP 20
    st.text AS [SQL]
    , cp.cacheobjtype                               ❶ Look in SQL
    , cp.objtype                                       text DMF
    , COALESCE(DB_NAME(st.dbid),                    ❷ Else in
        DB_NAME(CAST(pa.value AS INT))+'*',            attributes DMF
            'Resource') AS [DatabaseName]
    , cp.usecounts AS [Plan usage]                  ❸ Else default to
    , qp.query_plan                                    Resource database
FROM sys.dm_exec_cached_plans cp
CROSS APPLY sys.dm_exec_sql_text(cp.plan_handle) st
CROSS APPLY sys.dm_exec_query_plan(cp.plan_handle) qp
OUTER APPLY sys.dm_exec_plan_attributes(cp.plan_handle) pa
WHERE pa.attribute = 'dbid'
ORDER BY cp.usecounts DESC;
```

The relevant part of the query for obtaining the name of the database uses the built-in T-SQL COALESCE function. This returns the first non-NULL value from a nested list of potential values. In our case, we first try to retrieve the database id value (dbid) using the DMF sys.dm_exec_sql_text ❶. If this is NULL, we try to retrieve it using the DMF sys.dm_exec_plan_attributes ❷. If this also is NULL, it's assumed the query runs from the internal Microsoft database named 'Resource' ❸.

> **NOTE**   In the output, we identify those queries that are ad hoc by appending an asterisk to the database name; alternatively, we could look at the objtype column.

2.10   *Calculating DMV changes*

As was mentioned earlier, there are various ways of determining the effect of queries via the DMVs. Typically, the easiest method is to reset the DMVs before you do your work; then the DMV values will reflect your work. But this isn't always practical, especially on a production server.

Because DMV data is cumulative, you can deduce the effect of your queries by taking a snapshot of the relevant DMV columns, running your queries, and then taking another DMV snapshot. You can determine the effect of your queries by calculating the differences between the two DMV snapshots. In the next example, we'll get the delta between two DMV snapshots when determining the effect of a given stored procedure or batch of SQL (you should replace these with your own routines that you want to test).

You can use this common pattern for whichever aspect of performance is under investigation, like the longest-running or most-executed queries. The example in listing 2.8 determines the effect of running a given stored procedure (dbo.IWSR) and an inline SQL statement (SELECT * FROM dbo.appdate). Here specifically we'll look at elapsed time (the total time taken to run a SQL query).

Listing 2.8 Determine query effect via differential between snapshots

```
SET TRANSACTION ISOLATION LEVEL READ UNCOMMITTED           ❶ Get pre-work
                                                              snapshot
SELECT sql_handle, plan_handle, total_elapsed_time
      , execution_count, statement_start_offset, statement_end_offset
INTO #PreWorkSnapShot
FROM sys.dm_exec_query_stats
                                                           ❷ Run queries
EXEC dbo.IWSR
SELECT * FROM dbo.appdate
                                                           ❸ Get post-work
                                                              snapshot
SELECT sql_handle, plan_handle, total_elapsed_time
      , execution_count, statement_start_offset, statement_end_offset
INTO #PostWorkSnapShot
FROM sys.dm_exec_query_stats
                                                           ❹ Extract
                                                              delta
SELECT
  p2.total_elapsed_time - ISNULL(p1.total_elapsed_time, 0) AS [Duration]
  , SUBSTRING (qt.text,p2.statement_start_offset/2 + 1,
   ((CASE WHEN p2.statement_end_offset = -1
     THEN LEN(CONVERT(NVARCHAR(MAX), qt.text)) * 2
     ELSE p2.statement_end_offset
     END - p2.statement_start_offset)/2) + 1) AS [Individual Query]
  , qt.text AS [Parent Query]
  , DB_NAME(qt.dbid) AS DatabaseName                       ❺ RIGHT
FROM #PreWorkSnapShot p1                                     OUTER JOIN
RIGHT OUTER JOIN
#PostWorkSnapShot p2 ON p2.sql_handle =
        ISNULL(p1.sql_handle, p2.sql_handle)
AND p2.plan_handle = ISNULL(p1.plan_handle, p2.plan_handle)
AND p2.statement_start_offset =
        ISNULL(p1.statement_start_offset, p2.statement_start_offset)
AND p2.statement_end_offset =
        ISNULL(p1.statement_end_offset, p2.statement_end_offset)
CROSS APPLY sys.dm_exec_sql_text(p2.sql_handle) as qt
WHERE p2.execution_count != ISNULL(p1.execution_count, 0)
ORDER BY [Duration] DESC

DROP TABLE #PreWorkSnapShot
DROP TABLE #PostWorkSnapShot
```

The first part of listing 2.8 gets a pre-work snapshot of the relevant data from the DMV sys.dm_exec_query_stats and stores it in a temporary table named #PreWorkSnapShot ❶.

Next, we run the SQL query that we want to determine the effects of ❷. We then take another snapshot of DMV data (same columns as the first snapshot) and store the results in a temporary table named #PostWorkSnapShot ❸. Next, we calculate the differences between the DMV snapshots ❹, and finally we tidy up by dropping the temporary tables.

To calculate the difference between the snapshots, we first need to join them on the columns that uniquely identify the SQL statement in the query. This means the sql_handle, plan_handle, the statement_start_offset, and the statement_end_offset. Note that because the SQL query may not have run previously, we use a RIGHT OUTER JOIN between the pre-work snapshot and the post-work snapshot ❺. Additionally, because the data may not exist in the first snapshot, any calculations (for example, duration of query) will use only the values supplied by the second snapshot. We're interested in only those SQL statements that have executed between the snapshots, so we use a WHERE clause to get those statements that have different execution counts. Lastly, we sort the results by query duration.

The results of running the two embedded queries (EXEC dbo.IWSR and SELECT * FROM dbo.appdate) are given in figure 2.3. There are three output grids. The first grid shows the result of executing the stored procedure dbo.IWSR, the second grid shows the result of executing the inline SQL query SELECT * FROM dbo.appdate, and the last grid shows the DMV delta associated with each query. You'll note that the last grid also includes the pre-work DMV query itself; because this is also a SQL statement, it will be reported on!

The last grid in figure 2.3 shows the duration associated with each of the three queries we ran, ordered by duration. We could display many other indicators of performance, and we'll show these throughout this book. Hopefully, listing 2.8 illustrates how easy it is to calculate the effect of running queries on the relevant DMVs.

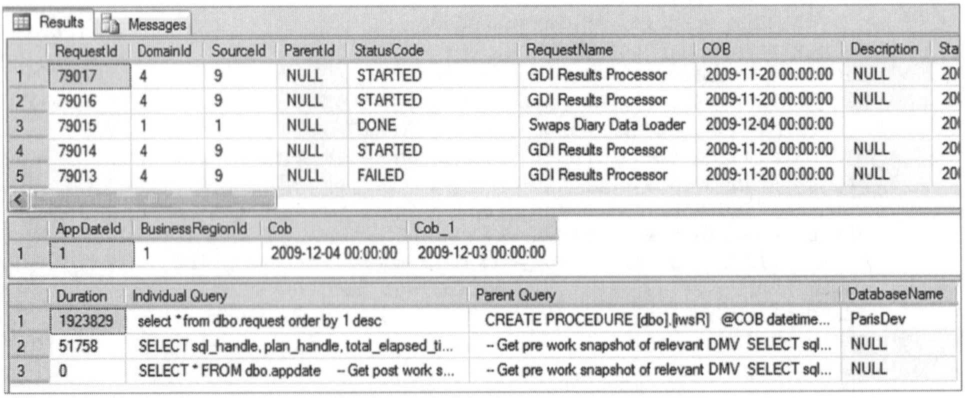
Results | Messages

	RequestId	DomainId	SourceId	ParentId	StatusCode	RequestName	COB	Description	Sta
1	79017	4	9	NULL	STARTED	GDI Results Processor	2009-11-20 00:00:00	NULL	20
2	79016	4	9	NULL	STARTED	GDI Results Processor	2009-11-20 00:00:00	NULL	20
3	79015	1	1	NULL	DONE	Swaps Diary Data Loader	2009-12-04 00:00:00		20
4	79014	4	9	NULL	STARTED	GDI Results Processor	2009-11-20 00:00:00	NULL	20
5	79013	4	9	NULL	FAILED	GDI Results Processor	2009-11-20 00:00:00	NULL	20

	AppDateId	BusinessRegionId	Cob	Cob_1
1	1	1	2009-12-04 00:00:00	2009-12-03 00:00:00

	Duration	Individual Query	Parent Query	DatabaseName
1	1923829	select * from dbo.request order by 1 desc	CREATE PROCEDURE [dbo].[iwsR] @COB datetime...	ParisDev
2	51758	SELECT sql_handle, plan_handle, total_elapsed_ti...	-- Get pre work snapshot of relevant DMV SELECT sql...	NULL
3	0	SELECT * FROM dbo.appdate -- Get post work s...	-- Get pre work snapshot of relevant DMV SELECT sql...	NULL

Figure 2.3 Results of running DMV delta code given in listing 2.8

It's also possible to replace the names of the routines under investigation with a time interval, allowing you to record the impact of all queries running over the period and their impact on the DMVs over that period. This is implemented with the WAITFOR DELAY command. The format of the command is WAITFOR DELAY 'hh:mm:ss', where hh refers to the number of hours to wait, mm is the number of minutes, and ss is the number of seconds. For example, to implement a delay of five minutes, you'd use the following:

```
WAITFOR DELAY '00:05:00'
```

Okay, so we've discussed a pattern you can use to determine the effect of a query. There are, however, some caveats to be aware of. The DMVs in the example have a server-wide scope, so if other queries are running on the server (on any of the databases), information about these will also be recorded. It's possible to get around these problems by running the example at a time when other queries aren't running, or filtering the results to include only your database (if you have exclusive access), or running on your own database where you have more control. That said, you can use this caveat to your advantage, because sometimes you might want to know the sum effect of all the queries running on the server.

When you run a query, a cached plan is produced. Knowing how to read this plan will increase your understanding of a performance problem and potentially offer solutions on improvement. We'll discuss this next.

2.11 Reading cached plans

When a SQL query executes, details of how it obtains its data or performs any modifications are recorded in the cached plan. This ensures that other similar queries can reuse this cached plan and not expend time on determining an appropriate access mechanism.

As described earlier, many of the scripts in this book will show the cached plan as part of the output. The cached plan is a great tool for determining why a query is behaving as it is and often provides clues on how you can improve performance.

2.11.1 Targeting the area of concern

In chapter 1, I provided an overview on what cached plans contain and how they're interpreted. In essence, a batch of SQL queries is represented by the query plan. Each query in the batch is assigned a high-level cost, which together total 100%. In addition, for each query, you can see the individual components that are also given a costing out of 100%. Typically, to find the troublesome area of concern in the cached plan, you first look for the query that has a high cost (relative to the batch), and then you look at the components within that query to discover the component with the high cost. This will often indicate the cause of the underlying problem.

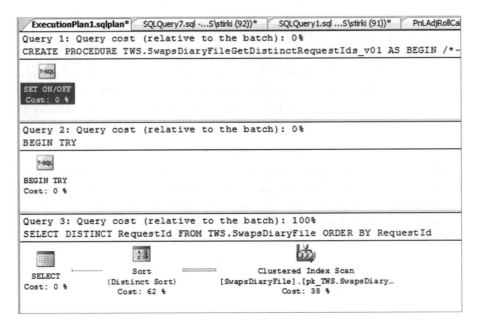

Figure 2.4   Cached plan showing cost by statement and within each statement

In the example given in figure 2.4, you can see that all the cost is associated with the third statement (Query 3), and within this, the Sort component is responsible for the majority of the cost.

The approach described here is ideal when you have the plan of a query that you've identified as being troublesome. Another approach will often prove useful in improving your queries: searching the cached plans directly for conditions that you know may cause problems. I'll provide various scripts to do this in chapter 5, for example, section 5.1, "Queries with missing statistics."

2.11.2   *Things to look out for*

Various conditions are known to impede query performance. I'll describe some of them here briefly, so you'll recognize them in your cached plan. Chapter 5 will provide detailed scripts to identify these conditions.

MISSING INDEXES

Indexes can have a dramatic effect on query performance. When the query optimizer wants to use an index but it isn't present, it records details of the missing index with the cached plan. In the XML version of the cached plan, missing indexes are identified by the XML element name of <MissingIndexes>. In the graphical version of the cached plan, they're represented as shown in figure 2.5 (as green text, immediately below the query text). Note that this graphical representation doesn't occur with SQL Server 2005.

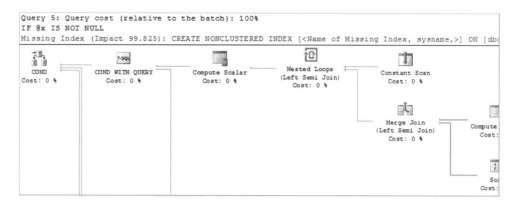

```
Query 5: Query cost (relative to the batch): 100%
IF @x IS NOT NULL
Missing Index (Impact 99.825): CREATE NONCLUSTERED INDEX [<Name of Missing Index, sysname,>] ON [dbo
```

Figure 2.5 Cached plan identifying a missing index

MISSING STATISTICS

Like indexes, statistics can have a dramatic effect on query performance. When the query optimizer wants to use statistics about a column but it isn't present, it records details of the missing column statistics in the cached plan. In the XML version of the cached plan, missing column statistics are identified by the XML element name <ColumnsWithNoStatistics>. In the graphical version of the cached plan, they're represented as a yellow triangle containing an exclamation mark. In figure 2.6 it can be seen immediately above the Table Scan text.

TABLE SCANS

When a query performs a table scan, it's bypassing any indexes that may be present and reading the underlying table, typically in its entirety. Although this may not be a concern for small tables, for larger tables it's worth investigating.

For small tables, even if an appropriate index is present, the optimizer may decide it's cheaper to bypass the index and perform a table scan instead. For larger tables, the table scan may occur because an index is missing or deemed to be inappropriate.

In the XML version of the cached plan, table scans are identified by the XML element name starting with <TableScan. In the graphical version of the cached plan, they're represented as shown in figure 2.7.

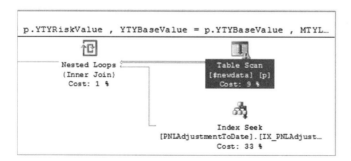

**Figure 2.6
Cached plan identifying a
missing column statistics**

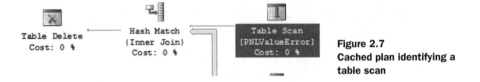

Figure 2.7
Cached plan identifying a table scan

INDEX LOOKUPS

Index lookups (also known as key look-ups) typically occur when a nonclustered index is used to partially access the required data but then needs to access the underlying clustered index to retrieve the rest of the required data. This can be expensive if the operation is performed many times.

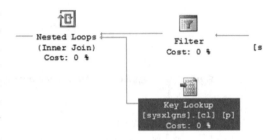

Figure 2.8   Cached plan identifying an index lookup

In the XML version of the cached plan, index lookups are identified by the XML element name starting with <IndexScan Lookup. In the graphical version of the cached plan, they're represented as shown in figure 2.8.

DATA TYPE CONVERSIONS

The data in the database tables is arranged in columns, each with a specified data type. If you query this data with an incorrect data type, the optimizer has to issue a convert data type call; this is often unnecessary and should be removed. In extreme cases, an inappropriate data type can result in an otherwise useful index not being used, causing a derogation in performance. In the XML version of the cached plan, data type conversions are identified in the XML by searching for the name CONVERT_IMPLICIT, as shown in figure 2.9; it doesn't have a corresponding graphical representation.

Later, in chapter 5, I'll provide a script that searches for these factors and more and discusses the consequences of these identified conditions. Such a script is given in section 5.1.

Next we'll look at how to build dynamic SQL queries to process a set of rows without using a cursor; we'll use this heavily in chapter 10 concerning the self-healing database.

```
<ColumnReference Column="Expr1000" />
<ScalarOperator ScalarString="CONVERT_IMPLICIT(int,[ParisQA06].[dbo].[DomainLondonOfficial](),0)">
  <Convert DataType="int" Style="0" Implicit="1">
```

Figure 2.9   Cached plan shown as XML, identifying an implicit data type conversion

2.12 Building dynamic SQL

Sometimes during development it can be difficult to create a set-based solution to a problem. Set-based solutions contain SQL that tells the engine what to do, not how to do it. A non-set-based solution typically involves processing each row individually. This approach is often not the most efficient algorithm. In addition, frequently you'll want to apply a given instruction to a set of data, for example, to obtain the number of rows in each of the tables on the database.

In both of these cases, you could use a cursor to obtain the result, but cursor usage is typically discouraged because it can lead to inefficient scripts. But it's possible to use another approach using dynamic SQL. This approach is used often in chapter 10.

The purpose of the example given here is to show the pattern used to dynamically generate SQL without a cursor. The next listing shows how you can apply instructions—in this case, getting the row count—to a set of data—in this case, the tables in the database.

Listing 2.9   Example of building dynamic SQL

```
SET TRANSACTION ISOLATION LEVEL READ UNCOMMITTED        ❶ Get table
                                                           details
SELECT
TABLE_CATALOG, TABLE_SCHEMA, TABLE_NAME
INTO #TableDetails
FROM INFORMATION_SCHEMA.tables
WHERE TABLE_TYPE = 'BASE TABLE'

DECLARE @DynamicSQL NVARCHAR(MAX)
SET @DynamicSQL = ''                                    ❷ Build up
                                                           dynamic SQL
SELECT
    @DynamicSQL = @DynamicSQL + CHAR(10)
    + ' SELECT COUNT_BIG(*)  as [TableName: '
    + TABLE_CATALOG + '.' + TABLE_SCHEMA + '. ' + TABLE_NAME
    + + '] FROM ' + QUOTENAME(TABLE_CATALOG) + '.'
    + QUOTENAME(TABLE_SCHEMA) + '. ' + QUOTENAME(TABLE_NAME)
FROM  #TableDetails
                                                        ❸ Run the
EXECUTE sp_executesql @DynamicSQL                          dynamic SQL

DROP TABLE #TableDetails
```

The first part of listing 2.9 gets the details of the tables we want to obtain the row count from. This information is stored in a temporary table named #TableDetails ❶. We then declare a dynamic variable of type NVARCHAR(MAX); this data type is needed for us to execute the dynamic SQL. The dynamic SQL is built up by concatenating the current value of the dynamic SQL with details of each row in the temporary table ❷. Finally, the dynamic SQL is executed ❸.

Next we'll look at how to print the content of large variables, which can be invaluable for debugging purposes.

2.13   *Printing the content of large variables*

As explained in the previous section, in chapter 10 the SQL to execute is built up dynamically. Sometimes, for example, to understand what's about to be updated, it makes sense to examine the content of this dynamic SQL before the underlying SQL is executed.

By default, the PRINT command will print out the first 4,000 characters of an NVARCHAR variable. This is the type needed to allow you to execute the dynamic SQL via the system routine sp_executesql. Because the content of your variable may be bigger than 4,000 characters, you need an algorithm to print out additional data.

You can extend the example given in the preceding section to provide the dynamic SQL that you can use as input to your print algorithm.

The first part of the next listing is the same as given in the previous section. It differs in that the EXECUTE statement has been commented out, and it's followed by the print algorithm.

Listing 2.10   Example of printing the content of large variables

```
SET TRANSACTION ISOLATION LEVEL READ UNCOMMITTED

SELECT                                                  Get table
TABLE_CATALOG, TABLE_SCHEMA, TABLE_NAME                 details
INTO #TableDetails
FROM INFORMATION_SCHEMA.tables
WHERE TABLE_TYPE = 'BASE TABLE'

DECLARE @DynamicSQL NVARCHAR(MAX)
SET @DynamicSQL = ''

SELECT                                                  Build up
    @DynamicSQL = @DynamicSQL + CHAR(10)                dynamic SQL
    + ' SELECT COUNT_BIG(*)  as [TableName: '
    + TABLE_CATALOG + '.' + TABLE_SCHEMA + '. ' + TABLE_NAME
    + + '] FROM ' + QUOTENAME(TABLE_CATALOG) + '.'
    + QUOTENAME(TABLE_SCHEMA) + '. ' + QUOTENAME(TABLE_NAME)
FROM  #TableDetails

--EXECUTE sp_executesql @DynamicSQL                     Run dynamic SQL
                                                        (commented out)
DECLARE @StartOffset INT
DECLARE @Length INT
SET @StartOffset = 0
SET @Length = 4000                                    ❶ Print
                                                        algorithm
WHILE (@StartOffset < LEN(@DynamicSQL))
BEGIN
    PRINT SUBSTRING(@DynamicSQL, @StartOffset, @Length)
    SET @StartOffset = @StartOffset + @Length
END

PRINT SUBSTRING(@DynamicSQL, @StartOffset, @Length)

DROP TABLE #TableDetails
```

To print the content of the variable @DynamicSQL, we extract its content in blocks of 4,000 characters, via the SUBSTRING command, altering the start position dynamically within the WHILE loop ❶.

Next we'll briefly discuss some of the more common acronyms and terms used throughout this book.

2.14   Common terms and acronyms

Each industry, and subspecialty in industry, develops its own language to describe its work efficiently and effectively. In order for you to get the most out of this book, I've listed some of the more common terms that will be used throughout this book in table 2.1.

Table 2.1   Common terms and their meaning

Term	Description
Ad hoc query	A query that isn't within a stored procedure.
Batch	A collection of one or more SQL statements that are run sequentially, typically separated by a GO statement.
Cached plan	A query plan that is to be reused. Often synonymous with *query plan*.
CLR	Common Language Runtime.
Data type	The type of data a variable can contain, for example, integer or varchar.
DMF	Dynamic Management Function.
DMV	Dynamic Management View.
DMV snapshot delta	Process used to obtain the difference between DMV counter values taken at different times. First a snapshot is made of the relevant DMV counters, a given time interval passes (or a SQL query or batch is run), then another DMV snapshot is taken, and finally the difference between the snapshots is calculated. Useful for determining the effect on the DMVs of a given time interval or query run during that time interval.
Index	Data structure used to provide fast access to the underlying data.
I/O	Input/output.
Lock	Protection mechanism, to prevent inconsistent data.
Query plan	Describes, in detail, how the query will be executed. Often synonymous with *cached plan*.
Script	A collection of one or more SQL queries, stored procedures, or a combination of both.
Server instance	It's possible to install multiple instances of SQL Server on a given Windows server. Each of these server instances has its own tempdb and set of DMVs. In the interest of simplicity, I'll refer to the word *server* in this book, but typically this will relate to the server instance.

Table 2.1 Common terms and their meaning *(continued)*

Term	Description
Snippet	A collection of SQL statements used to perform a piece of functionality. In this book, it's synonymous with *script*.
SSMS	SQL Server Management Studio.
Stored procedure	A collection of SQL statements wrapped in a container. This provides various advantages such as plan reuse, improved maintenance, and improved security.
T-SQL	Transact-SQL; this is Microsoft's flavor of SQL.

I needed to make a trade-off with the code snippets and their commentary. Many of the code snippets within each chapter are related, and this means there's a certain degree of repetition and overlap in both the code snippets and their related discussions. Rather than edit out this repetition, I've left it in, to allow each code snippet to be more self-contained. Hopefully, you'll appreciate this when you come to revisit the specific code examples in the future.

2.15 Known problems that may affect the scripts

During testing a few minor problems with the scripts were reported; these follow. Rather than amend the scripts to cater for these relatively rare and unusual conditions, a description of the problem together with any solution is given.

2.15.1 SQL Server compatibility level set to below 2005

The DMVs are part of SQL Server 2005 and higher. If you have a database with a compatibility level of 80 or lower (that is, you're simulating SQL Server 2000 and below) on a 2005 or 2008 SQL Server, running some of the scripts may fail.

For queries that loop over all the databases on the server (that is, use sp_MSForEachDB), an error may be reported, but the query still runs correctly on the other databases (that have a compatibility level of 90 and above).

If you run some scripts from within an SSMS window where the database drop-down list contains a database that has a compatibility level below 90 (that is, before SQL Server 2005), the query may fail. The solution in this case is to change the database in the database drop-down list to one that has a compatibility level of 90 or above.

2.15.2 An OFFLINE database

For queries that loop over all the databases on the server (that is, use sp_MSForEachDB), an error may be reported if one of the databases is marked as OFFLINE. The solution is to add an INNER JOIN to the script as follows:

```
INNER JOIN sys.databases d ON d.database_id = DB_ID()
                  AND state_desc = ''ONLINE''
```

This code joins to the sys.databases table on the database defined by the function DB_ID(), which is the current database, and also where the database is online. The code results in offline databases being excluded.

2.16 Summary

The purpose of this chapter was to explain the common patterns of code that will occur repeatedly within the code snippets in subsequent chapters. We discussed the following patterns:

- Using CROSS APPLY
- Restricting output to a given database
- Restricting output by using the TOP command
- Creating an empty temporary table structure
- Looping over the databases on a server
- Retrieving a query's cached plan and SQL text
- Extracting the Individual Query from the Parent Query
- Identifying the database used by ad hoc queries
- Calculating DMV changes
- Reading cached plans

You saw how you can restrict your results to a given database. This is important because often you're concerned only with a given database. We also obtained the database associated with ad hoc queries (because this isn't recorded in the usual DMV). Similarly, we discussed the TOP statement, also used to filter the results, to obtain the most important results. This is important because often a small number of queries are responsible for a large number of performance problems.

We discussed a quick method of creating temporary tables, which is needed when you want to loop over all the databases on the current server, extracting results as you go.

We demonstrated a simple method of extracting the Individual Query from its Parent Query as well as discussed in depth calculating the impact of queries on DMVs by obtaining the delta between two DMV snapshots.

Now that we've reviewed the common patterns that will be used repeatedly in the code snippets, let's move on to our first set of detailed scripts and investigate index-related DMVs.

Part 2

DMV discovery

In this part we'll examine in detail various aspects of performance problems relating to indexes, queries, the operating system, the Common Language Runtime, transactions, space usage, and much more. The code snippets will give you a head start in identifying and solving your performance problems. You'll investigate the concept of the self-healing database and use the provided code snippets to automate many maintenance aspects of your SQL Server. Implementing the code snippets and advice from this part of the book will provide you with a more optimally performing SQL Server.

Index DMVs

This chapter covers

- Background on the importance of indexes
- Code snippets identifying aspects of suboptimal indexes
- Discussions on how to optimize indexes
- Holistic approach to index usage

Indexes are used to improve the performance of data retrieval, to order data, and sometimes to enforce uniqueness. It's the first of these uses, improving data retrieval, that I'll focus on in this chapter. We'll use the DMVs to identify indexes that may be suboptimal or unnecessary, as well as indexes the optimizer would like to use but are missing. All these aspects of index optimality can affect the performance of your SQL queries, sometimes significantly. I'll provide discussions within each code snippet on index optimization.

After we've examined various code snippets relating to index DMVs, I'll summarize the conflicting requirements of indexes with regard to data retrieval and modification and offer a holistic view of how index usage can be balanced. Let's begin by examining why indexes are important.

3.1   *The importance of indexes*

Because tables in production systems may easily contain many millions of rows, reading an entire table's content without using indexes would be impractical. Without an index, the entire table may need to be read to satisfy any queries run against it. Indexes typically enable queries to run quickly and efficiently.

3.1.1   *Types of index*

The data in an index, or indeed a table, is held as rows, and these rows belong to a page. A page (or group of pages) is typically the unit of data transfer when data is read. A brief description of the types of indexes is given in table 3.1.

Table 3.1   Types of indexes

Type of index	Description
Clustered	This index is the table itself with the physical order of the rows defined. It's typically good for range-based queries.
Nonclustered	An index that contains a subset of a table's columns. It's typically good for retrieving a small subset of easily identified rows.
Covered	An index that contains all the data required by a query.
Composite	An index that's composed of more than one column.
Filtered	An index that's based on a WHERE clause. This feature is present only in SQL Server 2008 and higher.

Indexes are data structures that duplicate part of the data already held in the underlying table the index relates to. Although this duplication can be costly for updates, it provides a quick way of accessing the table's data. This is especially true when the index contains all the information the query needs. In this case, the table isn't accessed at all; only the index is accessed. This type of index is called a *covered* index.

A table can have many indexes, but only one contains all the columns and physically orders the table's rows. This is the *clustered* index. The clustered index is typically used for retrieving a range of rows between two values (for example, to retrieve all the invoices between two invoice dates). As such, the clustered index is often determined by the most important queries, which retrieve a range of data. Having the data physically contiguous will improve query performance, especially where you want most of the data on the row, because each retrieved page will have related relevant data. Tables without a clustered index are known as heaps.

Other indexes are called *nonclustered* indexes; these are separate from the underlying table. They typically contain columns that identify a specific subset of rows (for example, you can use them to retrieve invoices that have invoice numbers 240577, 040427, 060168, 240797). Nonclustered indexes contain a pointer back to the underlying clustered index; this can be useful when other data needs to be retrieved from the underlying table (this is shown as an index or key lookup in the cached plan).

Indexes that are made up of multiple columns are called *composite* indexes. Sometimes the optimizer will create such a composite index dynamically, combining data from two or more indexes, if it determines this will result in a faster query.

You can include some additional data columns with the index key columns. This can improve query performance because the information can be retrieved solely from the index, rather than having to visit both the index and the underlying table's data. Such columns are known as included columns.

SQL Server 2008 introduced the concept of *filtered* indexes. These allow you to create an index for a given WHERE clause. This is a powerful feature. In many cases, you're mostly concerned with either the most current data or data that has been added recently. If you create a filtered index on the relevant tables for the most recent data, you can have, in essence, the equivalent of a two-day-old database. Best of all, the statistics for the filtered indexes are more precise, giving a more complete representation of the data and hopefully giving better query performance.

3.1.2 Types of index access

Indexes can be accessed via seeks, scans, and lookups. These are explained briefly in table 3.2.

Table 3.2   Types of index access

Type of index access	Description
Seek	Selectively accesses discreet rows of data in an index
Scan	Accesses a range of index rows
Lookup	Selectively accesses discreet rows of data in index and then gets additional data from the index's underlying table via a lookup

Seeks involve selectively accessing discreet rows of the index. This is ideal for queries that can pinpoint their data relatively easily with a high degree of selectivity.

Index *scans* involve accessing the index at a given point, such as a start date, and reading the index's data until another given point is reached, such as an end date. This access mechanism is ideal for range queries, for example, selecting all the invoices within a given date range. In some cases, identifying index scans in the cached plans might indicate an index is missing; further investigation of the cached plan's SQL query should help determine whether this is the case.

Index *lookups* involve identifying part of the information you want in the index and then accessing the underlying table to obtain the rest of the data. Again, in some cases, identifying lookups in the cached plans might indicate an index is missing one or more columns. Such missing columns could be added to the index as included columns.

Ideally, when you're reviewing your SQL queries in preparation to moving them into a production environment, you should check a query's cached plan to determine if it's using the correct index access mechanism. Alternatively, you can search the available cached plans for index access mechanisms that might be inappropriate and check to see if they're valid for the underlying query. I'll provide such a code snippet to search cached plans in chapter 5, "Further query improvements."

3.1.3 *Factors affecting index performance*

Indexes are central to query performance. It's essential to ensure that the factors that affect the efficiency of an index are optimal. It's important to undertake regular housekeeping to ensure these factors are kept optimal.

Later, in section 3.7, I'll provide a script that identifies which indexes are used and how these indexes are used when a given SQL query or batch of SQL is run. This will allow you to optimize these known indexes for a given SQL query, hopefully resulting in faster queries. Some of the factors you can optimize to improve an index's performance are discussed in the following sections.

FILL FACTOR

Fill factor describes how full an index page is. When you're retrieving data, you want each page to have as much data on it as possible. This will allow you to fulfill a query's needs with minimum reads, less locking, and less CPU usage. Similarly, when you're identifying a group of rows that are to be subsequently updated, you want to be able to obtain as much data as possible per read operation. But when you need to insert data, which needs to be placed in sequence with related data, the index page should contain space for this. When there's no space in the index page, page splitting will occur, resulting in queries taking longer because lookups need to be performed.

Your dilemma is being able to balance the need for this additional space to cater for any inserts/updates with the need to retrieve as many rows as possible with each page read. You can reserve some space on each index page, so that new data can be inserted in the correct order. You do this by specifying the index's fill factor, which is used when the index is created or rebuilt. If the index is largely read-only, the optimal fill factor for it is 100. If the index is modified often, a fill factor of 70 may be more appropriate. These are only rough guidelines; you should test out the appropriate fill factor values on your own systems. The default fill factor value is 0; this is similar to a fill factor of 100, but some space is left in the upper levels of the index for inserted data.

Typically, reads outnumber writes on a database by a factor of at least 5 or 10, even on transaction-intensive systems. Database read performance tends to be inversely proportional to the index fill factor, so a fill factor of 50% means reads are twice as slow as when the fill factor is 100. You must take care not to overstate the role of index updates in determining the index's fill factor.

You can use the following query to see the fill factor of the indexes on the tables in the current database (the database where the query is run):

```
SELECT DB_NAME() AS DatabaseName
      , SCHEMA_NAME(o.Schema_ID) AS SchemaName
      , OBJECT_NAME(s.[object_id]) AS TableName
      , i.name AS IndexName
      , i.fill_factor
FROM   sys.dm_db_index_usage_stats s
INNER JOIN sys.indexes i ON s.[object_id] = i.[object_id]
                     AND s.index_id = i.index_id
INNER JOIN sys.objects o ON i.object_id = O.object_id
WHERE s.database_id = DB_ID()
    AND i.name IS NOT NULL
    AND OBJECTPROPERTY(s.[object_id], 'IsMsShipped') = 0
ORDER BY fill_factor DESC
```

An example of the type of output for this query is given in figure 3.1.

Later in this chapter, in section 3.5.1, I'll provide a more comprehensive script to show the importance of fill factor in greater detail.

STATISTICS

In many ways, statistics are at the heart of the decision-making engine that is SQL Server's optimizer. *Statistics* describe the distribution and density of column values. Unless you have relevant and up-to-date statistics, which are needed to estimate the probability of retrieving a row's column value, a relevant index may not be used or may be accessed incorrectly, resulting in suboptimal query performance.

You can see the summary statistics for a given index by running a version of the following command in SSMS:

```
DBCC SHOW_STATISTICS ([schema.tableName], indexName) WITH STAT_HEADER
```

To find statistics details for an index named IX_Deal_5, on a table named Deal, belonging to the schema dbo, you'd run the following command:

```
DBCC SHOW_STATISTICS ([dbo.deal], IX_Deal_5) WITH STAT_HEADER
```

Sample output for this query is shown in figure 3.2.

	DatabaseName	SchemaName	TableName	IndexName	fill_factor
1	ParisDev	dbo	MessageLog	IX_MessageLog_1	85
2	ParisDev	dbo	MessageLog	IX_MessageLog_2	85
3	ParisDev	dbo	Deal	IX_Deal_StructuredTradeID	80
4	ParisDev	dbo	StructuredTrade	IX_StructuredTrade_StructuredTradeTypeID	80
5	ParisDev	dbo	Component	IX_Component_OrgId	50
6	ParisDev	dbo	Component	IX_Component_InstrumentId	50
7	ParisDev	dbo	Component	IX_Component_BookCode	50
8	ParisDev	dbo	Component	IX_Component_3	50
9	ParisDev	dbo	Component	IX_Component_1	50
10	ParisDev	dbo	Component	IX_Component	50
11	ParisDev	dbo	Component	IX_Component_DealId_ComponendCode	0
12	ParisDev	dbo	Party	PK_Party_1	0

Figure 3.1 Output showing the fill factor of indexes

Figure 3.2   Output showing the summary statistics for the index IX_Deal_5

In the output, of particular relevance are the Updated, Rows, and Rows Sampled columns. Using these columns, you get an idea of how old the statistics are and how much data is present. The Updated column describes when the statistics for the IX_Deal_5 index were last updated. The Rows column describes the number of rows in the table, and the Rows Sampled column describes the number of rows sampled to get statistics. Because the number of rows sampled (585,510) is smaller than the number of rows (11,913,105), the detailed statistics are based on this sample (approximately 5% of the rows were sampled). Later in this chapter, in section 3.10, I'll provide a more comprehensive script to show statistics in greater detail.

Typically, you want indexes on those columns that are used in JOIN and WHERE clauses (the joins often imply that you should implement indexes on foreign keys). When an index is created, statistics about the columns in the index are also created. Statistics are updated when the data in the underlying tables changes. Typically, when a table's data changes by 20% (since the statistics were last updated), its statistics are automatically recalculated. Changes in the statistics also cause any queries that use the underlying table to be recompiled, using the new statistics to produce (hopefully) a better cached plan and a better SQL query.

Sometimes, especially for larger tables, waiting for the table to change by 20% takes too long, resulting in the usage of stale and suboptimal plans. I've known of many queries that could be improved almost immediately by updating the table's statistics. I'll provide a script later in this chapter, in section 3.7, that will identify the indexes used by a given routine or SQL batch. This will allow you to update the statistics of those given indexes before the queries are run, rather than doing a blanket table update. This will allow the statistics update to run faster or have a large sampling percentage that should help improve query performance.

Similarly, in section 3.10, I'll provide a script that will describe the current state of your index statistics. Investigating the percentage of rows changed and the last updated columns should help in determining whether the statistics should be updated more often than the default.

In chapter 10, "The self-healing database," I'll provide a script that automatically updates the index statistics in an intelligent manner. The script updates only the statistics of the indexes whose data has changed and does so using an intelligent sampling algorithm.

FRAGMENTATION

Logical index *fragmentation* describes the percentage of index entries that are out of sequence. This has an impact on indexes that are involved in scans, increasing the amount of work they have to do because the index data isn't contiguous. Where possible, you should remove this type of fragmentation by reorganizing or rebuilding the index. Typically, for indexes that have more than 30% fragmentation, an index rebuild is recommended. If the fragmentation percentage is between 10% and 30%, index reorganization is recommended.

You can use the following query to see the fragmentation percentage of the indexes on a table named currency, within a database named parisdev:

```
SELECT i.name AS IndexName
      , ROUND(s.avg_fragmentation_in_percent,2) AS [Fragmentation %]
FROM sys.dm_db_index_physical_stats(DB_ID('parisdev'),
OBJECT_ID('currency'), NULL, NULL, NULL) s
INNER JOIN sys.indexes i ON s.[object_id] = i.[object_id]
    AND s.index_id = i.index_id
```

Figure 3.3 shows an example of the type of output for this query.

Later in this chapter, in section 3.6, I'll provide a more comprehensive script to show the fragmentation in greater detail. In chapter 10 I'll provide a script that automatically defragments indexes in an intelligent manner. The script defragments only the indexes whose data has fragmented significantly, and it decides between an index rebuild or a reorganization based on the degree of fragmentation.

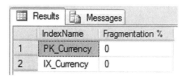

Figure 3.3 Output showing the fragmentation percentage of indexes

I/O SUBSYSTEM

If you know that certain indexes are typically used together, for example, in JOINs or WHERE clauses, it might be prudent to put them on a different physical disk with their own disk controllers. This will allow a higher degree of parallelism and a corresponding performance improvement. It may be worthwhile putting the most-frequently used indexes on their own disks for similar reasons; a script later in this chapter, in section 3.5, will identify these indexes.

This applies to frequently used tables as well as indexes, and where possible, tables that are used together should be placed on different disks.

COMPRESSION (2008)

SQL Server 2008 provides a facility to compress data, including data in indexes. By default, indexes aren't compressed when the underlying table is compressed; they have to be done separately. Compression ratios of 40% or more are common, allowing you to retrieve almost twice as much data per read operation.

If data is compressed, you can retrieve more data per page you read, so the performance of many queries should increase. You do need additional time to uncompress the data. You need to balance the positive aspect of retrieving more data per page with the negative impact of the time taken to uncompress the data. Luckily a GUI tool and associated stored procedures are provided that allow you to estimate the saving compression will provide. You can access the GUI tool from within SSMS by right-clicking a table, selecting Storage, and then selecting Manage Compression. You can use this tool to determine whether index compression is advantageous for your indexes.

Having discussed why indexes are important and factors that affect their importance, let's now look at which indexes could significantly improve the query performance but are missing.

3.2   *Costly missing indexes*

Indexes are typically the most important factor in identifying the relevant data rows quickly. They're used both for data retrieval and to identify data for subsequent modification. As much as an index has a big impact on quickly identifying rows of data, a missing index can have a corresponding detrimental impact on performance.

When SQL Server runs queries, it examines the query and tables/views and determines which indexes it would like to use. If these indexes are present, it typically uses them. But if these indexes aren't present, it makes a note of them with the cached plan in internal data structures that you can view via the DMVs.

> **Example of impact of implementing a missing index**
>
> A missing index can have a huge effect on performance. I've seen an example in a production system where a stored procedure was taking more than four hours to run, but when the missing indexes were applied, it ran in under five minutes.

3.2.1   *Finding the most important missing indexes*

Indexes are a principal means of improving the performance of SQL queries. But for various reasons, for example, changing systems, useful indexes may not always have been created. Running the SQL query given in the following listing will identify the top 20 indexes, ordered by impact (Total Cost), that are missing from your system.

Listing 3.1   Identifying the most important missing indexes

```
SET TRANSACTION ISOLATION LEVEL READ UNCOMMITTED
SELECT TOP 20
    ROUND(s.avg_total_user_cost *
            s.avg_user_impact
                * (s.user_seeks + s.user_scans),0)
                            AS [Total Cost]
    , d.[statement] AS [Table Name]
    , equality_columns
    , inequality_columns
    , included_columns
FROM sys.dm_db_missing_index_groups g
INNER JOIN sys.dm_db_missing_index_group_stats s
    ON s.group_handle = g.index_group_handle
```

❶ Calculate total cost of missing index

```
INNER JOIN sys.dm_db_missing_index_details d
    ON d.index_handle = g.index_handle
ORDER BY [Total Cost] DESC
```

In the listing, you can see that three DMVs are involved in identifying missing indexes; a brief description of each one is given in table 3.3.

Table 3.3 DMVs used to find missing indexes

DMV	Description
sys.dm_db_missing_index_details	Contains details of the database/schema/table the missing index relates to, together with how the index usage has been identified in queries (such as equality/inequality).
sys.dm_db_missing_index_group_stats	Contains details of how often the index would have been used, how it would be used (seek or scan), and a measure of the effectiveness of the index.
sys.dm_db_missing_index_groups	This is a linking DMV, linking the previous two DMVs together.

The joining of these three DMVs provides you with enough information to fully describe the missing indexes across all the databases on the server and assign an importance weighting (called Total Cost) to their usefulness. There are various ways of calculating the importance of an index. In this example, I combine the frequency of index usage (user_seeks and user_scans) with the measures of query improvement (avg_total_user_cost and avg_user_impact) ❶.

SQL Server Books Online defines the column avg_total_user_cost this way: Average cost of the user queries that could be reduced by the index in the group. Similarly, avg_user_impact is defined: Average percentage benefit that user queries could experience if this missing index group was implemented. The value means that the query cost would on average drop by this percentage if this missing index group was implemented. Combining these columns gives us a measure of expected query improvement.

The column user_seeks represents the number of SQL queries that would have used the index to seek data; it's not the number of times the index has been accessed. Similarly, user_scans represents the number of SQL queries that would have used the index to scan for data.

The results are ordered by the calculated total cost column, in descending order, so that the most important indexes are listed first. The T-SQL ROUND function is used to ensure the value of the total cost column is rounded up to remove any decimal places. The TOP command is used to restrict the output to the 20 most important missing indexes.

The column named TableName identifies the database/schema and table the index relates to. The columns equality_columns and inequality_columns contain

	Total Cost	TableName	equality_columns	inequality_columns	included_columns
1	35090665	[Paris].[dbo].[PositionGrid...	[DomainId]	[COB], [SourceId]	[PositionGridCellId], [Positi...
2	22405884	[Paris].[dbo].[Request]	[RequestDefinit...	NULL	[StatusCode], [COB]
3	17681267	[Paris].[dbo].[Deal]	[DealVersion]	[DealCode]	[DealId], [SourceId], [Part...
4	17186169	[Paris].[dbo].[PNLAdjustm...	NULL	[Status]	[PNLAdjustmentQueueId],....
5	9087210	[Paris].[dbo].[Mapping]	[MappingTypeI...	NULL	[FromValue], [ToValue]
6	8026926	[Paris].[dbo].[PNLValue]	NULL	[BaseValue]	[PNLValueId], [PositionGri...
7	6950941	[Paris].[dbo].[PNLAdjustm...	NULL	[Status]	[PNLAdjustmentQueueId],....
8	6906903	[Paris].[dbo].[RequestDeal...	[BatchNbr]	NULL	[RequestDealComponent...
9	6024897	[Paris].[dbo].[PNLAdjustm...	NULL	[Status]	[PNLAdjustmentQueueId],....
10	5988629	[Paris].[dbo].[PositionGrid...	[DomainId]	[SourceId]	[PositionGridCellId], [COB]...
11	5963443	[Paris].[dbo].[PNLAdjustm...	NULL	[BaseValue]	[PNLAdjustmentId], [Positi...
12	5944962	[Paris].[dbo].[RequestPNL...	[BatchNbr]	NULL	NULL

Figure 3.4   Output showing the most important missing indexes

the names of columns that should be used to create the index. The column named
included_columns identifies the columns that should be defined as included columns on the index.

An example of the type of output for this query is shown in figure 3.4.

3.2.2   *The impact of missing indexes*

Although you can use the output from the missing-indexes script to create the missing
indexes, and perhaps automate this, a word of caution is needed. The output doesn't
take into account the potentially conflicting requirements of all the queries that run
against the identified tables. The output relates to individual queries rather than their
sum cumulative actions. With this in mind, you need to balance the detrimental
effects that any index may have on any updates (INSERT/UPDATE/DELETE) with the
improved performance an index can bring. When you update a table's data, any relevant index will also need to be updated. This can add to the duration of the query,
transaction length, and locks, leading to potential problems with blocking (and associated client timeouts).

You'll need to test to determine whether the added missing indexes, on balance,
add value. The Database Tuning Advisor (DTA) is a good tool for amalgamating the
sum total effects of all the queries, to determine if an index should be added. That
said, on many occasions I've found the DTA to be both relatively conservative in its recommendations and time consuming to run.

The sys.dm_db_missing_index_group_stats DMV includes data for both user and
system usage. *System* relates to administration-like queries, whereas *user* queries relate
to application queries. Because we tend to be more interested in our own user queries, we ignore the system usage details in our script.

It's possible to create a DMV snapshot of queries (relating to duration, CPU, I/O,
and the like) and another relating to missing indexes. (How to create DMV snapshots
is shown in chapter 2, "Common patterns.") It should then be possible to correlate

the two snapshots, apply the missing indexes, and rerun the query to determine if the added indexes have improved performance.

You need to be careful with missing indexes that have a large number of columns in the included_columns column; this may be because someone is accessing the table via a SELECT * FROM tableName query. This in itself may be interesting, because it suggests the user may not know what data columns they want, or maybe they're being lazy in specifying the columns they want.

It's probably better, initially, to focus on those missing indexes that have a NULL value in the included_columns column. If the inequality_columns column is populated, it might be worthwhile searching your code base, which represents all your SQL queries taken as a whole, for the column identified. Often it's a good indicator of a SQL query that can be written more efficiently. For example, instead of specifying the column is *not* equal to something, it may be better to rewrite the query so it contains just the possible values.

If you want to focus your performance improvements on a given database, schema, or table, you could amend the missing-indexes query to look only at a given database, schema, or table you're interested in. For example, to retrieve missing index information for a database/schema/table called '[Paris].[dbo].[Component]', you could add the following to the query:

```
WHERE [statement] = '[Paris].[dbo].[Component]'
```

It's also possible to search the cached plans for missing indexes. I'll show a script for this later in the chapter on improving poor query performance, in section 5.2 ("Finding queries that have missing indexes"). Looking at these cached plans before and after the indexes have been implemented should provide valuable insight into the effectiveness of the index. In addition, when you open the cached plan in SSMS 2008, you can easily extract the missing index definition.

In chapter 10 I'll provide a script that automatically creates the SQL to build (and optionally implement) these missing indexes.

Having looked at useful indexes that are missing, we'll now look at the opposite view, indexes that exist but aren't being used at all for data retrieval.

3.3   *Unused indexes*

Indexes are great for improving the performance of retrieval-based queries. In addition, if an update query has a WHERE clause or a JOIN condition, it may use an index to identify the subset of rows to update, and this will improve the performance of the query.

But indexes can have a detrimental effect on updates. This occurs when a table is updated (via UPDATE, DELETE, or INSERT) and the index isn't used. In these cases, the index can have a detrimental effect on query performance, because the index may need to be updated too. This will add to the query duration, length of transaction, and locks, leading to blocking and potential client timeouts.

In essence, costly unused indexes force SQL Server to do unnecessary work. In addition to queries taking longer to execute, administrative functions like backups and restores will take longer to complete, and there's an additional cost associated with the storage of unnecessary data.

3.3.1   *Finding the most-costly unused indexes*

Superfluous indexes have a detrimental effect on the performance of your SQL queries, because they cause SQL Server to do unnecessary work. Running the SQL script given in the next listing will identify the top 20 most-costly unused indexes, ordered by the number of updates that have been applied to them.

Listing 3.2   The most-costly unused indexes

```
SET TRANSACTION ISOLATION LEVEL READ UNCOMMITTED

SELECT                                                         ◁─┐  Temp table to
    DB_NAME() AS DatabaseName                                   ❶  hold results
    , SCHEMA_NAME(o.Schema_ID) AS SchemaName
    , OBJECT_NAME(s.[object_id]) AS TableName
    , i.name AS IndexName
    , s.user_updates
    , s.system_seeks + s.system_scans + s.system_lookups
                        AS [System usage]
INTO #TempUnusedIndexes
FROM    sys.dm_db_index_usage_stats s
INNER JOIN sys.indexes i ON s.[object_id] = i.[object_id]
    AND s.index_id = i.index_id
INNER JOIN sys.objects o ON i.object_id = O.object_id
WHERE 1=2

EXEC sp_MSForEachDB 'USE [?];                                 ◁─┐  Loop around
INSERT INTO #TempUnusedIndexes                                 ❷  all databases
SELECT TOP 20
    DB_NAME() AS DatabaseName
    , SCHEMA_NAME(o.Schema_ID) AS SchemaName
    , OBJECT_NAME(s.[object_id]) AS TableName
    , i.name AS IndexName
    , s.user_updates
    , s.system_seeks + s.system_scans + s.system_lookups
                                    AS [System usage]
FROM    sys.dm_db_index_usage_stats s
INNER JOIN sys.indexes i ON s.[object_id] = i.[object_id]
    AND s.index_id = i.index_id
INNER JOIN sys.objects o ON i.object_id = O.object_id
WHERE s.database_id = DB_ID()
AND OBJECTPROPERTY(s.[object_id], ''IsMsShipped'') = 0
AND s.user_seeks = 0
    AND s.user_scans = 0
    AND s.user_lookups = 0
AND i.name IS NOT NULL                                          ❸  Identify most-costly
ORDER BY s.user_updates DESC'                                 ◁─   unused indexes

SELECT TOP 20 * FROM #TempUnusedIndexes ORDER BY [user_updates] DESC

DROP TABLE #TempUnusedIndexes
```

Here you can see that a single DMV and two system tables are involved in identifying the most-costly unused indexes; a brief description of each is shown in table 3.4.

Table 3.4 DMV/system tables to identify the most-costly unused indexes

DMV/tables	Description
sys.dm_db_index_usage_stats	Contains details of the different types of index operations, for example, number of updates by user queries
sys.indexes	Contains details for each index, for example, name and type
sys.objects	Contains details for each object, for example, schema name

By joining the DMV and two system tables, we have enough information to identify the most-costly unused indexes across all the databases on the server. The DMV and the sys.indexes system table are joined on their common key columns: object_id and index_id. The system tables sys.objects and sys.indexes are joined on the object_id key. The system table sys.objects is used to provide information about the schema the index relates to.

We use a common pattern to create the temporary table to hold the transient results. Again, we use another common pattern to loop over all the databases on the server. For more detail on these common patterns, see chapter 2.

The first part of the script creates an empty temporary table (named #Temp-UnusedIndexes) with the required structure of column names and data types ❶. We use the Microsoft-supplied stored procedure sp_MSForEachDB to execute a query on each database on the server ❷. The query we execute selects the 20 most-costly unused indexes on each database ❸. We put the results of each execution into the temporary table. Finally, we select the top 20 most-costly indexes across all the databases on the server.

The query we execute on each database identifies the top 20 most-costly unused indexes by selecting those indexes that haven't been used in any user queries to retrieve data (there are no seeks, scans, or lookups) but have been updated when the relevant columns in the underlying table have been updated. The results are sorted by the number of updates that user queries have caused to be applied to the index, in descending order.

> **NOTE**   We ignore any indexes whose name column is set to NULL. This is because they aren't indexes; they're heaps. Similarly, because we're interested in only our own user-created indexes, we filter out any indexes that relate to tables created by the SQL Server installation process (the column IsMsShipped has a value of 1). We include the calculated sum of any system usage columns in the output; this will allow us to determine if the index is necessary for any system processing and if further investigation is needed.

Sample output for this query is shown in figure 3.5.

	DatabaseName	SchemaName	TableName	IndexName	user_updates	System usage
1	ParisMini	dbo	MessageLog	IX_MessageLog_1	1559	0
2	ParisMini	dbo	MessageLog	IX_MessageLog_2	1559	0
3	ParisDev	dbo	Request	IX_Request_3	512	0
4	ParisDev	dbo	Request	IX_Request_1	252	0
5	ParisDev	dbo	Request	IX_Request_2	252	0
6	ParisDev	dbo	Mapping	IX_Mapping_4	168	0
7	ParisDev	dbo	Deal	IX_Deal_OrgId	132	0
8	ParisDev	dbo	Deal	IX_Deal_ProductGroupCode	132	0
9	ParisDev	dbo	Deal	IX_Deal_StructuredTradeID	132	0
10	ParisDev	Logging	ProcessLog	IX_Logging.ProcessLog_UniqueReference	130	0
11	ParisDev	dbo	PositionGridCell	IX_PositionGridCell_4	128	0

Figure 3.5   Output showing the most-costly unused indexes

3.3.2   *The impact of unused indexes*

There are various reasons why you might have indexes that aren't used for data retrieval. These include changing application functionality, changing database usage, inexperienced developers, and the lack of a project follow-up phase.

Often when a project starts, there's limited knowledge about the queries you want to run on the database and the indexes you need to fulfill these queries. Indexes may be created with a best-guess approach. As the project progresses, the needs of the project become more fully understood, and the queries and indexes become more stable. Indexes that were created early on may no longer be appropriate but are forgotten about or ignored, resulting in potential impedance on query performance.

Similarly, an application may change significantly, running new queries and requiring new indexes, but the old indexes are left in place. Perhaps a key player in the development team leaves, and the remaining developers are unsure of query and index usage. Maybe a combination of increased data volume and a change in the type of data results in another index being used for data retrieval.

For a variety of reasons, some projects are implemented by inexperienced staff. They may implement indexes without sufficient thought as to the queries that run against the tables. For example, they might assume an index is being used but have insufficient knowledge to inspect the cached plans, which show the index isn't being used (maybe a table scan is being used or a data type conversion is taking place; both can result in unused indexes).

All these reasons could potentially produce costly unused indexes. Because you know that costly unused indexes have a detrimental impact on performance, you should try to remove them where possible. I'd suggest running the query given in the previous script (listing 3.2) as part of the user acceptance testing plan and also when changes are made to the application, in order to determine if indexes are still required. It would also be prudent to run the script as a regular part of any database housekeeping, to ensure you identify any potential superfluous indexes and to remove them.

> ### Removing indexes
> Since SQL Server 2005, it has been possible to disable indexes rather than delete them. Disabling the index removes the index and its data but allows you to keep the definition of the index tied with its table, without having the complication of storing the definition elsewhere, should you wish to reapply it at a later date.

If you want to focus your performance improvements on a given database, schema, or table, you could amend the most-costly indexes script to look only at a given database, schema, or table you're interested in.

A note of caution is needed here. The DMVs contain data that has accumulated since the last SQL Server restart. You need to ensure that you have enough data, from all the queries that have run on the SQL Server, to ensure the indexes aren't used for data retrieval.

The DMV sys.dm_db_index_usage_stats contains entries only for indexes that have been used. Unused indexes are ones that have never been updated or used for retrieval. Although these unused indexes do no real harm, removing these indexes will simplify the schema. An OUTER JOIN between sys.indexes and sys.dm_db_index_usage_stats will identify these indexes. A script later in this chapter (see section 3.9) will identify these indexes.

3.4 High-maintenance indexes

High-maintenance indexes are indexes that are rarely used to retrieve data for user queries but may be updated when the underlying table's data is modified. In many ways they're similar to the most-costly unused indexes; they're relatively expensive and can have a negative effect on query performance, potentially increasing blocking and client timeouts.

3.4.1 Finding the top high-maintenance indexes

High-maintenance indexes, like unused indexes, can have a detrimental impact on SQL performance because they cause SQL Server to perform unnecessary work. Running the SQL script given in the following listing will identify the top 20 high-maintenance indexes, ordered by maintenance cost.

Listing 3.3   The top high-maintenance indexes

```
SET TRANSACTION ISOLATION LEVEL READ UNCOMMITTED

SELECT
    DB_NAME() AS DatabaseName                              ◁┐  Temp table to
    , SCHEMA_NAME(o.Schema_ID) AS SchemaName               ❶  hold results
    , OBJECT_NAME(s.[object_id]) AS TableName
    , i.name AS IndexName
    , (s.user_updates ) AS [update usage]
    , (s.user_seeks + s.user_scans + s.user_lookups)
                                AS [Retrieval usage]
```

```
    , (s.user_updates) -
      (s.user_seeks + s.user_scans + s.user_lookups) AS [Maintenance cost]
    , s.system_seeks + s.system_scans + s.system_lookups AS [System usage]
    , s.last_user_seek
    , s.last_user_scan
    , s.last_user_lookup
INTO #TempMaintenanceCost
FROM    sys.dm_db_index_usage_stats s
INNER JOIN sys.indexes i ON  s.[object_id] = i.[object_id]
    AND s.index_id = i.index_id
INNER JOIN sys.objects o ON i.object_id = O.object_id
WHERE 1=2

EXEC sp_MSForEachDB 'USE [?];
INSERT INTO #TempMaintenanceCost
SELECT TOP 20
    DB_NAME() AS DatabaseName
    , SCHEMA_NAME(o.Schema_ID) AS SchemaName
    , OBJECT_NAME(s.[object_id]) AS TableName
    , i.name AS IndexName
    , (s.user_updates ) AS [update usage]
    , (s.user_seeks + s.user_scans + s.user_lookups)
                    AS [Retrieval usage]
    , (s.user_updates) -
(s.user_seeks + user_scans +
                        s.user_lookups) AS [Maintenance cost]
    , s.system_seeks + s.system_scans + s.system_lookups AS [System usage]
    , s.last_user_seek
    , s.last_user_scan
    , s.last_user_lookup
FROM    sys.dm_db_index_usage_stats s
INNER JOIN sys.indexes i ON s.[object_id] = i.[object_id]
    AND s.index_id = i.index_id
INNER JOIN sys.objects o ON i.object_id = O.object_id
WHERE s.database_id = DB_ID()
    AND i.name IS NOT NULL
    AND OBJECTPROPERTY(s.[object_id], ''IsMsShipped'') = 0
    AND (s.user_seeks + s.user_scans + s.user_lookups) > 0
ORDER BY [Maintenance cost] DESC'

SELECT top 20 * FROM #TempMaintenanceCost ORDER BY [Maintenance cost] DESC

DROP TABLE #TempMaintenanceCost
```

➋ Loop around all databases

➌ Identify top high-maintenance indexes

In the script a single DMV and two system tables are involved in identifying the most-unused indexes. Table 3.5 gives a brief description of each.

Table 3.5   DMVs/system tables to identify the top high-maintenance indexes

DMV/table	Description
sys.dm_db_index_usage_stats	Contains details of the different types of index operations, for example, number of updates by user queries
sys.indexes	Contains details for each index, for example, name and type
sys.objects	Contains details for each object, for example, schema name

The joining of the DMV and system tables provides us with enough information to identify the top high-maintenance indexes across all the databases on the server. The DMV and the sys.indexes system table are joined on their common key columns, object_id and index_id. The system tables sys.objects and sys.indexes are joined on the object_id key. The system table sys.objects is used to provide information about the schema the index relates to.

We use a common pattern to create the temporary table to hold the transient results. Then we use another common pattern to loop over all the databases on the server. For more detail on these common patterns, see chapter 2.

The first part of the script creates an empty temporary table (named #Temp-MaintenanceCost) with the required structure of column names and data types ❶. We use the Microsoft-supplied stored procedure, sp_MSForEachDB, to execute a query on each database on the server ❷. The query we execute selects the top 20 high-maintenance indexes on each database ❸. We put the results of each execution into the temporary table. Finally we select the top 20 high-maintenance indexes across all the databases on the server.

The query we execute on each database identifies the top 20 high-maintenance indexes by subtracting the retrieval usage from the update usage. The update usage is given by the column user_updates, and the retrieval usage is calculated as the sum of the various user index access types (user_seeks + user_scans + user_lookups). The dates of the last seek, scan, and lookup are also included. These can be used to determine if the index lookup was a long time ago, increasing the probability that it can be disabled or removed. The results are sorted by the maintenance cost in descending order.

> **NOTE** We ignore any indexes whose name column is set to NULL. This is because they aren't indexes; they're heaps. Similarly, we're interested in only our own user-created indexes, so we filter out any indexes that relate to tables created by the SQL Server installation process (the column IsMsShipped has a value of 1).

Because we're interested in indexes that have at least some usage, we exclude indexes that haven't been used for data retrieval (we've already identified these, in the most-costly unused indexes script). We include the calculated sum of any system usage columns in the output; this will allow us to determine if the index is necessary for any system processing and if further investigation is needed.

Figure 3.6 shows an example of the type of output for this query.

3.4.2   *The impact of high-maintenance indexes*

In this section I've identified indexes that are used relatively infrequently compared to the number of index updates (which reflect updates to the underlying table's data). What you need to determine now is whether the cost of the index is too expensive compared with its usage and whether the index should be removed. If the

	DatabaseName	Sche...	TableName	IndexName	update usage	Retrieval usage	Maintenance cost	System usage	last_user_seek	last_user_scan	last_user_lookup
22	ParisDev	dbo	Instrumen...	PK_Instru...	5	5	0	0	2010-10-11 1...	NULL	NULL
23	ParisDev	dbo	PositionF...	PK_Positio...	1	1	0	1	2010-10-11 1...	NULL	NULL
24	ParisDev	dbo	OrgVersion	AK_dbo.Or...	2	2	0	0	2010-10-11 1...	NULL	NULL
25	ParisDev	dbo	RequestP...	PK_Requ...	1	1	0	2	2010-10-11 1...	NULL	NULL
26	ParisDev	dbo	DealCOBs	PK_DealC...	1	1	0	1	2010-10-11 1...	NULL	NULL
27	ParisDev	Loggi...	ProcessLog	PK_Loggin...	153	153	0	8	2010-10-11 1...	NULL	NULL
28	ParisDev	dbo	Depende...	PK_Depe...	1	1	0	0	NULL	NULL	2010-10-11 12...
29	ParisDev	dbo	Depende...	idxJobGro...	1	1	0	0	2010-10-11 1...	NULL	NULL
30	ParisDev	dbo	OrgNetw...	PK_OrgHi...	2	2	0	0	NULL	2010-10-11 ...	NULL

Figure 3.6   Output showing the top high-maintenance indexes

index is required to obtain a subset of the underlying data, it may be advisable to create a filtered index.

If you examine the column retrieval_usage, you can see how often the index is used. A small value might reflect a rare ad hoc query or even a query that previously used the index but no longer does, perhaps because of changes in the volume and/or type of data. You could use DMV snapshots here to determine if the indexes are still used for data retrieval. For more information on the use of DMV snapshots, please see the DMV snapshot section in chapter 2.

If you want to focus your performance improvements on a given database, schema, or table, you could amend the top high-maintenance indexes script to look only at a given database, schema, or table you're interested in.

It might be sensible to run the script regularly and see if its retrieval usage changes. If it doesn't, this suggests the index is no longer being used, and the index is eligible for removal.

3.5   *Most-frequently used indexes*

If you know which indexes are used most often, you can target these indexes for further optimization. This should have a positive impact on the performance of those queries that use these indexes. These index optimizations include ensuring that the index statistics are up to date and have a good sampling percentage, the fill factor is optimal for the type of index usage, and logical fragmentation is low.

3.5.1   *Finding the most-used indexes*

Optimizing the indexes that are used most often will have a proportionally better impact on SQL query performance than optimizing other indexes. Running the SQL script given in the following listing will identify the top 20 most-used indexes, ordered by usage.

> **Listing 3.4   The most-used indexes**

```
SET TRANSACTION ISOLATION LEVEL READ UNCOMMITTED

SELECT
    DB_NAME() AS DatabaseName
```

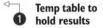
Temp table to hold results

```
    , SCHEMA_NAME(o.Schema_ID) AS SchemaName
    , OBJECT_NAME(s.[object_id]) AS TableName
    , i.name AS IndexName
    , (s.user_seeks + s.user_scans + s.user_lookups) AS [Usage]
    , s.user_updates
    , i.fill_factor
INTO #TempUsage
FROM sys.dm_db_index_usage_stats s
INNER JOIN sys.indexes i ON s.[object_id] = i.[object_id]
    AND s.index_id = i.index_id
INNER JOIN sys.objects o ON i.object_id = O.object_id
WHERE 1=2

EXEC sp_MSForEachDB 'USE [?];
INSERT INTO #TempUsage
SELECT TOP 20
    DB_NAME() AS DatabaseName
    , SCHEMA_NAME(o.Schema_ID) AS SchemaName
    , OBJECT_NAME(s.[object_id]) AS TableName
    , i.name AS IndexName
    , (s.user_seeks + s.user_scans + s.user_lookups) AS [Usage]
    , s.user_updates
    , i.fill_factor
FROM    sys.dm_db_index_usage_stats s
INNER JOIN sys.indexes i ON s.[object_id] = i.[object_id]
        AND s.index_id = i.index_id
INNER JOIN sys.objects o ON i.object_id = O.object_id
WHERE s.database_id = DB_ID()
    AND i.name IS NOT NULL
    AND OBJECTPROPERTY(s.[object_id], ''IsMsShipped'') = 0
ORDER BY [Usage] DESC'

SELECT TOP 20 * FROM #TempUsage ORDER BY [Usage] DESC

DROP TABLE #TempUsage
```

❷ Loop around all databases

❸ Identify most-used indexes

A single DMV and two system tables are used to identify the most-used indexes. A brief description of each is given in table 3.6.

Table 3.6   DMV/system tables to identify the most-used indexes

DMV/tables	Description
sys.dm_db_index_usage_stats	Contains details of the different types of index operations, for example, number of updates by user queries
sys.indexes	Contains details for ea.ch index, for example, name and type
sys.objects	Contains details for each object, for example, schema name

Joining the DMV and two system tables provides us with enough information to identify the most-used indexes across all the databases on the server. The DMV and the sys.indexes system table are joined on their common key columns, object_id and index_id. The system tables sys.objects and sys.indexes are joined on the object_id key.

The system table sys.objects is used to provide information about the schema the index relates to.

We use a common pattern to create the temporary table to hold the transient results. We use another common pattern to loop over all the databases on the server. For more details on these common patterns, see chapter 2.

The first part of the script creates an empty temporary table (named #TempUsage) with the required structure of column names and data types **❶**. We use the Microsoft-supplied stored procedure, sp_MSForEachDB, to execute a query on each database on the server **❷**. The query we execute selects the 20 most-used indexes on each database **❸**. We put the results of each execution into the temporary table. Finally, we select the top 20 most-used indexes across all the databases on the server.

The query we execute on each database identifies the top 20 most-used indexes by calculating the sum of all the user index access counts (user_seeks + user_scans + user_lookups) and sorting by this calculated sum in descending order. We also report on the index's fill_factor value; this will help us decide if we're using the appropriate fill factor in light of the amount of index data being read/updated.

Note that we ignore any heaps because they aren't indexes. Also, we're interested in only user-created indexes.

An example of the type of output for this query is shown in figure 3.7.

3.5.2 *The importance of the most-used indexes*

Knowing the most-commonly used indexes allows you to target your optimizations, confident in the knowledge that your changes should have a positive effect on the performance of those queries that use these most-popular indexes.

Indexes are used for data retrieval or to identify a subset of rows to modify. For the identified most-used indexes, you should ensure that the index's statistics are up to date and have a good sampling percentage. This should ensure that any queries that use the index have access to valid information about the probability of data values based on a column's data values. This is especially important for large tables where the automatic updating of statistics information may be suboptimal.

	DatabaseName	SchemaName	TableName	IndexName	Usage	user_updates	fill_factor
1	ParisDev	dbo	OrgNetwork	PK_OrgHierarchy	7993236	0	0
2	ParisDev	dbo	OrgNetwork	AK1_dbo.OrgNetwork_OrgHierarchyGroupId_ChildOrgId	7993213	0	0
3	ParisDev	dbo	Org	PK_Org	1486184	0	0
4	ParisMini	dbo	Source	IX_Source_1	160162	0	0
5	ParisMini	dbo	Currency	IX_Currency	109007	0	0
6	ParisMini	dbo	MappingType	IX_MappingType	77560	0	0
7	ParisDev	dbo	Product	PK_Product	8348	0	0
8	ParisDev	dbo	BusinessRegion	PK_BusinessRegion	6769	0	0
9	ParisDev	dbo	Bucket	PK_Bucket	3992	0	0
10	ParisDev	dbo	Source	IX_Source_1	3664	0	0
11	ParisDev	dbo	BucketGroupLink	IX_BucketGroupLink_1	3405	0	0
12	ParisDev	dbo	BucketType	PK_BucketType	2971	0	0

Figure 3.7 Output showing the most-used indexes

Similarly, you should look at the index's fill factor with a view to optimizing it, by ensuring you can get the most data per read, taking into account the number of updates the index is involved in. This should be easy to apply to tables and indexes that are relatively static, such as currency or country tables.

You might also consider placing the indexes on their own disk drive with their own disk controller, allowing queries to take advantage of concurrent access. If you're using SQL Server 2008, you might also consider these indexes for compression, because this will allow you to obtain more data for each read.

If you want to focus your performance improvements on a given database, schema, or table, you could amend the most-used-indexes query to look only at a given database, schema, or table you're interested in.

3.6 Fragmented indexes

Fragmentation relates to index entries that are out of sequence. For queries that access data sequentially, typically index scans, additional work is needed to retrieve the index's data. This additional work can result in longer-running queries, with potentially more blocking and client timeouts. Where possible, you should remove this fragmentation so you don't perform any unnecessary work.

3.6.1 Finding the most-fragmented indexes

The crux of this script is the DMV sys.dm_db_index_physical_stats. This DMV accepts various parameters, allowing fragmentation to be reported on at various levels of granularity, such as for a given database, table, or index. Under the hood, this DMV calls database console commands (DBCC), which can take a long time to execute. Consider this and its impact on resources when running this script. On my 4.5 terabyte database, with 128 GB of RAM, 16 CPUs, 600 indexes, and containing 255 tables, this script took more than an hour to execute.

The script we use to identify the most-fragmented indexes is shown here.

Listing 3.5 The most-fragmented indexes

```
SET TRANSACTION ISOLATION LEVEL READ UNCOMMITTED

SELECT                                                       Temp table to
    DB_NAME() AS DatbaseName                              ❶ hold results
    , SCHEMA_NAME(o.Schema_ID) AS SchemaName
    , OBJECT_NAME(s.[object_id]) AS TableName
    , i.name AS IndexName
    , ROUND(s.avg_fragmentation_in_percent,2) AS [Fragmentation %]
INTO #TempFragmentation
FROM sys.dm_db_index_physical_stats(db_id(),null, null, null, null) s
INNER JOIN sys.indexes i ON s.[object_id] = i.[object_id]
    AND s.index_id = i.index_id
INNER JOIN sys.objects o ON i.object_id = O.object_id
WHERE 1=2                                                     Loop around
                                                         ❷ all databases
EXEC sp_MSForEachDB 'USE [?];
INSERT INTO #TempFragmentation
```

```
SELECT TOP 20
    DB_NAME() AS DatbaseName
    , SCHEMA_NAME(o.Schema_ID) AS SchemaName
    , OBJECT_NAME(s.[object_id]) AS TableName
    , i.name AS IndexName
    , ROUND(s.avg_fragmentation_in_percent,2) AS [Fragmentation %]
FROM sys.dm_db_index_physical_stats(db_id(),null, null, null, null) s
INNER JOIN sys.indexes i ON s.[object_id] = i.[object_id]
    AND s.index_id = i.index_id
INNER JOIN sys.objects o ON i.object_id = O.object_id
WHERE s.database_id = DB_ID()
    AND i.name IS NOT NULL                                      ❸  Identify
    AND OBJECTPROPERTY(s.[object_id], ''IsMsShipped'') = 0         most-fragmented
ORDER BY [Fragmentation %] DESC'                                   indexes

SELECT top 20 * FROM #TempFragmentation ORDER BY [Fragmentation %] DESC

DROP TABLE #TempFragmentation
```

In the listing, a single DMV and two system tables are involved in identifying the most-fragmented indexes; a brief description of each is given in table 3.7.

Table 3.7   DMV/system tables to identify the most-fragmented indexes

DMV/tables	Description
sys.dm_db_index_physical_stats	Contains size and fragmentation information for the data and indexes for tables or views
sys.indexes	Contains details for each index, for example, name and type
sys.objects	Contains details for each object, for example, schema name

By joining the DMV and system tables, we have enough information to identify the most-fragmented indexes across all the databases on the server. The DMV and system tables are joined on their common key columns, object_id and index_id. The system tables sys.objects and sys.indexes are joined on the object_id key. The system table sys.objects is used to provide information about the schema the index relates to.

Again, we use a common pattern to create the temporary table to hold the transient results and another common pattern to loop over all the databases on the server. For more details on these common patterns, see chapter 2.

The first part of the script creates an empty temporary table (named #TempFragmentation) with the required structure of column names and data types ❶. We use the Microsoft-supplied stored procedure, sp_MSForEachDB, to execute a query on each database on the server ❷. The query we execute selects the 20 most-fragmented indexes on each database ❸. We put the results of each execution into the temporary table. Finally, we select the top 20 most-fragmented indexes across all the databases on the server.

	DatbaseName	SchemaName	TableName	IndexName	Fragmentation %
1	ParisPhil	TWS	SwapsDiaryError	IX_TWS.SwapsDiaryError_AllMandatoryQueriableColu...	97.24
2	ParisPhil	TWS	SwapsDiary	IX_TWS.SwapsDiary_AllMandatoryQueriableColumns	96.85
3	ParisPhil	Load	StagingRisk	idxGDIRisk_RequestId	95.87
4	ParisPhil	dbo	AuthorisationAuditPNL	IX_AuthorisationAuditPNL_OrgId	94.12
5	ParisPhil	Legacy	StagingPnl	idxLegacyPNL_RequestId	92.58
6	ParisPhil	ACBS	LL_RF_FAC_DETAIL	IDX_PORTFOLOI_ID	92.31
7	ParisPhil	Legacy	StagingRisk	idxLegacyRisk_RequestId	91.81
8	ParisPhil	dbo	Bucket	IX_Bucket_3	90.91
9	ParisPhil	dbo	Org	IX_Org	90.91
10	ParisPhil	dbo	BucketGroup	IX_BucketGroup	89.34
11	ParisPhil	Legacy	StagingRiskLog	idxLegacyRiskLog_RequestId	88.93
12	ParisPhil	dbo	OrgNetwork	PK_OrgHierarchy	87.5

Figure 3.8 Output showing the most-fragmented indexes

The query we execute on each database identifies the top 20 most-fragmented indexes using the column avg_fragmentation_in_percent and sorts by this column in descending order.

Note that we ignore any heaps because they aren't indexes. In addition, we're interested in only user-created indexes.

Figure 3.8 contains an example of the type of output for this query.

3.6.2 *The impact of fragmented indexes*

Having a low level of fragmentation is especially important for those queries that involve ranges, which retrieve data between two points. Fragmentation results in additional work being done. Where possible, you should remove fragmentation.

Typically, Microsoft recommends that indexes that have a fragmentation percentage in excess of 30% be rebuilt. Similarly, indexes with a fragmentation percentage between 10% and 30% should be reorganized.

It's possible to rebuild/reorganize indexes individually from within SSMS, by right-clicking the relevant index and selecting Rebuild. Although this is okay for selected indexes, for a more encompassing approach you should create a script and run the output automatically. You should run this script at regular intervals as part of the regular database housekeeping jobs. Note that you can perform these operations when the database is online, but it may have a negative impact on performance, so be sure to test a small change before it's applied more aggressively.

In chapter 10 I'll provide a script that automatically defragments indexes in an intelligent manner. The script defragments only the indexes whose data has fragmented significantly, and it decides between an index rebuild or a reorganization based on the degree of fragmentation.

It's possible to concentrate your efforts on a given database, table, or index by supplying relevant parameters to the sys.dm_db_index_physical_stats DMV.

We'll now look at which specific indexes are used by a given routine. This provides you with an opportunity to pre-optimize before the query is run.

3.7   *Indexes used by a given routine*

When you run your SQL queries or batches, some queries are more important than others. If you know which queries (stored procedure or a batch of one or more SQL statements) are your important ones and need to perform optimally, you can pre-optimize the indexes these queries use. If you can identify which indexes are used by a given batch of SQL, you can target these indexes for optimization. This should give you better performance where and when it matters.

When you run a SQL query, information about which indexes it uses and how it uses them (for example, updates, seeks, scans, or lookups) is stored. In addition, information about the number of rows affected by the running code is recorded. Using this information, you can target your performance improvements to those specific indexes, leading to better-performing code.

The purpose of the script described in this section is to identify the name and type of usage of indexes a SQL query uses and then suggest ways in which these targeted indexes can be improved.

Indexes are one of the main tools for improving SQL query performance. But information associated with indexes can become stale over time. Such information includes statistics, degree of logical fragmentation, and the fill factor. We'll discuss how these can be improved later in this section, but first we need to create the script to identify which indexes are used by a given SQL query.

3.7.1   *Finding the indexes used by a given routine*

If you know which indexes are used by a given routine, you can pre-optimize these indexes before the next time the routine is run, ensuring optimal performance. The script we use to identify the indexes used by a given routine is shown here.

Listing 3.6   Identifying indexes used by a given routine

```
SET TRANSACTION ISOLATION LEVEL READ UNCOMMITTED

SELECT
SchemaName = ss.name                                    ◁┐  Get pre-index
    , TableName = st.name                               ❶  counter values
    , IndexName = ISNULL(si.name, '')
    , IndexType = si.type_desc
    , user_updates = ISNULL(ius.user_updates, 0)
    , user_seeks = ISNULL(ius.user_seeks, 0)
    , user_scans = ISNULL(ius.user_scans, 0)
    , user_lookups = ISNULL(ius.user_lookups, 0)
    , ssi.rowcnt
    , ssi.rowmodctr
    , si.fill_factor
INTO #IndexStatsPre
FROM   sys.dm_db_index_usage_stats ius
```

```
RIGHT OUTER JOIN sys.indexes si ON  ius.[object_id] = si.[object_id]
         AND ius.index_id = si.index_id
INNER JOIN sys.sysindexes ssi ON si.object_id = ssi.id
         AND si.name = ssi.name
INNER JOIN sys.tables st ON st.[object_id] = si.[object_id]
INNER JOIN sys.schemas ss ON ss.[schema_id] = st.[schema_id]
WHERE ius.database_id = DB_ID()
    AND OBJECTPROPERTY(ius.[object_id], 'IsMsShipped') = 0

SELECT COB, COUNT(*) FROM dbo.request GROUP BY COB
```

❷ Run routine or native SQL

```
SELECT
SchemaName = ss.name
    , TableName = st.name
    , IndexName = ISNULL(si.name, '')
    , IndexType = si.type_desc
    , user_updates = ISNULL(ius.user_updates, 0)
    , user_seeks = ISNULL(ius.user_seeks, 0)
    , user_scans = ISNULL(ius.user_scans, 0)
    , user_lookups = ISNULL(ius.user_lookups, 0)
    , ssi.rowcnt
    , ssi.rowmodctr
    , si.fill_factor
INTO #IndexStatsPost
FROM    sys.dm_db_index_usage_stats ius
RIGHT OUTER JOIN sys.indexes si ON ius.[object_id] = si.[object_id]
         AND ius.index_id = si.index_id
INNER JOIN sys.sysindexes ssi ON si.object_id = ssi.id
         AND si.name = ssi.name
INNER JOIN sys.tables st ON st.[object_id] = si.[object_id]
INNER JOIN sys.schemas ss ON ss.[schema_id] = st.[schema_id]
WHERE ius.database_id = DB_ID()
    AND OBJECTPROPERTY(ius.[object_id], 'IsMsShipped') = 0

SELECT
DB_NAME() AS DatabaseName
    , po.[SchemaName]
    , po.[TableName]
    , po.[IndexName]
    , po.[IndexType]
    , po.user_updates - ISNULL(pr.user_updates, 0) AS [User Updates]
    , po.user_seeks - ISNULL(pr.user_seeks, 0) AS [User Seeks]
    , po.user_scans - ISNULL(pr.user_scans, 0) AS [User Scans]
    , po.user_lookups - ISNULL(pr.user_lookups , 0) AS [User Lookups]
    , po.rowcnt - pr.rowcnt AS [Rows Inserted]
    , po.rowmodctr - pr.rowmodctr AS [Updates I/U/D]
    , po.fill_factor
FROM #IndexStatsPost po LEFT OUTER JOIN #IndexStatsPre pr
        ON pr.SchemaName = po.SchemaName
            AND pr.TableName = po.TableName
            AND pr.IndexName = po.IndexName
            AND pr.IndexType = po.IndexType
WHERE ISNULL(pr.user_updates, 0) != po.user_updates
OR          ISNULL(pr.user_seeks, 0) != po.user_seeks
OR          ISNULL(pr.user_scans, 0) != po.user_scans
```

❸ Get post-index counter values

❹ Determine which index counters have changed

```
OR          ISNULL(pr.user_lookups, 0) != po.user_lookups
ORDER BY po.[SchemaName], po.[TableName], po.[IndexName];

DROP TABLE #IndexStatsPre
DROP TABLE #IndexStatsPost
```

Here you can see that a single DMV and four system tables are involved in identifying the indexes used by a given routine; a brief description of each is given in table 3.8.

Table 3.8 DMV/system tables to identify the index usage

DMV/tables	Description
sys.dm_db_index_usage_stats	Contains details of the different types of index operations, for example, number of updates by user queries
sys.indexes	Contains details for each index, for example, name and type
sys.sysindexes	Contains details of row counts and row changes (since last update statistics run)
sys.tables	Contains details of table objects, for example, name
sys.schemas	Contains details of schema objects, for example, name

By joining the DMV with the system tables, we have enough information to identify the indexes used by a given routine and how they're used. The DMV joins to the system table sys.indexes on their common key columns, object_id and index_id. The other system tables typically provide descriptive information.

The first part of the script stores the current value of various index counters into a temporary table (named #IndexStatsPre) ❶. We then run the SQL query or routine about which we want to discover indexes usage ❷. Next, we store the new value of various index counters into another temporary table (named #IndexStatsPost) ❸. Finally, we compare the temporary tables to determine which indexes have been used, how they've been used—for example, scan, seek, or lookup—and how much they have been used ❹. The results are sorted by schema name, table name, and index name.

The User column usage counts relate to the number of times the index was accessed by the running SQL query, not the number of rows within the index that were accessed. As an example, if a SQL query updates 10 rows (that are part of an index), it will have a User Updates value of 1 (because one UPDATE statement has been run) and will have an Update I/U/D value of 10 (because 10 rows have been modified—inserted, updated, or deleted) if the column updated is the leading column of the index. The Rows Inserted column will have a value of 0 because the number of rows hasn't changed.

Depending on how the query uses the index, it updates the relevant usage counters. A seek is a keyed access and is typically the most efficient method of retrieving a small number of selective rows of data. A scan occurs when an index is examined to

Results | Messages

	COB	(No column name)
1	2005-05-01 00:00:00	2
2	2005-05-15 00:00:00	1
3	2005-10-06 00:00:00	1
4	2005-10-07 00:00:00	1
5	2005-10-10 00:00:00	1

	DatabaseName	SchemaName	TableName	IndexName	IndexType	User Updates	User Seeks	User Scans	User Lookups	Rows Inserted	Updates I/U/D	fill_factor
1	Paris	dbo	Request	IX_Request_COB	NONCLUSTERED	0	0	1	0	0	0	0

Figure 3.9 Output showing the indexes used by a given routine

retrieve a range of rows. A lookup occurs when this index is used to look up data in another index.

The WHERE clause ensures only nonsystem indexes in the current database are examined. The results are sorted by schema name, table name, and then index name.

> **NOTE** When determining which indexes have been used, we use a RIGHT OUTER JOIN between the DMV sys.dm_db_index_usage_stats and the system table sys.indexes; this is necessary because the index may not have been used since the last reboot and may not be present in the DMV. Because of this, when you compare the temporary tables, you need to take into account any potential NULL values.

In addition, in the final step, there is a LEFT OUTER JOIN when calculating which indexes have changed their counter values. This is needed because indexes that may have been used by the routine may not have been used before.

Figure 3.9 shows sample output for this type of query.

3.7.2 *The importance of knowing which indexes are used*

This script allows you to determine which indexes are used, how they're used, and the number of rows affected when a given stored procedure or batch of SQL code is run. This information can be useful in targeting improvements to your T-SQL with a view to improving its performance.

Each index has a statistics object associated with it. This object includes information about the distribution and density of the index's columns, which is used by the optimizer to determine whether an index is used and how it's used (seek, scan, or lookup). For large tables, updating these statistics can be time consuming, so a smaller sample of rows is typically taken. If you know the specific indexes involved with a query, you can provide a greater sampling size and a better representation of the data, in the same amount of time, compared with a blanket statistics update for the table as a whole.

Large tables have an additional problem concerning statistics. Typically, a table's statistics are updated (automatically) only when 20% of its rows change. For large tables, this means their statistics can be stale for quite a while before they're updated. Using the previous targeted method of improvement should help ensure that the relevant statistics are kept up to date, and this should help improve query performance.

Logical index fragmentation indicates the percentage of entries in the index that are out of sequence. This isn't the same as the page-fullness type of fragmentation. Logical fragmentation has an impact on any order scans that use an index. Where possible, you should remove this fragmentation. You can achieve this by rebuilding or reorganizing the index. You can see the degree of fragmentation by examining the DMV sys.dm_db_index_physical_stats. Typically, if an index has over 30% fragmentation, a rebuild is recommended; if it's between 10% and 30%, a reorganization is recommended.

It's also advisable to ensure that the degree of physical fragmentation isn't excessive, because this will result in greater I/O with a corresponding decrease in performance.

Fill factor describes the number of entries on the page. For an index that's mostly read-only, you'd want the page to be relatively full, so you can get more data per read. Whereas for an index that has many update/inserts, you'd prefer a less-full page to prevent fragmentation that could hurt performance. You can use the output from this script to determine whether an index has mostly read access or not and then set the fill factor accordingly.

The type of index access can provide you with some interesting information. A large number of user lookups could indicate that additional columns should be added to the index via the INCLUDE keyword, because the index is being used to get data from the underlying table. User scans sometimes are indicative of a missing index; inspecting the underlying SQL query code will show whether a scan was intended or whether a more appropriate index needs to be created.

Indexes can cause updates to run more slowly. Because the updates may need to be applied to both the table and its indexes, this can have a significant impact when you make a large number of updates. If the indexes have many updates (see the User Updates column in the output) but few or no reads (see the other User columns), you can investigate whether you'd get better performance by removing the index. In some cases, it may be advisable to disable the index during updating and then enable it afterward. In essence, you should consider the combined total SQL query code that runs on the underlying tables before you consider adding or removing indexes.

If you know that certain indexes are used more than others, you might want to put them on different physical disks; this should give better concurrent access and improved data retrieval times. This is particularly relevant to indexes that are used repeatedly to join the same tables.

NOTE   If a table is relatively small, none of its indexes might be used. This is because it's cheaper for the optimizer to get the data directly via the table rather than from an index.

You can also use this script to confirm that certain indexes aren't being used by a SQL query. Investigating why an index isn't being used might result in the SQL query being rewritten or changing the index definition or even the deletion of an unnecessary index.

It may be worthwhile running the Database Tuning Advisor on the SQL query to ensure that the indexes you have are still appropriate or if additional ones should be added. Additionally, the missing indexes script described earlier can be useful in tracking down missing indexes.

Sometimes the values in the Rows Inserted and Updates I/U/D columns may not match what you might expect in the other User columns. This can have various causes including the following:

- For the Updates I/U/D column to be updated, the SQL query must change an entry in an index where the leading column is updated.
- The combined effect of updates/deletes/inserts needs to be considered.
- If statistics are updated when the utility is run, the Rows Inserted and Updates I/U/D columns get reset (sometimes leading to a negative value).
- Although an update statement may run (so it shows up in the User Updates column), it may not update any rows of data (so it doesn't show up in the Updates I/U/D column).
- A rolled-back transaction seems to affect the Rows Inserted and Updates I/U/D columns, whereas a committed transaction may not.

It might be advisable to run the SQL query under investigation twice because if the indexes haven't been loaded before, they'll give a NULL value in the Rows Inserted and Updates I/U/D columns.

A potential caveat of the method described is that it doesn't limit the index changes to only the SQL query under investigation. If any other code is running concurrently on the same database, its index accesses will also be recorded. One way around this problem is by running the SQL query on a standalone database or at a time when you know nothing else is running. That said, you can turn this caveat into an advantage because you may want to know about all index access on a given database.

3.8 Databases with most missing indexes

It's often the case that you have several different databases running on the same server. A consequence of this is that no matter how optimal your individual database may be, another database on the server, running suboptimally, may affect the server's resources, and this may impact the performance of your database. Remember, CPU, memory, and tempdb are shared across all the databases on the server. Now that you know about the importance of indexes on query performance, it makes sense to report on those databases with the most missing indexes, because they may be indirectly affecting the performance of your database.

It should be possible to amend the other queries in this chapter to provide counts of other aspects of indexing, to give you an indication of databases that perhaps need further attention.

3.8.1   *Finding which databases have the most missing indexes*

Excessive I/O is often reported as a root cause of poor system performance; often this relates to, and is exacerbated by, missing indexes. Identifying the databases that have the most missing indexes should help alleviate this problem. Running the SQL query given in the following listing will identify the databases with the most missing indexes, ordered by the number of missing indexes.

> **Listing 3.7   The databases with the most missing indexes**

```
SET TRANSACTION ISOLATION LEVEL READ UNCOMMITTED

SELECT
    DB_NAME(database_id) AS DatabaseName
    , COUNT(*) AS [Missing Index Count]
FROM sys.dm_db_missing_index_details
GROUP BY DB_NAME(database_id)
ORDER BY [Missing Index Count] DESC
```

Here a single DMV is used to identify the databases with the most missing indexes; a brief description of it is given in table 3.9.

Table 3.9   DMV to identify the databases with the most missing indexes

DMV	Description
sys.dm_db_missing_index_details	Contains details of the database/schema/table the missing index relates to, together with how the index usage has been identified in queries (for example, equality/inequality)

The sole DMV sys.dm_db_missing_index_details provides you with enough information to determine which databases are missing the most indexes, across all the databases on the server. The query counts the number of missing indexes per database and sorts the results by the number of missing indexes in descending order.

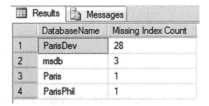

Figure 3.10   Output showing the databases with the most missing indexes

An example of the type of output for this query is shown in figure 3.10.

3.8.2   *The importance of other databases*

As mentioned earlier, your database may be highly optimized, but because you often have multiple databases sharing the same server, a suboptimal database running on the same server may impact the performance of the server and your database.

Often, one thing leads to another. A database that has a high number of missing indexes might also be indicative of a poorly designed database, undertaken by inexperienced staff, using poor-quality hardware. If this is the case, you could use the databases with the most-missing-indexes script as an indicator of general database quality and to identify those in need of further investigation.

3.9 Completely unused indexes

Earlier I presented a script that identified the most-costly unused indexes. These indexes aren't used for data retrieval, and they're expensive because they may need to be updated when the underlying table is updated. The script given here is different. It identifies indexes that haven't been used at all, neither for retrieval nor for update. These indexes don't have any effect on performance because they aren't used. They do, however, have an effect on the complexity of your database model, because you have additional indexes to understand. This is unnecessary, and you should try to remove them where possible.

> ### A word of caution
> The indexes identified as unused should be treated with caution. The algorithm used here to determine if an index is unused compares what's in the system table sys.indexes with the DMV sys.dm_db_index_usage_stats. The latter has entries only if a query accesses the index. It may be that the queries that would use these indexes have not yet been run (since the last SQL Server reboot); perhaps they're run on a quarterly or annual basis.

3.9.1 Finding which indexes aren't used at all

Unused indexes increase the complexity of your database model, resulting in longer and more complex analysis when you undertake maintenance work. Running the following SQL script will identify all the indexes that are unused on your server instance.

Listing 3.8 Indexes that aren't used at all

```
SET TRANSACTION ISOLATION LEVEL READ UNCOMMITTED         ❶ Temp table to
SELECT                                                      hold results
    DB_NAME() AS DatbaseName
    , SCHEMA_NAME(O.Schema_ID) AS SchemaName
    , OBJECT_NAME(I.object_id) AS TableName
    , I.name AS IndexName
INTO #TempNeverUsedIndexes
FROM sys.indexes I INNER JOIN sys.objects O ON I.object_id = O.object_id
WHERE 1=2

EXEC sp_MSForEachDB 'USE [?];                            ❷ Loop around
INSERT INTO #TempNeverUsedIndexes                          all databases
SELECT
    DB_NAME() AS DatbaseName
    , SCHEMA_NAME(O.Schema_ID) AS SchemaName
    , OBJECT_NAME(I.object_id) AS TableName
    , I.NAME AS IndexName
FROM sys.indexes I INNER JOIN sys.objects O ON I.object_id = O.object_id
```

```
LEFT OUTER JOIN sys.dm_db_index_usage_stats S ON S.object_id = I.object_id
        AND I.index_id = S.index_id
        AND DATABASE_ID = DB_ID()
WHERE OBJECTPROPERTY(O.object_id,''IsMsShipped'') = 0
  AND I.name IS NOT NULL
  AND S.object_id IS NULL'
```

❸ **Identify unused indexes**

```
SELECT * FROM #TempNeverUsedIndexes
ORDER BY DatbaseName, SchemaName, TableName, IndexName

DROP TABLE #TempNeverUsedIndexes
```

In the listing, you can see that a single DMV and two system tables are involved in identifying the databases that are unused. They're briefly described in table 3.10.

Table 3.10   DMV/tables to identify unused indexes

DMV/tables	Description
sys.dm_db_index_usage_stats	Contains details of the different types of index operations, for example, number of updates by user queries
sys.indexes	Contains details for each index, for example, name and type
sys.objects	Contains details for each object, for example, schema name

The first part of the script creates an empty temporary table (named #Temp-NeverUsedIndexes) with the required structure of column names and data types ❶. We use the Microsoft-supplied stored procedure, sp_MSForEachDB, to execute a query on each database on the server ❷. The query we execute selects all the unused indexes on each database. We put the results of each execution into the temporary table. Finally, we select the unused indexes across all the databases on the server ❸.

The DMV sys.dm_db_index_usage_stats is populated with details of any indexes that have been used in running our queries. If an index has not been used, it's not present in this DMV. The system table sys.indexes contains details of all the indexes present on a given database. The system table sys.objects is used to provide information about the schema the index relates to. You can determine which indexes are unused by comparing what's in the system table sys.indexes but not in the DMV sys.dm_db_index_usage_stats. We use the system table sys.objects to display the schema name of the index. The results are sorted by database name, schema name, table name, and index name.

> **NOTE**   When determining which indexes haven't been used, there's a LEFT OUTER JOIN between the system table sys.indexes and the DMV sys.dm_db_index_usage_stats. This is necessary because the index may not have been used since the last reboot and may not be present in the DMV. Checking for a NULL object_id in the DMV will ensure you obtain all the unused indexes.

Sample output for this query is shown in figure 3.11.

	DatbaseName	SchemaName	TableName	IndexName
462	ParisDev	dbo	LimitScalar	PK_LimitScalar
463	ParisDev	dbo	LimitScalar	IX_LimitScalar_1
464	ParisDev	dbo	LimitType	PK_LimitType
465	ParisDev	dbo	LimitType	IX_LimitType
466	ParisDev	dbo	LimitValueType	PK_LimitValueType
467	ParisDev	dbo	LimitValueType	IX_LimitValueType
468	ParisDev	dbo	LoanVersion	PK_LoanVersion
469	ParisDev	dbo	LoanVersion	NC_InstrumentId
470	ParisDev	dbo	MappingRuleType	PK_MappingRuleType

Figure 3.11 Output showing indexes that aren't used at all

3.9.2 *The importance of unused indexes*

The indexes identified as unused here should be treated with caution. It may be that the queries that would use these indexes haven't yet been run (since the last SQL Server reboot) and don't have an entry in the DMV sys.dm_db_index_usage_stats. As the time since the last reboot increases and the amount of data in the DMV increases, you can be more confident that the indexes aren't required. As a compromise, you could disable the identified used indexes, and if they subsequently appear in the list of missing indexes, you could reinstate them.

As noted earlier, these indexes haven't been used for either retrieval or update, so they have no effect on query performance. They do, however, have an effect on schema complexity. For example, you need to take them into account when analyzing the impact of changes. They result in unnecessary work and should be removed.

In chapter 10, I'll provide a script that automatically disables or deletes indexes that aren't used at all.

One of the major factors that affects whether an index is used or not is the index's statistics; this is discussed next.

3.10 *Your statistics*

Queries typically use indexes for WHERE clauses and JOIN conditions. Whether or not an index is used and how it's used are typically determined by the statistics on the columns in the index. If you know how often a given data value is likely to occur and its distribution in relation to other data values, you can provide an estimate to the optimizer that's used to determine which indexes are used by queries.

In many ways, statistical information is at least as important as the indexes it relates to, and so you should ensure it's up to date and representative of the underlying index data.

Statistics are typically automatically updated when 20% of the rows in a table have changed since the statistics were last updated. For small- to medium-size tables, the frequency of that statistics update may be adequate. But for larger tables, this automatic update may be insufficient. I've experienced many occasions where a query has taken many minutes to run only to be canceled because of its bad performance. Updating the relevant statistics has allowed the same query to subsequently run in a few seconds.

Although this script doesn't involve DMVs, I've included it here because knowledge of the current state of index statistics can have a profound effect on the use of indexes and the performance of SQL queries.

3.10.1 *Finding the state of your statistics*

Up-to-date statistics help ensure that the most appropriate index is chosen to obtain the underlying data. They also help ensure that the correct index access mechanism is chosen, for example, seek or lookup. Running the SQL script given in the following listing will identify the current state of your statistics.

> **Listing 3.9   What is the state of your statistics?**

```
SET TRANSACTION ISOLATION LEVEL READ UNCOMMITTED

SELECT
    ss.name AS SchemaName
  , st.name AS TableName
  , s.name AS IndexName
  , STATS_DATE(s.id,s.indid) AS 'Statistics Last Updated'
  , s.rowcnt AS 'Row Count'
  , s.rowmodctr AS 'Number Of Changes'
  , CAST((CAST(s.rowmodctr AS DECIMAL(28,8))/CAST(s.rowcnt AS
    DECIMAL(28,2)) * 100.0)
                      AS DECIMAL(28,2)) AS '% Rows Changed'
FROM sys.sysindexes s
INNER JOIN sys.tables st ON st.[object_id] = s.[id]
INNER JOIN sys.schemas ss ON ss.[schema_id] = st.[schema_id]
WHERE s.id > 100
  AND s.indid > 0
  AND s.rowcnt >= 500
ORDER BY SchemaName, TableName, IndexName
```

In the listing, you can see that three system tables are involved in identifying the current state of index statistics; a brief description of each is given in table 3.11.

Table 3.11   The state of your statistics

Tables	Description
sys.indexes	Contains details for each index, for example, name, type, row count, number of rows changed since statistics last updated
sys.tables	Contains table information, for example, name
sys.schemas	Contains details of schema objects, for example, name

The joining of the system tables provides enough information to identify when the index statistics were last updated and the percentage of rows that have changed since the last update of the statistics. The system table sys.sysindexes is joined to sys.tables on their key column id/object_id, and sys.tables is joined to sys.schemas on the schema_id column.

The script retrieves schema name, table name, index name, current row count, and number of changes. It calculates the number of rows changed as a percentage and uses the SQL function STATS_DATE to determine when the statistics for the index were last updated.

You filter out indexes with an index id (indId) of 0 because these aren't indexes; they're heaps. You also filter out indexes with fewer than 500 rows, because statistics are more important for larger tables. You also filter out system objects. The results are sorted by schema name, table name, and index name.

An example of the type of output for this query is shown in figure 3.12.

3.10.2 *The importance of statistics*

When the optimizer looks at how it will fulfill a user's query, it inspects the JOIN and WHERE clause and determines whether an index should be used. Statistics have an impact on both whether an index is used and how it would be used. Statistics describe the distribution and density of data values. Knowing the statistics for a given index column, you can estimate the probability of a given data value being used in a WHERE clause. Knowing this, the optimizer can choose a relevant index and decide how that index should be used, be it a seek, scan, or lookup.

You can see that statistics can have a profound effect on the performance of a query. Unfortunately, statistics can become stale; this is especially true of larger tables. An index's statistics tend to be updated automatically when 20% of its rows have changed. For large tables, this might take a considerable time, during which queries may run more slowly because of having stale statistics.

	SchemaName	TableName	IndexName	Statistics Last Updated	Row Count	Number Of Changes	% Rows Changed
1	ACBS	LL_RF_FAC_DE...	IDX_PORTFOLOI_ID	2010-01-26 10:51:04.853	11140	0	0.00
2	ACBS	LL_RF_FAC_DE...	IXD_UNQ_LL_RF_F...	2010-01-26 10:51:10.400	11140	0	0.00
3	ACBS	LL_RF_FAC_LIM...	IXD_UNQ_LL_RF_F...	2010-01-26 10:51:10.613	11170	0	0.00
4	ACBS	LL_RF_LOAN_I...	IDX_CLUST_LL_RF...	2010-01-26 10:51:11.730	17159	0	0.00
5	ACBS	LL_RF_LOAN_LI...	IXD_UNQ_LL_RF_L...	2010-01-26 10:51:11.423	20532	0	0.00
6	ACBS	StagingPNL	idxRequestId_ASP	2010-01-26 14:01:57.010	633975	0	0.00
7	ACBS	StagingPNLLog	idxRequestId_ASPL	2010-01-26 14:01:55.503	633975	0	0.00
8	dbo	ACBSLoan	PK_ACBSLoan	2010-01-25 18:00:06.420	1553	0	0.00
9	dbo	AuthorisationAudi...	IX_AuthorisationAudit...	2010-01-25 18:00:06.640	8338	0	0.00
10	dbo	AuthorisationAudi...	PK_PNLAuthorisatio...	2010-01-25 18:00:06.467	8338	0	0.00
11	dbo	BondVersion	IX_BondVersion_2	2010-01-25 18:00:06.793	96146	15815	16.45
12	dbo	BondVersion	PK_BondVersion	2010-01-25 18:00:06.717	96146	15815	16.45
13	dbo	Bucket	IX_Bucket	2010-01-25 18:00:13.730	1925	10	0.52

Figure 3.12 Output showing the current state of your statistics

To determine whether the statistics should be updated, you should look at the column % Rows Changed together with the Statistics Last Updated column. For a large table, perhaps the statistics need to be updated on a daily basis. I've found this to be the case where the current date is part of the index key.

You could use the output to automatically update the statistics of individual indexes. Because you have the individual index names, you could target your updates to the relevant indexes. This will allow you to have a faster statistics update or a higher sampling percentage within the same time period as a blanket table update.

In chapter 10 I'll provide a script that automatically updates the index statistics in an intelligent manner. The script updates only the statistics of the indexes whose data has changed and does so using an intelligent sampling algorithm.

We've discussed various aspects of indexes in detail in this chapter. One of the themes that comes through is the conflict between the usefulness of indexes in retrieving data and their cost in terms of unnecessary updates. We'll examine this theme next.

3.11   *A holistic approach to managing indexes*

Indexes have a significant contribution to make to the discussion relating to balancing transactional and reporting systems. Typically, queries in transactional systems update a small number of rows relatively quickly. If they need to update additional indexes (required for reporting), the update will add time to the query duration, transaction time, and resource locks. By contrast, queries in reporting systems typically retrieve a large number of rows, run for long time periods, and often require many indexes. If both of these conflicting systems are present on the same database, you should try to balance these two contradictory requirements.

Ideally, you'd have the two systems (transactional and reporting systems) on different databases and preferably on different servers. The transactional system could feed the reporting system with periodic updates.

If system separation isn't feasible, you should take steps to minimize the adverse effects of indexes. This would include ensuring that unused or high-maintenance indexes are removed (see the scripts given earlier for this). In addition, indexes that are used heavily or for important queries should be optimized, with reference to their statistics, fill factor, and fragmentation (again, you have scripts to discover these things).

Another solution might be to disable reporting indexes during the transactional processing and reenable them during the reporting processing. You could also see how indexes are used in terms of reads/writes and compare this with the number of I/O reads/writes.

Databases tend to have a bias toward either reporting or transactional processing. Even with transactional systems, the database typically has more reads than writes, often by a factor of at least 5 or 10, so you need to be careful not to overestimate the cost of index updates (unless you have lots of indexes on a table!). Database read performance tends to be inversely proportional to the index fill factor, so a fill factor of 50% means reads are twice as slow as when the fill factor is 100.

3.12 Summary

Indexes are critical to query performance. In this chapter we've discussed the different types of indexes along with the different index access mechanisms.

I've provided a variety of scripts that use DMVs to identify indexes that may be suboptimal, unnecessary, or even missing. We've discussed several factors that relate to indexes that can be used to optimize the identified indexes, resulting in faster-performing queries.

Indexes are a vital element in determining how a table's data is accessed, thus impacting query performance. Having looked at various useful aspects of indexes, we'll now move on to looking at the execution of SQL queries in the next chapter.

Improving poor query performance

This chapter covers

- Query execution
- Identifying different aspects of poorly performing queries
- How to improve poorly performing queries

Slow-performing queries can have a costly impact on systems. When queries run slowly, transactions and locks are held longer, leading to an increased possibility of blocking, which can cause other queries in turn to run more slowly. All of this can lead to more client application timeouts.

Identifying the slowest queries will allow you to make targeted improvements, confident in the knowledge that any improvement to these queries will have the biggest overall impact on performance.

As well as looking at slow-running queries, we'll look at other aspects of queries that could be indicative of an underlying problem or could be used to target improvements. Various aspects of queries that make use of the CLR are discussed separately in chapter 7, "Common Language Runtime DMVs."

So that you'll get the most from the scripts described in this chapter, first I'll explain how and why SQL queries are cached.

4.1 Understanding executed queries

When a SQL query is run for the first time, the optimizer has to determine an optimal way of satisfying the query. Typically, the optimizer looks at the record counts, available indexes, and statistics to determine the access paths necessary to fulfill the query easily and quickly. The optimizer takes time to do this work. Rather than having to perform this work for queries that are the same (except for different parameters), the optimizer creates a cached plan that describes the access mechanism. This plan can be reused by all subsequent similar queries.

Stored procedures have cached plans and so do many ad hoc queries. With ad hoc queries, reuse can be restricted based on the parameters supplied and the simplicity of the query. Cached plans allow subsequent reruns of the queries to run more quickly, because the access method is already known. Although this is fine for queries where the underlying data doesn't change significantly (in terms of the distribution and density of data values), there can be problems when the underlying data does change.

In addition, when the cached plan is created, it's based on the parameters initially supplied to it. If these initial parameter values are atypical (for example, getting data where data volumes are based on a holiday), then subsequent reuse of the plan is likely to be suboptimal. Indeed, when a query suddenly starts to run slowly, it's often advisable to recompile it, because its cached plan may have been based on atypical parameters. Note that when the data in the underlying tables changes significantly (typically 20% of the table changes), the statistics are automatically updated. This leads to any related SQL queries being recompiled and a new cached plan created when the queries are next run.

I'll have a lot more to say about this in the next chapter when we identify and discuss which queries are running slower than normal in section 5.5, "Slower-than-normal queries."

4.1.1 Aggregated results

It's important to remember that the DMVs accumulate metrics since the last SQL Server reboot or restart. Often you may want to clear the DMVs to give you a clean starting point from which to take your measurements. Clearing the DMVs on production systems is generally not recommended. Instead, you can infer the effects of your SQL queries on the DMVs by using DMV snapshots. For more information about this method of measuring the effects on DMVs without resetting them, see "Calculating DMV changes" in chapter 2.

4.1.2 Clearing the cached plans

If a SQL query hasn't been run on SQL Server since the last reboot, it won't be present in the DMVs. This is especially important if you're using the DMVs to determine whether an object (for example, a stored procedure, table, or index) hasn't been used and could be removed.

It's possible to save DMV data periodically into user-defined tables; an example of this is given in chapter 11, section 11.7, "Who's doing what and when?" Also, in SQL Server 2008 and higher, you might want to consider using the Data Collector, which stores server-wide data, including that relating to DMVs, into a centralized data warehouse for later analysis. Several tools also store DMV data (for example, DMVStats).

In addition to the aforementioned caveats, there are other cases where the DMVs, or some of them, may be cleared. These cases are reboots, a flushed cache, and memory pressure.

REBOOTS/RESTARTS

When SQL Server is rebooted, or the service is stopped and restarted, any DMV data is lost.

FLUSHED CACHE

Issuing certain DBCC commands (for example, DBCC FreeProcCache) will cause the cached plans to be flushed out. Any SQL queries that run subsequently will re-create the cached plans anew. Such commands were discussed in the section "Clearing DMVs" in chapter 1. Typically, you use these commands to provide a clean starting point for any DMV work. An alternative to this approach, which doesn't involve clearing the DMVs, is to use DMV snapshots, as already discussed.

MEMORY PRESSURES

Memory is a finite resource on SQL Server. Keeping a large number of cached plans can quickly fill the available memory, especially in systems that create lots of SQL queries that differ subtly (for example, having different environment settings), resulting in separate cached plans for each one. When SQL Server observes this pressure on its memory, it uses an algorithm to remove the least-used cached plans.

4.2   Finding a cached plan

As you've seen in the previous section, when a SQL query (batch or stored procedure) is run, the optimizer determines how it will fulfill its needs. Typically, the optimizer looks at the number of rows in the tables, the indexes, and statistics, and determines the best way to access the table's data.

Viewing the cached plan associated with a SQL query is a great way to discover why a query is behaving as it is. For example, why is the query taking too long? Is it using an index or a table scan? Is an index being used appropriately (an index seek rather than an index scan)?

4.2.1   How to find a cached plan

Cached plans contain detailed information about how a given query request is to be fulfilled. Running the SQL script given in listing 4.1 will retrieve the first 20 cached plans that contain the text "PartyType" ❶. "PartyType" in the following listing is the text we know is in the cached plan we want to investigate further. Typically, this filter, if specific enough, will retrieve only the cached plan we're interested in.

Listing 4.1 How to find a cached plan

```
SET TRANSACTION ISOLATION LEVEL READ UNCOMMITTED

SELECT TOP 20
      st.text AS [SQL]
    , cp.cacheobjtype
    , cp.objtype
    , COALESCE(DB_NAME(st.dbid),
         DB_NAME(CAST(pa.value AS INT))+'*',
         'Resource') AS [DatabaseName]
    , cp.usecounts AS [Plan usage]
    , qp.query_plan                              Join cached plan,
FROM sys.dm_exec_cached_plans cp                 text, and plan
CROSS APPLY sys.dm_exec_sql_text(cp.plan_handle) st
CROSS APPLY sys.dm_exec_query_plan(cp.plan_handle) qp
OUTER APPLY sys.dm_exec_plan_attributes(cp.plan_handle) pa
WHERE pa.attribute = 'dbid'                      ❶ Text to search
  AND st.text LIKE '%PartyType%'                    plan for
```

In the listing, one DMV and three DMFs are involved in finding a cached plan; a brief description of each is given in table 4.1.

Table 4.1 DMV/DMFs to find a cached plan

DMV/DMF	Description
sys.dm_exec_cached_plans	Contains cached query plans
sys.dm_exec_sql_text	DMF that returns the SQL text identified by a given SQL handle or plan handle
sys.dm_exec_query_plan	DMF that returns the cached plan, in XML format, identified by a given plan handle
sys.dm_exec_plan_attributes	DMF used to obtain the underlying database for ad hoc or pre-pared queries (as opposed to stored procedures)

The joining of the DMV and DMFs provides us with enough information to identify the cached plans for the specified text pattern given by the LIKE clause, across all the databases on the server. The DMV sys.dm_exec_cached_plans provides the plan_handle used to CROSS APPLY to all three DMFs. The cached plan's plan_handle is passed to the DMF sys.dm_exec_sql_text to retrieve the text of the SQL query. Similarly, the cached plan's plan_handle is passed to the DMF sys.dm_exec_query_plan to retrieve the cached plan of the query. Finally, the cached plan's plan_handle is passed to the DMF sys.dm_exec_plan_attributes to decode the underlying database name for any ad hoc or prepared queries.

We use a common pattern to extract the underlying database name for any ad hoc or prepared queries. For more detail on these common patterns, see chapter 2.

The query we execute selects the first 20 queries that contain the text "PartyType" in the SQL query, across all databases on the server. This query can be very useful when searching the SQL queries for a given comment, for example, a given change number, change implementer, or date of change.

> ### LIKE pattern matching
>
> There's one thing to be careful of when searching for names that are wrapped in square brackets or have an underscore, as is sometimes the case in SQL Server function names, for example [dbo].[Some_Function_Name]. When a LIKE statement is used, it interprets the underscore to mean any single character and the square brackets to means any single character within the set.
>
> It's possible to escape these characters so they can be used, by preceding the relevant string in with a backslash (\). For example, to find routines that contain the text "dba_," the LIKE statement would be
>
> ```
> LIKE '%dba\_%' ESCAPE '\'
> ```

An example of the type of output for this query is shown in figure 4.1.

You could amend the script presented in listing 4.1 to filter for cached plans on a given database only. You can also filter on the objtype to look only at nonstored procedure SQL queries, if you're interested in the number of ad hoc queries running on the server.

The code snippet presented allows you to search for a cached plan that contains a given piece of text. Later, in the next chapter (in sections 5.1 to 5.4), I'll present another code snippet that allows you to search inside the cached plans for indicators of poor performance.

	SQL	cacheobjtype	objtype	DatabaseName	Plan usage	query_plan
1	CREATE FUNCTION [dbo].[PartyTypeCl...	Compiled Plan	Proc	ParisQA03	8	<ShowPlanXML xmlns="htt...
2	----------------------------------...	Compiled Plan	Proc	ParisQA03	8	<ShowPlanXML xmlns="htt...
3	CREATE FUNCTION [dbo].[PartyTypeCl...	Compiled Plan	Proc	ParisQA03	8	<ShowPlanXML xmlns="htt...
4	----------------------------------...	Compiled Plan	Proc	ParisQA03	8	<ShowPlanXML xmlns="htt...
5	CREATE FUNCTION [dbo].[PartyTypeCl...	Compiled Plan	Proc	ParisGDI3	2	<ShowPlanXML xmlns="htt...
6	----------------------------------...	Compiled Plan	Proc	ParisGDI3	2	<ShowPlanXML xmlns="htt...
7	CREATE FUNCTION [dbo].[PartyTypeCl...	Compiled Plan	Proc	ParisGDI3	2	<ShowPlanXML xmlns="htt...
8	----------------------------------...	Compiled Plan	Proc	ParisGDI3	2	<ShowPlanXML xmlns="htt...
9	----------------------------------...	Compiled Plan	Proc	ParisGDI3	3931	<ShowPlanXML xmlns="htt...
10	-- use of alter going forward allows us ...	Compiled Plan	Proc	ParisGDI3	3931	NULL

Figure 4.1   Output showing cached plans that contain the text "PartyType"

4.3 Finding where a query is used

When you first join a new organization, you may need to quickly understand the business's SQL queries and database structures. You may also need to perform impact analysis of query changes or investigate production problems where the only lead is an error message relating to the table or partial query information.

In all these cases, knowing where a given SQL query is used, what stored procedures it's in, and how it was executed should help you gain a better understanding of the problem and help in providing a solution.

4.3.1 Identifying where a query is used

Identifying where a given query is used can give you a better understanding of system usage and can help provide faster problem resolution. Running the SQL script given in the following listing will identify the first 20 queries ❶ that contain the text you're searching for, in this case, "insert into dbo.deal." ❷

Listing 4.2 Finding where a query is used

```
SET TRANSACTION ISOLATION LEVEL READ UNCOMMITTED

SELECT TOP 20                                              ❶ Extract SQL
  SUBSTRING (qt.text,(qs.statement_start_offset/2) + 1,      statement
  ((CASE WHEN qs.statement_end_offset = -1
    THEN LEN(CONVERT(NVARCHAR(MAX), qt.text)) * 2
      ELSE qs.statement_end_offset
    END - qs.statement_start_offset)/2) + 1) AS [Individual Query]
  , qt.text AS [Parent Query]
  , DB_NAME(qt.dbid) AS DatabaseName
  , qp.query_plan
FROM sys.dm_exec_query_stats qs
CROSS APPLY sys.dm_exec_sql_text(qs.sql_handle) as qt
CROSS APPLY sys.dm_exec_query_plan(qs.plan_handle) qp
WHERE SUBSTRING (qt.text,(qs.statement_start_offset/2) + 1,
  ((CASE WHEN qs.statement_end_offset = -1
    THEN LEN(CONVERT(NVARCHAR(MAX), qt.text)) * 2
    ELSE qs.statement_end_offset
    END - qs.statement_start_offset)/2) + 1)      ❷ Text to search
LIKE '%insert into dbo.deal%'                         plan for
```

Here one DMV and two DMFs are involved in identifying where a query is used. Table 4.2 offers a brief description of each.

Table 4.2 DMV/DMFs used to identify where a query is used.

DMV/DMF	Description
sys.dm_exec_query_stats	Contains aggregated performance statistics for cached plans
sys.dm_exec_sql_text	DMF that returns the SQL text identified by a given sql_handle or plan_handle
sys.dm_exec_query_plan	DMF that returns the cached plan, in XML format, identified by a given plan_handle

By joining the DMV and DMFs we have sufficient information to identify where the queries are used, across all the databases on the server. The DMV sys.dm_exec_query_stats is joined to the DMFs via the CROSS APPLY keyword. The query's sql_handle is passed to the DMF sys.dm_exec_sql_text to retrieve the text of the SQL query. Similarly, the query's plan_handle is passed to the DMF sys.dm_exec_query_plan to retrieve the cached plan of the query. We use a common pattern to extract the Individual Query from the Parent Query.

The query we execute selects the 20 queries that contain the SQL text, across all databases on the server. We can restrict the results further by specifying the database we want to search.

Sample output for this query is shown in figure 4.2.

Knowing where a given SQL query is used is useful when examining the impact of changes or when you want to gain a better understanding of a system. For example, you might want to know where a given table is updated or inserted into or which stored procedure contains a given line of SQL or text. The cached plan supplied with the output should prove useful in helping you improve the query's performance.

Let's now look at a code snippet that you'll want to run often. It identifies queries that take the longest time to run; these are primary candidates for performance improvements.

4.4   Long-running queries

Probably the most common request from users about their queries is, "Why is my query running so slowly?" There can be many reasons why a query is running slowly. In this section I'll show you how to obtain a list of the slowest queries and discuss what you can do to improve their performance.

The DMV sys.dm_exec_query_stats records various metrics about the performance of SQL queries. It's important to explain the different metrics here because there are various measures of slowness. For most users, slowness is measured by the total duration of a query. The DMV sys.dm_exec_query_stats records this in the column total_elapsed_time (as microseconds). This total_elapsed_time consists of both the amount of time spent on the CPU doing work (recorded in the column total_worker_time) and the time spent waiting to execute.

	Individual Query	Parent Query	DatabaseName	query_plan
1	INSERT INTO dbo.Deal ([D...	/*------- ...	Paris	NULL
2	INSERT INTO dbo.DealCo...	/*------- ...	Paris	NULL
3	INSERT INTO dbo.Deal ([D...	/*------- ...	Paris	NULL
4	INSERT INTO dbo.DealCo...	/*------- ...	Paris	NULL

Figure 4.2   Output showing the results of searching for a given query

Time waiting to execute can be viewed as time being blocked, because the query should be running but for some reason it can't get onto the CPU. There are many reasons why the query may be waiting to execute, including waiting to acquire a lock on a resource and waiting for I/O to complete.

We have three different measures of query performance: total duration, time on the CPU, and time being blocked. We'll examine each of these individually in scripts within this section. First we'll concentrate on total duration, because this is how users typically report a query as being slow.

4.4.1 Finding the queries that take the longest time to run

If you can identify slow-running queries, you should be able to target your improvements and increase the performance of the server as a whole. Running the SQL script given in the next listing will identify the top 20 queries ❶ that take the longest time to run, as ordered by total_elapsed_time ❷.

Listing 4.3 The queries that take the longest time to run

```
SET TRANSACTION ISOLATION LEVEL READ UNCOMMITTED

SELECT TOP 20
  CAST(qs.total_elapsed_time / 1000000.0 AS DECIMAL(28, 2))
                               AS [Total Duration (s)]
, CAST(qs.total_worker_time * 100.0 / qs.total_elapsed_time
                         AS DECIMAL(28, 2)) AS [% CPU]
, CAST((qs.total_elapsed_time - qs.total_worker_time)* 100.0 /
      qs.total_elapsed_time AS DECIMAL(28, 2)) AS [% Waiting]
, qs.execution_count
, CAST(qs.total_elapsed_time / 1000000.0 / qs.execution_count
            AS DECIMAL(28, 2)) AS [Average Duration (s)]    ❶ Extract SQL
, SUBSTRING (qt.text,(qs.statement_start_offset/2) + 1,         statement
  ((CASE WHEN qs.statement_end_offset = -1
     THEN LEN(CONVERT(NVARCHAR(MAX), qt.text)) * 2
     ELSE qs.statement_end_offset
     END - qs.statement_start_offset)/2) + 1) AS [Individual Query]
, qt.text AS [Parent Query]
, DB_NAME(qt.dbid) AS DatabaseName
, qp.query_plan
FROM sys.dm_exec_query_stats qs
CROSS APPLY sys.dm_exec_sql_text(qs.sql_handle) as qt
CROSS APPLY sys.dm_exec_query_plan(qs.plan_handle) qp
WHERE qs.total_elapsed_time > 0                          ❷ Sort by slowest
ORDER BY qs.total_elapsed_time DESC                         queries
```

In the listing, one DMV and two DMFs are involved in identifying the queries that take the longest time to run. A brief description of each is given in table 4.3.

Table 4.3   DMV/DMFs to identify the queries that take the longest time to run

DMV/DMF	Description
sys.dm_exec_query_stats	Contains aggregated performance statistics for cached plans
sys.dm_exec_sql_text	DMF that returns the SQL text identified by a given sql_handle
sys.dm_exec_query_plan	DMF that returns the cached plan, in XML format, identified by a given plan_handle

Joining the DMV and DMFs provides enough information to identify the queries that take the longest to run, across all the databases on the server. The DMV sys.dm_exec_query_stats is joined to the DMFs via the CROSS APPLY keyword. The query's sql_handle is passed to the DMF sys.dm_exec_sql_text to retrieve the text of the SQL query. Similarly, the query's plan_handle is passed to the DMF sys.dm_exec_query_plan to retrieve the cached plan of the query. We use a common pattern to extract the Individual Query, which the timings relate to, from the Parent Query.

If there isn't much data in the DMVs or some of the DMV columns have a zero value, you might encounter a "divide by zero" error. To prevent this, a WHERE clause is added to the script to ensure that all queries have a total_elapsed_time value of greater than zero. This won't affect the results, because queries that execute in zero time won't be slow queries.

The query we execute selects the 20 queries that take the longest time to run, across all databases on the server. The query calculates the total elapsed duration in seconds, by dividing the total_elapsed_time column by 1,000,000 because this column's value relates to microseconds. We use the T-SQL CAST function to output the result to two decimal places. Similarly, the average elapsed time is expressed in seconds, by dividing the total_elapsed_time column by 1,000,000 and then dividing again by the number of times the query has executed (execution_count).

The percentage of time the query spent waiting on resources, as opposed to executing on the CPU, is also calculated by multiplying the difference between total_elapsed_time and total_worker_time by 100 and dividing the result by the total_elapsed_time. Similarly, we calculate the percentage of the time the query spends doing work on the CPU by multiplying the total_worker_time by 100 and dividing the result by the total_elapsed_time. In both cases, we use the T-SQL CAST function to display the result to two decimal places.

Having these values will allow us to determine whether the query has spent most of its time waiting or executing. This will be useful in determining whether the query's slowness is a result of internal or external factors.

The name of the database, the Individual Query, the Parent Query, and the query's cached plan are also output. The output is sorted by total_elapsed_time in descending order.

Figure 4.3 shows an example of the type of output for this query.

	Total Duration (s)	% CPU	% Waiting	execution_count	Average Duration (s)	Individual Query	Parent Query	Database Name	query_plan
1	1057.32	63.66	36.34	33	32.04	WITH pnl_cte(Repor...	/* ─────...	Paris	NULL
2	772.38	2.51	97.49	10	77.24	SELECT "Cob","Domain...	SELECT "Cob","Domai...	NULL	<ShowPlanXM
3	592.22	2.35	97.65	15068	0.04	UPDATE t SET [Org...	– use of alter going f...	Paris	NULL
4	557.41	51.72	48.28	1493	0.37	INSERT INTO #RiskPre...	──── – use of alter goi...	Paris	NULL
5	545.52	76.40	23.60	2	272.76	INSERT #OutputHolder (...	CREATE PROCEDUR...	Paris	<ShowPlanXM
6	544.97	86.35	13.65	1	544.97	SELECT p.*,o.OrgHierar...	SELECT p.*,o.OrgHierar...	NULL	<ShowPlanXM
7	418.45	0.03	99.97	26	16.09	SELECT DISTINCT de...	CREATE PROCEDURE ...	Paris	<ShowPlanXM
8	400.14	88.73	11.27	15068	0.03	SELECT @RequestDeal...	CREATE PROC [dbo].[...	Paris	<ShowPlanXM
9	390.56	92.20	7.80	2	195.28	SELECT yc.compone...	CREATE PROCEDUR...	Paris	<ShowPlanXM

Figure 4.3 Output showing the queries that take the longest time to run

4.4.2 *The impact of long-running queries*

I'm sure you'll agree that obtaining details of the queries taking the longest time to run via DMVs is significantly easier than doing the same thing with the typical alternative: the SQL Server Profiler utility. You must start SQL Server Profiler before the queries are run or, as often happens, before the queries are rerun. It also makes more use of system resources, and because of this, DBAs are often reluctant to use it on production systems. When the Profiler is finished (it may take some time), the results need to be amalgamated, and this can be cumbersome when the SQL queries have different parameters and routine signatures.

To do the same thing with DMVs, you query the already populated DMVs. If you're interested in the slowest queries in a given time period, you can use the DMV snapshot technique discussed in chapter 2.

> **The accumulative effect of short-duration queries**
> An interesting observation seen easily with DMVs is the accumulative effect of queries that individually take only a small amount of time to run but collectively can have a significant impact. When the SQL Server Profiler is used, it's common to filter out queries that take less than a given time to run. In this case, the cumulative effect of these queries would be missed.

Now that we've identified the queries that take the longest time to run, the next step is to determine why they're running so slowly. Finally, we'll look at how to improve them.

One of the columns output from the script is named % waiting; this column is useful for determining whether most of the query's time was spent doing work or waiting on another resource. If the % waiting value is relatively high, say over 60%, the query is spending less time on the CPU doing work and more time waiting on other resources before it can do its work. This points to external factors as the primary source of the query's slowness.

Similarly, if the % waiting column is relatively low, say below 40%, the query is spending more time on the CPU doing work than waiting on resources; this points more to internal factors as the cause of the query's slowness. For queries that have a % waiting in the range of 40% to 60%, we should look at both external and internal factors. This approach is summarized in table 4.4.

Table 4.4   **Percentage waiting and cause of slowness**

% waiting	Cause of slowness
> 60%	External factors
< 40%	Internal factors
Between 40% and 60%	Both external and internal factors

Okay, what are these factors we should be looking at? For queries that have a high % waiting value, the query is unable to get onto the CPU to do its work. The external factors (external in that they're outside this query's control) that are stopping this query from getting to the CPU include other queries using the CPU, waiting on I/O to complete, blocking by other queries, and lock escalation. You can verify that interaction with other queries is the cause of the slowness by running the query on a stand-alone database or at a time when other queries aren't running. Indeed, one solution to improving the performance of blocked queries is to run them at a time when system usage is low.

For queries with a low % waiting value, the query has gotten on the CPU and is doing a lot of work. Internal factors that can affect the query's performance include missing indexes, inappropriate index usage (for example, a repeated seek instead of a scan), stale statistics, and data type conversions (this can lead to an index not being used).

Alternatively, the query could be processing a lot more data than usual. Later, in chapter 5, we'll examine the case where the queries are running slower than normal, taking into account the amount of I/O involved.

For external factors, you can see the cause of the waits via the DMV sys.dm_os_wait_stats. If you create a DMV snapshot delta when you run your slow queries, you'll discover the cause of the waiting for your specific queries. For more information on how to create a DMV snapshot delta, see "Calculating DMV changes" in chapter 2.

It may be possible to improve the performance of queries that have a high % waiting value by lowering the amount of locking the query performs. For read-only queries, which make no changes to the underlying data, appending WITH(NOLOCK) after each table name in the query will result in the query taking no locks or honoring any locks on the table, both of which should improve performance. For example, to select rows from a table named dbo.Deal, without any locking, run the following command:

```
SELECT * FROM dbo.Deal WITH(NOLOCK)
```

For update queries, if the queries run at the same time as other queries that might update the same data, adding WITH(NOLOCK) can cause problems and should be avoided. But if an update query deals with a subset of data that isn't updated by other queries that run at the same time (perhaps you handle accounts starting with letters A–M and someone else handles accounts starting with letters N–Z), appending WITH(NOLOCK) to the table name should be advantageous.

It's possible to apply one statement to the top of a script that behaves in the same way as appending WITH(NOLOCK) to each table. You can accomplish this with the following command:

```
SET TRANSACTION ISOLATION LEVEL READ UNCOMMITTED
```

For queries with a low % waiting value, their slowness is more affected by internal factors. These might include missing indexes, stale statistics, incorrect fill factor, and fragmented indexes. You can get more insight into the factors that are limiting a query's performance by looking at the query's cached plan. The cached plan is provided as one of the output columns in the script. Please see chapter 3, "Index DMVs," for a consideration of these internal factors and how to correct them. It's also worthwhile looking at the plan for any oddities such as data type conversions or key lookups. Data type conversions relate to an incorrect type of data being used, in which case SQL Server will do a conversion; this might result in an otherwise useful index being ignored. I'll provide a script in chapter 5, section 5.3 ("Finding queries that have implicit data type conversions"), that will enable you to search cached plans for such oddities for subsequent correction.

Sometimes, no matter what you change, the query's performance doesn't improve. As a last resort I suggest you rewrite the query into smaller steps. Providing simpler SQL queries often gives the optimizer more options, resulting in an improved plan with better performance.

Often queries take a long time to run because they're being blocked by other queries or are waiting on resources. We'll investigate this in the next section.

4.5　Queries that spend a long time being blocked

A SQL query may run quickly when it's the only query running on the server; this behavior may change dramatically when it's running together with other queries. Queries use shared resources, such as CPU and I/O subsystems, which may result in limited resources being available for other queries. In addition, update queries need to protect their rows while they're being changed and wrap a transaction around the rows being changed. These changes result in both fewer resources for other queries and a potential for blocking while the query performs its changes. For the purpose of this discussion, I'll use the terms *blocking* and *waiting* interchangeably.

The DMV sys.dm_exec_query_stats records metrics that allow you to determine how much of a query's run duration is spent being blocked. To calculate the amount of blocking, subtract the total_worker_time from the total_elapsed_time.

> **Is blocking the same as waiting?**
> When a query can't run, SQL Server records details of why it can't run. If a query is prevented from running because another query has access to the resources it wants, this is usually taken to be *blocking*. When a query is prevented from running due to other factors, such as waiting for I/O to complete, this is usually taken to mean *waiting*. In essence, blocking is a type of waiting that relates to locks and can be thought of as a subset of waiting. In most situations, you can treat the terms *blocking* and *waiting* as synonymous.

4.5.1 *Finding the queries that spend the longest time being blocked*

If you can identify the queries that spend the longest time being blocked, you can target these for improvement, perhaps providing a different access mechanism to the underlying data or providing a less-stringent locking regime. Both of these should improve concurrency and throughput. Running the SQL script given in the following listing calculates the time blocked ❶, for the top 20 most-blocked queries ❷, as ordered by Total time blocked (s) ❸.

Listing 4.4   The queries spend the longest time being blocked

```
SET TRANSACTION ISOLATION LEVEL READ UNCOMMITTED

SELECT TOP 20                                                        ❶ Calculate time
  CAST((qs.total_elapsed_time - qs.total_worker_time) /                blocked
        1000000.0 AS DECIMAL(28,2)) AS [Total time blocked (s)]
  , CAST(qs.total_worker_time * 100.0 / qs.total_elapsed_time
        AS DECIMAL(28,2)) AS [% CPU]
  , CAST((qs.total_elapsed_time - qs.total_worker_time)* 100.0 /
        qs.total_elapsed_time AS DECIMAL(28, 2)) AS [% Waiting]
  , qs.execution_count
  , CAST((qs.total_elapsed_time  - qs.total_worker_time) / 1000000.0
    / qs.execution_count AS DECIMAL(28, 2)) AS [Blocking average (s)]
  , SUBSTRING (qt.text,(qs.statement_start_offset/2) + 1,
  ((CASE WHEN qs.statement_end_offset = -1                            ❷ Extract SQL
    THEN LEN(CONVERT(NVARCHAR(MAX), qt.text)) * 2                       statement
    ELSE qs.statement_end_offset
    END - qs.statement_start_offset)/2) + 1) AS [Individual Query]
  , qt.text AS [Parent Query]
  , DB_NAME(qt.dbid) AS DatabaseName
  , qp.query_plan
FROM sys.dm_exec_query_stats qs
CROSS APPLY sys.dm_exec_sql_text(qs.sql_handle) as qt
CROSS APPLY sys.dm_exec_query_plan(qs.plan_handle) qp
WHERE qs.total_elapsed_time > 0                                       ❸ Sort by most
ORDER BY [Total time blocked (s)] DESC                                  time blocked
```

In this example, one DMV and two DMFs are involved in identifying the queries that spend the longest time being blocked. A brief description of each is given in table 4.5.

Table 4.5   DMV/DMFs to reveal the queries that take the longest time being blocked

DMV/DMF	Description
sys.dm_exec_query_stats	Contains aggregated performance statistics for cached plans
sys.dm_exec_sql_text	DMF that returns the SQL text identified by a given sql_handle or plan_handle
sys.dm_exec_query_plan	DMF that returns the cached plan, in XML format, identified by a given plan_handle

By joining the DMV and DMFs, we have adequate information to identify the queries that spend the longest time being blocked, across all the databases on the server. The DMV sys.dm_exec_query_stats is joined to the DMFs via the CROSS APPLY keyword. The query's sql_handle is passed to the DMF sys.dm_exec_sql_text to retrieve the text of the SQL query. Similarly, the query's plan_handle is passed to the DMF sys.dm_exec_query_plan to retrieve the cached plan of the query. We use a common pattern to extract the Individual Query, which the timings relate to, from the Parent Query.

If there isn't much data in the DMVs or some of the DMV columns have a zero value, it's possible to encounter a "divide by zero" error. To prevent this, a WHERE clause is added to the script that ensures all queries have a total_elapsed_time value of greater than zero.

The query we execute selects the 20 queries that are blocked the most, across all databases on the server. The query calculates the Total Time Blocked in seconds, by subtracting the total_worker_time column from the total_elapsed_time column and dividing the result by 1,000,000 because the column's value relates to microseconds. We use the T-SQL CAST function to output the result to two decimal places. Similarly, the Blocking Average is expressed in seconds, by subtracting the total_worker_time column from the total_elapsed_time column, dividing the result by 1,000,000, and then dividing again by the number of times the query has executed (execution_count).

The other column outputs are % CPU, % Waiting, DatabaseName, Individual Query, Parent Query, and the query's cached plan (query_plan). The output is sorted by Total time blocked in descending order.

If you're interested in which queries are the most blocked, as a percentage of the total time it takes to run the query, you can get this information by editing the existing script to sort by % waiting in descending order. This will allow you to target your improvement efforts on the external factors described in the previous section.

Sample output for this query is shown in figure 4.4.

The results are sorted by the Total time blocked and show the queries that have spent the most time being blocked. We also record the percentage of time the query spent on the CPU (% CPU column) and the percentage of time the query spent being blocked (% Waiting column).

	Total time blocked (s)	% CPU	% Waiting	execution_count	Blocking average (s)	Individual Query	Parent Query	Database Name	query_plan
1	8343.13	0.01	99.99	1	8343.13	SELECT DealId...	CREATE PRO...	ParisDev	<ShowPlanXM
2	3689.94	0.00	100.00	12	307.50	WAITFOR(REC...	– sp_readreque...	msdb	<ShowPlanXM
3	1950.33	3.93	96.07	18733	0.10	SELECT @PrinI...	CREATE PR...	ParisDev	<ShowPlanXM
4	464.00	40.49	59.51	1	464.00	INSERT INTO [...	CREATE PRO...	Paris	<ShowPlanXM
5	162.23	39.03	60.97	1	162.23	DELETE FROM...	CREATE PRO...	Paris	NULL
6	80.84	11.33	88.67	21044	0.00	SELECT @Accr...	CREATE PRO...	ParisDev	<ShowPlanXM
7	66.18	33.33	66.67	1	66.18	INSERT INTO [...	/–––––––––...	ParisDev	<ShowPlanXM
8	60.08	13.19	86.81	18733	0.00	SELECT @Prev...	CREATE PR...	ParisDev	<ShowPlanXM
9	55.30	12.89	87.11	14	3.95	SELECT td.CO...	CREATE PRO...	ParisDev	<ShowPlanXM
10	52.36	15.41	84.59	6	8.73	SELECT @C...	CREATE PRO...	Paris	<ShowPlanXM

Figure 4.4 Output showing the queries that spend the longest time being blocked

For more details on how you can improve the performance of the most-blocked queries, please read the previous section on the impact of queries that take the longest time to run.

When a query isn't waiting or being blocked, it's typically using the CPU. In the next section I'll identify which queries are using the most CPU and suggest why this might reflect various performance problems, along with some possible solutions.

4.6   *CPU-intensive queries*

Queries need to coexist with other queries running at the same time. Therefore they need to share resources such as CPU. If a query is making high usage of the CPU, it means there may be less CPU resources for other queries, resulting in blocking and poorer-performing queries. High CPU usage may also be a sign of problems, such as a suboptimal cached plan or missing indexes.

The DMV sys.dm_exec_query_stats records how long a query spends on the CPU, in the column total_worker_time; this forms the basis of our code snippet.

4.6.1   *Finding the queries that use the most CPU*

If you can identify the queries that use the most CPU, you can inspect their cached plans for indications of why they're so CPU intensive, with a view to improving their performance. It may be because they're doing a lot of calculations, and perhaps this work could be offloaded to a CLR function (see chapter 7 for more information about this). Running the SQL script given in the next listing will identify the top 20 queries ❶ that use the most CPU, as ordered by Total CPU time (s) ❷.

Listing 4.5   The queries that use the most CPU

```
SET TRANSACTION ISOLATION LEVEL READ UNCOMMITTED

SELECT TOP 20
    CAST((qs.total_worker_time) / 1000000.0 AS DECIMAL(28,2))
                                    AS [Total CPU time (s)]
  , CAST(qs.total_worker_time * 100.0 / qs.total_elapsed_time
                        AS DECIMAL(28,2)) AS [% CPU]
  , CAST((qs.total_elapsed_time - qs.total_worker_time)* 100.0 /
        qs.total_elapsed_time AS DECIMAL(28, 2)) AS [% Waiting]
```

```
    , qs.execution_count
    , CAST((qs.total_worker_time) / 1000000.0
      / qs.execution_count AS DECIMAL(28, 2)) AS [CPU time average (s)]
    , SUBSTRING (qt.text,(qs.statement_start_offset/2) + 1,
      ((CASE WHEN qs.statement_end_offset = -1
        THEN LEN(CONVERT(NVARCHAR(MAX), qt.text)) * 2
        ELSE qs.statement_end_offset
        END - qs.statement_start_offset)/2) + 1) AS [Individual Query]
    , qt.text AS [Parent Query]
    , DB_NAME(qt.dbid) AS DatabaseName
    , qp.query_plan
FROM sys.dm_exec_query_stats qs
CROSS APPLY sys.dm_exec_sql_text(qs.sql_handle) as qt
CROSS APPLY sys.dm_exec_query_plan(qs.plan_handle) qp
WHERE qs.total_elapsed_time > 0
ORDER BY [Total CPU time (s)] DESC
```

❶ Extract SQL statement

❷ Sort by most CPU used

In the listing, you can see that one DMV and two DMFs are involved in identifying the queries that use the most CPU. A brief description of each is shown in table 4.6.

Table 4.6   DMV/DMFs to identify the queries that use the most CPU

DMV/DMF	Description
sys.dm_exec_query_stats	Contains aggregated performance statistics for cached plans
sys.dm_exec_sql_text	DMF that returns the SQL text identified by a given sql_handle or plan_handle
sys.dm_exec_query_plan	DMF that returns the cached plan, in XML format, identified by a given plan_handle

The joining of the DMV and DMFs provides us with enough information to identify the queries that use the most CPU, across all the databases on the server. The DMV sys.dm_exec_query_stats is joined to the DMFs via the CROSS APPLY keyword. The query's sql_handle is passed to the DMF sys.dm_exec_sql_text to retrieve the text of the SQL query. Similarly, the query's plan_handle is passed to the DMF sys.dm_exec_query_plan to retrieve the cached plan of the query. We use a common pattern to extract the Individual Query, which the timings relate to, from the Parent Query.

If there isn't much data in the DMVs or some of the DMV columns have a zero value, you might encounter a "divide by zero" error. To prevent this, a WHERE clause added to the script ensures that all queries have a total_elapsed_time value of greater than zero.

The query we execute selects the 20 queries that use the most CPU, across all databases on the server. The query calculates the Total CPU time in seconds, by dividing the total_worker_time column by 1,000,000 because the column's value relates to microseconds. We use the T-SQL CAST function to output the result to two decimal places. Similarly, the CPU Time Average is expressed in seconds, by dividing the total_worker_time column by 1,000,000 and then dividing again by the number of times the query has executed (execution_count).

Figure 4.5   Output showing the queries that use the most CPU

The other column outputs are % CPU, % Waiting, DatabaseName, the Individual Query, the Parent Query, and the query's cached plan. The output is sorted by Total CPU time (s) in descending order.

If you're interested in which queries use the most CPU as a percentage of the total time it takes to run the query, you can get this information by editing the existing script to sort by % CPU in descending order. This will allow you to target your improvement efforts on the internal factors described in the previous section.

An example of the type of output for this query is shown in figure 4.5.

The results are sorted by the Total CPU time (s) and show the queries that have spent the most time using the CPU. We also record the percentage of time the query spent on the CPU (% CPU column) and the percentage of time the query spent being blocked (% Waiting column).

For more detail on how you can improve the performance of the queries that use the most CPU, read the previous section on the impact of queries that take the longest time to run.

In addition to using the CPU to target queries that might reflect an underlying performance problem, it's possible to use the amount of I/O in a similar manner. We'll investigate this next.

4.7   I/O-hungry queries

Rather than looking at SQL query performance from the perspectives of query duration, blocking, and CPU, you can look at performance from an I/O viewpoint. This is particularly interesting because often I/O is the limiting factor on many database systems, where emphasis tends to be placed mainly on CPU and memory.

The core functionality of database systems is to retrieve data, and this is reflected in the amount of I/O involved. You can look at the queries that use the most I/O to determine whether they can be changed to retrieve data more efficiently. Perhaps an index is missing or is incomplete, or perhaps the SQL is incorrect or not specific enough, resulting in additional I/O.

A high I/O value suggests that the server may be doing unnecessary work, potentially increasing the number of locks on tables and indexes, leading to blocking and timeouts in client applications.

The DMV sys.dm_exec_query_stats records metrics that allow you to determine how much I/O a query uses. The DMV includes details of both physical and logical reads and writes. Here we'll concentrate on logical reads/writes, because typically after the first read from the physical device, the data will already be in memory.

4.7.1 Finding the queries that use the most I/O

If you identify those queries that use the most I/O, inspecting their cached plans might provide clues as to why they're using a lot of I/O. This might be because an index is missing or being used inappropriately because the statistics are stale. Running the SQL script given in the following listing will identify the top 20 queries ❶ that use the most I/O, as ordered by Total IO ❷.

Listing 4.6   The queries that use the most I/O

```
SET TRANSACTION ISOLATION LEVEL READ UNCOMMITTED
SELECT TOP 20
  [Total IO] = (qs.total_logical_reads + qs.total_logical_writes)
  , [Average IO] = (qs.total_logical_reads + qs.total_logical_writes) /
                                            qs.execution_count
  , qs.execution_count
  , SUBSTRING (qt.text,(qs.statement_start_offset/2) + 1,        ◁─┐  Extract SQL
  ((CASE WHEN qs.statement_end_offset = -1                         ❶ statement
    THEN LEN(CONVERT(NVARCHAR(MAX), qt.text)) * 2
    ELSE qs.statement_end_offset
    END - qs.statement_start_offset)/2) + 1) AS [Individual Query]
  , qt.text AS [Parent Query]
  , DB_NAME(qt.dbid) AS DatabaseName
  , qp.query_plan
FROM sys.dm_exec_query_stats qs
CROSS APPLY sys.dm_exec_sql_text(qs.sql_handle) as qt
CROSS APPLY sys.dm_exec_query_plan(qs.plan_handle) qp      ❷  Sort by
ORDER BY [Total IO] DESC                                   ◁─┘  Total IO
```

In this script, one DMV and two DMFs are involved in identifying the queries that use the most I/O. A brief description of each is given in table 4.7.

Table 4.7   DMV/DMFs to identify the queries that use the most I/O

DMV/DMF	Description
sys.dm_exec_query_stats	Contains aggregated performance statistics for cached plans
sys.dm_exec_sql_text	DMF that returns the SQL text identified by a given sql_handle or plan_handle
sys.dm_exec_query_plan	DMF that returns the cached plan, in XML format, identified by a given plan_handle

By joining the DMV and DMFs, we have enough information to identify the queries that use the most IO, across all the databases on the server. The DMV sys.dm_exec_query_stats is joined to the DMFs via the CROSS APPLY keyword. The query's sql_handle is passed to the DMF sys.dm_exec_sql_text to retrieve the text of the SQL query. Similarly, the query's plan_handle is passed to the DMF sys.dm_exec_query_ plan to retrieve the cached plan of the query. We use a common pattern to extract the Individual Query, which the timings relate to, from the Parent Query.

The query we execute selects the 20 queries that use the most I/O, across all databases on the server. The query calculates the Total IO by summing the columns total_logical_reads and total_logical_writes. Similarly, the Average IO is calculated by dividing the sum of the total_logical_reads and total_logical_writes by the number of times the query has executed (execution_count).

The other column outputs are DatabaseName, Individual Query, Parent Query, and the query's cached plan (query_plan). The output is sorted by Total IO in descending order.

An example of the type of output for this query is shown in figure 4.6.

4.7.2   *Reducing the impact of queries that use the most I/O*

The results are sorted by the Total IO and show the queries that have used the most I/O. We also record the Average IO per query. When the execution_count is relatively high and the Average IO relatively low, this suggests the query is being called repeatedly, getting a small amount of data per call. You may be able to optimize the query to get more data in fewer calls. This should reduce the Total IO value, resulting in a better-performing query. Looking at the Parent Query in the output will allow you to determine if this is possible.

Some SQL queries may have a high Total IO value because they're getting a lot of data, rather than getting a small amount of data repeatedly. If you examine the Individual Query column in the script's output, you may see some queries that start with SELECT *; often this is used because users don't know what data they need (maybe at the start of a project). You should correct this to retrieve only the data column required and thus reduce the Total IO value.

You should also examine the SQL given in the Individual Query column for an appropriate WHERE clause. Again, you should ensure you're retrieving only the subset of rows required.

	Total IO	Average IO	execution_count	Individual Query	Parent Query	DatabaseName	query_plan
1	1730286	865143	2	SELECT * FROM my.[...	SELECT * FROM my.[Or...	NULL	≤ShowPlanXM
2	945360	5	171984	set @levelofparent = (s...	CREATE FUNCTION [d...	Paris	≤ShowPlanXM
3	864788	864788	1	SELECT * FROM my.[...	SELECT * FROM my.[Or...	NULL	≤ShowPlanXM
4	864670	864670	1	SELECT * FROM my.[...	SELECT * FROM my.[Or...	NULL	≤ShowPlanXM
5	733104	6	122160	set @parent = (select t...	CREATE FUNCTION [d...	Paris	≤ShowPlanXM
6	733104	6	122160	set @levelofchild = (sel...	CREATE FUNCTION [d...	Paris	≤ShowPlanXM
7	595872	5	113736	set @parent = (select t...	CREATE FUNCTION [d...	Paris	≤ShowPlanXM
8	349488	6	58248	set @returnname=(sele...	CREATE FUNCTION [d...	Paris	≤ShowPlanXM
9	279564	279564	1	insert into #pnladjdatad...	-- use of alter going for...	Paris	≤ShowPlanXM
10	145060	145060	1	insert into #pnladjdatad...	-- use of alter going for...	Paris	≤ShowPlanXM

Figure 4.6   Output showing the queries that use the most I/O

If the Parent Query value is a function, it may be useful to search your code base (all your SQL code) to see how this function is used. If the function is embedded in SQL queries that are involved in various table joins, the function will be called for each row in the resultant table. It's often possible to cache this function value and supply the cached value to the query in the WHERE clause. This will reduce the amount of I/O and improve the performance of the query. I've known of many queries whose performance has been significantly improved by caching any embedded function calls they contain.

You should examine the query_plan column in the script's output for any entries that might suggest the query is performing suboptimally; these include table scan, index scan, stale statistics, and any implicit data conversions. I'll provide scripts in chapter 5, sections 5.1 to 5.4, to search for these items in the cached plans and also detail why they're typically detrimental factors.

It could prove useful to match the tables given in the Individual Query output with the tables specified in the missing indexes DMVs (see section 3.2, "Costly missing indexes," in chapter 3). Often a missing index will result in a corresponding increase in I/O. Similarly, comparing this script's output with the output from the queries that use the most I/O or CPU or have the longest duration or the most blocking may show how interlinked these "poor" queries are.

Another potential indicator of poor query performance might be the number of times a query is executed; this is especially true when the query involved is a function that's used in a JOIN condition. Let's examine this next.

4.8   Frequently executed queries

If you know which queries are executed most often, you can target the objects that they use (for example, indexes, statistics, and tables) to ensure they're optimal. Making improvements to the objects identified by these targeted queries should have a positive impact on performance because you know they're used often by queries.

In addition, if you can find a way to rewrite these SQL queries more efficiently (for example, caching function values), they'll have a positive effect each time they're used.

The DMV sys.dm_exec_query_stats records details of the number of times a given SQL query has been executed.

4.8.1   Finding the queries that have been executed the most often

Identifying the most-executed queries allows you to target improvements, which will be applied repeatedly as the queries are executed. Running the SQL script given in the following listing will identify the top 20 queries ❶ that are executed the most, as ordered by execution_count ❷ (see annotated lines in the next listing).

Listing 4.7   The queries that have been executed the most often

```
SET TRANSACTION ISOLATION LEVEL READ UNCOMMITTED

SELECT TOP 20
    qs.execution_count
    , SUBSTRING (qt.text,(qs.statement_start_offset/2) + 1,
    ((CASE WHEN qs.statement_end_offset = -1
      THEN LEN(CONVERT(NVARCHAR(MAX), qt.text)) * 2
      ELSE qs.statement_end_offset
      END - qs.statement_start_offset)/2) + 1) AS [Individual Query]
    , qt.text AS [Parent Query]
    , DB_NAME(qt.dbid) AS DatabaseName
    , qp.query_plan
FROM sys.dm_exec_query_stats qs
CROSS APPLY sys.dm_exec_sql_text(qs.sql_handle) as qt
CROSS APPLY sys.dm_exec_query_plan(qs.plan_handle) qp
ORDER BY qs.execution_count DESC;
```

❶ Extract SQL statement

❷ Sort by most executed

In this listing, one DMV and two DMFs are involved in identifying the queries that are executed most often. A brief description of each is given in table 4.8.

Table 4.8   DMV/DMFs that identify the queries that are executed most often

DMV/DMF	Description
sys.dm_exec_query_stats	Contains aggregated performance statistics for cached plans
sys.dm_exec_sql_text	DMF that returns the SQL text identified by a given sql_handle or plan_handle
sys.dm_exec_query_plan	DMF that returns the cached plan, in XML format, identified by a given plan_handle

The joining of the DMV and DMFs provides enough information to identify the queries that are executed most often, across all the databases on the server. The DMV sys.dm_exec_query_stats is joined to the DMFs via the CROSS APPLY keyword. The query's sql_handle is passed to the DMF sys.dm_exec_sql_text to retrieve the text of the SQL query. Similarly, the query's plan_handle is passed to the DMF sys.dm_exec_query_plan to retrieve the cached plan of the query. We use a common pattern to extract the Individual Query, which the execution count relates to, from the Parent Query.

The query we execute selects the 20 queries that are executed most often, across all databases on the server. The other columns of output are DatabaseName, Parent Query, and the query's cached plan (query_plan). The output is sorted by execution_count in descending order.

An example of the type of output for this query is shown in figure 4.7.

	execution_count	Individual Query	Parent Query	DatabaseName	query_plan
1	8397467	SELECT @ParentOrgId ...	CREATE FUNCTION [dbo].[OrgNa...	Paris	≤ShowPlanXML xn
2	7659493	set @levelofparent = (sel...	CREATE FUNCTION [dbo].[OrgNam...	Paris	≤ShowPlanXML xn
3	5425356	set @parent = (select top(...	CREATE FUNCTION [dbo].[OrgNam...	Paris	≤ShowPlanXML xn
4	5425356	set @levelofchild = (selec...	CREATE FUNCTION [dbo].[OrgNam...	Paris	≤ShowPlanXML xn
5	5054224	set @parent = (select top(...	CREATE FUNCTION [dbo].[OrgNam...	Paris	≤ShowPlanXML xn
6	2994288	IF @pRequiredLevel > IS...	CREATE FUNCTION [dbo].[OrgNa...	Paris	≤ShowPlanXML xn
7	2605269	set @returnname=(select ...	CREATE FUNCTION [dbo].[OrgNam...	Paris	≤ShowPlanXML xn
8	2267120	SELECT @Id = ProductH...	CREATE FUNCTION [dbo].[OfficialP...	Paris	≤ShowPlanXML xn
9	2102122	SELECT @OrgName = O...	CREATE FUNCTION dbo.OrgName(...	Paris	≤ShowPlanXML xn
10	1829914	SET @ReturnOrgName =...	CREATE FUNCTION [dbo].[OrgNa...	Paris	≤ShowPlanXML xn

Figure 4.7   Output showing the queries that are executed most often

4.8.2   *Reducing the impact of queries that are executed most often*

Knowing which SQL queries are executed most often provides you with a target for improvement, because you know that if you can improve the performance of these queries, it could have a significant impact on overall performance.

To identify areas of potential performance improvement, you can inspect the SQL text to ensure the following:

- There's no unnecessary sorting. Sometimes you may add an ORDER BY clause in your testing. It may not be necessary because often sorting takes place on the client.
- You're retrieving only the columns you need. During the initial phase of a project, you're unsure of the data you want, so you might issue a SELECT * for expediency. You should correct this.
- You have an appropriate WHERE clause. Again, you want to ensure that you're retrieving only the subset of rows you require.

Inspecting the cached plan associated with the query will allow you to check to see if any suboptimal operations are being performed. I'll present a script that does this in the next chapter. Again, to identify areas of potential performance improvement, you can check for the following:

- Missing indexes.
- Inappropriate index usage. Check for any index scans or lookups.
- Missing statistics.
- Implicit data type conversions.
- Unnecessary sorting. A hash join often suggests an index is missing.

You can also check these items:

- You have indexes on the join columns. When creating a database schema, although indexes are created by default on primary keys, they are *not* created on foreign keys.

■ Statistics are up to date and have a good sampling percentage. A script in chapter 3 displays the current status of your database statistics.

If the Parent Query in the output is a function, it may be that it's part of a JOIN or WHERE clause, and as such it will get called repeatedly for each row in the resultant join. This can have a detrimental effect on performance, and where possible the function value should be cached and the cached value used in the JOIN, in place of the function call.

In many cases, it's possible to see correlations in the output of the different DMV scripts given in this book. For example, a missing index may result in the queries that use the underlying tables having high I/O and CPU values.

4.9   The last run of a query

Often it's useful to know when a SQL query or stored procedure was last run. Similarly, it might be useful to know when a table was last updated or accessed. You might want to know this information when determining how a table came to be updated or to understand why some queries were run out of sequence, giving spurious results.

The DMV sys.dm_exec_query_stats records information that's useful in determining when a query was first run (typically, since the last reboot) and last run. You can limit your search by specifying the name of a stored procedure or an individual SQL statement. Similarly, you can specify an object name, for example, a table or view, and determine when this was last updated or read from.

4.9.1   Determining when a query was last run

As part of a larger piece of analysis work, it can often be useful to determine when a given query was last run. Running the SQL script given in the following listing will identify the top 20 times a given SQL query ❶ was run, as ordered by last_execution_time ❷. We identify the relevant query by supplying part of it as a filter via the WHERE clause.

> **Listing 4.8   Finding when a query was last run**

```
SET TRANSACTION ISOLATION LEVEL READ UNCOMMITTED

SELECT DISTINCT TOP 20
    qs.last_execution_time
    , qt.text AS [Parent Query]                              ❶ Name of
    , DB_NAME(qt.dbid) AS DatabaseName                          routine we're
FROM sys.dm_exec_query_stats qs                                 looking for
CROSS APPLY sys.dm_exec_sql_text(qs.sql_handle) as qt
WHERE qt.text LIKE '%CREATE PROCEDURE%List%PickList%'  ◁──  ❷ Sort by last
ORDER BY qs.last_execution_time DESC                    ◁──     time run
```

Here, one DMV and one DMF are involved in identifying when a query was last run. Table 4.9 provides a brief description of each.

Table 4.9   DMV/DMF to identify when a query was last run

DMV/DMF	Description
sys.dm_exec_query_stats	Contains aggregated performance statistics for cached plans
sys.dm_exec_sql_text	DMF that returns the SQL text identified by a given sql_handle

By joining the DMV and DMF, we have enough information to identify when the query was last run, across all the databases on the server. The DMV sys.dm_exec_query_stats is joined to the DMF via the CROSS APPLY keyword. The query's sql_handle is passed to the DMF sys.dm_exec_sql_text to retrieve the text of the SQL query.

The query we execute selects the 20 queries that contain the SQL text specified by the WHERE clause, across all databases on the server. You can restrict the output further by specifying the name of the database you're interested in. By specifying the CREATE PROCEDURE literal as part of the search criteria, you'll retrieve only one entry. If you were to specify just the stored procedure name (%List%PickList%) in this example, you'd expect at least two entries, because in addition to the stored procedure entry itself, you'll also have entries for any client SQL that calls this stored procedure.

Again, you need to be careful when you specify the WHERE criteria for a stored procedure, because the square brackets and underscore have special meaning for the LIKE statement. Searching for "CREATE PROC%[dbo].[usp_PickList]" may not give you the results you expect, because the square brackets are interpreted as "match any of the characters inside the square brackets."

Sample output for this query is shown in figure 4.8.

4.9.2   *Variations on searching for queries*

In addition to searching for when a given routine was last run, you can search for when a given SQL statement was last run. This might be useful if you want to determine which SQL queries updated or read from a given table or view.

For example, you can use the code snippet given in the next listing to determine when a table named dbo.Underlying last had rows added to it (this illustrates both when a given SQL query was run and when a table was last updated).

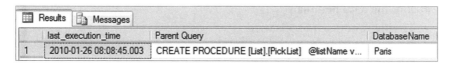

Figure 4.8   Output showing when a query was last run

Listing 4.9   Finding when a table was last inserted

```
SET TRANSACTION ISOLATION LEVEL READ UNCOMMITTED
SELECT TOP 20
    qs.last_execution_time
    , SUBSTRING (qt.text,(qs.statement_start_offset/2) + 1,
      ((CASE WHEN qs.statement_end_offset = -1
        THEN LEN(CONVERT(NVARCHAR(MAX), qt.text)) * 2
        ELSE qs.statement_end_offset
        END - qs.statement_start_offset)/2) + 1) AS [Individual Query]
    , qt.text AS [Parent Query]
    , DB_NAME(qt.dbid) AS DatabaseName
FROM sys.dm_exec_query_stats qs
CROSS APPLY sys.dm_exec_sql_text(qs.sql_handle) as qt
WHERE SUBSTRING (qt.text,(qs.statement_start_offset/2) + 1,
  ((CASE WHEN qs.statement_end_offset = -1
    THEN LEN(CONVERT(NVARCHAR(MAX), qt.text)) * 2
    ELSE qs.statement_end_offset
    END - qs.statement_start_offset)/2) + 1)
LIKE '%INSERT INTO dbo.Underlying%'
ORDER BY qs.last_execution_time DESC
```

❶ SQL query we're looking for

Sort by last time run

The listing is very similar to the other scripts we've created. The main point to note is that the WHERE clause specifies the SQL statement or object we want information about ❶.

It's also possible to determine which queries have run between two given points of time. There's a caveat with this, however, in that if a query is run outside the time limit you specify, it won't be in your results (because the DMV sys.dm_exec_query_stats only records when it was *last* run).

Similarly, the DMV sys.dm_exec_query_stats also records when a query was first used; this is shown in the column creation_time. Again there's a caveat: the times relate only to the time since SQL Server was last rebooted, providing the cached plan hasn't been removed because of memory pressure or other factors.

4.10   Summary

This chapter has provided several SQL scripts that can use be used to identify problematic SQL queries from different perspectives. Each perspective identifies queries that would benefit from further investigation, with the aim of improving their performance. Such scripts include the following:

- Finding a cached plan
- Finding where a query is used
- Which queries run the longest
- Which queries are blocked the most
- Which queries use the most CPU
- Which queries use the most I/O
- Which queries are executed the most often
- Which stored procedures are not used

For each script, we discussed the importance of the area under investigation, the impact of the factors discussed, and ways of improving the highlighted queries.

It's possible to extend the DMV snapshot pattern given in chapter 2 ("Common patterns"), in listing 2.7, to create DMV deltas for many of the scripts given in this chapter. This will allow you to determine the effect of a query on a wide range of DMV metrics.

You can do many more things with execution-based DMVs, such as determining which plans have missing statistics or which queries are running slower than normal. These and other examples are discussed in the next chapter.

Further query improvements

This chapter covers

- Identifying missing statistics and indexes
- Identifying queries running slower than normal
- Determining which SQL queries run over a given time period
- Capturing the relationships between DMV snapshot deltas

The previous chapter discussed scripts that allow you to discover information about the worst queries and how you might improve them. I'd now like to discuss a series of scripts that are typically not explicitly concerned with finding the slowest or worst item but rather indicate possible areas of concern and as such deserve to be examined in further detail.

We'll look at how to search the cached plans for details of missing statistics and missing indexes. Implementing these identified missing items could make a profound improvement on the performance of your SQL queries.

When SQL Server encounters a variable that has a different data type than expected, it needs to spend time converting the data type. This is unnecessary and can degrade performance. I'll provide a script to identify these mismatched data types.

I'll also show you how to identify queries that are running slower than normal and provide a discussion of why this might have happened, together with some possible solutions.

Because SQL queries typically don't run in isolation, it can be important to know which queries are running over a given time period. This is especially true where blocking and locking are concerns. We'll discuss a script that shows which SQL queries are running over a given time period.

Another script determines the effect of running queries on several DMVs. This will allow you to combine and reinforce the results from these different DMVs, giving you better insight into any problems.

Finally, I'll show you how to discover what SQL is currently running. Although I provided a script for this in chapter 1, the version given here is an updated version that uses DMVs only. Let's get started by examining which SQL queries have missing statistics.

5.1   Queries with missing statistics

Previously we discussed the impact of statistics on query performance. In essence, statistics contain details about the distribution and density of column values in a table or index. The optimizer uses this information to estimate the probability of access of a given column's value and thus provide an estimate of the cost of obtaining the underlying data.

Statistics are created automatically for indexes. In addition, when the optimizer comes across a column that's used in a JOIN condition or a WHERE clause, and no index exists, the optimizer will usually create statistics on the column. There are conditions that prevent statistics from being created or updated, and we'll discuss these later in this section. Sometimes, non-index-related statistics, including missing statistics, are indicators of missing indexes, and inspecting the DMVs that reveal missing indexes should confirm this.

It's possible to search the cached plans for queries that have missing statistics. Next up is a script that does just that.

5.1.1   Finding queries that have missing statistics

Statistics play a major role in the performance of SQL queries. I've witnessed huge increases in performance when missing statistics have subsequently been created. Running the SQL script given in the following listing will identify the top 20 queries with missing statistics, ordered by usecounts, which represents the number of times the cached plan has been used.

Listing 5.1   Finding queries with missing statistics

```
SET TRANSACTION ISOLATION LEVEL READ UNCOMMITTED

SELECT TOP 20
    st.text AS [Parent Query]
```

```
     , DB_NAME(st.dbid)AS [DatabaseName]
     , cp.usecounts AS [Usage Count]
     , qp.query_plan
FROM sys.dm_exec_cached_plans cp
CROSS APPLY sys.dm_exec_sql_text(cp.plan_handle) st
CROSS APPLY sys.dm_exec_query_plan(cp.plan_handle) qp
WHERE CAST(qp.query_plan AS NVARCHAR(MAX))
  LIKE '%<ColumnsWithNoStatistics>%'
ORDER BY cp.usecounts DESC
```

❶ Cast plan

❷ Search for missing statistics

In the listing, one DMV and two DMFs are involved in identifying the queries that contain missing statistics. A brief description of each is given in table 5.1.

Table 5.1   DMV/DMFs to identify the queries that contain missing statistics

DMV/DMF	Description
sys.dm_exec_cached_plans	Contains cached plans
sys.dm_exec_sql_text	DMF that returns the SQL text identified by a given sql_handle or plan handle
sys.dm_exec_query_plan	DMF that returns the cached plan, in XML format, identified by a given plan_handle

The joining of the DMV and DMFs provides you with enough information to identify the queries that contain missing statistics, across all the databases on the server. The DMV sys.dm_exec_cached_plans contains a plan_handle that's passed to the DMF sys.dm_exec_sql_text to retrieve the text of the SQL query. Similarly, the query's plan_handle is passed to the DMF sys.dm_exec_query_plan to retrieve the cached plan of the query.

The key to understanding this script is converting the cached plan, which is stored as XML, into a NVARCHAR(MAX) ❶, which can then be searched using the SQL LIKE statement ❷. Although it's possible to use XPATH to query more specifically and obtain the results more quickly, using the current approach allows for a more generic method of searching the cached plans and aids future maintenance. Using a similar script, you can search for other items in the cached plans.

The query we execute selects the top 20 queries that contain missing statistics, ordered by how often the plan has been used, across all databases on the server. You can restrict the results further by specifying the database you want to search, or indeed part of the SQL text. You can further filter your results by making use of DMV deltas to examine changed plans that run in a given time period. Chapter 2, "Common patterns," contains more information on how to do this.

An example of the type of output for this query is given in figure 5.1.

You'll need to open up the cached plan to discover the individual statement that's involved with the missing statistics. If the plan opens as XML (this is the default with SQL Server 2005), you may need to store the plan to the filesystem by saving it with an extension of .sqlplan, which will allow you to reopen it as a visual cached plan (in diagram mode). In SQL Server 2008, clicking the cached plan opens it in diagram mode.

	Parent Query	DatabaseName	Usage Count	query_plan
1	– use of alter going forward allows us...	Paris	10120	<ShowPlanXML xmlns
2	– use of alter going forward allows us...	Paris	10120	<ShowPlanXML xmlns
3	CREATE PROCEDURE [Report].[Ris...	Paris	129	<ShowPlanXML xmlns
4	CREATE PROCEDURE [Report].[Get...	Paris	109	<ShowPlanXML xmlns
5	–[Report].[RiskVARDCM] '13-Mar-08', ...	Paris	65	<ShowPlanXML xmlns
6	CREATE PROCEDURE PNLAdjustm...	Paris	60	<ShowPlanXML xmlns
7	– use of alter going forward allows us...	Paris	55	<ShowPlanXML xmlns
8	CREATE PROCEDURE [List].[PickLis...	Paris	50	<ShowPlanXML xmlns
9	/*----------------------------...	Paris	43	<ShowPlanXML xmlns
10	/*----------------------------...	Paris	33	<ShowPlanXML xmlns

Figure 5.1   Output showing the results of searching for queries with missing statistics

You can search the diagram mode cached plan visually for a Table Scan with a yellow triangle next to it, as shown in figure 5.2. Alternatively, you can search the XML version of the cached plan for the text "<ColumnsWithNoStatistics>." Both methods will allow you to see the individual SQL statement that uses tables that relate to the missing statistics.

5.1.2   *The importance of statistics*

Where possible, especially for important queries, you should consider creating statistics on the identified column. This will enable the optimizer to make better decisions about the underlying data used by your queries. For example, to create a statistics object named EmailAddressStats on a column named EmailAddress in a table named dbo.Contact, with 5% sampling, use the following command:

```
CREATE STATISTICS EmailAddressStats
ON dbo.Contact (EmailAddress) WITH SAMPLE 5 PERCENT
```

Creating statistics data takes time, especially on large tables. Because of this, we often obtain statistics based on a sample of data. In the example given here, 5% of the rows

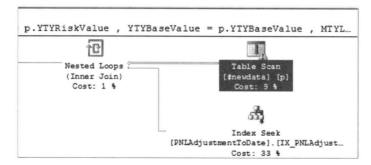

Figure 5.2   Cached plan identifying missing column statistics

in the underlying table were examined to obtain the statistics for the column EmailAddress.

Up-to-date statistics are often vitally important to the performance of SQL queries, especially on larger tables. A script in a previous chapter detailed how to obtain the date the statistics were last updated along with how much the data has changed since the statistics were last taken. You can use the output from this script to automatically update the relevant statistics, rather than wait for SQL Server to automatically update the statistics after 20% of the data has changed. An example of this is given in chapter 10.

Typically, statistics are updated for a given table, using a command that's similar to the CREATE STATISTICS command, for example:

```
UPDATE STATISTICS dbo.Contact WITH SAMPLE 5 PERCENT
```

This command will update all the statistics objects on the table named dbo.Contact, with a sampling of 5%. Although this might be okay for many circumstances, if you know which indexes a SQL query uses, you can target the update of the statistics associated with these specific indexes. Because you'll typically target fewer indexes, you should be able to use a larger sampling percentage, compared with when you issue a generic statistics update at the table level, for the statistics to update in the same time period. We discussed a script in the previous chapter to identify which indexes are used by a given routine, and that will allow us to make these targeted improvements.

5.1.3 *Default statistics properties*

By default, creating and updating statistics are enabled on SQL Server. Although it isn't recommended, you can disable these options. I've known cases where these options were purposely disabled so that queries would run slower, with the intention of investigating these queries to determine what indexes need to be created. Similarly, because updating the statistics can take a significant amount of time, I've seen the default options disabled with a view to providing updated statistics at a later time.

> **NOTE** Another database option allows the statistics to be updated later automatically; this is the AutoUpdateStatisticsAsync property. Unless you have unusual needs, I'd suggest you keep the default value of these properties.

You can see the current state of your statistics options by running the script given in the following listing.

> **Listing 5.2 Finding your default statistics options**

```
SET TRANSACTION ISOLATION LEVEL READ UNCOMMITTED

SELECT name AS DatabaseName
     , is_auto_create_stats_on AS AutoCreateStatistics
     , is_auto_update_stats_on AS AutoUpdateStatistics
```

```
    , is_auto_update_stats_async_on
                    AS AutoUpdateStatisticsAsync
FROM sys.databases
ORDER BY DatabaseName
```

All the default statistics properties are obtained from the sys.databases table. To view the database entries in this table, you need VIEW ANY DATABASE server-level permission. Alternatively, you'll be able to see the rows only for the database in which you're running.

An example of the type of output for this query is shown in figure 5.3. Looking at the figure, you can see that all databases have AutoCreateStatistics and AutoUpdate-Statistics enabled and AutoUpdateStatisticsAsync disabled.

It's important to keep your statistics up to date; this ensures that the optimizer can make appropriate decisions based on the distribution and density of the current data values and thus produce good-quality cached plans. I provided a SQL script to determine when your statistics were last updated and the amount of change they had undergone since that time in chapter 3, section 3.10.

In chapter 10 I'll provide a script that automatically updates the index statistics in an intelligent manner. The script updates only the statistics of the indexes whose data has changed and does so using an intelligent sampling algorithm.

In a similar way to finding queries that have missing statistics, you can find queries with missing indexes. We'll discuss these next.

5.2 Finding queries that have missing indexes

Indexes are essential for the normal running of production databases; without indexes many database queries would be unfeasible. In chapter 3 we discussed the DMVs for finding missing indexes. These DMVs provide an amalgamated view of the various missing indexes, without reference to the individual queries involved.

	DatabaseName	AutoCreateStatistics	AutoUpdateStatistics	AutoUpdateStatisticsAsync
1	AdventureWorks	1	1	0
2	AdventureWorksDW	1	1	0
3	IWSTest	1	1	0
4	master	1	1	0
5	model	1	1	0
6	msdb	1	1	0
7	Paris	1	1	0
8	ParisDev	1	1	0
9	ParisMini	1	1	0
10	ParisModelPersist	1	1	0
11	QuestSoftware	1	1	0
12	tempdb	1	1	0

Figure 5.3 Default statistics properties

In the script discussed here, we'll identify the individual SQL statements that the missing indexes apply to.

The script used to discover missing indexes is essentially the same as the one discussed previously that was used to find queries with missing statistics, but the LIKE clause needs to be replaced with the following:

```
LIKE '%<MissingIndexes>%'
```

We already discussed the importance and consequences of missing indexes in chapter 3. These are the additional benefits of searching the cached plans for missing indexes:

- You have the ability to provide more filter criteria, for example, include only SQL text that matches a certain pattern.
- If you have SQL Server 2008, selecting the cached plan from the output gives a visual display of the plan, including details of the missing index. If you right-click the missing index text (in green) and select Missing Index Details, it will create a script of the missing index.
- You know these indexes belong to SQL that has run since the last SQL server reboot.

In a similar way to finding queries that have missing indexes, you can find queries that have implicit (silent) data type conversions. These can have a detrimental effect on query performance and are discussed next.

5.3 *Finding queries that have implicit data type conversions*

Typically, you use the same column name across different tables (and views) to denote the same item of data. For example, you'd expect a column named DomainId to have the same meaning and same data type in all the tables it's part of. But databases often contain columns with the same name that have been defined with different data types. These mismatched columns can cause problems.

Columns with the same name, in different tables, are typically used to link tables together (as key/foreign keys). If the data types are not the same, the optimizer has to do additional work to make the columns comparable. SQL Server will silently convert one of the data types. This additional work is unnecessary overhead. In some cases it can also mean an otherwise useful index is not used, resulting in a further decrease in performance.

An incorrectly defined column can affect data integrity, potentially invalidating both the underlying table and any client applications because the data may be inconsistent and can be a source of application errors. For example, if a column should have been defined as data type int but has been defined as a tinyint, a large value will cause an overflow error.

Having different data types for the same column has implications for maintainability. Client applications (for example, stored procedures or ADO.NET clients) often need to define the types. If the column has mismatched data types, which column's data type should the client use without extending the problem into the client arena?

5.3.1   *Finding implicit data conversions*

The script used to discover SQL queries that contain implicit data type conversions is essentially the same as that used to find queries that have missing statistics, discussed previously. But the LIKE clause needs to be replaced with the following:

```
LIKE '%CONVERT_IMPLICIT%'
```

As you examine your output, you might be surprised at the amount of background work SQL Server does in ensuring that the data types become compatible; I know I was. Where possible, these column type mismatches should be reconciled at the source. If you allow me to digress from DMVs for a short while, in the next section I'll explain how you can do this.

5.3.2   *Finding disparate column data types*

You can use the INFORMATION_SCHEMA views to compare the different data types for the same named column, across all the tables and views in a database. The script you use to find columns with disparate data types is shown here.

Listing 5.3   Finding disparate columns with different data types

```
SET TRANSACTION ISOLATION LEVEL READ UNCOMMITTED

SELECT
    COLUMN_NAME                                              Calculate prevalence
    ,[%] = CONVERT(DECIMAL(12,2),COUNT(COLUMN_NAME)*      ❶ of column name
        100.0 / COUNT(*)OVER())
INTO #Prevalence
FROM INFORMATION_SCHEMA.COLUMNS
GROUP BY COLUMN_NAME

SELECT DISTINCT                                              Do the columns
        C1.COLUMN_NAME                                    ❷ differ?
    , C1.TABLE_SCHEMA
    , C1.TABLE_NAME
    , C1.DATA_TYPE
    , C1.CHARACTER_MAXIMUM_LENGTH
    , C1.NUMERIC_PRECISION
    , C1.NUMERIC_SCALE
    , [%]
FROM INFORMATION_SCHEMA.COLUMNS C1
INNER JOIN INFORMATION_SCHEMA.COLUMNS C2 ON C1.COLUMN_NAME =
                        C2.COLUMN_NAME
INNER JOIN #Prevalence p ON p.COLUMN_NAME = C1.COLUMN_NAME
WHERE ((C1.DATA_TYPE != C2.DATA_TYPE)
    OR (C1.CHARACTER_MAXIMUM_LENGTH != C2.CHARACTER_MAXIMUM_LENGTH)
    OR (C1.NUMERIC_PRECISION != C2.NUMERIC_PRECISION)
```

```
      OR (C1.NUMERIC_SCALE != C2.NUMERIC_SCALE))
ORDER BY [%] DESC, C1.COLUMN_NAME, C1.TABLE_SCHEMA, C1.TABLE_NAME

DROP TABLE #Prevalence
```

In this script, one table is involved in identifying columns with mismatched data types; a brief description of it is shown in table 5.2.

Table 5.2   The table used to identify columns with mismatched data types

Table	Description
INFORMATION_SCHEMA.COLUMNS	Contains details about the columns of the tables/views in a database

The script first creates a temporary table, named #Prevalence, which contains details of each column in any table in the current database as well as with the prevalence of that column name across the different tables ❶. The purpose of this table is to give a weighting to the results, allowing the disparate columns to be sorted by their prevalence.

The main part of the script is a self join on INFORMATION_SCHEMA.COLUMNS, on the COLUMN_NAME column. It selects rows that have the same column name but differ in data type (and other precision-based details) ❷. The results are sorted by the prevalence of the named column in descending order. Finally, the temporary table is dropped.

Figure 5.4 contains a sample of the type of output for this query.

The results show how the data type for the same named column varies across tables. Here you can see that the column DomainId has been defined variously as a tinyint, smallint, int, and varchar. Some columns will be identified as having mismatched data types, but they're really columns having the same name that describe different things. In this case, it's better to give them different names. For example, the column IsYearEnd might be a bit in one table and a varchar(3) in another table; the latter should be renamed IsYearEndChar. Some of the columns identified

	COLUMN_NAME	TABLE_SCHEMA	TABLE_NAME	DATA_TYPE	CHARACTER_MAXIMUM_LENGTH	NUMERIC_PRECISION	NUMERIC_SCALE	%
198	DomainId	dbo	RequestDefin...	smallint	NULL	5	0	3.75
199	DomainId	dbo	RiskAdjustme...	smallint	NULL	5	0	3.75
200	DomainId	dbo	RiskError	tinyint	NULL	3	0	3.75
201	DomainId	dbo	RiskTotalSu...	smallint	NULL	5	0	3.75
202	DomainId	dbo	RiskValueSu...	smallint	NULL	5	0	3.75
203	DomainID	Legacy	StagingPnlLog	int	NULL	10	0	3.75
204	DomainID	Legacy	StagingRiskL...	int	NULL	10	0	3.75
205	DomainId	Load	IPNL1	tinyint	NULL	3	0	3.75
206	DomainId	Load	IPNLError1	varchar	100	NULL	NULL	3.75
207	DomainId	Load	IRisk1	tinyint	NULL	3	0	3.75
208	DomainId	Load	IRiskError1	tinyint	NULL	3	0	3.75

Figure 5.4   Mismatched data columns

might be the result of a view's definition being out of date. In this case, using sp_refreshview will correct this problem.

The identified mismatched columns should be corrected. It should be a simple matter to identify the correct data type for a given column. It might take longer to correct any client's applications that use the column.

> **ON A PREEMPTIVE NOTE** This script can be used as part of a QA process to ensure any columns in new or amended tables are defined consistently across different tables, before being migrated to a production environment.

The script described here allows you to quickly identify which columns have mismatched data types across tables in a database. Recognizing and correcting these columns will improve performance, data integrity, and maintainability.

In a similar way to finding queries that have implicit data type conversions, you can find queries that contain table scans. These may indicate inappropriate or missing indexes, leading to a decrease in performance. Table scans are discussed next.

5.4 Finding queries that have table scans

Often, especially for larger tables, you hope to use indexes to quickly access the data you require. Without indexes, the query has to scan the table to obtain its data. Identifying and resolving the cause of these table scans should ensure that your indexes and queries are correct.

The script used to discover SQL queries that contain table scans is essentially the same as that used to find queries that have missing statistics (discussed previously), but the LIKE clause needs to be replaced with the following:

```
LIKE '%<TableScan%'
```

For relatively small tables, the optimizer may decide it's cheaper to scan the table than to use an index. A missing index or inappropriate indexes might also cause the optimizer to use table scans. As an example of an inappropriate index, if a query needs to retrieve a lot of data, some of which it can get from an index and the rest from the underlying table, because it can be costly to repeatedly get the data from the underlying table via an index (key) lookup, it's often more appropriate to bypass the index completely and scan the underlying table for the required data. To remedy this situation, it may be necessary to create a new index that contains the required data or consider adding the required columns as INCLUDEd columns on the index.

Searching the cached plans for table scans could prove useful in corroborating that indexes are missing or are of an inappropriate type. It may also catch inappropriate SELECT statements without a WHERE condition.

5.5 Slower-than-normal queries

As part of your normal monitoring, it makes sense to ensure that the runtime duration of your queries doesn't deviate significantly from the expected norm. Identifying slower-than-normal queries will allow you to target your efforts and correct any performance problems in a timely manner.

A query can start to run slower for many reasons, including an increased number of users (resulting in more waiting on resources), increased volume of data to process, too much context switching for parallel queries, and slower hardware.

5.5.1 *Finding queries that are running slower than normal*

The script we use to identify queries that are running slower than normal is shown in the following listing.

Listing 5.4   Finding queries that are running slower than normal

```
SET TRANSACTION ISOLATION LEVEL READ UNCOMMITTED           ❶ Get raw
                                                               values
SELECT TOP 100
  qs.execution_count AS [Runs]
  , (qs.total_worker_time - qs.last_worker_time) / (qs.execution_count - 1)
        AS [Avg time]
  , qs.last_worker_time AS [Last time]
  , (qs.last_worker_time - ((qs.total_worker_time - qs.last_worker_time) /
        (qs.execution_count - 1))) AS [Time Deviation]
  , CASE WHEN qs.last_worker_time = 0
      THEN 100
      ELSE (qs.last_worker_time - ((qs.total_worker_time -
        qs.last_worker_time) / (qs.execution_count - 1)))  * 100
      END
        / (((qs.total_worker_time - qs.last_worker_time) /
              (qs.execution_count - 1.0))) AS [% Time Deviation]
  ,qs.last_logical_reads + qs.last_logical_writes + qs.last_physical_reads
                            AS [Last IO]
  , ((qs.total_logical_reads + qs.total_logical_writes +
        qs.total_physical_reads) -
          (qs.last_logical_reads + last_logical_writes
              + qs.last_physical_reads))
                    / (qs.execution_count - 1) AS [Avg IO]
  , SUBSTRING (qt.text,(qs.statement_start_offset/2) + 1,
    ((CASE WHEN qs.statement_end_offset = -1
      THEN LEN(CONVERT(NVARCHAR(MAX), qt.text)) * 2
      ELSE qs.statement_end_offset
      END - qs.statement_start_offset)/2) + 1) AS [Individual Query]
  , qt.text AS [Parent Query]
  , DB_NAME(qt.dbid) AS [DatabaseName]
INTO #SlowQueries
FROM sys.dm_exec_query_stats qs
CROSS APPLY sys.dm_exec_sql_text(qs.plan_handle) qt
WHERE qs.execution_count > 1
  AND qs.total_worker_time != qs.last_worker_time
ORDER BY [% Time Deviation] DESC

SELECT TOP 100 [Runs]                          ❷ Calculate IO Deviation
      , [Avg time]                                and % IO Deviation
      , [Last time]
      , [Time Deviation]
```

```
    , [% Time Deviation]
    , [Last IO]
    , [Avg IO]
    , [Last IO] - [Avg IO] AS [IO Deviation]
    , CASE WHEN [Avg IO] = 0
            THEN 0
      ELSE ([Last IO]- [Avg IO]) * 100 / [Avg IO]
      END AS [% IO Deviation]
    , [Individual Query]
    , [Parent Query]
    , [DatabaseName]
INTO #SlowQueriesByIO
FROM #SlowQueries
ORDER BY [% Time Deviation] DESC

SELECT TOP 100
    [Runs]
    , [Avg time]
    , [Last time]
    , [Time Deviation]
    , [% Time Deviation]
    , [Last IO]
    , [Avg IO]
    , [IO Deviation]
    , [% IO Deviation]
    , [Impedance] = [% Time Deviation] - [% IO Deviation]
    , [Individual Query]
    , [Parent Query]
    , [DatabaseName]
FROM #SlowQueriesByIO
WHERE [% Time Deviation] - [% IO Deviation] > 20
ORDER BY [Impedance] DESC

DROP TABLE #SlowQueries
DROP TABLE #SlowQueriesByIO
```

③ Calculate Impedance

Here one DMV and one DMF are used to identify the queries that are running slower than normal. A brief description of each is given in table 5.3.

Table 5.3   DMV/DMF to identify queries that are running slower than normal

DMV/DMF	Description
sys.dm_exec_query_stats	Contains aggregated performance statistics for cached plans
sys.dm_exec_sql_text	DMF that returns the SQL text identified by a given sql_handle or a plan_handle

By joining the DMV and DMF, we obtain enough information to identify the queries that are running slower than normal, across all the databases on the server. The DMV sys.dm_exec_query_stats plan_handle is passed to the DMF sys.dm_exec_sql_text to retrieve the text of the SQL query. We use a common pattern to extract the Individual Query from the Parent Query.

The _elapsed_time columns record how long the query took, taking into account any waiting on resources. The _worker_time columns record how long the query took, ignoring any waiting on resources; instead, they're concerned only with the time spent using the CPU.

In this script, we'll look only at queries that are slower based on the _worker_time columns ❶. This will allow us to ignore many of the variable factors that affect query duration, allowing us instead to create and discuss a simplified script to quickly determine whether a query is running slower than normal, based on the amount of CPU it has used.

To determine whether a query is running slower than normal, we need to calculate the average duration of the query and compare it to its last run value, adjusted for the amount of data it has processed ❷.

The number of runs (execution_count) and the total worker time (total_worker_time) both include data relating to the last run. In order to create a more representative average, the number of runs is reduced by 1, and the total worker time has the last run time subtracted from it.

The average duration of the query is calculated by subtracting the last_worker_time from the total_worker_time and dividing the result by execution_count – 1.

The algorithm used to determine whether a query is running slower than average is

```
%Slower = (LAST - AVG) x 100 / AVG
```

where LAST represents the duration of the last query and AVG represents the average duration of the query.

For example, if the average query duration (AVG) is 40 ms, and the last query duration (LAST) is 160 ms, then

```
%Slower = (160 - 40) x 100 / 40 = 300%
```

The duration of a query is affected by the amount of data it processes; this volume of data is reflected in the various I/O columns of sys.dm_exec_query_stats. This utility calculates the slowness of a query (Impedance) by combining the duration of the query with the amount of I/O performed ❸. Again, the total I/O values include the last run values and need to be adjusted.

To see the SQL text of the Individual Query statement along with its Parent Query, we call the Dynamic Management Function (DMF) sys.dm_exec_sql_text, passing it the query's plan_handle as the function parameter. We can extract the Individual Query using the statement start and end offset values that are part of the DMV sys.dm_exec_query_stats. The DMF sys.dm_exec_sql_text contains the id of the database the query related to; this is also shown. Note that the WHERE clause selects only queries that have been executed at least twice.

For maintainability, the calculation of % IO deviation is separated from the main query. The data is sorted by Impedance to show the TOP 100 queries running

	Runs	Avg time	Last time	Time Deviation	% Time Dev...	Last IO	Avg IO	IO Deviation	% IO Dev...	Impedance	Individual Query	Parent Query	Database Name
1	7692	14	977	963	6878	4	4	0	0	6878	set @returnn...	CREATE FU...	Paris
2	32	31	977	946	3051	3	3	0	0	3051	select @Deal...	CREATE FU...	ParisDev
3	29	69	977	908	1315	0	0	0	0	1315	SET @Proce...	CREATE T...	ParisDev
4	23	1198	15625	14427	1204	0	0	0	0	1204	SET @Proce...	CREATE T...	ParisDev
5	36	83	977	894	1077	5	5	0	0	1077	SELECT sv.n...	SELECT sv....	NULL
6	23	88	977	889	1010	0	0	0	0	1010	SET @Proce...	CREATE T...	ParisDev
7	12	88	977	889	1010	5	4	1	25	985	SELECT @B...	CREATE ...	ParisDev
8	48	103	977	874	848	0	0	0	0	848	SET @Proce...	CREATE T...	Paris
9	29	104	977	873	839	0	0	0	0	839	SET @Proce...	CREATE T...	ParisDev
10	10	108	977	869	804	2	2	0	0	804	SELECT @A...	CREATE P...	ParisDev

Figure 5.5   Output showing queries taking longer than normal to run

slower than normal. This is a reflection of time deviation, taking into account IO deviation ❸.

An example of the type of output for this query is given in figure 5.5.

5.5.2 *The importance of queries that are running slower than normal*

The script described here allows you to quickly identify which queries are running slower than expected, after taking into account the volume of data processed.

Because this script concerns itself with _worker_time rather than _elapsed_time, you can ignore many of the reasons why the query might be running slower (for example, concurrency and blocking) and concentrate on why the query is using more CPU (that is, worker_time) to fulfill its needs.

If many of the queries to be recompiled have a large impedance value, but their absolute time using the CPU is relatively small, it might be sensible to include only queries that have a duration above a certain threshold. You can achieved this by adding a filter to the WHERE clause of the first query in listing 5.4, for example, to include queries where their last run exceeded five seconds on the CPU:

```
AND qs.last_worker_time > 5000000
```

Perhaps the most common reason why a query starts to run slower (often suddenly) relates to parameters sniffing. Here the query plan is optimized based on the value of the parameters when the query is first used. You can imagine that a parameter that retrieves only a few rows would produce a different plan than a parameter that retrieves many rows.

Various solutions exist to create cached plans that are more optimal for the passed parameters; these are shown in table 5.4.

Table 5.4   Options for improving cached plans

Option	Example
Execute the stored procedure with the RECOMPILE option; this doesn't replace the query's current cached plan.	`EXEC sprocName WITH RECOMPILE`

Table 5.4 Options for improving cached plans *(continued)*

Option	Example
| Add WITH RECOMPILE to the body of the stored procedure signature; this causes the stored procedure to be recompiled on every usage. | ```
CREATE PROC sprocName WITH
RECOMPILE
``` |
| Use the optimizer hint RECOMPILE on an Individual Query within a stored procedure. | ```
SELECT col3 FROM table1 WHERE
col3 = @param1 OPTION (RECOMPILE)
``` |
| Use the optimizer hint OPTIMIZE FOR. This allows you to create a plan based on more typical parameter values. | ```
SELECT col3 FROM table1 WHERE
col3 = @param1 OPTION
(OPTIMIZE FOR (@param1=71))
``` |
| Use plan guides. This allows you to reuse a known good query plan and provides a degree of stability. | |

Should WITH RECOMPILE be used by default for long-running queries?

I've often wondered if long-running queries and stored procedures should by default contain the WITH RECOMPILE option. With queries that run quickly, the amount of time spent recompiling the query might make up a significant amount of the queries' time. But with long-running queries, for example, reporting queries, the amount of time spent in recompilation becomes increasingly less important as the query duration increases.

It really depends on how much the data has changed since the statistics were last updated, together with the initial parameters used when the plan was first compiled.

Because data can change without the statistics being automatically updated, and because the first-supplied parameters to a routine might be atypical, it makes sense to investigate using the WITH RECOMPILE option on long-running queries.

Let's change tack now and look at stored procedures that aren't used. Having them in the database has implications for maintenance and analysis.

5.6 *Unused stored procedures (2008 only)*

When you undertake analysis on database systems, such as determining the effect of changing a column from 20 characters to 50 characters in length, you often have to scan, search, and evaluate many objects (for example, tables and stored procedures). Having extraneous objects only complicates an already difficult task. SQL Server 2008 has a DMV named sys.dm_exec_procedure_stats that records performance statistics for cached stored procedures.

Examining this DMV will allow you to determine how often a stored procedure is run. Conversely, it can also be used indirectly to determine which stored procedures aren't used.
```

5.6.1 Finding unused stored procedures

Unused stored procedures, like unused indexes, unnecessarily increase the complexity of your database system. Running the SQL script given in the following listing will identify these unused stored procedures, ordered by name.

Listing 5.5 Finding unused stored procedures

```
SET TRANSACTION ISOLATION LEVEL READ UNCOMMITTED

SELECT s.name, s.type_desc
FROM sys.procedures s
LEFT OUTER JOIN sys.dm_exec_procedure_stats d          ❶ Determine which
            ON s.object_id = d.object_id                 stored procedures
WHERE d.object_id IS NULL                                haven't run
ORDER BY s.name
```

In the listing, one DMV and one system table are involved in identifying unused stored procedures. A brief description of each is given in table 5.5.

Table 5.5 The DMV/system table used to identify unused stored procedures

DMV/table	Description
sys.dm_exec_procedure_stats	Contains aggregated performance statistics for cached stored procedures
sys.procedures	Contains a row for each object that is a procedure, for example, SQL stored procedure, extended stored procedure, CLR stored procedure, and replication filter procedure

Joining the DMV and system table gives us enough information to determine which stored procedures aren't used in the current database in which the query is run. The DMV sys.dm_exec_procedure_stats and the system table sys.procedures are joined on their common key column object_id. Because we want to know which stored procedures are in the sys.procedures table but not in the sys.dm_exec_procedure_stats DMV, we issue a LEFT OUTER JOIN, thus preserving the left-hand table (sys.procedures). We filter out rows that have an entry in the sys.dm_exec_procedure_stats DMV by using a WHERE clause that checks for NULL ❶ in the corresponding right-hand object (sys.dm_exec_procedure_stats). This is a fast and common pattern for determining what's in one table but not another. The results are ordered, for convenience, by stored procedure name.

Sample output for this query is shown in figure 5.6.

As with finding unused indexes, it's important to remember that DMVs contain only data since the last reboot. It may be that the stored procedure (and index) aren't in the DMV because they haven't been used since the last reboot.

Taking that warning into account, it makes sense to remove (or at least archive) the unused stored procedures. This should reduce the schema complexity and help with any future maintenance analysis.

	name	type_desc
1	dba_ShowIndexUsage	SQL_STORED_PROCEDURE
2	dba_UpdateStatistics2	SQL_STORED_PROCEDURE
3	DMVDiffs	SQL_STORED_PROCEDURE
4	GetStatus	SQL_STORED_PROCEDURE
5	iws999	SQL_STORED_PROCEDURE
6	StagingRequestTest	SQL_STORED_PROCEDURE
7	WMQWrapper	CLR_STORED_PROCEDURE

Figure 5.6 Output showing unused stored procedures

Sometimes when investigating production problems, it's useful to know which SQL queries are running. This helps in solving looping problems or concurrency problems. I'll present a script next that will show which SQL queries are run over a given time period.

5.7 Looking for SQL queries run during a specific interval

You can use the DMV snapshot delta pattern discussed in chapter 2 to discover which queries run over a given time period. Knowing which queries run at regular time periods can be useful, allowing you to ensure that related objects (for example, indexes) are optimized prior to their use. It might also allow you to discover the causes of any concurrency problems or looping and assist in their resolution.

5.7.1 What runs over a given time period?

Knowing what's running over a given time interval can be a great starting point in diagnosing performance problems. Running the SQL script given in the following listing will identify which queries are running over a given time period. In this example, the time period is five minutes; you may want to alter this time interval to suit your needs.

Listing 5.6 Which queries run over a given time period

```
--ThisRoutineIdentifier99

SET TRANSACTION ISOLATION LEVEL READ UNCOMMITTED

SELECT sql_handle, plan_handle, total_elapsed_time          -- 1 Get pre-work snapshot
       , total_worker_time, total_logical_reads, total_logical_writes
       , total_clr_time, execution_count, statement_start_offset
       , statement_end_offset
INTO #PreWorkSnapShot
FROM sys.dm_exec_query_stats

WAITFOR DELAY '00:05:00'                                     -- 2 Time delay period

SELECT sql_handle, plan_handle, total_elapsed_time          -- 3 Get post-work snapshot
       , total_worker_time, total_logical_reads, total_logical_writes
       , total_clr_time, execution_count, statement_start_offset
       , statement_end_offset
```

```
INTO #PostWorkSnapShot
FROM sys.dm_exec_query_stats
SELECT
  p2.total_elapsed_time - ISNULL(p1.total_elapsed_time, 0) AS [Duration]
  , p2.total_worker_time - ISNULL(p1.total_worker_time, 0) AS [Time on CPU]
  , (p2.total_elapsed_time - ISNULL(p1.total_elapsed_time, 0)) -
               (p2.total_worker_time - ISNULL(p1.total_worker_time, 0))
                         AS [Time blocked]
  , p2.total_logical_reads - ISNULL(p1.total_logical_reads, 0) AS [Reads]
  , p2.total_logical_writes - ISNULL(p1.total_logical_writes, 0)
                         AS [Writes]
  , p2.total_clr_time - ISNULL(p1.total_clr_time, 0) AS [CLR time]
  , p2.execution_count - ISNULL(p1.execution_count, 0) AS [Executions]
  , SUBSTRING (qt.text,p2.statement_start_offset/2 + 1,
         ((CASE WHEN p2.statement_end_offset = -1
            THEN LEN(CONVERT(NVARCHAR(MAX), qt.text)) * 2
            ELSE p2.statement_end_offset
            END - p2.statement_start_offset)/2) + 1) AS [Individual Query]
  , qt.text AS [Parent Query]
  , DB_NAME(qt.dbid) AS DatabaseName
  , qp.query_plan
FROM #PreWorkSnapShot p1
RIGHT OUTER JOIN
#PostWorkSnapShot p2 ON p2.sql_handle =
         ISNULL(p1.sql_handle, p2.sql_handle)
AND p2.plan_handle = ISNULL(p1.plan_handle, p2.plan_handle)
AND p2.statement_start_offset =
         ISNULL(p1.statement_start_offset, p2.statement_start_offset)
AND p2.statement_end_offset =
         ISNULL(p1.statement_end_offset, p2.statement_end_offset)
CROSS APPLY sys.dm_exec_sql_text(p2.sql_handle) as qt
CROSS APPLY sys.dm_exec_query_plan(p2.plan_handle) qp
WHERE p2.execution_count != ISNULL(p1.execution_count, 0)
  AND qt.text NOT LIKE '--ThisRoutineIdentifier99%'
ORDER BY [Duration] DESC

DROP TABLE #PreWorkSnapShot
DROP TABLE #PostWorkSnapShot
```

④ Extract delta

⑤ RIGHT OUTER JOIN

This script uses one DMV and two DMFs to identify which queries run in a given time period. They're described briefly in table 5.6.

Table 5.6   DMV/DMFs that identify the queries that run in a given time period

DMV/DMF	Description
sys.dm_exec_query_stats	Contains aggregated performance statistics for cached plans
sys.dm_exec_sql_text	DMF that returns the SQL text identified by a given sql_handle or plan_handle
sys.dm_exec_query_plan	DMF that returns the cached plan, in XML format, identified by a given plan_handle

The script takes a pre-work snapshot of the relevant columns of the sys.dm_exec_query_stats DMV ❶. It then waits for a given time period to pass ❷ before taking a similar post-work DMV snapshot ❸. It then calculates the difference between the snapshots ❹ and joins to the sys.dm_exec_sql_text and sys.dm_exec_query_plan DMFs to obtain additional useful information. A RIGHT OUTER JOIN is used to join the pre-work and post-work snapshots ❺; this is because some of the SQL queries may not be in the initial pre-work snapshot.

The joining of the pre-work snapshot, post-work snapshot, and the DMFs provides us adequate information to identify the queries that run in a given time period, across all the databases on the server. The pre-work snapshot and post-work snapshot are joined on their common key columns plan_handle, sql_handle, statement_start_offset, and statement_end_offset.

The query's sql_handle is passed to the DMF sys.dm_exec_sql_text to retrieve the text of the SQL query. Similarly, the query's plan_handle is passed to the DMF sys.dm_exec_query_plan to retrieve the cached plan of the query. We use a common pattern to extract the Individual Query, which the timings relate to, from the Parent Query. An example of the type of output for this query is shown in figure 5.7.

The results in figure 5.7 are sorted by query duration. You can amend the script to sort by the column you're interested in. In addition, you might want to filter the results by database or some text pattern matching.

NOTE   The script starts with the literal –ThisRoutineIdentifier99; this allows our diagnostics script itself to be filtered out of subsequent processing.

It can prove quite illuminating to take DMV snapshots at regular time periods and store the results into temporary tables for later analysis. Using this method, it's possible to determine which queries run, which indexes are used, when most I/O occurs, and when most blocking occurs between the given time periods.

This particular script could be helpful in determining the effect of moving from one version of SQL Server to another. You could run a batch of SQL queries on the current version of SQL Server and record the results in a datastore. Then you could upgrade the version of SQL Server and run the batch of SQL again, storing it in

	Duration	Time on CPU	Time blocked	Reads	Writes	CLR time	Executions	Individual Query	Parent Query	DatabaseName	query_plan
1	1543771	1529938	13833	1150138	0	0	2	select localcurrency...	select localcurre...	NULL	<ShowPlan
2	59265	59264	1	4817	72	0	1	insert into @temp ex...	create procedure ...	NULL	<ShowPlan
3	6520	5433	1087	29	0	0	1	insert into @perfcou...	create procedur...	NULL	<ShowPlan
4	5654	2753	2901	44	0	0	16	FETCH API_CURSO...	FETCH API_CUR...	NULL	<ShowPlan
5	2519	2520	-1	34	0	0	1	insert into @results e...	create procedur...	NULL	<ShowPlan
6	1890	1890	0	55	0	0	1	select @str = value fr...	create procedure ...	NULL	<ShowPlan
7	1089	1090	-1	52	0	0	4	SELECT @current_r...	CREATE PROCE...	msdb	<ShowPlan
8	668	668	0	0	0	0	4	IF (EXISTS (SELECT...	CREATE PROCE...	msdb	<ShowPlan
9	645	645	0	24	0	0	4	INSERT INTO msdb...	CREATE PROCE...	msdb	NULL
10	602	603	-1	20	0	0	4	SELECT @current_r...	CREATE PROCE...	msdb	<ShowPlan

Figure 5.7 Output showing the queries that run in a given time period

another datastore. Finally, you could match the two datastores on the columns of the database, Individual Query and Parent Query. This will allow you to determine whether the metrics have changed between the two versions, helping you make the decision to upgrade.

In chapter 11 I'll provide a script that can be used to determine the effect of moving from one version of SQL Server to another, allowing comparison on metrics at the database, batch (or stored procedure), or individual statement level.

Assessing the effect of running a SQL query

The current script allows you to determine which SQL queries run in a given time period. You can amend that script to determine the effect of a given SQL query or batch on the DMVs, for example, how much I/O is used or how long it takes to run. You'd need to replace the line of code that has the WAITFOR DELAY command with the SQL query or batch you want to determine the effect of.

5.8 Relationships between DMV snapshot deltas

Up to now we've tended to look at DMV changes in isolation. Although this is fine while we gain an understanding of specific areas, we can get a better understanding of the impact of queries if we examine the effect of our queries on several DMVs at the same time.

In this section, we report on several DMV snapshots to illustrate the combined effect of our queries. This is useful as a starting point in correlating the changes in the different DMVs.

5.8.1 Amalgamated DMV snapshots

Often performance problems have an effect on multiple DMVs concurrently. The output from the DMVs can be used to corroborate each other. Running the SQL script given in listing 5.7 will report how various DMVs change over a given time interval. In this example, the time period is five minutes; you may want to alter this time interval to suit your needs. The DMVs examined are missing indexes, query stats, performance counters, and wait statistics.

Listing 5.7 Amalgamated DMV snapshots

```
--ThisRoutineIdentifier

SET TRANSACTION ISOLATION LEVEL READ UNCOMMITTED          ①  Pre-work
                                                              snapshots
SELECT                                                    ◁─ Missing
  index_group_handle, index_handle                           indexes
  , avg_total_user_cost, avg_user_impact, user_seeks, user_scans  ② counters
INTO #PreWorkMissingIndexes
FROM sys.dm_db_missing_index_groups g
INNER JOIN sys.dm_db_missing_index_group_stats s
   ON s.group_handle = g.index_group_handle
```

```
SELECT
  sql_handle, plan_handle, total_elapsed_time, total_worker_time
  , total_logical_reads, total_logical_writes, total_clr_time
  , execution_count, statement_start_offset, statement_end_offset
INTO #PreWorkQuerySnapShot
FROM sys.dm_exec_query_stats

SELECT
  [object_name], [counter_name], [instance_name]
  , [cntr_value], [cntr_type]
INTO #PreWorkOSSnapShot
FROM sys.dm_os_performance_counters

SELECT
  wait_type, waiting_tasks_count
  , wait_time_ms, max_wait_time_ms, signal_wait_time_ms
INTO #PreWorkWaitStats
FROM sys.dm_os_wait_stats

WAITFOR DELAY '00:05:00'

SELECT wait_type, waiting_tasks_count, wait_time_ms
  , max_wait_time_ms, signal_wait_time_ms
INTO #PostWorkWaitStats
FROM sys.dm_os_wait_stats

SELECT [object_name], [counter_name], [instance_name]
  , [cntr_value], [cntr_type]
INTO #PostWorkOSSnapShot
FROM sys.dm_os_performance_counters

SELECT sql_handle, plan_handle, total_elapsed_time, total_worker_time
  , total_logical_reads, total_logical_writes, total_clr_time
  , execution_count, statement_start_offset, statement_end_offset
INTO #PostWorkQuerySnapShot
FROM sys.dm_exec_query_stats

SELECT index_group_handle, index_handle
  , avg_total_user_cost, avg_user_impact, user_seeks, user_scans
INTO #PostWorkMissingIndexes
FROM        sys.dm_db_missing_index_groups g
INNER JOIN  sys.dm_db_missing_index_group_stats s
    ON s.group_handle = g.index_group_handle

SELECT
  p2.total_elapsed_time - ISNULL(p1.total_elapsed_time, 0) AS [Duration]
  , p2.total_worker_time - ISNULL(p1.total_worker_time, 0) AS [Time on CPU]
  , (p2.total_elapsed_time - ISNULL(p1.total_elapsed_time, 0)) -
          (p2.total_worker_time - ISNULL(p1.total_worker_time, 0))
                                      AS [Time blocked]
  , p2.total_logical_reads - ISNULL(p1.total_logical_reads, 0) AS [Reads]
  , p2.total_logical_writes - ISNULL(p1.total_logical_writes, 0)
                                      AS [Writes]
  , p2.total_clr_time - ISNULL(p1.total_clr_time, 0) AS [CLR time]
  , p2.execution_count - ISNULL(p1.execution_count, 0) AS [Executions]
  , SUBSTRING (qt.text,p2.statement_start_offset/2 + 1,
    ((CASE WHEN p2.statement_end_offset = -1
      THEN LEN(CONVERT(NVARCHAR(MAX), qt.text)) * 2
```

3 **Query stats counters**

4 **OS counters**

5 **Wait stats counters**

6 **Put your query or SQL batch here (or a time delay)**

7 **Post-work snapshots**

8 **Calculate snapshot deltas**

```
          ELSE p2.statement_end_offset
          END - p2.statement_start_offset)/2) + 1) AS [Individual Query]
    , qt.text AS [Parent Query]
    , DB_NAME(qt.dbid) AS DatabaseName
FROM #PreWorkQuerySnapShot p1
RIGHT OUTER JOIN
#PostWorkQuerySnapShot p2 ON p2.sql_handle =
      ISNULL(p1.sql_handle, p2.sql_handle)
    AND p2.plan_handle = ISNULL(p1.plan_handle, p2.plan_handle)
    AND p2.statement_start_offset =
      ISNULL(p1.statement_start_offset, p2.statement_start_offset)
    AND p2.statement_end_offset =
      ISNULL(p1.statement_end_offset, p2.statement_end_offset)
CROSS APPLY sys.dm_exec_sql_text(p2.sql_handle) as qt
WHERE p2.execution_count != ISNULL(p1.execution_count, 0)
    AND qt.text NOT LIKE '--ThisRoutineIdentifier%'

SELECT
    p2.wait_time_ms - ISNULL(p1.wait_time_ms, 0) AS wait_time_ms
    , p2.signal_wait_time_ms - ISNULL(p1.signal_wait_time_ms, 0)
                        AS signal_wait_time_ms
    , ((p2.wait_time_ms - ISNULL(p1.wait_time_ms, 0))
                - (p2.signal_wait_time_ms
                    - ISNULL(p1.signal_wait_time_ms, 0))) AS RealWait
    , p2.wait_type
FROM #PreWorkWaitStats p1
RIGHT OUTER JOIN
#PostWorkWaitStats p2 ON p2.wait_type = ISNULL(p1.wait_type, p2.wait_type)
WHERE p2.wait_time_ms - ISNULL(p1.wait_time_ms, 0) > 0
    AND p2.wait_type NOT LIKE '%SLEEP%'
    AND p2.wait_type != 'WAITFOR'
ORDER BY RealWait DESC

SELECT
    ROUND((p2.avg_total_user_cost - ISNULL(p1.avg_total_user_cost, 0))
        * (p2.avg_user_impact - ISNULL(p1.avg_user_impact, 0)) *
            ((p2.user_seeks - ISNULL(p1.user_seeks, 0))
                + (p2.user_scans - ISNULL(p1.user_scans, 0))),0)
                        AS [Total Cost]
    , p2.avg_total_user_cost - ISNULL(p1.avg_total_user_cost, 0)
                        AS avg_total_user_cost
    , p2.avg_user_impact - ISNULL(p1.avg_user_impact, 0) AS avg_user_impact
    , p2.user_seeks - ISNULL(p1.user_seeks, 0) AS user_seeks
    , p2.user_scans - ISNULL(p1.user_scans, 0) AS user_scans
    , d.statement AS TableName
    , d.equality_columns
    , d.inequality_columns
    , d.included_columns
FROM #PreWorkMissingIndexes p1
RIGHT OUTER JOIN
#PostWorkMissingIndexes p2 ON p2.index_group_handle =
      ISNULL(p1.index_group_handle, p2.index_group_handle)
                        AND p2.index_handle =
      ISNULL(p1.index_handle, p2.index_handle)
INNER JOIN   sys.dm_db_missing_index_details d
    ON p2.index_handle = d.index_handle
```

```
WHERE           p2.avg_total_user_cost - ISNULL(p1.avg_total_user_cost, 0) > 0
  OR p2.avg_user_impact - ISNULL(p1.avg_user_impact, 0) > 0
  OR p2.user_seeks - ISNULL(p1.user_seeks, 0) > 0
  OR p2.user_scans - ISNULL(p1.user_scans, 0) > 0
ORDER BY [Total Cost] DESC

SELECT
  p2.object_name, p2.counter_name, p2.instance_name
  , ISNULL(p1.cntr_value, 0) AS InitialValue
  , p2.cntr_value AS FinalValue
  , p2.cntr_value - ISNULL(p1.cntr_value, 0) AS Change
  , (p2.cntr_value - ISNULL(p1.cntr_value, 0)) * 100 / p1.cntr_value
                                  AS [% Change]
FROM #PreWorkOSSnapShot p1
RIGHT OUTER JOIN
#PostWorkOSSnapShot p2 ON p2.object_name =
       ISNULL(p1.object_name, p2.object_name)
    AND p2.counter_name = ISNULL(p1.counter_name, p2.counter_name)
    AND p2.instance_name = ISNULL(p1.instance_name, p2.instance_name)
WHERE p2.cntr_value - ISNULL(p1.cntr_value, 0) > 0
  AND ISNULL(p1.cntr_value, 0) != 0
ORDER BY [% Change] DESC, Change DESC

DROP TABLE #PreWorkQuerySnapShot                    ⟵  Tidy up
DROP TABLE #PostWorkQuerySnapShot
DROP TABLE #PostWorkWaitStats
DROP TABLE #PreWorkWaitStats
DROP TABLE #PreWorkOSSnapShot
DROP TABLE #PostWorkOSSnapShot
DROP TABLE #PreWorkMissingIndexes
DROP TABLE #PostWorkMissingIndexes
```

The listing is an amalgamation of various DMV snapshot deltas that are discussed in their relevant sections of this book. Rather than discuss each DMV snapshot in detail here, including the SQL involved, I ask you to read the relevant entry in the other sections of this book.

In essence, various pre-work DMV snapshots are taken ❶. These include DMVs that relate to

- Missing indexes ❷
- Query stats ❸
- OS counters ❹
- Wait stats ❺

Next, you should run the query that you want to gather DMV information about ❻. This can be a single SQL statement, a batch of SQL, or a time delay. After this, the post-work DMV snapshots are taken ❼, and finally, the various DMV snapshot deltas are calculated ❽.

In our example, we use a time period; this allows a given time period to elapse before we take a post-work snapshot. This will allow us to determine what's happening over given time periods and could be extended if the results were captured periodically into a datastore for further processing. If you know which SQL queries are running at regular times on your server, it's possible to preempt the processing and provide optimal conditions for your SQL queries to run (for example, provide up-to-date statistics).

Notice that the script start with the literal –ThisRoutineIdentifier. This is done so we can filter out the queries involved in our particular diagnostics script from the query stats DMV. A RIGHT OUTER JOIN is used to join the various pre-work and post-work snapshots, and this is because some of the SQL queries may not be in the initial pre-work snapshot.

You could extend the list of DMVs involved in the snapshots with your favorite DMVs. Depending on your particular interests, you might want to change the sort order of the queries in the query DMV to sort by number of reads or writes, time blocked, or time on CPU, according to what aspect of the query you're interested in.

An example of the type of output for this query is given in figure 5.8.

The next step would be to correlate the various DMV snapshots against each other. Some example correlations that could be expected include the following:

- A query that has a large number of reads to perhaps have missing indexes or inappropriate index usage (for example, it's using an index scan instead of a seek)
- Queries that have a large Time blocked value to relate to the wait_type in the waitstats DMV delta
- Individual queries that are called often and involve temporary tables, resulting in a high number of recompiles (shown in the performance counter DMV snapshot delta)

	Duration	Time on CPU	Time blocked	Reads	Writes	CLR time	Executions	Individual Query	Parent Query	DatabaseName
1	3062520	674973	2387547	173953	2	0	1	select * FROM my.PnL p–YearT...	select * FROM my.P...	NULL
2	187884	169157	18727	22733	323	0	1	SELECT sql_handle, plan_ha...	SET TRANSACTIO...	NULL
3	114435	1934	112501	64748	0	0	1	INSERT #tempFunctionTable ...	CREATE PROCE...	Paris
4	48190	48189	1	4114	62	0	1	insert into @temp exec(@com...	create procedure sy...	NULL
5	20572	19450	1122	2841	174	0	1	SELECT [object_name], [cou...	SET TRANSACTIO...	NULL

	wait_time_ms	signal_wait_time_ms	RealWait	wait_type
1	120000	0	120000	BROKER_TASK_STOP
2	60000	0	60000	SQLTRACE_BUFFER_FLUSH
3	2093	0	2093	PAGEIOLATCH_SH
4	281	0	281	ASYNC_NETWORK_IO

	Total Cost	avg_total_user_cost	avg_user_impact	user_seeks	user_scans	TableName	equality_columns	inequal
1	0	-8.40990914241502E-06	-0.00999999999999801	1	0	[Paris].[Legacy].[FLOW]	[COB], [CCY_ID], [INDEX_NAME]	[FIXING
2	0	0.00693484269942779	-0.019999999999996	1	0	[Paris].[dbo].[PositionFactor]	[FactorId]	NULL

	object_name	counter_name	instance_name	InitialValue	FinalValue	Change	% Change
1	SQLServer:Plan Cache	Cache Hit Ratio	Object Plans	852	897	45	5
2	SQLServer:Plan Cache	Cache Hit Ratio Base	Object Plans	852	897	45	5
3	SQLServer:Plan Cache	Cache Hit Ratio Base	Temporary Tables & Table Variables	977	989	12	1
4	SQLServer:Plan Cache	Cache Hit Ratio	Temporary Tables & Table Variables	931	941	10	1

Figure 5.8 Output showing various DMV snapshot deltas

It's appropriate here to remember the limitations of DMVs. The DMVs will record information about all queries that are currently running on the server. If you're interested in only a given database, you can filtering the results to include queries only for that database, or run the query under investigation when you know nothing else is running on the database or server, or perhaps run the queries on your own server.

5.9   *Currently running queries*

Previously we've looked at static historic DMV data; now we'll look at which SQL queries are currently running. This can be useful when you're trying to debug what's happening on your database servers. Often, running this script when a problem is occurring, for example, when a query is running slowly, will illuminate the underlying cause of the problem as well as give you greater insight into your processing.

5.9.1   *What's running now?*

Sometimes we get calls from users informing us that their queries don't seem to be progressing quickly enough. In these cases it makes sense to examine what's currently running on the server. Running the SQL script given in the following listing will identify what's currently running on the server.

Listing 5.8   What queries are running now

```
SELECT
    es.session_id, es.host_name, es.login_name                    ❶ Who's running
                                                                      a query
    , er.status, DB_NAME(database_id) AS DatabaseName
    , SUBSTRING (qt.text,(er.statement_start_offset/2) + 1,       ❷ What they're
      ((CASE WHEN er.statement_end_offset = -1                        doing
        THEN LEN(CONVERT(NVARCHAR(MAX), qt.text)) * 2            What resources ❸
        ELSE er.statement_end_offset                                are used
        END - er.statement_start_offset)/2) + 1) AS [Individual Query]
    , qt.text AS [Parent Query]
    , es.program_name, er.start_time, qp.query_plan
    , er.wait_type, er.total_elapsed_time, er.cpu_time, er.logical_reads

    , er.blocking_session_id, er.open_transaction_count, er.last_wait_type
    , er.percent_complete
FROM sys.dm_exec_requests AS er
INNER JOIN sys.dm_exec_sessions AS es ON es.session_id = er.session_id
CROSS APPLY sys.dm_exec_sql_text( er.sql_handle) AS qt
CROSS APPLY sys.dm_exec_query_plan(er.plan_handle) qp           Miscellaneous
WHERE es.is_user_process=1                                      but useful  ❹
    AND es.session_Id NOT IN (@@SPID)
ORDER BY es.session_id
```

In the listing, two DMVs and two DMFs are involved in identifying which queries are currently running. A brief description of each is given in table 5.7.

Table 5.7 DMVs/DMFs to identify queries that are running now

DMV/DMF	Description
sys.dm_exec_requests	Contains details about each request executing on SQL Server
sys.dm_exec_sessions	Contains details about each authenticated session on SQL Server
sys.dm_exec_query_plan	DMF that returns the cached plan, in XML format, identified by a given plan_handle
sys.dm_exec_sql_text	DMF that returns the SQL text identified by a given sql_handle or plan_handle

The columns we report on tell us who's running the query ❶, what queries they're running ❷, whether the query is running or waiting on a resource ❸, and details of any blocking or transactions ❹.

The joining of the DMVs and DMFs provides us with enough information to determine which SQL queries are currently running, across all databases on the server. The DMVs sys.dm_exec_requests and sys.dm_exec_sessions are joined on their common key column session_id. The request's sql_handle is passed to the DMF sys.dm_exec_sql_text to retrieve the text of the SQL query. Similarly, the request's plan_handle is passed to the DMF sys.dm_exec_query_plan to retrieve the cached plan of the query. We use a common pattern to extract the Individual Query from the Parent Query.

The query is concerned only with requests that belong to users, as opposed to system requests; thus we include requests where the column is_user_request is equal to 1. We also filter out the currently running script from the results.

An example of the type of output for this query is provided in figure 5.9.

The output can prove useful in determining the cause of any conflicts. It can also be useful in ensuring whether a given point in a SQL batch has passed. Running this script periodically, perhaps into a semi-permanent table, will allow you to make decisions about your SQL batch and possibly avoid concurrency problems. It's possible to amend the script to include only those SQL queries that are running on the database you're interested in.

	session_id	host_na...	login_name	status	DatabaseName	Individual Query	Parent Query	program_name	start_time	query_plan
1	69	FMDX1...	MARKETS\CO...	runnable	Paris	insert into #AllPN...	DECLARE @COB s...	Microsoft SQL Server ...	2010-03-08 13:...	NULL
2	76	FMDX1...	MARKETS\Sti...	suspended	IWSTest	UPDATE [dbo].[f...	(@1 varchar(8000))UP...	Microsoft SQL Server ...	2010-03-08 13:...	<ShowPlan/
3	85	FMDX1...	MARKETS\Sti...	suspended	IWSTest	select *from dbo....	select *from dbo.fxR...	Microsoft SQL Server ...	2010-03-08 13:...	<ShowPlan/
4	86	FMF-V3...	MARKETS\D...	suspended	ParisDev	insert into #riskad...	CREATE PROCEDU...	.Net SqlClient Data Pro...	2010-03-08 13:...	<ShowPlan/
5	103	FMDX1...	MARKETS\R...	suspended	IWSTest	select *from dbo....	select *from dbo....	Microsoft SQL Server ...	2010-03-08 12:...	<ShowPlan/

Figure 5.9 Output showing which SQL queries are currently running

5.10 *Recompiled queries*

One of the advantages of creating a cached plan is that the data access mechanism for the query is determined once and reused. This typically saves time when the queries run subsequently, because it can reuse the already-created cached plan.

When you run one or more SQL statements, or indeed a stored procedure, each SQL statement is represented in the cached plan. If a statement needs to be recompiled, only the relevant statements are recompiled.

Recompilation takes additional time and can be responsible for CPU spikes and blocking. You can examine the DMVs to determine which individual SQL statements have been recompiled the most, with a view to determining the cause of the recompilation and finding ways of reducing it.

Sometimes, for example, when you want to run a long-running reporting query, recompiling a query may have a positive effect on performance. This is especially true where the distribution of the underlying data differs significantly from the data that was present when the cached plan was created. You can use the script we created in chapter 3, section 3.10, to help determine whether the underlying data has changed noticeably. Earlier in this chapter we discussed various methods of explicitly recompiling a query.

A great article covering many aspects of cached plans titled "Plan Caching in SQL Server 2008" is available from Microsoft; you can find it at mng.bz/8BX7. It also contains much that's applicable to SQL Server 2005.

5.10.1 *Finding the most-recompiled queries*

Although there are valid reasons for recompiling queries, in most cases you'd hope to be able to reuse an existing cached plan. Examining the queries that are recompiled the most can highlight why the query is being recompiled, providing an opportunity to reduce it and improve performance. Running the SQL script given in the following listing will identify the top 20 most-recompiled queries, ordered by plan_generation_num (which indicates the number of times a query has been recompiled) ❶.

Listing 5.9 Determining your most-recompiled queries

```
SET TRANSACTION ISOLATION LEVEL READ UNCOMMITTED

SELECT TOP 20
    qs.plan_generation_num
  , qs.total_elapsed_time
  , qs.execution_count
  , SUBSTRING (qt.text,(qs.statement_start_offset/2) + 1,
    ((CASE WHEN qs.statement_end_offset = -1
      THEN LEN(CONVERT(NVARCHAR(MAX), qt.text)) * 2
      ELSE qs.statement_end_offset
      END - qs.statement_start_offset)/2) + 1) AS [Individual Query]
  , qt.text AS [Parent Query]
```

```
      , DB_NAME(qt.dbid) AS DatabaseName
      , qs.creation_time
      , qs.last_execution_time
FROM sys.dm_exec_query_stats qs
CROSS APPLY sys.dm_exec_sql_text(qs.sql_handle) as qt        ❶  Sort by number of
ORDER BY plan_generation_num DESC                               recompilations
```

In this script, one DMV and one DMF are used to identify the most-recompiled queries; a brief description of each is given in table 5.8.

Table 5.8   DMV/DMF to identify the most recompiled queries

DMV/DMF	Description
sys.dm_exec_query_stats	Contains aggregated performance statistics for cached plans
sys.dm_exec_sql_text	DMF that returns the SQL text identified by a given sql_handle or plan handle

The sys.dm_exec_query_stats DMV contains the query's sql_handle, which is passed to the DMF sys.dm_exec_sql_text to retrieve the text of the SQL query. To report on the most-recompiled queries, we sort the results by the plan_generation_num in descending order. The column execution_count represents the number of times the query has been executed since it was last recompiled.

Figure 5.10 shows sample output for this query.

A SQL statement might be recompiled for many reasons; we discussed many of these in this chapter, in the section "Slower-than-normal queries." In addition, SQL statements that contain temporary tables will be recompiled. This is to be expected because the optimizer needs to know about the distribution and density of data values in the temporary table in order to create a good cached plan. Changing various environmental variables, via your SQL connection, may cause a recompilation. Changes in the objects referenced by the plan, for example, dropping an index, may also cause the plan to be recompiled.

	plan_generation_num	total_elapsed_ti...	execution_count	Individual Query	Parent Query	DatabaseName	creation_time	last_execution_time
1	6049	875000	17	UPDATE t SET t.Pr...	– use of alter go...	ParisDev	2010-03-30 13:16:40.867	2010-03-30 13:16:53.870
2	6048	8790	29	UPDATE t SET t.C...	– use of alter go...	ParisDev	2010-03-30 13:16:34.850	2010-03-30 13:16:54.170
3	6047	193360	29	INSERT INTO #tmpCur...	– use of alter go...	ParisDev	2010-03-30 13:16:34.827	2010-03-30 13:16:54.163
4	6046	595704	29	INSERT INTO dbo.Map...	– use of alter go...	ParisDev	2010-03-30 13:16:34.783	2010-03-30 13:16:54.147
5	6045	188477	29	if exists (select 1 from #...	– use of alter go...	ParisDev	2010-03-30 13:16:34.773	2010-03-30 13:16:54.140
6	6044	204102	29	UPDATE t SET t.Ris...	– use of alter go...	ParisDev	2010-03-30 13:16:34.750	2010-03-30 13:16:54.133
7	6043	1791992	29	UPDATE t SET t.R...	– use of alter go...	ParisDev	2010-03-30 13:16:34.653	2010-03-30 13:16:54.083
8	6042	525391	29	INSERT INTO dbo.Map...	– use of alter go...	ParisDev	2010-03-30 13:16:34.610	2010-03-30 13:16:54.067
9	6041	179688	29	if exists (select 1 from #...	– use of alter go...	ParisDev	2010-03-30 13:16:34.603	2010-03-30 13:16:54.060
10	6040	195313	29	UPDATE t SET t.Un...	– use of alter go...	ParisDev	2010-03-30 13:16:34.580	2010-03-30 13:16:54.053

Figure 5.10   Output showing the most-recompiled queries

5.11 *Summary*

This chapter discussed some of the more peripheral questions you might want answered about your database. We discussed how to discover queries that have missing statistics, missing indexes, table scans, and mismatched data types, together with the implications these may have on performance.

You saw how you can identify queries that are running slower than normal and learned various possible solutions to remedy these. We also discussed a DMV-only version of a routine that identifies which SQL queries are currently running. This should prove useful in debugging production systems that involve blocking and concurrency issues.

Because SQL queries affect multiple DMVs when they're run, it made sense to examine the combined effect of these changed DMVs and discuss any relationship you could expect.

Having looked at indexes and cached plans in detail, next we'll look at the performance of databases from a different perspective. We'll examine why the queries are unable to run. This should highlight troublesome databases that need further investigation, along with the reasons for the suboptimal performance. Although this approach is separate from using cached plans and indexes, you'll find they can be combined to give a more complete picture of the problem and potential solutions.

Operating system DMVs

This chapter covers

- Identifying why your queries are waiting
- Obtaining performance counter information
- Capturing DMV data periodically

SQL Server provides several operating system–related DMVs that allow you to understand, at the server level, why your queries are waiting. Investigating these in conjunction with the SQL queries that are running should enable you to identify the problem areas and provide solutions to improve your SQL queries. I'll provide a script to show your most common waits, both at the server level and those that occur when you run a given SQL query or batch.

Another DMV allows you to access the Windows internal performance counters for various SQL Server–related objects. These performance counters provide information on many aspects of Windows components. Inspecting these counters will often highlight areas of concern that can be targeted for improvement.

Correlating the wait types with various performance counters is a well-known and much-used method of performance tuning. We'll examine the causes of waiting together with the changes in the performance counters to suggest reasons for the problems and how to rectify them.

6.1   Understanding server waits

The previous two chapters discussed scripts that allow you to discover information about poorly performing SQL at the query level. When a SQL query is executing, the time it spends on the CPU is recorded in the column total_work_time in the DMV sys.dm_exec_query_stats. In addition, there are times when the query is ready to run but is unable to, for a variety of reasons, including waiting for I/O to complete. At the query level, you can determine the amount of waiting from the difference between the total_elapsed_time and total_work_time columns in the sys.dm_exec_query_stats DMV.

SQL Server also records the reason for any waiting at the server instance level, in the sys.dm_os_wait_stats DMV. Inspecting this DMV will provide you with a high-level view of the main causes of waiting on a given SQL Server; this will allow you to target further investigation based on the prominent wait types.

When a SQL query runs, it typically requires resources, for example, exclusive access to a given set of data. If the query can't run, perhaps because it doesn't have access to these resources, it enters a wait state. SQL Server keeps a record of this waiting, by wait type, accumulated since the last reboot or clearing of the sys.dm_os_wait_stats DMV. Inspecting this DMV provides you with a starting point for investigating the chief causes of any waiting.

For your testing, it's often convenient to reset the values in the sys.dm_os_wait_stats DMV. It's possible to clear this DMV using the following DBCC command:

```
DBCC SQLPERF ('sys.dm_os_wait_stats', CLEAR)
```

Alternatively, rather than resetting the DMV, which can be problematic on production servers, you can deduce the effect of queries on the sys.dm_os_wait_stats DMV by creating a DMV snapshot delta. An example script to do this is described later in this chapter, in section 6.3.

> **THE MEANING OF WAIT TYPES**   To decode the meaning of the various wait types, what they mean, what problems they represent, and how these problems might be solved, I recommend you read the "SQL Server 2005 Waits and Queues" white paper. Although the paper refers to SQL Server 2005, it's still applicable to SQL Server 2008. The white paper is available here: mng.bz/8gl4.

6.2   Identifying your most common waits

When a SQL query is able to run but isn't on the CPU, it's waiting. SQL Server keeps a record of these waits by wait type. Analyzing these wait types will provide you with a high-level indication of problematic resources that can be targeted for improvement.

When a query is waiting on a resource, its status is set to suspended. When the resource that a waiting query had been waiting on becomes available, the query is placed in a queue and enters a runnable status. But it still might take time before it actually runs; this is because there may be other queries in the queue that have propriety or the CPU is busy doing other work. The time the query spends waiting to run while it's in the queue is also recorded in the sys.dm_os_wait_stats DMV, in the column signal_wait_time_ms. It's possible to determine the amount of time that was spent waiting on a resource and the amount of time spent waiting to get onto the CPU by subtracting the signal_wait_time_ms from the wait_time_ms. You can use this to highlight CPU pressure, where the CPU is spending a large amount of time at or near peak performance.

6.2.1   *Why are you waiting?*

Identifying the cause of your server's waits is a great starting point for analyzing, at a high level, why your queries are waiting and thus giving suboptimal performance. Running the SQL script shown here will identify the top 20 causes of waiting on your server instance, ordered by wait_time_ms ❶.

Listing 6.1   Why are you waiting?

```
SET TRANSACTION ISOLATION LEVEL READ UNCOMMITTED

SELECT TOP 20
  wait_type, wait_time_ms, signal_wait_time_ms
  , wait_time_ms - signal_wait_time_ms AS RealWait
  , CONVERT(DECIMAL(12,2), wait_time_ms * 100.0 / SUM(wait_time_ms) OVER())
                                                   AS [% Waiting]
  , CONVERT(DECIMAL(12,2), (wait_time_ms - signal_wait_time_ms) * 100.0
                     / SUM(wait_time_ms) OVER()) AS [% RealWait]
FROM sys.dm_os_wait_stats
WHERE wait_type NOT LIKE '%SLEEP%'
  AND wait_type != 'WAITFOR'           ❶  Order by time
ORDER BY wait_time_ms DESC                 spent waiting
```

In the listing, you can see that one DMV is involved in identifying the most common causes of waiting; a brief description of it is shown in table 6.1.

Table 6.1   DMV for identifying the most common waits

DMV	Description
sys.dm_os_wait_stats	Contains information about all the waits encountered by threads of execution

The script lists the top 20 wait types on the SQL Server, ordered by the time spent waiting, in descending order. We filter out any waits that contain the word SLEEP because these are not really waits in the context of our investigation. Similarly, we filter out any WAITFOR wait types because these are intentional waits prescribed by the developer. We use the OVER clause to calculate the percentages for a given wait type relative to all the wait types. The columns output by the script are described in table 6.2.

Table 6.2   Wait state column descriptions

Column	Description
wait_type	Name of the wait type.
wait_time_ms	Total time spent waiting in milliseconds.
signal_wait_time_ms	Total time spent waiting to get on the CPU, when no longer waiting on original cause of wait.
RealWait	Total time spent waiting on original resource. This is wait_time_ms less signal_wait_time_ms.
% Waiting	How much time this wait_type spent waiting as a percentage of all waits.
% RealWait	How much time this RealWait spent waiting as a percentage of all waits.

The column wait_time_ms records the total time a given wait type spent waiting; this includes both the original cause of the waiting (for instance, waiting on I/O to complete) and the time it took to get the thread back onto the CPU to continue its work (recorded separately as signal_wait_time_ms). Calculating the real time spent waiting (in the column % RealWait) should give you an indication of any CPU pressures. You can see this more clearly when there's a big discrepancy in the values in the columns % Waiting and % RealWait, for a given wait type.

An example of the type of output for this query is shown in figure 6.1.

The output in figure 6.1 shows that the most common wait type was CXPACKET, which was responsible for more than half of the total wait time (50.94%) of all of the different wait types shown. The difference between the columns % Waiting and % RealWait are relatively minor, suggesting that in general this SQL Server's CPU was not under pressure.

Although it's possible to filter out some of the more innocuous wait types, for example, SQLTRACE_BUFFER_FLUSH, I've included them here because they often provide a marker against which you can infer the importance and impact of the

	wait_type	wait_time_ms	signal_wait_time_ms	RealWait	% Waiting	% RealWait
1	CXPACKET	9371237484	390091546	8981145938	50.94	48.82
2	BROKER_TASK_STOP	2686659343	20419484	2666239859	14.61	14.49
3	CLR_AUTO_EVENT	1829417125	859	1829416266	9.95	9.95
4	SQLTRACE_BUFFER_FLUSH	1005315796	163671	1005152125	5.47	5.46
5	DBMIRRORING_CMD	732828875	5429984	727398891	3.98	3.95
6	OLEDB	590214031	0	590214031	3.21	3.21
7	PAGEIOLATCH_SH	377560453	2872515	374687938	2.05	2.04
8	DBMIRROR_SEND	267063000	3540937	263522063	1.45	1.43
9	IO_COMPLETION	213656093	279734	213376359	1.16	1.16
10	BACKUPIO	212229859	8450093	203779766	1.15	1.11

Figure 6.1   Output showing the most common wait type

other wait types. For example, because SQLTRACE_BUFFER_FLUSH is typically an inoffensive wait type, items that occur below it will typically have little importance. Many of the wait types shown are relatively common; an overview of some of the more common wait types is given next.

6.2.2 Common wait types

A list of some of the more common wait types, together with a description of their meaning and an indication of the problem area they relate to, is given in table 6.3.

Table 6.3   Common wait types descriptions

Wait type	Description
CXPACKET	When a query runs in parallel, some of the threads finish before others; these finished threads result in a waiting status of CXPACKET. For OLAP systems CXPACKET waits are to be expected, but if the value of this wait is over 10% of the total waits, it may need correcting. For OLTP systems parallelism is less important and may be detrimental to performance; if the value of this wait is over 5% of the total waits, it may need correcting. It's possible to lower the Degree of Parallelism (DOP) setting at either the server level or on individual queries to reduce the amount of parallelism. Alternatively or additionally, you might want to alter the value of the Cost Threshold for Parallelism setting.
LCK_x	Occurs when a task is waiting on a locked resource. Indicates blocking problems. Often a side effect of inappropriate transaction isolation level or long-running transactions. Can also relate to memory shortage or excessive I/O.
ASYNC_IO_COMPLETION	Occurs while waiting for asynchronous I/O to finish. Disk subsystem may be suboptimal. Consider moving files/file groups to less-used drives. Investigate queries with the most I/O and longest blocking. Consider applying appropriate missing indexes (knowing which queries have run). Check for index or table full scan performance counters.
ASYNC_NETWORK_IO	Occurs on network writes when task is blocked behind the network. May be due to network issues between SQL Server and the client application or because the application is processing results inefficiently.
LATCH_x	These are short-term synchronization objects (lightweight locks). Often caused by internal contention on internal caches, cached data pages, and other in-memory objects (as opposed to I/O buffer). Often indicates memory problems.
PAGELATCH_x	Latch used to synchronize access to buffer pages. Typically indicates cache contention.
PAGEIOLATCH_x	Occurs while waiting for data page I/O operations to complete. I/O system is busy. Typically represents disk-to-memory problems.

Table 6.3   Common wait types descriptions (continued)

Wait type	Description
IO_COMPLETION	Due to slow client response. Occurs while waiting for non-data page I/O operations to complete. Disk subsystem may be suboptimal. Investigate bulk inserts. Check for growth in database files. Check for queries with most I/O. Investigate missing indexes. Check sys.dm_io_virtual_file_stats to target specific files (and thus the underlying database tables) for stalls.
WRITELOG	Occurs while waiting for the log flush to finish. These typically occur when a transaction commits or a checkpoint is taken. Check log files on sys.dm_io_virtual_file_stats for stalls. Consider moving log files to less-used disks.
SOS_SCHEDULER_YIELD	Occurs when a task voluntarily yields the scheduler to another task. A high value often indicates CPU pressure.
SQLTRACE_BUFFER_FLUSH	Occurs when the SQL Trace task pauses between flushes. If user-initiated traces aren't active, this value represents the default trace. This can be used as a benchmark against which the impact of other waits can be compared.

A little later in this chapter, in section 6.9, we'll link these common wait types with changes in the performance counters. This is a well-known method of investigating performance problems. In essence, you should use your most-common wait types to select a set of performance counters (often looking at queues in particular) to highlight and corroborate your performance problems.

Because the DMV sys.dm_os_wait_stats accumulates data, it may make sense to use DMV snapshots to determine the effect of a given query or what's happening during a given time period. An example of this is given next.

6.3   *Identifying your most common waits—snapshot version*

The DMV sys.dm_os_wait_stats is useful for discovering the cumulative effect of the causes of waiting since SQL Server was last rebooted, restarted, or cleared programmatically. But being cumulative, it doesn't record trend or discreet time interval information. You can use the DMV snapshot approach given in chapter 2 ("Common patterns") to determine the specific waits that occur when you run a given SQL query or batch of SQL or indeed to determine the waits over a given time period. This should allow you to highlight, and target for investigation and improvement, any waits that occur while you're running specific SQL queries or for a given time interval.

There's a caveat with this approach (and some proposed solutions too). The DMV sys.dm_os_wait_stats records information at the server level and thus will record all other activity on the server. This may or may not be a problem depending on how these other queries influence the wait type values. It's possible to reduce the effect of external influences by running your queries on a standalone server or at a time when you know other queries won't be running.

6.3.1 *Why are you waiting? (snapshot version)*

Because the wait states DMV is accumulative, if you want to determine the effects of a given set of queries or a given time period, it makes sense to calculate the difference between two DMV snapshots. Running the SQL script given in the following listing will identify the waits that occur over a given 10-minute period, ordered by RealWait.

> **Listing 6.2 Why are you waiting? (snapshot version)**

```
SET TRANSACTION ISOLATION LEVEL READ UNCOMMITTED

SELECT wait_type, waiting_tasks_count
  , wait_time_ms, max_wait_time_ms, signal_wait_time_ms
INTO #PreWorkWaitStats
FROM sys.dm_os_wait_stats

WAITFOR DELAY '00:10:00'

SELECT wait_type, waiting_tasks_count
  , wait_time_ms, max_wait_time_ms, signal_wait_time_ms
INTO #PostWorkWaitStats
FROM sys.dm_os_wait_stats

SELECT
  p2.wait_time_ms - ISNULL(p1.wait_time_ms, 0) AS wait_time_ms
  , p2.signal_wait_time_ms - ISNULL(p1.signal_wait_time_ms, 0)
                                           AS signal_wait_time_ms
  , ((p2.wait_time_ms - ISNULL(p1.wait_time_ms, 0))
        - (p2.signal_wait_time_ms - ISNULL(p1.signal_wait_time_ms, 0)))
                                           AS RealWait
  , p2.wait_type
FROM #PreWorkWaitStats p1
RIGHT OUTER JOIN
#PostWorkWaitStats p2 ON p2.wait_type = ISNULL(p1.wait_type, p2.wait_type)
WHERE p2.wait_time_ms - ISNULL(p1.wait_time_ms, 0) > 0
  AND p2.wait_type NOT LIKE '%SLEEP%'
  AND p2.wait_type != 'WAITFOR'
ORDER BY RealWait DESC

DROP TABLE #PostWorkWaitStats
DROP TABLE #PreWorkWaitStats
```

① Get pre-query DMV counters

② Do something here (SQL query or time delay)

③ Get post-query DMV counters

④ Calculate changes in wait states counters

⑤ Sort by real wait

The DMV snapshot approach given in this example is based on the DMV snapshot pattern explained more fully in chapter 2. First, we take a snapshot of the relevant DMV counters **①**, then we run a query or wait for a given time period to elapse **②**, and then we take another DMV snapshot **③**. The DMV snapshots are compared to determine what has changed **④**, and the results are sorted by the RealWait column **⑤**.

The DMV and columns used are the same as described in the previous script. In this example, we find out the waits that occur over a given time period, 10 minutes in this example. You may want to alter this time interval to suit your needs. If

Results | Messages

	wait_time_ms	signal_wait_time_ms	RealWait	wait_type
1	1200000	16	1199984	BROKER_TASK_STOP
2	600000	0	600000	SQLTRACE_BUFFER_FLUSH
3	244500	15703	228797	CXPACKET
4	22422	282	22140	PAGEIOLATCH_SH
5	14844	375	14469	ASYNC_NETWORK_IO
6	1625	32	1593	LATCH_EX
7	156	0	156	MSQL_XP
8	78	0	78	OLEDB
9	141	94	47	PAGELATCH_EX

Figure 6.2 Output showing the most common wait type (snapshot version)

you want to examine the wait types associated with a given SQL statement or batch of SQL, you can replace the WAITFOR command given in the script with relevant SQL statements.

Sample output for this query is shown in figure 6.2.

The output in figure 6.2 shows that the most common wait type was BROKER_TASK_STOP. In all the different wait types, the values in the column signal_wait_time_ms are small relative to the column wait_time_ms. This suggests that during the running of this script, this SQL Server CPU wasn't under pressure.

Although it may be interesting to observe the different wait types that occur at different periods, ideally you want to know which SQL queries are running that produce these wait types. We discuss this in the next section.

6.4 *Identifying why queries wait*

You've just seen how to get a DMV snapshot delta for a given time interval. In the chapter concerning execution-based DMVs, you saw how to determine which queries are being blocked the most. If you combine both scripts, you'll have both details of the most-blocked queries and the reason why these queries were blocked. This will form our next script. If you know why your queries are waiting, you'll have a starting point from which to make improvements.

> **NOTE** In the example given, the WAITFOR DELAY command is used to record details of any queries and waits that occur for the duration of the WAITFOR command. It's possible to replace the WAITFOR command with your own specific SQL query or batch of SQL, to get the waits associated with your queries.

6.4.1 *Discovering why your queries are waiting*

Knowing why your queries are waiting provides valuable diagnostic information. You can enhance this by knowing which SQL queries have been run over the period under examination. Running the SQL script given in listing 6.3 will identify both the type of waits that are occurring and the queries that have run, over the given time period. In this example, the time period is five minutes; you may want to alter this time interval to suit your needs.

Listing 6.3 Why your queries are waiting

```
--ThisRoutineIdentifier                                      ◁─┐  Script
SET TRANSACTION ISOLATION LEVEL READ UNCOMMITTED           ❶  identifier

SELECT                                                       ◁─┐  Pre-work
  sql_handle, plan_handle, total_elapsed_time, total_worker_time    query
  , total_logical_reads, total_logical_writes, total_clr_time    ❷ counters
  , execution_count, statement_start_offset, statement_end_offset
INTO #PreWorkQuerySnapShot
FROM sys.dm_exec_query_stats

SELECT
  wait_type, waiting_tasks_count                            ◁─┐  Pre-work wait
  , wait_time_ms, max_wait_time_ms, signal_wait_time_ms     ❸ states counters
INTO #PreWorkWaitStats
FROM sys.dm_os_wait_stats
                                                            ❹  Do something here
WAITFOR DELAY '00:05:00'                                    ◁─  (query or delay)

SELECT
  wait_type, waiting_tasks_count, wait_time_ms              ◁─┐  Post-work wait
  , max_wait_time_ms, signal_wait_time_ms                   ❺ states counters
INTO #PostWorkWaitStats
FROM sys.dm_os_wait_stats                                    ❻  Post-work
                                                                 query counters
SELECT                                                       ◁─
  sql_handle, plan_handle, total_elapsed_time, total_worker_time
  , total_logical_reads, total_logical_writes, total_clr_time
  , execution_count, statement_start_offset, statement_end_offset
INTO #PostWorkQuerySnapShot
FROM sys.dm_exec_query_stats

SELECT                                                       ◁─┐  Calculate
  p2.wait_time_ms - ISNULL(p1.wait_time_ms, 0) AS wait_time_ms   wait states
  , p2.signal_wait_time_ms - ISNULL(p1.signal_wait_time_ms, 0)   counters
            AS signal_wait_time_ms                          ❼ changes
  , ((p2.wait_time_ms - ISNULL(p1.wait_time_ms, 0))
      - (p2.signal_wait_time_ms - ISNULL(p1.signal_wait_time_ms, 0)))
                                                AS RealWait
  , p2.wait_type
FROM #PreWorkWaitStats p1
RIGHT OUTER JOIN
#PostWorkWaitStats p2 ON p2.wait_type = ISNULL(p1.wait_type, p2.wait_type)
WHERE p2.wait_time_ms - ISNULL(p1.wait_time_ms, 0) > 0
  AND p2.wait_type NOT LIKE '%SLEEP%'
  AND p2.wait_type != 'WAITFOR'                             ❽  Calculate query
ORDER BY RealWait DESC                                           counters
                                                                 changes
SELECT                                                       ◁─
  p2.total_elapsed_time - ISNULL(p1.total_elapsed_time, 0) AS [Duration]
  , p2.total_worker_time - ISNULL(p1.total_worker_time, 0) AS [Time on CPU]
```

```
      , (p2.total_elapsed_time - ISNULL(p1.total_elapsed_time, 0)) -
            (p2.total_worker_time - ISNULL(p1.total_worker_time, 0))
                                                    AS [Time blocked]
      , p2.total_logical_reads - ISNULL(p1.total_logical_reads, 0) AS [Reads]
      , p2.total_logical_writes - ISNULL(p1.total_logical_writes, 0)
                                                    AS [Writes]
      , p2.total_clr_time - ISNULL(p1.total_clr_time, 0) AS [CLR time]
      , p2.execution_count - ISNULL(p1.execution_count, 0) AS [Executions]
      , SUBSTRING (qt.text,p2.statement_start_offset/2 + 1,
        ((CASE WHEN p2.statement_end_offset = -1
          THEN LEN(CONVERT(NVARCHAR(MAX), qt.text)) * 2
          ELSE p2.statement_end_offset
          END - p2.statement_start_offset)/2) + 1) AS [Individual Query]
      , qt.text AS [Parent Query]
      , DB_NAME(qt.dbid) AS DatabaseName
FROM #PreWorkQuerySnapShot p1
RIGHT OUTER JOIN
#PostWorkQuerySnapShot p2 ON p2.sql_handle =
        ISNULL(p1.sql_handle, p2.sql_handle)
AND p2.plan_handle = ISNULL(p1.plan_handle, p2.plan_handle)
AND p2.statement_start_offset =
        ISNULL(p1.statement_start_offset, p2.statement_start_offset)
AND p2.statement_end_offset =
        ISNULL(p1.statement_end_offset, p2.statement_end_offset)
CROSS APPLY sys.dm_exec_sql_text(p2.sql_handle) as qt
WHERE p2.execution_count != ISNULL(p1.execution_count, 0)
  AND qt.text NOT LIKE '--ThisRoutineIdentifier%'
ORDER BY [Time blocked] DESC

DROP TABLE #PostWorkWaitStats
DROP TABLE #PreWorkWaitStats
DROP TABLE #PostWorkQuerySnapShot
DROP TABLE #PreWorkQuerySnapShot
```

We give the script a script identifier that uniquely identifies it ❶; this allows us to filter this query from the results. We take pre-work snapshots of the query ❷ and wait states DMV counters ❸. We then run the query that we want details about (this could be an individual query or a batch or a time interval) ❹, and we take post-work snapshots of the wait states ❺ and query DMV ❻ counters. Then we calculate the change in the DMV counters for both the wait states ❼ and query DMV counters ❽.

Listing 6.3 calculates which waits are associated with which queries that run over the given time interval.

Figure 6.3 shows an example of the type of output for this query.

The first grid in figure 6.3 shows the wait types that occurred when the script was run. Similarly, the second grid shows the most-blocked queries during the same time period. The next step in any analysis would be to run the most-blocked queries individually and record the wait types associated with each, with a view to correcting the underlying problem. For example, if when the most-blocked query runs alone it's associated with the CXPACKET wait, then it may be that the query needs to have a hint added to it that specifies the degree of parallelism (DOP). For further details of the

	wait_time_ms	signal_wait_time_ms	RealWait	wait_type
1	2484594	216734	2267860	CXPACKET
2	743047	3312	739735	PAGEIOLATCH_SH
3	599984	63	599921	BROKER_TASK_STOP
4	300000	0	300000	SQLTRACE_BUFFER_FLUSH
5	54125	2781	51344	LATCH_EX
6	2875	218	2657	ASYNC_NETWORK_IO
7	2031	0	2031	OLEDB
8	375	31	344	LATCH_SH

	Duration	Time on CPU	Time blocked	Reads	Writes	CLR time	Executions	Individual Query	Parent Query	DatabaseName
1	5654708	11701	5643007	313684	0	0	2	SELECT * FROM MY....	SELECT * FROM MY.PNL p ...	NULL
2	2172499	315738	1856761	72187	24	0	1	SELECT ChildOrgId A...	CREATE PROCEDURE [Lega...	Paris
3	1340595	61298	1279297	11157	169	0	1	SELECT COB , p.Or...	/*------------------------...	Paris
4	368524	9583	358941	9506	0	0	1	SELECT "Cob" ,"Do...	SELECT "Cob" ,"DomainId" ,"...	NULL
5	4666103	4399050	267053	847739	0	0	2	SELECT [o].[OrgHier...	CREATE procedure [Extract_...	Paris
6	501120	311000	190120	6879	2	0	2	select m.FromValue ...	-- use of alter going forward al...	Paris
7	703446	514513	188933	6932	0	0	2	select m.FromValue ...	-- use of alter going forward al...	Paris
8	193414	9288	184126	8819	0	0	1	SELECT "Cob" ,"Do...	SELECT "Cob" ,"DomainId" ,"...	NULL
9	134359	7218	127141	6585	0	0	1	SELECT "Cob" ,"Do...	SELECT "Cob" ,"DomainId" ,"...	NULL

Figure 6.3   Output showing the most-blocked queries as well as the most-common wait type in a given time interval

meaning of the wait types, what they represent, and how they can be used to improve your server and queries, see the "Waits and Queues" Microsoft white paper mentioned earlier.

We've discussed waits from a server viewpoint and now from a given SQL query workload viewpoint. Next, we'll discuss how to discover what the currently running SQL statements are waiting on.

6.5   *Queries that are waiting*

In chapter 5, section 5.9 contains a script to identify currently running queries. The output from this script also includes two wait-related columns. The column wait_type identifies why the query is currently waiting, and the column last_wait_type identifies the last wait type (even for running queries). An example of the output from the script in section 5.9 is shown in figure 6.4, with both a waiting query and a runnable query. Note that the wait columns have been rearranged for this figure.

Figure 6.4 shows that the query with a session_id of 96 has a status of suspended and a wait_type of CXPACKET. The query with the session_id of 100 has a status of runnable and a NULL wait type. An explanation of the various status column values is given in table 6.4.

	session_id	host_name	login_name		status	DatabaseName	wait_type	last_wait_type	Individual Query	Parent Query
1	96	FMDX2...	MAF	J...	suspended	Paris	CXPACKET	CXPACKET	SELECT * FROM my.P...	--For trades loaded via th
2	100	FMDX1...	MAF	IN3	runnable	Paris	NULL	SOS_SCHE...	SELECT * ,CASE r.LocalC...	set transaction isolation le

Figure 6.4   Output showing a currently waiting query

Table 6.4   Query status values

Status	Description
Running	The query is using CPU.
Runnable	The query is not waiting on a resource. It's in a queue ready to run, but some other query is using the CPU.
Suspended	The query is waiting on some resource.
Sleeping	SQL Server is waiting for the next command.

In relation to the wait-related DMV sys.dm_os_wait_stats, the time a query spends suspended and runnable is collectively recorded in the wait_time_ms column for the relevant wait type. The time a query spends in a runnable status is recorded in the signal_wait_time_ms column for the relevant wait type.

Examining the specific wait types associated with the submitted queries should provide a lead in identifying how to improve the performance of those specific queries. Further details of how to do this are given in the Microsoft "Waits and Queues" white paper.

6.6   *Finding what's blocking running SQL*

Many SQL queries run fine in isolation, but in the real world SQL queries need to interact with other running queries. The queries compete for resources, often leading to temporary blocking. This is normal and to be expected. But if you notice queries running slowly, it's possible to identify the queries involved and perhaps reschedule them so they don't run concurrently or to decode the resource the queries are competing for, possibly removing the contention. For example, if an index is the cause of contention, it's possible to create another index that could remove this contention, allowing both queries to progress.

In chapter 1, you saw a script that involved a simple monitor; it referred to a utility named dba_BlockTracer that showed queries involved in blocking. The script given in this section is similar, but it uses DMVs only (the other script used sys.sysprocesses), so it should be more viable in the future.

6.6.1   *What's blocking my SQL query?*

When users call to ask why their queries are running slowly, I often turn to this script to quickly determine if blocking is the cause. Running the SQL script given in the following listing will identify what and who are causing the blocking and what and who are being blocked.

Listing 6.4   What is blocked?

```
SELECT
    Blocking.session_id as BlockingSessionId
    , Sess.login_name AS BlockingUser
```

 Blocker details

```
, BlockingSQL.text AS BlockingSQL
, Waits.wait_type WhyBlocked
, Blocked.session_id AS BlockedSessionId
, USER_NAME(Blocked.user_id) AS BlockedUser
, BlockedSQL.text AS BlockedSQL
, DB_NAME(Blocked.database_id) AS DatabaseName
FROM sys.dm_exec_connections AS Blocking
INNER JOIN sys.dm_exec_requests AS Blocked
     ON Blocking.session_id = Blocked.blocking_session_id
INNER JOIN sys.dm_os_waiting_tasks AS Waits
     ON Blocked.session_id = Waits.session_id
RIGHT OUTER JOIN sys.dm_exec_sessions Sess
     ON Blocking.session_id = sess.session_id
CROSS APPLY sys.dm_exec_sql_text(Blocking.most_recent_sql_handle)
                              AS BlockingSQL
CROSS APPLY sys.dm_exec_sql_text(Blocked.sql_handle) AS BlockedSQL
ORDER BY BlockingSessionId, BlockedSessionId
```

The script shows details of the query that is causing the blocking ❶, specifically the session id, the query text, and the reason for the wait/blocking. This is followed by details of the query that's blocked ❷, including the session id, the username, and the query being blocked.

In this script, four DMVs and one DMF are used to identify which queries are being blocked. Table 6.5 gives a brief description of each.

Table 6.5   DMVs/DMF to identify queries that are blocked

DMV/DMF	Description
sys.dm_exec_connections	Contains details about connections established on SQL Server
sys.dm_exec_requests	Contains details about each request executing on SQL Server
sys.dm_os_waiting_tasks	Contains details about the wait queues of tasks that are waiting on some resource
sys.dm_exec_sessions	Contains details about each authenticated session on SQL Server
sys.dm_exec_sql_text	DMF that returns the SQL text identified by a given sql_handle

By joining the DMVs and DMF, we have enough information to determine which SQL queries are causing blocking and which queries are being blocked, across all databases on the server. The DMVs sys.dm_exec_connections, sys.dm_exec_requests, and sys.dm_os_waiting_tasks are joined on their common key column session_id (blocking_session_id in the case of sys.dm_exec_requests). These DMVs have a RIGHT OUTER JOIN to the DMV sys.dm_exec_sessions; this is because the blocking queries are typically running and will be present in the sys.dm_dm_os_waiting_tasks DMV.

The blocking query's most_recent_sql_handle is passed to the DMF sys.dm_exec_sql_text to retrieve the text of the blocking SQL query. Similarly, the blocked query's sql_handle is passed to the DMF sys.dm_exec_sql_text to retrieve the text of the blocked SQL query.

	BlockingSessionId	BlockingUser	BlockingSQL		WhyBlocked	BlockedSessionId	BlockedUser	BlockedSQL	DatabaseName
1	101	MARKETS\Randa...	USE IWSTEST	b...	LCK_M_U	76	MARKETS\Stirkl	(@1 varchar(8000))UP...	IWSTest
2	101	MARKETS\Randa...	USE IWSTEST	b...	LCK_M_S	103	dbo	select * from dbo....	IWSTest
3	103	MARKETS\Randa...	select * from dbo.fxR...		LCK_M_S	85	MARKETS\Stirkl	select * from dbo.fxR...	IWSTest

Figure 6.5   Output showing which SQL queries are blocking and being blocked

Sample output for this query is shown in figure 6.5.

In the output, you can see that SessionId 101 is blocking SessionId 76. The users causing the blocking and being blocked are both identified. Similarly, the SQL queries involved in the blocking are identified. You can also see that SessionId 103 is also being blocked by SessionId 101, and SessionId 85 is being blocked by SessionId 103.

It might prove useful to run this script together with the one given in chapter 5 (section 5.9) to get more complete and detailed information about what specific lines of SQL are causing the blocking and being blocked. The two sets of output can be interlinked via their common session_id.

> **Using cached plans for blocking queries**
>
> It might be useful to mention here that when blocking occurs (or waiting, for that matter), developers often examine the cached plan for clues on how to speed up the query. Although this approach is common, you should note that the cached plan's metrics don't take into account interaction with other running queries. So while you might improve the performance of the section of SQL in a batch that has the highest cost, it may have little impact on a piece of SQL that has little cost but is involved in blocking. In this case, it makes more sense to run the batch of SQL inside a wrapper that records the duration of each SQL statement within the batch and target these for improvement. In essence, this gives you instrumentation inside your SQL code. An example of this is given in section 6.10.

Having looked at how useful wait states can be in identifying the cause of performance problems, we'll now look at the SQL Server performance counter. These two aspects of DMVs, taken together, can provide combined supportive information for identifying problems and providing potential solutions.

6.7   *SQL Server performance counters*

Performance Monitor is a well-known tool for collecting detailed operating system information. Such information includes metrics relating to memory, processor, I/O, and the network. The tool is invariably known by the shorter name of *PerfMon* or *SysMon*. PerfMon allows you to monitor counters that relate to various hardware and software resources. The objects provide a grouping for the detailed contained counters; for example, to monitor the amount of blocking, you'd look at the object named SQLServer:General Statistics and then the counter Processes Blocked.

Monitoring the changes in these counters is a useful step in determining the cause of a problem.

Another column provided by Performance Monitor is named instance_name. This typically contains the database name the counter relates to. If you wanted to collect details about all the databases, you'd look at the instance_name of _Total or else you'd look at the corresponding counters for the database you're interested in.

SQL Server provides a DMV named sys.dm_os_performance_counters that enables you to view these counters from within SQL Server. But unlike its Windows counterpart, you can see only those objects that relate to SQL Server. Although this might limit its usefulness, it does enable you to obtain and examine some useful information from within SQL Server.

You could monitor many hundreds of counters, but as with much of life, targeting a few specific areas will give you most return for the time invested. A list of the more useful objects and counters, together with a description of their meaning and an indication of the problem area they relate to, is given in table 6.6.

Table 6.6   Useful SQL Server performance-monitoring objects/counters

Object	Counter
SQLServer:AccessMethods	Full Scans/sec. Occurs when an entire table or index is scanned. Often indicates excessive I/O. Look at missing indexes DMV to fix the problem. Also check SQL; maybe too many rows are being requested.
	Forwarded Records/sec. Indicates tables without clustered index. Inserted rows have pointers due to split. Corrected by using fixed-length records.
	Table Lock Escalations/sec. Records the number of times locks on a table were escalated. Large values can indicate design problems.
SQLServer:Latches	Total Latch Wait Time (ms). Latches are short-term synchronization objects. Often indicate I/O bottleneck or memory pressures.
SQLServer:SQL Statistics	Batch Requests/sec. Shows amount of SQL submitted per second. Compare with SQL Compilations/sec to determine how often these queries are compiled/ recompiled.
	SQL Compilations/sec. High value, compared with Batch Requests/sec; indicates inefficient reuse of cached plans.
	SQL Re-Compilations/sec. High value, compared with Batch Requests/sec; indicates inefficient reuse of cached plans.
SQLServer:Buffer Manager	Buffer Cache Hit Ratio. Percentage of time the requested pages are already in the cache. If low (< 98%), may indicate memory pressures. May be fixed by adding more memory.
	Page Life Expectancy. Time in seconds that data pages stay in the SQL Server cache. Low value is < 300. May indicate memory problems or missing indexes.

Table 6.6   Useful SQL Server performance-monitoring objects/counters *(continued)*

Object	Counter
SQLServer:Memory Manager	Memory Grants Pending. Indicates insufficient memory for the user to run their query. Ideally, this value should be around zero. May be solved by adding more memory.
	Target Server Memory (KB). Total physical memory available to SQL Server. Ideally, its value should be close to the amount of physical memory on the server.
	Total Server Memory (KB). Amount of physical memory currently assigned to SQL Server. Should be high if SQL Server is running on a dedicated box (i.e., no IIS or Exchange present). Ideally, should be close in value to Target Server Memory (KB).
SQLServer:General Statistics	Processes Blocked. Number of currently blocked processes. Large values indicate concurrency problems.
SQLServer:Locks	Lock Waits/sec. Indicative of transactions, hence should be low. Memory pressure or missing index might increase values.

Some of the counters are cumulative, although others are per second. Examining each of these sets of counters will require a different understanding. For per-second values, ideally the values should be recorded per second (or some other short time period). You can achieve this by storing the DMV snapshot into a temporary table each second; a GO statement followed by an appropriate number (for example, GO 60) will enable this to occur easily. An example of this is given later in this chapter (section 6.12).

When examining the changes in values, it's important to measure them with reference to a default or benchmark set of values. This set of values contains the typical values for your system; having this set of values allows you to make a considered judgment when the values change. In its absence, you might be able to infer the impact of the changed values by comparing the performance counter values in the period immediately before or after you run your queries.

Examining the values for specific performance counters should provide a lead to identify both the cause of the problem and how to improve the performance of those specific queries. Further details of how to do this are given in the Microsoft "Waits and Queues" white paper mentioned earlier.

Many other non-SQL performance counters should be monitored with a view to corroborating or rejecting your understanding of the potential causes of the performance problems. Let's look at some of the more useful counters.

6.7.1   *Important non-SQL performance counters*

The list of counters provided by the sys.dm_os_performance_counters DMV is relatively small when compared with those available within the Windows environment. Although the list provided by the DMV might be useful for determining the cause of some SQL Server–based issues, often you'll want to use PerfMon to record counters that relate to memory, processor, disk, and network. A list of the more useful objects and counters used for monitoring, as well as a description of their meaning and an indication of the problem area they relate to, is given in table 6.7.

Table 6.7   Useful non-SQL performance-monitoring objects/counters

Object	Counter
Memory	Available Bytes. The amount of free RAM on server. If it has a relatively low value, this indicates memory is a limiting factor. Check to see if other applications (apart from SQL Server) are running on the server.
	Pages/sec. Shows amount of Windows paging. Values should ideally be close to zero.
Physical Disk	% Disk Time. The percentage of time the disk is busy. It will have peaks but should be below 10%. Performance is better if the data is already in the buffer.
	Avg. Disk Queue Length. If value is high (> 2 per disk), indicates I/O bandwidth problem.
	Current Disk Queue Length. If value is high (> 2 per disk), indicates I/O subsystems can't keep up with the workload.
Processor	% Processor Time. Percentage of time the CPU is doing work. Sustained periods where the values exceed 80% indicate CPU bottleneck.
	% User Time. Percentage of time CPU spends doing user work. If the value exceeds 70% consistently, it indicates a CPU bottleneck with the SQL Server workload. Check to see if other applications (apart from SQL Server) are running on the server.
Network Interface (network card)	Bytes Total/sec. Rate at which the bytes are transferred on the network interface card (NIC). A value below 50% of the card's capacity should be acceptable. There will be peaks.

Where possible, all these performance counters (both SQL Server and non–SQL Server) should be included as a minimum in any monitoring to help determine the underlying cause of any performance problems. Ideally, you should create a benchmark, which contains the counters' values over a typical 24-hour period. Then when you experience performance problems, you can start recording the performance counters again and compare them with the benchmark. This should highlight areas that underlie the problem and provide targeted areas for improvement.

If you do decide to use the more-extensive performance counters provided by the Windows environment, I'd encourage you to use the Performance Analysis of Logs (PAL) tool for analyzing the output. This tool highlights the peaks and troughs in your logs and provides plenty of commentary on their potential causes.

6.8 *Effect of running SQL queries on the performance counters*

When SQL queries run, they require various resources, and this resource usage is reflected in the changing values in the underlying operating system performance counters. Examining the changes in these counters should identify what factors may be limiting the performance of your queries. Correcting these will improve their performance.

You can determine how the performance counters change over a given time period by calculating the difference between two DMV snapshots, taken at the start and end of a time interval. Running the SQL script given here will show how the performance counters change over the given time interval. In this example, the time period is five minutes; you may want to alter this time interval to suit your needs.

Listing 6.5   Effect of queries on performance counters

```
SET TRANSACTION ISOLATION LEVEL READ UNCOMMITTED     ❶ Get pre-work
                                                        performance counters
SELECT
  [object_name], [counter_name], [instance_name]
  , [cntr_value], [cntr_type]
INTO #PreWorkOSSnapShot
FROM sys.dm_os_performance_counters                  ❷ Wait a given
                                                        time interval
WAITFOR DELAY '00:05:00'

SELECT                                               ❸ Get post-work
  [object_name], [counter_name], [instance_name]        performance counters
  , [cntr_value], [cntr_type]
INTO #PostWorkOSSnapShot
FROM sys.dm_os_performance_counters                  ❹ Calculate
                                                        changes
SELECT
  p2.object_name, p2.counter_name, p2.instance_name
  , ISNULL(p1.cntr_value, 0) AS InitialValue
  , p2.cntr_value AS FinalValue
  , p2.cntr_value - ISNULL(p1.cntr_value, 0) AS Change
  , (p2.cntr_value - ISNULL(p1.cntr_value, 0)) * 100 / p1.cntr_value
                                             AS [% Change]
FROM #PreWorkOSSnapShot p1
RIGHT OUTER JOIN
#PostWorkOSSnapShot p2 ON p2.object_name =
              ISNULL(p1.object_name, p2.object_name)
    AND p2.counter_name = ISNULL(p1.counter_name, p2.counter_name)
    AND p2.instance_name = ISNULL(p1.instance_name, p2.instance_name)
WHERE p2.cntr_value - ISNULL(p1.cntr_value, 0) > 0
   AND ISNULL(p1.cntr_value, 0) != 0
ORDER BY [% Change] DESC, Change DESC

DROP TABLE #PreWorkOSSnapShot
DROP TABLE #PostWorkOSSnapShot
```

The script shown in listing 6.5 takes a pre-work snapshot of all of the performance counters ❶. It then waits a given time interval (five minutes in the script example) ❷ and takes a post-work snapshot ❸. The script then determines the percentage change in value for each of the counters, for each object, for each instance ❹. The results are sorted by the percentage change in value in descending order.

Although sorting by the percentage change in value may be adequate for showing the changes in performance counters in a generic manner, it may not be adequate for a more detailed investigation. In particular, some counters may have a small percentage change in value but have a significant impact on performance. Additionally, the percentage change in value is too dependent on the counter's initial value. For these reasons, the initial and final values of the performance counters are also output; this will provide raw data for any subsequent analysis.

An example of the type of output for this script is shown in figure 6.6.

The example script shows the change in performance counter values over a given time interval. Although this might be useful in cases where you want to determine what's happening with a batch of SQL that runs periodically, it's possible to replace the WAITFOR command with a SQL query or batch of SQL that you want to determine the effects of. I'll show how to do this in section 6.10.

Next, we'll examine how both the performance counters and wait states change over a given time interval, and you'll see how the results support and corroborate each other.

6.9 How performance counters and wait states relate

In addition to determining the effect of queries on performance counters, it's possible to determine what effect these queries have on wait states. This is interesting because performance counters and wait states are often used together to target the underlying cause of slow query performance.

Previously, we examined how wait states and queries change over a given time interval. Similarly, here we'll examine how performance counters and wait states change over a given time period. Running the SQL script given in the following listing will identify the changes in the wait states and performance counters over the given time interval.

	object_name	counter_name	instance_name	InitialValue	FinalValue	Change	% Change
1	SQLServer:Wait Statistics	Memory grant queue waits	Waits started per second	1	4	3	300
2	SQLServer:Wait Statistics	Page latch waits	Waits started per second	105	210	105	100
3	SQLServer:Wait Statistics	Network IO waits	Waits in progress	1	2	1	100
4	SQLServer:Exec Statistics	Extended Procedures	Execs started per second	1	2	1	100
5	SQLServer:Wait Statistics	Memory grant queue waits	Cumulative wait time (ms) per second	2000	3000	1000	50
6	SQLServer:Wait Statistics	Memory grant queue waits	Waits in progress	2	3	1	50
7	SQLServer:Memory Manager	Memory Grants Pending		2	3	1	50
8	SQLServer:Plan Cache	Cache Hit Ratio Base	SQL Plans	646	731	85	13
9	SQLServer:Plan Cache	Cache Hit Ratio	SQL Plans	317	359	42	13
10	SQLServer:Buffer Manager	Buffer cache hit ratio base		6059	6506	447	7

Figure 6.6 Output showing the change in performance counter values

Listing 6.6   Changes in performance counters and wait states

```
SET TRANSACTION ISOLATION LEVEL READ UNCOMMITTED
SELECT
  [object_name], [counter_name], [instance_name]
  , [cntr_value], [cntr_type]
INTO #PreWorkOSSnapShot
FROM sys.dm_os_performance_counters

SELECT
  wait_type, waiting_tasks_count
  , wait_time_ms, max_wait_time_ms, signal_wait_time_ms
INTO #PreWorkWaitStats
FROM sys.dm_os_wait_stats

WAITFOR DELAY '00:05:00'

SELECT
  wait_type, waiting_tasks_count, wait_time_ms
  , max_wait_time_ms, signal_wait_time_ms
INTO #PostWorkWaitStats
FROM sys.dm_os_wait_stats

SELECT
  [object_name], [counter_name], [instance_name]
  , [cntr_value], [cntr_type]
INTO #PostWorkOSSnapShot
FROM sys.dm_os_performance_counters

SELECT
  p2.wait_time_ms - ISNULL(p1.wait_time_ms, 0) AS wait_time_ms
  , p2.signal_wait_time_ms - ISNULL(p1.signal_wait_time_ms, 0)
                       AS signal_wait_time_ms
  , ((p2.wait_time_ms - ISNULL(p1.wait_time_ms, 0)) -
      (p2.signal_wait_time_ms - ISNULL(p1.signal_wait_time_ms, 0)))
                       AS RealWait
  , p2.wait_type
FROM #PreWorkWaitStats p1
RIGHT OUTER JOIN
#PostWorkWaitStats p2 ON p2.wait_type = ISNULL(p1.wait_type, p2.wait_type)
WHERE p2.wait_time_ms - ISNULL(p1.wait_time_ms, 0) > 0
  AND p2.wait_type NOT LIKE '%SLEEP%'
  AND p2.wait_type != 'WAITFOR'
ORDER BY RealWait DESC

SELECT
  p2.object_name, p2.counter_name, p2.instance_name
  , ISNULL(p1.cntr_value, 0) AS InitialValue
  , p2.cntr_value AS FinalValue
  , p2.cntr_value - ISNULL(p1.cntr_value, 0) AS Change
  , (p2.cntr_value - ISNULL(p1.cntr_value, 0)) * 100 / p1.cntr_value
                       AS [% Change]
FROM #PreWorkOSSnapShot p1
RIGHT OUTER JOIN
#PostWorkOSSnapShot p2 ON p2.object_name =
                ISNULL(p1.object_name, p2.object_name)
```

❶ Get pre-work performance counters

❷ Get pre-work wait states counters

❸ Wait a given time interval

❹ Get post-work performance counters

❺ Get post-work wait states counters

❻ Calculate changes in wait states

❼ Calculate changes in performance counters

```
    AND p2.counter_name = ISNULL(p1.counter_name, p2.counter_name)
    AND p2.instance_name = ISNULL(p1.instance_name, p2.instance_name)
WHERE p2.cntr_value - ISNULL(p1.cntr_value, 0) > 0
  AND ISNULL(p1.cntr_value, 0) != 0
ORDER BY [% Change] DESC, Change DESC

DROP TABLE #PostWorkWaitStats
DROP TABLE #PreWorkWaitStats
DROP TABLE #PreWorkOSSnapShot
DROP TABLE #PostWorkOSSnapShot
```

The script shown in listing 6.6 takes a pre-work snapshot of all of the performance counters ❶ and the wait states ❷. It then waits a given time interval ❸ (five minutes in the script example; you may want to alter this time interval to suit your needs) and takes a post-work snapshot for both the performance counters ❹ and the wait states ❺.

The script then determines the change in value of the wait states ❻ and calculates the percentage change in value for each of the performance counters, for each object, for each instance ❼.

Figure 6.7 shows sample output for this script.

Examining the changes in both the wait states and performance counters should reveal some factors that require future investigation, which should then lead to performance improvements.

Having looked at how performance counters and wait states change while SQL queries run, it would be nice to know what specific queries are running and causing these changes. I'll provide a script to do that next.

	wait_time_ms	signal_wait_time_ms	RealWait	wait_type
1	60000	0	60000	SQLTRACE_BUFFER_FLUSH
2	60000	0	60000	BROKER_TASK_STOP
3	4735	485	4250	CXPACKET
4	172	0	172	ASYNC_NETWORK_IO
5	31	31	0	SOS_SCHEDULER_YIELD

	object_name	counter_name	instance_name	InitialValue	FinalValue	Change	% Change
1	SQLServer:Plan Cache	Cache Hit Ratio	Object Plans	546	735	189	34
2	SQLServer:Plan Cache	Cache Hit Ratio Base	Object Plans	546	735	189	34
3	SQLServer:Plan Cache	Cache Hit Ratio	_Total	2638	2838	200	7
4	SQLServer:Plan Cache	Cache Hit Ratio Base	_Total	3313	3535	222	6
5	SQLServer:Buffer Manager	Buffer cache hit ratio		5578	5837	259	4
6	SQLServer:Buffer Manager	Buffer cache hit ratio base		5586	5845	259	4
7	SQLServer:Plan Cache	Cache Hit Ratio Base	SQL Plans	713	738	25	3
8	SQLServer:Plan Cache	Cache Objects in use	SQL Plans	26	27	1	3
9	SQLServer:Plan Cache	Cache Objects in use	_Total	26	27	1	3
10	SQLServer:Plan Cache	Cache Hit Ratio	SQL Plans	102	105	3	2

Figure 6.7 Output showing the change in wait state and performance counter values

6.10   SQL queries and how they change the performance counters and wait states

Previously we determined the effect of queries on performance counters and determined what effect these queries have on both wait states and performance counters. You can go one step further and display which queries have run. This will allow you to correlate the individual SQL queries with the changes in the wait states and performance counters.

Reporting the changes in performance counters, wait states, and queries over a given time period should allow you to identify the relationship between performance counters and wait states and determine how they're influenced by the running queries. Running the SQL script given next will identify how the performance counters, wait states, and queries interact.

Listing 6.7   Queries that change performance counters and wait states

```
SET TRANSACTION ISOLATION LEVEL READ UNCOMMITTED          ❶ Get pre-work
                                                             query counters
SELECT
  sql_handle, plan_handle, total_elapsed_time, total_worker_time
  , total_logical_reads, total_logical_writes, total_clr_time
  , execution_count, statement_start_offset, statement_end_offset
INTO #PreWorkQuerySnapShot
FROM sys.dm_exec_query_stats

SELECT                                                       Get pre-work
  [object_name], [counter_name], [instance_name]             performance
  , [cntr_value], [cntr_type]                              ❷ counters
INTO #PreWorkOSSnapShot
FROM sys.dm_os_performance_counters

SELECT                                                       Get pre-work
  wait_type, waiting_tasks_count                             wait states
  , wait_time_ms, max_wait_time_ms, signal_wait_time_ms    ❸ counters
INTO #PreWorkWaitStats
FROM sys.dm_os_wait_stats

WAITFOR DELAY '00:05:00'                                  ❹ Wait a given
                                                             time interval

SELECT                                                     ❺ Get post-work wait
  wait_type, waiting_tasks_count, wait_time_ms               states counters
  , max_wait_time_ms, signal_wait_time_ms
INTO #PostWorkWaitStats
FROM sys.dm_os_wait_stats

SELECT                                                       Get post-work
  [object_name], [counter_name], [instance_name]          ❻ performance counters
  , [cntr_value], [cntr_type]
INTO #PostWorkOSSnapShot
FROM sys.dm_os_performance_counters                       ❼ Get post-work
                                                             query counters
SELECT
  sql_handle, plan_handle, total_elapsed_time, total_worker_time
  , total_logical_reads, total_logical_writes, total_clr_time
  , execution_count, statement_start_offset, statement_end_offset
```

```
INTO #PostWorkQuerySnapShot
FROM sys.dm_exec_query_stats
SELECT
  p2.total_elapsed_time - ISNULL(p1.total_elapsed_time, 0) AS [Duration]
  , p2.total_worker_time - ISNULL(p1.total_worker_time, 0) AS [Time on CPU]
  , (p2.total_elapsed_time - ISNULL(p1.total_elapsed_time, 0)) -
                (p2.total_worker_time - ISNULL(p1.total_worker_time, 0))
                                                    AS [Time blocked]
  , p2.total_logical_reads - ISNULL(p1.total_logical_reads, 0) AS [Reads]
  , p2.total_logical_writes - ISNULL(p1.total_logical_writes, 0)
                                                    AS [Writes]
  , p2.total_clr_time - ISNULL(p1.total_clr_time, 0) AS [CLR time]
  , p2.execution_count - ISNULL(p1.execution_count, 0) AS [Executions]
  , SUBSTRING (qt.text,p2.statement_start_offset/2 + 1,
    ((CASE WHEN p2.statement_end_offset = -1
    THEN LEN(CONVERT(NVARCHAR(MAX), qt.text)) * 2
    ELSE p2.statement_end_offset
    END - p2.statement_start_offset)/2) + 1) AS [Individual Query]
  , qt.text AS [Parent Query]
  , DB_NAME(qt.dbid) AS DatabaseName
FROM #PreWorkQuerySnapShot p1
RIGHT OUTER JOIN
#PostWorkQuerySnapShot p2 ON p2.sql_handle =
        ISNULL(p1.sql_handle, p2.sql_handle)
   AND p2.plan_handle = ISNULL(p1.plan_handle, p2.plan_handle)
   AND p2.statement_start_offset =
        ISNULL(p1.statement_start_offset, p2.statement_start_offset)
AND p2.statement_end_offset =
        ISNULL(p1.statement_end_offset, p2.statement_end_offset)
CROSS APPLY sys.dm_exec_sql_text(p2.sql_handle) as qt
WHERE p2.execution_count != ISNULL(p1.execution_count, 0)
   AND qt.text NOT LIKE '--ThisRoutineIdentifier%'
ORDER BY [Duration] DESC

SELECT
  p2.wait_time_ms - ISNULL(p1.wait_time_ms, 0) AS wait_time_ms
  , p2.signal_wait_time_ms - ISNULL(p1.signal_wait_time_ms, 0)
                                        AS signal_wait_time_ms
  , ((p2.wait_time_ms - ISNULL(p1.wait_time_ms, 0)) -
        (p2.signal_wait_time_ms - ISNULL(p1.signal_wait_time_ms, 0)))
                                        AS RealWait
  , p2.wait_type
FROM #PreWorkWaitStats p1
RIGHT OUTER JOIN
#PostWorkWaitStats p2 ON p2.wait_type = ISNULL(p1.wait_type, p2.wait_type)
WHERE p2.wait_time_ms - ISNULL(p1.wait_time_ms, 0) > 0
   AND p2.wait_type NOT LIKE '%SLEEP%'
   AND p2.wait_type != 'WAITFOR'
ORDER BY RealWait DESC

SELECT
  p2.object_name, p2.counter_name, p2.instance_name
  , ISNULL(p1.cntr_value, 0) AS InitialValue
  , p2.cntr_value AS FinalValue
```

8 **Calculate changes in query counters**

9 **Calculate changes in wait states**

10 **Calculate changes in performance counters**

```
    , p2.cntr_value - ISNULL(p1.cntr_value, 0) AS Change
    , (p2.cntr_value - ISNULL(p1.cntr_value, 0)) * 100 / p1.cntr_value
                                               AS [% Change]
FROM #PreWorkOSSnapShot p1
RIGHT OUTER JOIN
#PostWorkOSSnapShot p2 ON p2.object_name =
        ISNULL(p1.object_name, p2.object_name)
    AND p2.counter_name = ISNULL(p1.counter_name, p2.counter_name)
    AND p2.instance_name = ISNULL(p1.instance_name, p2.instance_name)
WHERE p2.cntr_value - ISNULL(p1.cntr_value, 0) > 0
  AND ISNULL(p1.cntr_value, 0) != 0
ORDER BY [% Change] DESC, Change DESC

DROP TABLE #PreWorkQuerySnapShot
DROP TABLE #PostWorkQuerySnapShot
DROP TABLE #PostWorkWaitStats
DROP TABLE #PreWorkWaitStats
DROP TABLE #PreWorkOSSnapShot
DROP TABLE #PostWorkOSSnapShot
```

The script shown in listing 6.7 takes a pre-work snapshot of all of the query counters ❶, performance counters ❷, and wait states ❸. It then waits a given time interval ❹ (five minutes in the script example; you may want to alter this time interval to suit your needs) and then takes a post-work snapshot for the wait states ❺, performance counters ❻, and query counters ❼. The script determines the change in value of the query counters ❽ and wait states ❾ and then calculates the percentage change in value for each of the performance counters ❿.

To get detailed information about any of the specific DMV snapshots shown, see the relevant section of this book for that DMV snapshot. Here we're interested in any relationship between the DMV snapshots rather than the individual DMV snapshots themselves.

An example of the type of output for this script is shown in figure 6.8.

The first grid shown in figure 6.8 shows the queries that ran during the given time interval, sorted by query duration. The second grid shows the wait states that occurred

	Duration	Time on CPU	Time blocked	Reads	Writes	CLR time	Executions	Individual Query	Parent Query	DatabaseName
1	2929	2929	0	6	0	0	3	SELECT 'object_name' = RTRIM...	CREATE PROCEDURE sp_sqlag...	msdb
2	0	0	0	2	0	0	1	IF (NOT EXISTS (SELECT *	CREATE PROCEDURE sp_sqlag...	msdb
3	0	0	0	2	0	0	1	SELECT @step_name = step_n...	CREATE PROCEDURE sp_sqlag...	msdb
4	0	0	0	6	0	0	1	INSERT INTO msdb.dbo.sysjobh...	CREATE PROCEDURE sp_sqlag...	msdb
5	0	0	0	2	0	0	1	SELECT @job_name = name, ...	CREATE PROCEDURE sp_sqlag...	msdb

	wait_time_ms	signal_wait_time_ms	RealWait	wait_type
1	60000	0	60000	SQLTRACE_BUFFER_FLUSH
2	60000	0	60000	BROKER_TASK_STOP
3	16	0	16	WRITELOG

	object_name	counter_name	instance_name	InitialValue	FinalValue	Change	% Change
1	SQLServer:Databases	Log Flush Wait Time	_Total	15	30	15	100
2	SQLServer:Plan Cache	Cache Objects in use	_Total	26	27	1	3
3	SQLServer:Plan Cache	Cache Objects in use	SQL Plans	26	27	1	3
4	SQLServer:Plan Cache	Cache Hit Ratio Base	SQL Plans	829	842	13	1
5	SQLServer:General S...	Active Temp Tables		251	254	3	1
6	SQLServer:Buffer Ma...	Page lookups/sec		2111601...	211160...	9268	0

Figure 6.8   Output showing the change in performance counter values for the identified queries

during the same time interval, sorted by wait_time_ms. The last grid shows the change in the various SQL Server performance counters over the same time interval, sorted by percentage change in value. You can infer that the changed values in the wait states and performance counters are a result of running the queries. You could determine the effects of specific queries by replacing the WAITFOR statement in the script with the SQL query you want to examine.

Once you know which queries in particular are troublesome, you could wrap the DMV snapshot code around the particular statement(s) to get more detailed information about that query.

6.11   *Correlating wait states and performance counters*

Wait states and performance counters often display an association with each other; this relationship can be used to corroborate either of them. A list of some of the more common associations is given in table 6.8. For a more detailed description of the waits states and performance counters, please see the relevant section earlier in this chapter.

Table 6.8   Associations between wait states and performance-monitoring objects/counters

Wait state	Performance counter
ASYNC_IO_COMPLETION	Physical Disk: Avg. Disk Queue Length Physical Disk: Current Disk Queue Length Memory: Available Bytes Memory: Pages/sec
IO_COMPLETION	Physical Disk: Avg. Disk Queue Length Physical Disk: Current Disk Queue Length Memory: Available Bytes Memory: Pages/sec
LATCH_xx	Memory: Available Bytes Memory: Pages/sec
LOGMGR	Physical Disk: Avg. Disk Queue Length Physical Disk: Current Disk Queue Length
PAGEIOLATCH_xx	Physical Disk: Avg. Disk Queue Length Physical Disk: Current Disk Queue Length
PAGELATCH_xx	Physical Disk: Avg. Disk Queue Length Physical Disk: Current Disk Queue Length
WRITELOG	Physical Disk: Avg. Disk Queue Length Physical Disk: Current Disk Queue Length

Having identified how the wait states and performance counters relate, we'll now discuss how to capture DMV snapshot information on a regular basis, allowing for further analysis.

6.12   *Capturing DMV data periodically*

The scripts you've seen so far typically involve taking a DMV snapshot of relevant metrics, doing some work (for example, running a query or waiting a given time interval), and then taking another DMV snapshot. Finally, you compare the two DMV snapshots to determine what effect the query or time interval has on the DMV delta.

With DMV data in general, and performance counters in particular (especially the per-second ones), it can prove instructive to record the DMV metrics on a more regular basis. The script you can use to record DMV snapshots periodically is given here.

Listing 6.8   Recording DMV snapshots periodically

```
SET TRANSACTION ISOLATION LEVEL READ UNCOMMITTED

CREATE TABLE #PerfCounters                             ◁─┐   Create temp
(    RunDateTime datetime NOT NULL,                      │   table to hold
     object_name nchar(128) NOT NULL,                 ❶   periodic results
     counter_name nchar(128) NOT NULL,
     instance_name nchar(128) NULL,
     cntr_value bigint NOT NULL,
     cntr_type int NOT NULL
)
ALTER TABLE #PerfCounters                             ❷   Add datetime
ADD CONSTRAINT DF_PerFCounters_RunDateTime            ◁─    constraint
     DEFAULT (getdate()) FOR RunDateTime
GO                                                    ❸   Extract
                                                          relevant
INSERT INTO #PerfCounters                             ◁─   DMV data
        (object_name,counter_name,instance_name,cntr_value,cntr_type)
(SELECT object_name,counter_name,instance_name,cntr_value,cntr_type
FROM sys.dm_os_performance_counters)
                                                      ❹   Wait given
WAITFOR DELAY '00:00:01'                              ◁─    time interval
GO 20                                                 ◁─┐
                                                          Repeat last
SELECT * FROM #PerfCounters                               two statements
ORDER BY RunDateTime, object_name,counter_name,instance_name  ❺  (20 times here)

DROP TABLE #PerfCounters
```

The first section of the script in listing 6.8 creates a temporary table (named #Perf-Counters) to hold the DMV metrics ❶. We add a constraint to the table to automatically fill in the date and time the rows were added ❷. Note that the first GO statement runs this batch of two commands.

Next, we take a snapshot of the counters in the sys.dm_os_performance_counters DMV and insert these into the table #PerfCounters ❸. We then wait a given time interval (one second in this example) ❹. We run a GO command followed by the number 20 ❺. GO 20 repeats the last SQL commands before the previous GO statement. In our example, the INSERT and WAITFOR statements are executed a total of 20 times. Thus, we collect the performance counters each second, for 20 seconds. It

	RunDateTime	object_name	counter_name	instance_name	cntr_value	cntr_type
1	2010-11-25 09:34:16.450	SQLServer:Buffer Manager	AWE lookup maps/sec		0	272696576
2	2010-11-25 09:34:16.450	SQLServer:Buffer Manager	AWE stolen maps/sec		0	272696576
3	2010-11-25 09:34:16.450	SQLServer:Buffer Manager	AWE unmap calls/sec		0	272696576
4	2010-11-25 09:34:16.450	SQLServer:Buffer Manager	AWE unmap pages/sec		0	272696576
5	2010-11-25 09:34:16.450	SQLServer:Buffer Manager	AWE write maps/sec		0	272696576

Figure 6.9   Output showing the DMV snapshot data for performance counters

should be a simple matter of exporting the results of this script into Excel or some other analysis tool to investigate how the various counters change over time.

Although the example given in listing 6.8 relates specifically to how the performance counter values change over time, you can use the pattern shown to examine in greater detail how any of the various DMV data changes over time.

Ideally, you'd use the more generic start and end DMV snapshots to record large changes in counters, over one large time period, and then target specific highlighted counters for greater investigation using this more periodic script.

Sample output for this script is shown in figure 6.9.

You can use this script as a template for recording information about other DMVs on a regular basis.

6.13   *Summary*

In this chapter we examined the causes of why SQL Server queries must wait to run. I provided scripts to examine both the accumulated types of waiting and also a DMV snapshot delta to determine the waiting that's occurring over a given time interval. Linked to this, I provided a script to determine the wait states that occur when a given SQL query or batch of SQL is run. I also described some of the more common wait types, what problems they represent, and how these might be corrected.

In addition to exploring wait states, I provided a script to show the changes in SQL Server operating system counters, over a given time period or when a SQL query is run. We combined scripts to determine how the wait states and performance counters change when a given query runs or a time interval passes. The association between the wait states and performance counters can be seen in the various script outputs.

I provided a pattern to enable you to take DMV snapshots periodically. This should allow you to collect more-detailed information and target specific counters.

Having looked at how the various operating system–related DMVs can be used to highlight and target various performance problems, next we'll investigate Common Language Runtime (CLR)–related DMVs.

Common Language
Runtime DMVs

SQL is great for performing set-based processing, where one or more rows of data are manipulated in accordance with set theory. In the early days, Structured Query Language (SQL) was extended, typically by third parties looking for commercial advantage, to benefit from an increasingly technical environment. These nonstandard, third-party-based SQL extensions were often embedded into a host programming language to enhance its programmability. Extending the reach of SQL has a long history, culminating in the current movement of using the Common Language Runtime (CLR) to extend SQL programmability.

Although this book is primarily about DMVs, I want to stray a little from the CLR-based DMVs initially. I feel that in order for you to understand the CLR-based DMVs, coupled with the fact that many SQL practitioners may not be so familiar with CLR code, it would be best to first provide a background to CLR processing. In addition, in this chapter I'll create a small SQL CLR class, which will provide regular expression functionality, allowing complex pattern matching to be used within SQL queries. I hope this will offer a gentle introduction to the subject as well as provide a useful piece of functionality.

Microsoft provides the .NET Framework and Visual Studio for creating code that will use the CLR. The .NET Framework is a set of libraries from Microsoft that facilitates the reuse of many well-written, well-tested classes (a *class* is a template for an object, which allows you to do something useful). The CLR is a runtime environment that manages the execution of the .NET code. The terms *CLR* and *.NET* in relation to SQL are often used interchangeably. Although this may be technically incorrect, it does follow the spirit of usage.

7.1   *Introducing the CLR*

Microsoft has incorporated the CLR into SQL Server itself, enabling you to write code in one of the many .NET languages, for example, Visual Basic .NET or C#, that can easily be used from within your SQL queries. The main point to note is that the CLR gives you access to many already-written classes that provide useful functionality that would otherwise not be available or are difficult to program with SQL alone. Also, when used correctly, CLR code typically provides improved performance.

CLR code won't replace the standard set-based processing or data access that SQL excels at. That said, there are cases where the CLR can exceed SQL performance. For example, using a datareader (this is a container that points to the current row in a group of rows) within CLR code is typically faster than SQL cursor processing—not that I'm advocating SQL cursor processing as a standard solution.

The dividing line between when to use SQL code and when to use CLR code can sometimes seem blurred. There are certain things that SQL code just cannot do (for example, complex regular expressions). There are some things that SQL code does much better than CLR code (for example, set-based processing), and there are some things that CLR code does much better. Apart from the obvious areas of their respective advantages, if you're unsure about which to use, it's best to test out any code using both SQL and CLR.

One obvious disadvantage of the CLR is it requires you to learn a new programming language and environment. But with the increasing usage of the CLR code within SQL Server, you could turn this into an advantage for your resume.

In summary, SQL code excels at

- Data access
- Set-based processing

CLR code is typically very good at

- Complex calculation
- String manipulation
- Shredding XML
- Accessing external resources
- Iterative logic

> **An example of how powerful the CLR can be**
>
> I recently experienced a problem with some SQL code that shredded some XML, and it had become a noticeable bottleneck. Putting the required functionality into a CLR function enabled it to run around 200 times faster and consequently removed the bottleneck.

The CLR can be used to create various types of programming constructs, including functions, stored procedures, and triggers. In practice, it's used mostly to create functions that can be called from within SQL code.

7.2   *A simple CLR example*

The main aim of the CLR code example given here is to illustrate how easy it is to create functions in CLR code that can be used within SQL code. The code provides regular expression functionality, allowing complex pattern matching.

7.2.1   *Creating a simple CLR class*

Although the SQL LIKE keyword can be useful in pattern matching, it can be relatively limited when compared to regular expression functionality. The following instructions show how to create a simple CLR class that contains regular expression functions that can be used within SQL queries. Hopefully you'll find the resultant functions useful in your everyday work.

The following example explains how to create a CLR function using Visual Studio 2010 Professional Edition (a version for Visual Studio 2008 is given immediately after). To create the regular expression class, do the following:

1 From within Visual Studio 2010, choose File > New > Project > Database > SQL Server.
2 Select the Visual C# SQL CLR Database project and enter a name for the project, for example, CLRRegularExpression. Click the .NET Framework drop-down list, and select a version of the CLR that's appropriate for your version of SQL Server (for SQL Server 2005 and 2008, this means .NET Framework 2.0 to 3.5). For now, select .NET Framework 3.5, and then click OK.
3 Add a database reference. This is the database in which you want to create the CLR function. You can change this later, if necessary. Click OK.
4 You'll see a pop-up asking if you want to enable debugging on the connection; click No.
5 Choose Project > Add User-Defined Function.
6 Replace the code in the created class with the code supplied in listing 7.1.
7 Choose Build > Build (yourProjectName). This creates a DLL (called an assembly) from the CLR class.
8 Choose Build > Deploy (yourProjectName). This deploys your class and its functions to the database you specified previously.

The following example explains how to create a CLR function using Visual Studio 2008 Professional Edition. To create the regular expression class, do the following:

1 From within Visual Studio 2008, choose File > New > Project > Visual C# > Database.

2 Select the SQL Server project, and enter a name for the project, for example, CLRRegularExpression. Click OK.

3 Add a database reference. This is the database in which you want to create the CLR function. You can change this later if necessary. Click OK.

4 You'll see a pop-up asking if you want to enable debugging on the connection; click No.

5 Choose Project > Add User-Defined Function.

6 Replace the code in the created class with the code supplied in listing 7.1.

7 Choose Build > Build (yourProjectName). This creates a DLL (called an assembly) from the CLR class.

8 Choose Build > Deploy (yourProjectName). This deploys your class and its functions to the database you specified previously.

The C# code used to create regular expression functions that can be used within SQL Server is given in the following listing.

Listing 7.1   C# code to create regular expression functionality for use within SQL Server

```
using System.Data.SqlTypes;
using Microsoft.SqlServer.Server;
using System.Text.RegularExpressions;

namespace CLRRegEx
{

public partial class CLRRegEx
{

private const string sDigitsOnly = @"^\d+$";                    ❶ Constants for
private const string sEmailRegEx =                                 regular expression
                @"^\w+([-+.']\w+)*@\w+([-.]\w+)*\.\w+([-.]\w+)*$";  patterns
private const string sWebAddressRegEx =
                @"^http(s)?://([\w-*]+\.)+[\w-*]+(/[\w- ./?%&=*]*)?$";

[SqlFunction(IsDeterministic = true,                           ❷ Email pattern-
➥DataAccess = DataAccessKind.None)]                              matching function
public static SqlBoolean RegExEmailIsValid(SqlString sSource)
{
    if (sSource.IsNull)
        return SqlBoolean.Null;
    else
        return (SqlBoolean)Regex.IsMatch(sSource.Value, sEmailRegEx
                , RegexOptions.IgnoreCase);
}

[SqlFunction(IsDeterministic = true,                           ❸ Digits-only pattern-
➥DataAccess = DataAccessKind.None)]                              matching function
```

```
public static SqlBoolean RegExDigitsOnly(SqlString sSource)
{
    if (sSource.IsNull)
        return SqlBoolean.Null;
    else
        return (SqlBoolean)Regex.IsMatch(sSource.Value, sDigitsOnly
                , RegexOptions.CultureInvariant);
}

[SqlFunction(IsDeterministic = true,
➥DataAccess = DataAccessKind.None)]
public static SqlBoolean WebAddressIsValid(SqlString sSource)
{
    if (sSource.IsNull)
        return SqlBoolean.Null;
    else
        return (SqlBoolean)Regex.IsMatch(sSource.Value, sWebAddressRegEx
                , RegexOptions.IgnoreCase);
}

 [SqlFunction(IsDeterministic = true,
 ➥DataAccess = DataAccessKind.None)]
public static SqlString RegExReplace(SqlString sSource, SqlString sPattern
, SqlString sReplacement)
{
    if (sSource.IsNull || sPattern.IsNull || sReplacement.IsNull)
        return SqlString.Null;
    else
        return (SqlString)Regex.Replace(sSource.Value, sPattern.Value
                , sReplacement.Value);
}

 [SqlFunction(IsDeterministic = true,
 ➥DataAccess = DataAccessKind.None)]
public static SqlBoolean RegExMatch(SqlString sSource, SqlString sRegEx)
{
    if (sSource.IsNull || sRegEx.IsNull)
        return SqlBoolean.Null;
    else
        return (SqlBoolean)Regex.IsMatch(sSource.Value, sRegEx.Value
                , RegexOptions.CultureInvariant);
}

};
}
```

❹ Web address pattern-matching function

❺ Pattern-matching and replace function

❻ Generic regular expression function

In the listing, we first declare some constants that will be used by the regular expression patterns ❶. Each of the five functions has a similar structure. You can deduce each function's usage from the name of the function. For example, RegExEmail-IsValid ❷ accepts a passed variable (sSource in the C# code), and validates it against a known pattern for valid email addresses. Similarly, RegExDigitsOnly ❸ determines if the passed variable contains only digits, and the function WebAddressIs-Valid ❹ determines if the passed variable represents a valid email address format.

The function RegExReplace ❺ accepts a variable and a pattern to match against, and matches are replaced with the value specified in the variable sReplacement. Finally, the most generic function is RegExMatch ❻; this accepts an input variable and a pattern to match against. It returns true if a match occurs or false if there's no match. Examples of the use of each of these functions will be given shortly.

You can see the deployed assembly and its associated functions from within SSMS. Figure 7.1 shows this on my local database. Under the Programmability\Assemblies folder, you can see the assembly we created named CLRRegularExpression; under the Programmability\Functions\Scalar-valued Functions folder, you can see the five regular expression functions.

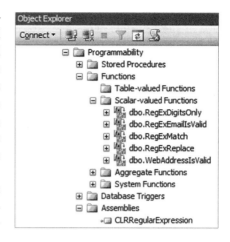

Figure 7.1 Viewing assembly and CLR functions from within SQL Server Management Studio

It's also possible to determine which functions are in a SQL CLR assembly and see their source code by using .NET reflection. The standard tool for inspecting assemblies and revealing their source code is Red Gate's Reflector tool. An add-in for Reflector permits you to view what functions exist within a SQL CLR assembly and also to view the function's source code. This can be useful when you're unsure about which CLR functions are associated with which SQL CLR assemblies. The add-in also provides a drop-down box to display the source code in various .NET languages; this might be useful as a simple language-conversion utility or if you're more familiar with Visual Basic than C#. An example of the output from this add-in is shown in figure 7.2.

You can also view details of the assembly and functions just created from within SSMS by querying the sys.assemblies and sys.assembly_files tables. The former gives details of the assembly name, its permission set, and creation/modified dates. The latter contains details of the actual assembly code in hexadecimal format. Some additional files (including the associated debug and information files) are also included. Figure 7.3 shows these details.

Now that we've created our regular expression assembly and its associated functions, you'll see how to use them in your SQL queries.

7.2.2 *Using the SQL CLR regular expression functions*

With the regular expression assembly and its five functions under our belts, I now want to show how they're used from within SSMS. But before I can do this, you need to enable CLR integration within SQL Server. You can do this with the commands given in the following listing.

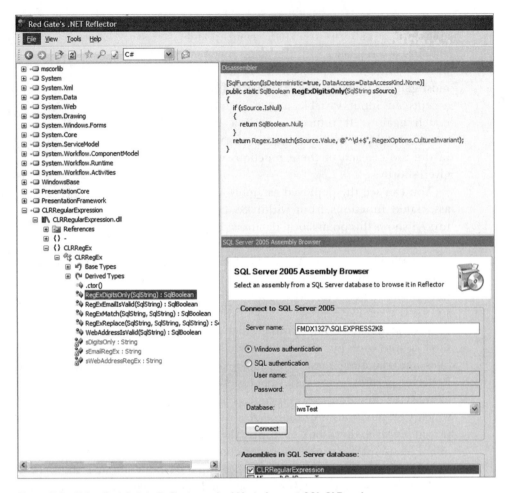

Figure 7.2   Using Red Gate's Reflector and add-in to inspect SQL CLR code

Figure 7.3   Viewing details of the created assembly in the system tables

Listing 7.2 Enabling CLR integration within SQL Server

```
EXEC sp_configure 'show advanced options', 1

RECONFIGURE

EXEC sp_configure 'clr_enabled', 1

RECONFIGURE
```

Now that CLR integration is enabled, you can run various SQL queries from within SSMS to test each of the CLR regular expression functions. The script given in the following listing contains examples of such tests, together with notes of their expected outcome.

Listing 7.3 Using the CLR regular expression functionality

```
SELECT dbo.RegExDigitsOnly('123456');                      ⟵ Pass      ❶
SELECT dbo.RegExDigitsOnly('123456789abc');                ⟵ Fail

SELECT dbo.RegExEmailIsValid('ian_stirk@yahoo.com');       ⟵ Pass      ❷
SELECT dbo.RegExEmailIsValid('ian_stirk@yahoo');           ⟵ Fail

SELECT dbo.WebAddressIsValid
➦ ('http://www.manning.com/stirk');         | Pass          ❸
SELECT dbo.WebAddressIsValid
➦ ('http://wwwmanningcom');                  | Fail

SELECT dbo.RegExReplace('Q123AS456WE789', '[^0-9]', 'a');  ⟵❹

SELECT dbo.RegExMatch('123456789', '^[0-9]+$');            ⟵ Pass      ❺
SELECT dbo.RegExMatch('12345678abc9', '^[0-9]+$');         ⟵ Fail
```

The script shows how the SQL CLR regular expression functions can be used from within SQL Server. Most examples show data that will pass and also data that would fail the regular expression check. The first example relates to checking to see if the data contains only digits ❶; this is followed by a check for a valid email address ❷ and then a check for a valid web address ❸. We then present an example of how data can be replaced; specifically this example replaces any nondigits with the character 'a' ❹. Finally, we use the generic regular expression function ❺.

Now that we've created, built, deployed, and tested the CLR functions, I'll briefly highlight some areas of .NET CLR programming that may be a cause of concern in relation to CLR performance.

7.3 *.NET Framework performance concerns*

The .NET Framework is Microsoft's preferred development platform. Regarding .NET code performance, table 7.1 lists some areas of concern relating to performance and some possible solutions. Developers who already have experience with .NET development can use this table as a reminder, and as such, it's not meant to be extensive or detailed. Yet it should highlight typical areas of concern for .NET performance.

For most applications, the performance bottleneck is typically the database. We're very lucky in that we specialize in an area where performance can be improved. In addition, most of the scripts given in this book are aimed at improving database performance. The areas given in table 7.1 relate to nondatabase .NET performance tips.

Table 7.1 .NET application performance tips

Area	Problem/solution
Loops	Loops are a typical area of concern; if a problem exists within a loop, it can be repeated many times. Where possible ensure that any values that can be cached are done outside the loop.
Data types	Each variable has an explicit or implied data type (the latter occurring increasingly with the recent var data type). Ensure that the correct data type is used, or else unnecessary time will be spent converting between types.
Reference/value types	This is similar to the data type problem, but objects reside on the heap and value types reside on the stack. Converting between reference and value types (and vice versa) results in extra code being written for boxing and unboxing, degrading performance.
IDispose	.NET takes care of memory resources when code exits. For other resources you should implement the IDispose pattern to ensure that nonmemory resources are disposed of adequately.
using	Because it can be troublesome to remember to implement IDispose and any associated error handling (try/catch), the using keyword is used to combine this functionality.
Correct data structures	You should use the correct data structure for the correct processing. The dictionary should be used for key/value data, and a list should be used for holding sequential data.
StringBuilder	Strings can't change their values. When they appear to do so, a new string is being created behind the scene, leaving the original string occupying memory until it's cleaned up by the garbage collector. To get around this problem, you can use the StringBuilder, which is built for changing data.
Generics	Generics allow you to create a structure that can be implemented in specific data types. Not only does this provide type safety (for example, you can't add a string to a structure that implements integers), but generics are also faster than their object counterparts.
Make chunky calls	Typically, the number of calls made is more important for performance than the amount of data passed for the same overall data volumes. Aim to retrieve more data with fewer calls.

Table 7.1   .NET application performance tips *(continued)*

Area	Problem/solution
Return multiple resultsets	In some ways this is the next level of making chunky calls. Where possible, have a stored procedure return multiple result-sets that can be looped around and processed on the client.
Cache data when possible	A lot of data doesn't change often; where possible this data should be cached. A callback mechanism can be implemented to update the cache when the underlying data changes.
Error handling	Don't use error handling to control the normal flow of logic. Exceptions should be exceptional.
Connection pooling	Where possible, ensure that the database connection string is the same between users of an application, because this facilitates connection reuse.
Reflection	Although reflection is very flexible, it's relatively slow and bulky compared with native code, and you should avoid using it if possible.

We've looked at some of the more prominent areas of concern relating to .NET programming and performance. Now let's examine how SQL Server reports this CLR code in terms of long-running queries.

7.4   *Time-consuming CLR queries*

Although the underlying DMVs identified in this section relate to query execution, and should perhaps therefore reside in the chapter on execution-related DMVs, it seems more appropriate to include them in this CLR chapter because they relate to code that executes within the CLR.

All code statements, even those running within the CLR, can have performance problems. If you can identify which statements spend the most time in the CLR, you can target these for performance improvement. The next example script identifies those queries.

The DMV sys.dm_exec_query_stats records various metrics about the performance of SQL queries, including the ones that use the CLR. The column total_clr_time records the total time a given query spends in the CLR.

7.4.1   *Finding the queries that spend the most time in the CLR*

Identifying which queries spend most of their time in the CLR can be useful because it typically identifies those queries that are CPU intensive and provides another avenue of performance improvement via the .NET environment. Running the SQL script given in the following listing will identify the top 20 queries that spend most of their time within the CLR, ordered by total_clr_time.

Listing 7.4   The queries that spend the most time in the CLR

```
SET TRANSACTION ISOLATION LEVEL READ UNCOMMITTED

SELECT TOP 20
  qs.total_clr_time
  , qs.total_elapsed_time AS [Duration]
  , qs.total_worker_time AS [Time on CPU]
  , qs.total_elapsed_time - qs.total_worker_time  AS [Time waiting]
  , qs.total_logical_reads
  , qs.total_logical_writes
  , qs.execution_count
  , SUBSTRING (qt.text,qs.statement_start_offset/2 + 1,
    ((CASE WHEN qs.statement_end_offset = -1
      THEN LEN(CONVERT(NVARCHAR(MAX), qt.text)) * 2
      ELSE qs.statement_end_offset
      END - qs.statement_start_offset)/2) + 1) AS [Individual Query]
  , qt.text AS [Parent Query]
  , DB_NAME(qt.dbid) AS DatabaseName
FROM sys.dm_exec_query_stats qs
CROSS APPLY sys.dm_exec_sql_text(sql_handle) as qt
WHERE qs.total_clr_time > 0
ORDER BY qs.total_clr_time DESC
```

① Get CLR duration

② Extract SQL statement

③ Sort by time in the CLR

The listing shows how to extract the time spent in the CLR **①** and also shows the individual SQL query that contains the SQL CLR function name **②**. The results are sorted by the total_clr_time **③** because we're interested in the queries that spend the most time in the CLR.

The listing uses one DMV and one DMF to identify the queries that spend the most time in the CLR. Table 7.2 provides a brief description of each.

Table 7.2   DMV/DMF to identify the queries that spend the most time in the CLR

DMV/DMF	Description
sys.dm_exec_query_stats	Contains aggregated performance statistics for cached query plans
sys.dm_exec_sql_text	DMF that returns the SQL text identified by a given sql_handle

By joining the DMV and DMF, we have enough information to identify the queries that spend the most time in the CLR, across all the databases on the server. The query's sql_handle is passed to the DMF sys.dm_exec_sql_text to retrieve the text of the SQL query. Note that unlike other similar queries, here we don't obtain the cached plan, because this query spends its time in the CLR. We use a common pattern, as discussed in chapter 2, to extract the Individual Query, which the timings relate to, from the Parent Query. An example of the type of output for this query is shown in figure 7.4.

The query we execute selects the top 20 queries that spend the most time in the CLR, across all databases on the server. The total duration, time on the CPU, time

	total_clr_time	Duration	Time on CPU	Time waiting	total_logical_reads	total_logical_writes	execution_count	Individual Query	Parent Query	Database Name
1	154719684	2285807010	872986394	1412820616	36838406	791278	6972	INSERT INTO #RiskPr...	-- use of alter going forw...	Paris
2	57411655	904017382	562435876	562435876	13211973	278525	4649	INSERT INTO #RiskPr...	-- use of alter going forw...	Paris_COB
3	12528419	268654321	96280139	172374182	1200947	376	17212	insert into #DealPrep	-- use of alter going forwar...	Paris
4	4685075	222459213	82618595	139840618	1193272	200	17212	insert into #Component...	-- use of alter going forwar...	Paris
5	3169973	77209216	26234119	50975097	329404	196	5005	insert into #DealPrep	-- use of alter going forwar...	Paris_COB
6	3032049	96458705	33798994	62659711	528749	135	10240	INSERT INTO #PNLPr...	-- use of alter going forwar...	Paris
7	1133204	62209108	21965285	40243823	327693	125	5005	insert into #Component...	-- use of alter going forwar...	Paris_COB
8	123412	5155541	1455063	3700478	23375	6	356	INSERT INTO #PNLPr...	-- use of alter going forwar...	Paris_COB

Figure 7.4   Output showing the queries that spend the most time in the CLR

waiting, number of reads, number of writes, name of the database, the Individual Query, and the Parent Query are also output. The output is sorted by total_clr_time in descending order. Note that the Individual Query given in the output contains the CLR code, which is typically hosted in a SQL query statement.

7.4.2   Impact of time-consuming CLR queries

Typically, the column in the output named Individual Query will contain the name of a CLR function. You'll notice other columns in the output, including Time on CPU, Time waiting, total_logical_reads, total_logical_writes, execution_count, and Database-Name. The script provided could be amended to obtain other interesting information, including the most-executed CLR queries, CLR queries with the most I/O, and CLR queries with the most waiting. The script could also be filtered on a given database name.

Often when you run code, you have an idea of where the performance bottleneck is. Although experience is often valuable, there's no substitute for profiling your code to determine exactly where the real bottleneck is. I'm sure there will be times when the bottleneck is in some unexpected area.

Having identified the queries that spend the most time in the CLR, the next step would be to identify the individual lines of code within the CLR function that take the most time or could be a bottleneck.

Unfortunately, SQL Server doesn't provide a method of determining duration of the individual lines of SQL CLR code. One reason for this is security. The way to get around this limitation is to copy the CLR code into another Visual Studio project and then insert debug timing-related code between the various lines of code (this is called instrumentation). Running the code from a test client will output the timings between the lines of code, enabling you to determine which lines of code are taking the longest to run.

Alternately, there are high-end versions of Visual Studio that come with profiling tools, for example, Visual Studio 2008 Developer Edition or Visual Studio 2010 Premium Edition. These editions contain tools for profiling your .NET code, enabling you to easily determine the slowest parts of your code.

Several third-party tools also provide performance metrics for your .NET code. A well-known tool is supplied by Red Gate Software, called ANTS Performance Profiler. Details about this tool, together with a 14-day free trial copy of the software, are available from Red Gate's website.

Typically, your CLR code will make minimum use of database access and database manipulation, because this is what T-SQL excels at. But there are times when the CLR code will need to perform data access operations; these will result in a corresponding increase in the number of reads and writes associated with the query. Similarly, there will be times when the query will have to wait on another resource, and this will be recorded in the Time waiting column in the output. Examining any index's usage may provide opportunities for improving performance by ensuring the following:

- Index statistics are up to date.
- Indexes are not fragmented.
- There are no missing indexes.
- There are minimum indexes if an update is performed.

You've seen how to identify the queries that spend most of their time inside the CLR. Although this is fine for getting an overall view, it can be useful to determine the CLR usage during a given time interval or when a given query is run. This could provide targeted tuning information for that specific time or query. I'll show how this is done next.

7.5   Queries spending the most time in the CLR (snapshot version)

In addition to determining which queries spend the most time in the CLR, there may be certain time periods when it's critical to determine what processing is occurring within the CLR with a view to optimizing it. Similarly, there may be occasions when you need to know what CLR functionality is used when a given SQL query or batch of SQL statements is run.

There is a caveat with this approach (and some proposed solutions too). The DMV sys.dm_exec_query_stats records information at the database level and thus will record all other activity on the database. It's possible to reduce the effect of external influences by running your queries on a standalone database or at a time when you know other queries won't be running.

7.5.1   Finding queries that spend the most time in the CLR (snapshot version)

Because the DMVs are accumulative, if you want to determine which queries spend the most time within the CLR over a given time period, it makes sense to calculate the difference between two DMV snapshots. The snapshots are taken at the start and end of the time interval. Running the SQL script given in the next listing will identify the queries that use the CLR the most over a given 10-minute period, ordered by CLR time.

> **Listing 7.5   The queries that spend the most time in the CLR (snapshot version)**

```
SET TRANSACTION ISOLATION LEVEL READ UNCOMMITTED                  ❶ Get pre-query
                                                                     DMV counters
SELECT
  sql_handle, plan_handle, total_elapsed_time, total_worker_time
  , total_logical_reads, total_logical_writes, total_clr_time
  , execution_count, statement_start_offset, statement_end_offset
INTO #PreWorkQuerySnapShot
FROM sys.dm_exec_query_stats
                                    ❷ Do something here
WAITFOR DELAY '00:10:00'              (query/time interval)
                                                   ❸ Get post-query
SELECT                                               DMV counters
  sql_handle, plan_handle, total_elapsed_time, total_worker_time
  , total_logical_reads, total_logical_writes, total_clr_time
  , execution_count, statement_start_offset, statement_end_offset
INTO #PostWorkQuerySnapShot
FROM sys.dm_exec_query_stats
                                              ❹ Calculate changes
SELECT                                           in CLR counters
  p2.total_elapsed_time - ISNULL(p1.total_elapsed_time, 0) AS [Duration]
  , p2.total_worker_time - ISNULL(p1.total_worker_time, 0) AS [Time on CPU]
  , (p2.total_elapsed_time - ISNULL(p1.total_elapsed_time, 0)) -
          (p2.total_worker_time - ISNULL(p1.total_worker_time, 0))
                                                    AS [Time blocked]
  , p2.total_logical_reads - ISNULL(p1.total_logical_reads, 0) AS [Reads]
  , p2.total_logical_writes - ISNULL(p1.total_logical_writes, 0)
                                                    AS [Writes]
  , p2.total_clr_time - ISNULL(p1.total_clr_time, 0) AS [CLR time]
  , p2.execution_count - ISNULL(p1.execution_count, 0) AS [Executions]
  , SUBSTRING (qt.text,p2.statement_start_offset/2 + 1,
    ((CASE WHEN p2.statement_end_offset = -1
      THEN LEN(CONVERT(NVARCHAR(MAX), qt.text)) * 2
      ELSE p2.statement_end_offset
      END - p2.statement_start_offset)/2) + 1) AS [Individual Query]
  , qt.text AS [Parent Query]
  , DB_NAME(qt.dbid) AS DatabaseName
FROM #PreWorkQuerySnapShot p1
RIGHT OUTER JOIN
#PostWorkQuerySnapShot p2 ON p2.sql_handle =
        ISNULL(p1.sql_handle, p2.sql_handle)
  AND p2.plan_handle = ISNULL(p1.plan_handle, p2.plan_handle)
  AND p2.statement_start_offset =
        ISNULL(p1.statement_start_offset, p2.statement_start_offset)
  AND p2.statement_end_offset =
        ISNULL(p1.statement_end_offset, p2.statement_end_offset)
CROSS APPLY sys.dm_exec_sql_text(p2.sql_handle) as qt
WHERE p2.execution_count != ISNULL(p1.execution_count, 0)
  AND p2.total_clr_time - ISNULL(p1.total_clr_time, 0) <>0
ORDER BY [CLR time] DESC                              ⟵
                                                      Sort by time
DROP TABLE #PreWorkQuerySnapShot                    ❺ spent in CLR
DROP TABLE #PostWorkQuerySnapShot
```

The DMV snapshot approach given in this example is based on the DMV snapshot pattern explained more fully in chapter 2. The DMV and columns used are the same

	Duration	Time on CPU	Time blocked	Reads	Writes	CLR time	Executions	Individual Query	Parent Query	Database Name
1	59876909	33515984	26360925	966350	14903	5725550	502	INSERT INTO #RiskPrep (Req...	– use of alter goi...	Paris
2	4734955	3904972	829983	50228	5	530331	501	insert into #DealPrep (RequestI...	– use of alter going...	Paris
3	6878925	3485823	3393102	48327	1	197987	501	insert into #ComponentPrep (Re...	– use of alter going...	Paris

Figure 7.5   Output showing the queries that spend most of the time in the CLR (snapshot version)

as described in the previous script example. In this example, we take a pre-work snapshot of the DMV query counters ❶, wait a given amount of time (10 minutes in this example) ❷, and then take another snapshot of the DMV query counters ❸. Finally we determine which CLR queries have run ❹, sorted by the CLR time ❺. If you want to examine the CLR functions associated with a given SQL statement or batch of SQL, you can replace the WAITFOR command given in the script with relevant SQL statements.

Sample output for this query is shown in figure 7.5.

The output in figure 7.5 shows the queries that spend most of their time in the CLR during a given time interval. We record information about the number of reads, number of writes, time on CPU, time waiting, and database name.

If you know that these queries are run at critical times, you can try to optimize them by using the output columns to provide clues as to where to optimize. For example, if a large number of reads are occurring, you'd want to ensure that the table's indexes are optimal (by checking for any missing indexes, that statistics are up to date, and index fragmentation is low). Similarly, examining the wait states DMV might lead you to discover why the queries are waiting (recorded in the Time blocked column). This interplay between the different DMVs is discussed next.

7.6   *Relationships between CLR DMVs and other DMVs*

Up to now we've tended to look at CLR metrics in isolation. Although this is fine while you gain an understanding of specific areas, you can get a better appreciation of the impact of queries if you examine the effect of your queries on several DMVs at the same time.

In this section, we report on several DMV snapshots that illustrate the combined effect of our CLR-based queries. This can be a useful starting point in correlating the changes in the different DMVs and highlighting areas of concern and subsequent optimization.

In common with previous scripts, here we'll examine how the CLR queries interact with other DMVs. Specifically we'll look at how they interact with missing indexes, performance counters, and wait states. Running the SQL script given in the following listing will identify the relationship between the queries that use the CLR and the other DMVs, over a given time interval. In this example, the time period is 10 minutes, but you may want to alter this time interval to suit your needs.

Listing 7.6   Relationships between DMVs and CLR queries

```
SET TRANSACTION ISOLATION LEVEL READ UNCOMMITTED
SELECT
  g.index_group_handle, g.index_handle
  , s.avg_total_user_cost
  , s.avg_user_impact, s.user_seeks, s.user_scans
INTO #PreWorkMissingIndexes
FROM sys.dm_db_missing_index_groups g
INNER JOIN   sys.dm_db_missing_index_group_stats s
    ON s.group_handle = g.index_group_handle

SELECT
  sql_handle, plan_handle, total_elapsed_time, total_worker_time
  , total_logical_reads, total_logical_writes, total_clr_time
  , execution_count, statement_start_offset, statement_end_offset
INTO #PreWorkQuerySnapShot
FROM sys.dm_exec_query_stats

SELECT
  [object_name], [counter_name], [instance_name]
  , [cntr_value], [cntr_type]
INTO #PreWorkOSSnapShot
FROM sys.dm_os_performance_counters

SELECT
  wait_type, waiting_tasks_count
  , wait_time_ms, max_wait_time_ms, signal_wait_time_ms
INTO #PreWorkWaitStats
FROM sys.dm_os_wait_stats

WAITFOR DELAY '00:10:00'

SELECT wait_type, waiting_tasks_count, wait_time_ms
  , max_wait_time_ms, signal_wait_time_ms
INTO #PostWorkWaitStats
FROM sys.dm_os_wait_stats

SELECT [object_name], [counter_name], [instance_name]
      , [cntr_value], [cntr_type]
INTO #PostWorkOSSnapShot
FROM sys.dm_os_performance_counters

SELECT sql_handle, plan_handle, total_elapsed_time, total_worker_time
  , total_logical_reads, total_logical_writes, total_clr_time
  , execution_count, statement_start_offset, statement_end_offset
INTO #PostWorkQuerySnapShot
FROM sys.dm_exec_query_stats

SELECT g.index_group_handle, g.index_handle, s.avg_total_user_cost
  , s.avg_user_impact, s.user_seeks, s.user_scans
INTO #PostWorkMissingIndexes
FROM        sys.dm_db_missing_index_groups g
INNER JOIN  sys.dm_db_missing_index_group_stats s
    ON s.group_handle = g.index_group_handle

SELECT
  p2.total_elapsed_time - ISNULL(p1.total_elapsed_time, 0) AS [Duration]
```

① Pre-work missing indexes counters

② Pre-work query stats counters

③ Pre-work OS counters

④ Pre-work wait states counters

⑤ Do something here (query/time interval)

⑥ Post-work snapshots

⑦ Calculate snapshot deltas

```
        , p2.total_worker_time - ISNULL(p1.total_worker_time, 0) AS [Time on CPU]
        , (p2.total_elapsed_time - ISNULL(p1.total_elapsed_time, 0)) -
                (p2.total_worker_time - ISNULL(p1.total_worker_time, 0))
                                                        AS [Time blocked]
        , p2.total_logical_reads - ISNULL(p1.total_logical_reads, 0) AS [Reads]
        , p2.total_logical_writes - ISNULL(p1.total_logical_writes, 0)
                                                            AS [Writes]
        , p2.total_clr_time - ISNULL(p1.total_clr_time, 0) AS [CLR time]
        , p2.execution_count - ISNULL(p1.execution_count, 0) AS [Executions]
        , SUBSTRING (qt.text,p2.statement_start_offset/2 + 1,
          ((CASE WHEN p2.statement_end_offset = -1
            THEN LEN(CONVERT(NVARCHAR(MAX), qt.text)) * 2
            ELSE p2.statement_end_offset
            END - p2.statement_start_offset)/2) + 1) AS [Individual Query]
        , qt.text AS [Parent Query]
        , DB_NAME(qt.dbid) AS DatabaseName
FROM #PreWorkQuerySnapShot p1
RIGHT OUTER JOIN
#PostWorkQuerySnapShot p2 ON p2.sql_handle =
        ISNULL(p1.sql_handle, p2.sql_handle)
  AND p2.plan_handle = ISNULL(p1.plan_handle, p2.plan_handle)
  AND p2.statement_start_offset =
        ISNULL(p1.statement_start_offset, p2.statement_start_offset)
  AND p2.statement_end_offset =
        ISNULL(p1.statement_end_offset, p2.statement_end_offset)
CROSS APPLY sys.dm_exec_sql_text(p2.sql_handle) as qt
WHERE p2.execution_count != ISNULL(p1.execution_count, 0)
  AND p2.total_clr_time - ISNULL(p1.total_clr_time, 0) <>0
ORDER BY [CLR time] DESC

SELECT
    p2.wait_time_ms - ISNULL(p1.wait_time_ms, 0) AS wait_time_ms
    , p2.signal_wait_time_ms - ISNULL(p1.signal_wait_time_ms, 0)
                                        AS signal_wait_time_ms
    , ((p2.wait_time_ms - ISNULL(p1.wait_time_ms, 0)) -
            (p2.signal_wait_time_ms
                - ISNULL(p1.signal_wait_time_ms, 0))) AS RealWait
    , p2.wait_type
FROM #PreWorkWaitStats p1
RIGHT OUTER JOIN
#PostWorkWaitStats p2 ON p2.wait_type = ISNULL(p1.wait_type, p2.wait_type)
WHERE p2.wait_time_ms - ISNULL(p1.wait_time_ms, 0) > 0
  AND p2.wait_type NOT LIKE '%SLEEP%'
  AND p2.wait_type != 'WAITFOR'
ORDER BY RealWait DESC

SELECT
    ROUND((p2.avg_total_user_cost - ISNULL(p1.avg_total_user_cost, 0))
        * (p2.avg_user_impact - ISNULL(p1.avg_user_impact, 0)) *
            ((p2.user_seeks - ISNULL(p1.user_seeks, 0)) + (p2.user_scans -
                ISNULL(p1.user_scans, 0))),0) AS [Total Cost]
    , p2.avg_total_user_cost - ISNULL(p1.avg_total_user_cost, 0)
                                            AS avg_total_user_cost
    , p2.avg_user_impact - ISNULL(p1.avg_user_impact, 0) AS avg_user_impact
    , p2.user_seeks - ISNULL(p1.user_seeks, 0) AS user_seeks
    , p2.user_scans - ISNULL(p1.user_scans, 0) AS user_scans
```

```
    , d.statement AS TableName
    , d.equality_columns
    , d.inequality_columns
    , d.included_columns
FROM #PreWorkMissingIndexes p1
RIGHT OUTER JOIN
#PostWorkMissingIndexes p2 ON p2.index_group_handle =
      ISNULL(p1.index_group_handle, p2.index_group_handle)
      AND p2.index_handle = ISNULL(p1.index_handle, p2.index_handle)
INNER JOIN sys.dm_db_missing_index_details d
    ON p2.index_handle = d.index_handle
WHERE p2.avg_total_user_cost - ISNULL(p1.avg_total_user_cost, 0) > 0
  OR p2.avg_user_impact - ISNULL(p1.avg_user_impact, 0) > 0
  OR p2.user_seeks - ISNULL(p1.user_seeks, 0) > 0
  OR p2.user_scans - ISNULL(p1.user_scans, 0) > 0
ORDER BY [Total Cost] DESC

SELECT
  p2.object_name, p2.counter_name, p2.instance_name
  , ISNULL(p1.cntr_value, 0) AS InitialValue
  , p2.cntr_value AS FinalValue
  , p2.cntr_value - ISNULL(p1.cntr_value, 0) AS Change
  , (p2.cntr_value - ISNULL(p1.cntr_value, 0)) * 100 / p1.cntr_value
                                  AS [% Change]
FROM #PreWorkOSSnapShot p1
RIGHT OUTER JOIN
#PostWorkOSSnapShot p2 ON p2.object_name =
        ISNULL(p1.object_name, p2.object_name)
    AND p2.counter_name = ISNULL(p1.counter_name, p2.counter_name)
    AND p2.instance_name = ISNULL(p1.instance_name, p2.instance_name)
WHERE p2.cntr_value - ISNULL(p1.cntr_value, 0) > 0
  AND ISNULL(p1.cntr_value, 0) != 0
ORDER BY [% Change] DESC, Change DESC

DROP TABLE #PreWorkQuerySnapShot
DROP TABLE #PostWorkQuerySnapShot
DROP TABLE #PostWorkWaitStats
DROP TABLE #PreWorkWaitStats
DROP TABLE #PreWorkOSSnapShot
DROP TABLE #PostWorkOSSnapShot
DROP TABLE #PreWorkMissingIndexes
DROP TABLE #PostWorkMissingIndexes
```

In this script we create DMV snapshots for missing indexes ❶, CLR queries ❷, performance counters ❸, and wait states ❹. We then wait for a given time period to pass ❺. The corresponding post-work DMV snapshots are then taken ❻. We follow this by calculating and showing the changes in the DMVs' counter values ❼.

Inspecting the output of this script will enable you to discern if there's any relationship between the DMV snapshots. As always, note that the DMVs typically record server-wide information. This must be taken into account, reduced, or eliminated when interpreting the results. It may be advisable to also include a DMV snapshot of all queries that are running in the given time interval in order to eliminate or estimate their influence.

Results | Messages

	Duration	Time on CPU	Time blocked	Reads	Writes	CLR time	Executions	Individual Query	Parent Query	DatabaseName
1	991184350	447342636	543841714	17270983	367095	77085219	8640	INSERT INTO #RiskPrep (...	-- use of alter going for...	Paris
2	105355386	38443954	66911432	459461	27	4849125	10759	insert into #DealPrep (Requ...	-- use of alter going forwa...	Paris
3	79542656	30644695	48897961	433006	37	1777031	10759	insert into #ComponentPrep (...	-- use of alter going forwa...	Paris
4	30131763	8894258	21237505	188184	192	1079245	2112	INSERT INTO #PNLPrep (...	-- use of alter going forwa...	Paris

	wait_time_ms	signal_wait_time_ms	RealWait	wait_type
1	57232031	1193187	56038844	CXPACKET
2	29064422	703609	28360813	BACKUPIO
3	14145015	205969	13939046	BROKER_TASK_STOP
4	12992141	0	12992141	MSQL_XP

	Total Cost	avg_total_user_cost	avg_user_impact	user_seeks	user_scans	TableName	equality_columns	inequality_columns	included_columns
1	17337	26.1902256144923	19.47	34	0	[Paris].[Load].[Staging...	[RequestId]	NULL	[StagingID], [UnderlyingId], ...
2	7581	20.352941263582	11.64	32	0	[Paris].[dbo].[RequestR...	[RequestRiskAu...	NULL	[AddedToQueue], [StartTim...
3	223	0.3830803011032...	64.75	9	0	[Paris].[Legacy].[Stagin...	[request_id]	NULL	[cob], [factor_id], [underlyin...
4	39	1.29476668563289	0.3900000000...	77	0	[Paris].[dbo].[RequestR...	[RequestRiskAu...	[StatusCode]	NULL

	object_name	counter_name	instance_name	InitialValue	FinalValue	Change	% Change
1	SQLServer:Buffer Manager	Reserved pages		178	34216	34038	19122
2	SQLServer:Transactions	Transactions		40	958	918	2295
3	SQLServer:Buffer Partition	Free pages	006	8	99	91	1137
4	SQLServer:Wait Statistics	Thread-safe m...	Waits started...	36	368	332	922

Figure 7.6 Output showing the impact of CLR functions on DMV snapshots

Figure 7.6 shows an example of the type of output for this query.

The output in figure 7.6 shows four grids, each representing a DMV snapshot over the given time interval. The first shows the queries that spend the most time in the CLR. The second grid shows the wait states changes, the third shows any missing indexes, and the fourth shows the SQL Server performance counters. To get detailed information about any of the specific DMV snapshots shown, see the relevant section of this book for that DMV snapshot.

Here we're interested in any relationships between the DMV snapshots rather than the individual DMV snapshots themselves. For example, a high Time blocked column value in the first grid (CLR queries) might relate to the high value of the BACKUPIO wait type in the second grid (wait_type). Similarly, if the queries access the database, the queries may be in need of indexes, which are identified in the second grid (missing indexes). Many other potential relationships may exist and warrant further investigation. Next, we'll look at how to obtain information about the CLR running on your SQL Server.

7.7 Getting information about SQL Server CLR integration

The DMV sys.dm_clr_properties is a name/value pair container that has a row for each property related to the SQL Server CLR integration. Issuing a simple SELECT statement against the DMV on my local SQL Server gives the results shown in figure 7.7.

Results | Messages

	name	value
1	directory	C:\WINDOWS\Microsoft.NET\Framework64\v2.0.50727\
2	version	v2.0.50727
3	state	CLR is initialized

Figure 7.7 Output showing SQL Server CLR integration details

The output shows the directory where the CLR is installed, its version, and its current state. The state row is useful for determining the cause of any errors when CLR integration on the server isn't working or is in a state of transition. The values of the state row include the following:

- Mscoree is not loaded (temporary state, when the server starts). Mscoree is a DLL containing core .NET Framework functions.
- Mscoree is loaded (temporary state, when the server starts).
- Locked CLR version with mscoree (occurs when the hosted CLR isn't being used and thus hasn't been initialized).
- CLR is initialized. (This is the desired state. Note that you still might need to enable CLR integration; for information on how to do this, see listing 7.2 in the section "Using the SQL CLR regular expression functions.")
- CLR initialization permanently failed. (Memory pressure is the most typical cause, followed by communication failure between SQL Server and the CLR.)
- CLR is stopped (occurs when SQL Server is shutting down).

Prior to version 4 of the CLR, various versions of the .NET Framework were released, but starting with version 2, most provided additional libraries to extend the .NET Framework rather than the underlying core CLR DLL, which remained at version 2. Presumably, as later versions of the CLR are released, this DMV will contain version-specific details.

Let's now look at how you can obtain specific information about the SQL CLR assemblies you've deployed.

7.8   Getting information about your SQL CLR assemblies

You can discover some useful information about the installed SQL CLR assemblies by combining the CLR-based DMVs with the assembly system tables. The script you use to obtain information about SQL CLR assemblies follows.

Listing 7.7   Obtaining information about SQL CLR assemblies

```
SET TRANSACTION ISOLATION LEVEL READ UNCOMMITTED
SELECT
  DB_NAME(d.db_id) AS DatabaseName
  , USER_NAME(d.user_id) UserName
  , a.name AS AssemblyName
  , f.name AS AssemblyFileName
  , a.create_date AS AssemblyCreateDate
  , l.load_time  AS AssemblyLoadDate
  , d.appdomain_name
  , d.creation_time AS AppDomainCreateTime
  , a.permission_set_desc
  , d.state
  , a.clr_name
  , a.is_visible
```

```
FROM sys.dm_clr_loaded_assemblies AS l
INNER JOIN sys.dm_clr_appdomains d
         ON l.appdomain_address = d.appdomain_address
INNER JOIN sys.assemblies AS a
         ON l.assembly_id = a.assembly_id
INNER JOIN sys.assembly_files AS f
         ON a.assembly_id = f.assembly_id
ORDER BY DatabaseName, UserName, AssemblyName
```

Here you can see that two DMVs and two system tables are involved in obtaining SQL CLR assembly information. A brief description of each is given in table 7.3.

Table 7.3   DMVs/system tables for getting SQL CLR information

DMV/table	Description
sys.dm_clr_loaded_assemblies	Shows which managed user assemblies have been loaded
sys.dm_clr_appdomains	Shows details of loaded application domains, including their state, creation date, name, and the database they reside in
sys.assemblies	Contains details of the assembly's name, its unique CLR name, its creation date, and the permissions set for the assembly
sys.assembly_files	Shows details of where the assembly is installed, together with the contents of the assembly

The joining of the DMVs and system tables provides you with enough data to obtain information about SQL CLR assemblies, across all databases on the server. The DMVs sys.dm_clr_loaded_assemblies and sys.dm_clr_appdomains are joined on their common key column appdomain_address. The system table sys.assemblies is joined to the sys.dm_clr_loaded_assemblies DMV on their common key assembly_id. Finally, the system table sys.assembly_files is joined to the system table sys.assemblies on their common key assembly_id.

Sample output for this query is shown in figure 7.8.

The output can be useful in determining which assemblies are loaded on which databases, where they're physically located, what version of the assembly is present, and the permissions set required by the assemblies.

Figure 7.8   Output showing detailed SQL CLR assembly information

7.9 *Summary*

In this chapter we discussed how SQL functionality has been extended by integrating CLR functionality into SQL Server. I created a simple CLR class with regular expression functionality, which illustrated how this extra functionality can be provided relatively easily. We created, built, deployed, and tested the CLR class. I showed how various aspects of the class could be discerned via SSMS or third-party tools, including the Reflector tool.

One of the prime aims of this book is to look at SQL performance from a different angle, namely, via DMVs. In discussing CLR SQL functions, it makes sense to look at aspects of CLR performance that are known to cause problems, allowing you to produce better CLR code.

As with other SQL queries discussed in other chapters, this chapter allowed you to discover which queries spend most of the time in the CLR. I also provided a DMV snapshot version of this script and subsequently extended it to examine the relationships between other related DMVs. Finally, we looked at how to obtain SQL CLR integration information and details of the various assemblies running in SQL Server.

Blocking is an important consideration in examining performance problems, especially within the context of transactions. We'll look at this next.

Resolving transaction issues

This chapter covers

- Transactions, locks, blocks, and deadlocks
- Sessions, connections, and requests
- Methods to minimize contention and improve concurrency and performance

A query may run fast when it runs alone, taking advantage of all available resources without the impact of other running queries. But in the real world it needs to interact with other running queries, each requiring resources and coordination to reduce contention.

To enable queries to run concurrently, resources need to be shared, and data needs to be protected so it's able to give consistent and correct values. Therefore, there's often a trade-off between data consistency and concurrency. Many factors can affect both consistency and concurrency, and we'll discuss these throughout this chapter.

To protect the consistency of data, SQL Server issues locks against resources such as a row or page of data within a database table. These locks can lead to blocking, resulting in reduced performance, concurrency, and scalability. Circular blocking between queries can lead to a deadlock, which results in SQL Server terminating one of the queries and rolling back its changes.

A transaction is a unit of work. A unit of work is a set of SQL queries that are treated as a unit; for example, either they all commit or none of them commit their changes to the database. You can consider the movement of money from one bank account to another as two pieces of work, but to ensure consistency, they're treated as a single unit of work, or one transaction.

Transactions affect how units of work are carried out; this influences the locking strategy and subsequent blocking. Locks are held by transactions. To ensure that the data used or modified by two or more queries is consistent, locks are taken out on the underlying data.

Before we can get into some interesting and useful scripts, it makes sense to examine the features that will allow you to understand more fully the output from the scripts. We'll do this in the following sections, starting with an overview of transactions.

8.1 Transaction overview

A database transaction is a group of SQL queries that are treated as a single unit of work. If any one of the queries fails, the whole group of SQL queries is treated as failed, and any data changed by the queries is rolled back, leaving the database in the same position as before these queries ran.

By default, each SQL statement is treated as a transaction. It's possible to enroll a group of SQL queries into a transaction with the keywords BEGIN TRAN. If the queries are successful, the transaction is committed using the keyword COMMIT, and if the queries are unsuccessful, any changes are removed using the keyword ROLLBACK. A typical pattern used to implement this approach is given in the following listing.

Listing 8.1 Transaction processing pattern

```
BEGIN TRY
    BEGIN TRAN
        SELECT 1/0
        PRINT 'Success'
    COMMIT
END TRY
BEGIN CATCH
    ROLLBACK
    PRINT 'An error has occurred'
END CATCH
```

This code starts with the keywords BEGIN TRY, which is the start of the error-handling block. A transaction is initiated with the keywords BEGIN TRAN. What follows next is typically a group of SQL queries that you want to treat as a unit of work. In this example, for illustrative purposes the command SELECT 1/0 will cause an error to be raised. The raised error causes the execution of the code to jump into the BEGIN CATCH block. Here, the transaction is rolled back (ROLLBACK keyword), and an error message is printed. If the statement SELECT 1/0 is replaced with SELECT 1/1, the code executes successfully and the transaction is committed (via the keyword COMMIT).

NOTE In the real world, the transaction would encompass a group of queries that would modify the underlying data. For illustrative purposes, our example contains only a few simple SQL statements.

Each SQL query, even a simple SELECT, takes out locks on various structures within the database (we'll discuss these structures shortly). By grouping queries within a transaction, we typically increase the amount and scope of these locks, resulting in potentially more blocking, decreased performance (of the other queries), and less concurrency. Toward the end of this chapter we'll examine ways in which these locks and blocking can be reduced, with a view to allowing greater concurrency, performance, and scalability while balancing any reduction in data consistency.

As you can see, the cost of providing data consistency is reduced performance (even if nothing else is running, a query will still issue locks) and reduced concurrency.

As a general point, in our example scripts we'll often obtain the individual SQL queries involved in the blocking. Note that the locks may have been taken out by earlier SQL statements, because the transaction may apply across batches of SQL queries.

8.2   *A simple transaction-based case study*

In order to discuss the impact of locks and blocking in this chapter, I want to introduce a simple case study, which will be used in the subsequent example scripts. If you want to follow the output produced by the subsequent scripts given in this chapter, be sure to run the following scripts as detailed.

First, run the script given in the following listing within SQL Server Management Studio (SSMS). The script creates a test database (named IWS_TEMP), changes your SSMS session to this newly created database, and creates a single table (named dbo.tblCountry).

Listing 8.2   Creating the sample database and table

```
CREATE DATABASE IWS_Temp
GO

USE IWS_Temp

CREATE TABLE [dbo].[tblCountry](
    [CountryId] [int] IDENTITY(1,1) NOT NULL,
    [Code] [char](3) NOT NULL,
    [Description] [varchar](50) NOT NULL)
```

Next, open another window in SSMS, and enter and run the script given in listing 8.3. The script changes the SSMS window to use your newly created database, and then a new transaction is started (with the BEGIN TRANSACTION command). Then it inserts a single row into the tblCountry table.

Listing 8.3   Starting an open transaction

```
USE IWS_TEMP

BEGIN TRANSACTION

INSERT INTO [dbo].[tblCountry] ([Code], [Description])
VALUES('ENG', 'ENGLAND')
```

Because this transaction has been started but not committed or rolled back, it's described as *open*. This means it contains locks against the table dbo.tblCountry that will impact other queries that run against this table. This will allow us to investigate and discuss the impact of locks, blocking, and transactions.

Open another window in SSMS, and enter and run the script given in listing 8.4. The SQL query changes the SSMS window to use your newly created database and then attempts to select data from the tblCountry table. Notice that the query doesn't complete; this is because it conflicts with the session that's inserting a row but has not committed or rolled back its open transaction.

Listing 8.4   Selecting data from a table that has an open transaction against it

```
USE IWS_TEMP

SELECT * FROM [dbo].[tblCountry]
```

You can look at the locks that have been taken out by the previous two queries (the insert and select queries) by entering and running the script given in the following listing in SSMS.

Listing 8.5   Observing the current locks

```
SELECT DB_NAME(resource_database_id) AS DatabaseName, request_session_id
  , resource_type, request_status, request_mode
FROM sys.dm_tran_locks
WHERE request_session_id !=@@spid
ORDER BY request_session_id
```

The script decodes the database name from the supplied resource_database_id. It displays the session id (request_session_id), which maps to the two windows within SSMS that are running the two sessions. Note that this session_id represents the process id (spid) discussed in previous chapters. The resource that's being locked (resource_type) or requested, together with the request_mode, is also shown. The results are sorted by request_session_id.

An example of the output from this script is shown in figure 8.1.

Don't worry if you don't understand all these terms and their values at the moment; all will be revealed as we progress with this chapter.

In outline, the output shows that session 52 (the one that contains BEGIN TRANS) is requesting an exclusive lock (request mode of X) on a given row (resource_type of RID), and various other less-restrictive locks have been taken on the page and database. All the locks for session 52 have been granted (request_status of GRANT).

	DatabaseName	request_session_id	resource_type	request_status	request_mode
1	IWS_Temp	52	DATABASE	GRANT	S
2	IWS_Temp	52	RID	GRANT	X
3	IWS_Temp	52	PAGE	GRANT	IX
4	IWS_Temp	52	OBJECT	GRANT	IX
5	IWS_Temp	53	DATABASE	GRANT	S
6	IWS_Temp	53	OBJECT	GRANT	IS
7	IWS_Temp	53	RID	WAIT	S
8	IWS_Temp	53	PAGE	GRANT	IS

Figure 8.1   Output showing details of locks between sessions over various resources

Meanwhile, session 53 (the one that's trying to select from tblCountry) is issuing a shared lock (request mode of S) on a given row (resource_type of RID), but it's still waiting to get that lock (request_status of WAIT). Again, session 53 has various other less-restrictive locks that have been taken on the page and database.

We'll discuss the output in greater detail later, in section 8.7, when I've given a better explanation of locking, blocking, and deadlocks, which follows next.

8.3   Locks, blocks, and deadlocks

The terms *locks*, *blocks*, and *deadlocks* are often used incorrectly. Although the terms are related, each has a specific meaning. When data is being queried, locks are taken out on the underlying data to ensure data consistency. For example, you wouldn't want two people updating the same data at the same time. If a user issues an update query, the data related to the query will be protected by locks; this may cause another user to wait until the first query has finished doing its work. The second user's query will be blocked by the first user's query. If two queries are holding locks on resources that the other query wants, resulting in circular blocking, SQL Server will detect it as a deadlock. There's no nice way out of a deadlock, so SQL Server terminates one of the queries and rolls back its transaction.

You can see the link between locks, blocks, and deadlocks. We'll now examine these in greater detail, starting with locks.

8.3.1   Locks

Locks in SQL Server are normal and to be expected. Locks can be taken out at various levels of the database structural hierarchy, affecting the scope of the locks. At the top level is the database itself; at the bottom level is an individual row of data. When we examine the locks via the DMVs later, in section 8.7, you'll see which locks have been taken out on which database structures. A brief overview of the structures that can be locked is given in table 8.1.

Table 8.1   Database structure hierarchy

Structure	Description
Database	This structure represents the database. Locks held against the database can be most restrictive for concurrency but optimal for data consistency.
Table	Within the database, locks can be taken out on individual tables.
Heap or B-tree	Heaps are tables without a clustered index. A B-tree object typically refers to a partition.
Extent	An extent is a group of contiguous pages.
Page	A page holds rows of data.
Key	A key is a row within an index.
Row	A row is a single row of data within a table.

Locks can be taken out at various levels within this structural hierarchy, and each lock can have a different impact via its severity (for example, an exclusive lock is more restrictive than a shared lock).

The different types of lock that can be taken are listed in table 8.2. The letter(s) given in parentheses after the lock type represent how the lock type is shown in the columns of the various transaction/lock-related DMVs.

Table 8.2   Types of lock

Lock type	Description
Shared (S)	Used for read-only queries. Other read-only queries can access the data concurrently, but modifying queries (DELETE, UPDATE, INSERT) are prevented, to ensure data consistency. By default, the shared lock is released after the data has been read.
Update (U)	This lock means the data is being read with the aim of modifying the data. It applies to an UPDATE query, which can be viewed as a SELECT to get the data and then an UPDATE to modify it. Other queries that have a shared lock on this data can run concurrently.
Exclusive (X)	Exclusive access to a resource. This ensures only one query can INSERT/DELETE/UPDATE the data at any given time. Other queries can't access the data being modified.
Intent shared (IS)	Indicates a shared lock has been taken at a lower level in the resource hierarchy.
Intent exclusive (IX)	Indicates an exclusive lock has been taken at a lower level in the resource hierarchy.
Shared with intent exclusive (SIX)	Indicates an intent exclusive lock has been taken at a lower level in the resource hierarchy.

Table 8.2   Types of lock *(continued)*

Lock type	Description
Schema modification (Sch-M)	Typically this is acquired when a query wants to modify a table. This lock prevents other queries from accessing the table.
Schema stability (Sch-S)	This lock is typically taken when a query needs access to metadata about a table, for example, for query compilation.
Bulk update (BU)	Relates to bulk load operations.
Key range	Relates to holding locks across a wider range of rows than normal.

A NOTE ABOUT THE INTENT LOCKS   When a lock is taken on a relatively low-level object, for example, a row or a page, related intent locks are also taken in the higher-level object in the database structure hierarchy. This enables SQL Server to determine quickly, using the higher-level information, whether any new query will cause potential locking conflicts on the lower levels.

Locking uses resources, and coordination is needed to manage any conflicts. As the number of locks taken out by a query increases, this coordination can become more difficult. In this case, SQL Server will often escalate a lock held on a low-level resource to a higher level, for example, from a row lock to a page lock. The locks that were held at the lower level are then released. This results in the use of fewer resources but also potentially more blocking (and less concurrency) because the whole page of rows is now locked. Lock escalation typically occurs when more than 5,000 locks have been taken. We'll discuss lock escalation and its implications toward the end of this chapter.

Now that you've seen the database structures that can be locked and the different types of locks that can be taken out, we're in a position to examine blocks and deadlocks.

8.3.2   Blocks

Blocking is a consequence of locking. When a query runs, locks are taken out on resources to ensure consistency of data. But when another query wants to access the same resources, it may be blocked, leading to decreased performance and less scalability.

> **NOTE**   Some of these blocks are recorded as waits on locked resources (see the code in chapter 6 for more details on how to view these). It's possible to use these waits to determine whether locking is a consistent and important problem needing attention.

Often the terms *blocking* and *waiting* are used interchangeably. Blocking is a specific type of waiting that relates to locks. Blocking is a subset of waiting.

By default, SQL Server will wait until the blocking has finished before proceeding. If the client is a Windows or web client, the blocked query typically waits a given time before failing with a timeout error.

It's also possible to record blocking that occurs for longer than a given time period by setting the blocked process threshold within the system configuration. This enables SQL Profiler to record details of any blocks that occur over the given wait threshold.

It's also possible to record details of blocking via the SQL Server performance counters. More details about how to do this, together with the meaning of these counters, are given in chapter 6.

Blocking and waiting are similar concepts and the terms are typically interchangeable. With this in mind, it might be profitable to also look at chapters 4 and 5 for the wait-related scripts.

8.3.3 *Deadlocks*

Deadlocks are an extreme version of blocking, where typically two queries each hold a lock on a resource and each then requires the resource held by the other query. Deadlocks can be thought of as circular blocking. It's possible to discover which SQL queries were involved in the deadlock by turning on trace flag 1222 either as part of the SQL Server startup script or from within SSMS, using the following command: DBCC TRACEON (1222, -1). In the latter case, the trace flag is on only until SQL Server is restarted.

If trace flag 1222 is on when a deadlock occurs, information about the deadlock is written to the SQL Server error log. The log includes details of the individual queries involved in the deadlock, together with their stack trace, details of the resources involved in the deadlock, the transaction isolation level, the sql_handle, and the plan_handle (so you can get the SQL query and the cached plan from the DMVs if needed).

Because deadlocks can occur because of scheduling conflicts, for example, when two SQL batches are accessing similar resources at the same time, it's possible to capture the error in a TRY/CATCH block and resubmit the query. An example of this is given in listing 8.6. Note that in SQL Server 2008 you can enter an initial value for a variable on the same line as its declaration. You'll need to change this if you're using SQL Server 2005. Also note that you should replace dbo.SomeRoutine with the name of your routine.

Listing 8.6 Template for handling deadlock retries

```
DECLARE @CurrentTry INT = 1
DECLARE @MaxRetries INT = 3
DECLARE @Complete BIT = 0

WHILE (@Complete = 0)
BEGIN                              ❶  Try block
    BEGIN TRY
```

```
        EXEC dbo.SomeRoutine
        SET @Complete = 1
    END TRY                                          ❷  Catch error
BEGIN CATCH                                        ⤶
        DECLARE @ErrorNum INT
        DECLARE @ErrorMessage      NVARCHAR(4000)
        DECLARE @ErrorState INT
        DECLARE @ErrorSeverity     INT

        SET @ErrorNum = ERROR_NUMBER()
        SET @ErrorMessage = ERROR_MESSAGE()
        SET @ErrorState = ERROR_STATE()
        SET @ErrorSeverity = ERROR_SEVERITY()
                                                     ❸  Handle
        IF (@ErrorNum = 1205) AND (@CurrentTry < @MaxRetries)  ⤶  deadlock
        BEGIN
            IF @@TRANCOUNT > 0
              ROLLBACK TRANSACTION
            SET @CurrentTry = @CurrentTry + 1
            WAITFOR DELAY '00:00:10'
                                              ❹  Raise
        END                                   ⤶  error
        ELSE                                 ⤶
        BEGIN
            IF @@TRANCOUNT > 0
              ROLLBACK TRANSACTION
            SET @Complete = 1
            RAISERROR ('An error has occurred'
                    , @ErrorSeverity
                    , @ErrorState)
        END
    END CATCH
END
```

In the example given, the routine named dbo.SomeQuery is executed. If an error is raised within the TRY block ❶, execution is passed to the CATCH block ❷. Here, the error code is examined; if its value is 1205, it means a deadlock has occurred ❸. In the case of a deadlock, any transactions are rolled back, the query waits a given time period, and then the query is re-executed. This is attempted a given number of times (three times in the example). If a deadlock still occurs, a message can be logged and the code exited with a RAISERROR ❹.

Please note that this example is only a template used to indicate the flow of processing. In a real-world implementation, better logging would be required.

Every five seconds or so, the deadlock manager runs, looking for blocks that can't be resolved because they are deadlocks. SQL Server chooses one of the queries to terminate and roll back; this is usually the query that's easiest to roll back, for example, the one that has done the fewest updates. You can influence which query is rolled back when a deadlock is detected by setting a deadlock priority indicator in the query. An example of this is SET DEADLOCK_PRIORITY LOW. Other values include NORMAL and HIGH. In SQL Server 2008, you can use a number in the range -10 to 10 to indicate a finer-grained deadlock priority.

You can also obtain details relating to deadlocks via the SQL Server performance counters. More details about how to do this, together with the meaning of these counters, is given in chapter 6.

Later, at the end of this chapter, we'll discuss how blocking can be reduced and, by extension, how deadlocks can be reduced.

Other important aspects that are useful in understanding transactions are typically ascribed as the ACID properties of transactions. We'll discuss these next.

8.4 The ACID properties of transactions

Transactions are often described as having ACID properties. The initialism *ACID* represents the atomic, consistent, isolated, and durable properties of transactions. An overview of each of the ACID properties is given in table 8.3.

> **NOTE** The isolation level in particular impacts the locks taken on resources, and you can influence this within your queries and change how queries interact.

Table 8.3 ACID requirements

Property	Description
Atomic	The group of queries is treated as a unit; either they are all successful or none of them are.
Consistent	After the transaction has been committed or rolled back, the database must be in a consistent state (for example, indexes updated, constraints satisfied).
Isolated	A transaction shouldn't interact with uncommitted data of other transactions. It should behave as if it's the only transaction running.
Durable	Any changes made are durable.

Having discussed the ACID properties of transactions, we'll now investigate the isolated property, with particular reference to its values and how it impacts locking.

8.5 Transaction isolation levels

The lock types described previously protect the data being queried from the impact of other concurrently running queries. The level of isolation between concurrent queries can also be affected by the isolation level of the query. For example, it's possible to read uncommitted data that's currently involved in an update transaction. The isolation level is typically set using the SQL keywords SET TRANSACTION ISOLATION LEVEL; we've used this repeatedly in our scripts to prevent unnecessary locking.

An overview of the different types of isolation levels and their impact is given in table 8.4. The first four entries are most commonly used; they specify isolation level in terms of increasing restriction. The latter two entries are currently relatively little used.

Table 8.4   Isolation levels

Isolation level	Description
Read Uncommitted	This causes SELECT statements to ignore most locks and not take out any locks.
Read Committed	This is the default isolation level. A query will wait until data has been committed or rolled back before SELECTing it.
Repeatable Read	Any locks caused by SELECTs are held until the end of the transaction.
Serializable	Locks are taken out not only on the rows being selected/updated but also on nearby rows; this prevents the insertion of data that might affect the query.
Read Committed Snapshot	This relates to keeping a copy of any prechanged data, enabling better concurrency. Statement based.
Snapshot	This relates to keeping a copy of any prechanged data, enabling better concurrency. Transaction oriented.

Often, the more restrictive the isolation level, the greater the performance of a given query, but the worse the performance and scalability of other queries or the system as a whole.

You can set the isolation level for a given batch of SQL queries. Similarly, you can do the same thing by implementing table hints on individual tables within the queries. A common technique for reporting-based queries is to set the isolation level to Read Uncommitted or implement the corresponding NOLOCK table hint. Notice in most of our DMV scripts that the first statement sets the transaction isolation level to Read Uncommitted; this ensures that the script doesn't hold any locks and doesn't get delayed by any locks.

Having discussed the various transaction isolation levels, next we'll discuss sessions, connections, and requests, because these tie the locks to the running queries.

8.6   *Sessions, connections, and requests*

In this section we'll briefly discuss sessions, connections, and requests because they provide valuable information for discussing transaction and locks next in this chapter. Each is represented by a corresponding DMV.

Sessions contain information about the client and host, for example, when the session started, the program used to start the session (such as Microsoft Office), the hostname (name of the client workstation initiating the session), the login name, and if any requests are running for this session. The associated DMV is named sys.dm_exec_sessions. A session can have one or more connections.

A *connection* contains information about connections established to SQL Server, for example, the method of connection and the number of reads and writes. The associated DMV is named sys.dm_exec_connections. A connection can have one or more requests.

A *request* contains information about SQL queries executing on SQL Server, for example, the id of the SQL query executing, its start time, its status, the id of any session blocking it, and the reason for any waiting. The associated DMV is named sys.dm_exec_requests.

You can see what information is contained in these DMVs, together with the relationships between them, by running the script given in the following listing.

Listing 8.7 Information contained in sessions, connections, and requests

```
SET TRANSACTION ISOLATION LEVEL READ UNCOMMITTED

SELECT *
FROM sys.dm_exec_sessions s
LEFT OUTER JOIN sys.dm_exec_connections c
    ON s.session_id = c.session_id
LEFT OUTER JOIN sys.dm_exec_requests r
    ON c.connection_id = r.connection_id
WHERE s.session_id > 50
```

A LEFT OUTER JOIN is used to link the session and connection because there may not be a connection for the corresponding session. Similarly, a LEFT OUTER JOIN is used to link the connection and request because there may not be a request for the corresponding connection. In both cases, you can see the maximum amount of information that's present. We look only at sessions that have a session_id greater than 50; this is because session_id values up to 50 are system session_ids, and we're typically interested only in our application sessions.

Both the session and request DMVs provide column values for the various environmental settings, for example, Arithabort and Ansi_Nulls. Examination of these values can prove very insightful when investigating why SQL queries run slower in SSMS compared with other clients such as Excel.

Now that we've discussed the theory background, you should be in a better position to interpret and understand the output from some useful scripts relating to transaction, locking, and blocking.

8.7 Finding locks

Earlier in this chapter, while introducing the simple transaction-based case study, I ran a simple query to show details of locks between queries over various resources. The purpose of this section is to explain in more detail the output and give you a better understanding of locks. The following discussion relates to the simple case study given at the start of this chapter, so ensure that you have this running if you want to follow the discussion. Once you understand how to interpret the output, it will help in understanding more complex situations.

The script we use to discover which locks are currently held follows.

Listing 8.8   How to discover which locks are currently held

```
SET TRANSACTION ISOLATION LEVEL READ UNCOMMITTED

SELECT DB_NAME(resource_database_id) AS DatabaseName
  , request_session_id
  , resource_type
  , CASE
      WHEN resource_type = 'OBJECT'
      THEN OBJECT_NAME(resource_associated_entity_id)
      WHEN resource_type IN ('KEY', 'PAGE', 'RID')
      THEN (SELECT OBJECT_NAME(OBJECT_ID)
              FROM sys.partitions p
              WHERE p.hobt_id = l.resource_associated_entity_id)
  END AS resource_type_name
  , request_status
  , request_mode
FROM sys.dm_tran_locks l
WHERE request_session_id !=@@spid
ORDER BY request_session_id
```

❶ Decode resource

The script involves a single DMV, sys.dm_tran_locks. The database id is resolved into the underlying database name using the SQL function DB_NAME. Similarly, the underlying resource name is resolved in the CASE statement, decoding the resource_type to the appropriate resource being locked ❶. In this case, the contended resource is the table tblCountry.

Sample output for this query is shown in figure 8.2.

The output shows the contention between our two sessions; note that your session ids may be different. Session 51 contains the BEGIN TRANSACTION statement together with the INSERT statement. Because it ran first, it has taken out an exclusive lock on the row; this is shown in the second row of the output. The resource type is RID (row id), which indicates a row-level lock; the request_mode of X shows it's an exclusive lock. In order to help prevent conflicts from occurring, locks with lesser impact are taken in objects above the row in the database structure hierarchy. In this case, you can see that session 51 has an intent exclusive lock (IX in the request_mode column) on the PAGE resource. Similarly, the database itself has a shared (S) lock.

	DatabaseName	request_session_id	resource_type	resource_type_name	request_status	request_mode
1	IWS_Temp	51	DATABASE	NULL	GRANT	S
2	IWS_Temp	51	RID	tblCountry	GRANT	X
3	IWS_Temp	51	PAGE	tblCountry	GRANT	IX
4	IWS_Temp	51	OBJECT	tblCountry	GRANT	IX
5	IWS_Temp	54	DATABASE	NULL	GRANT	S
6	IWS_Temp	54	OBJECT	tblCountry	GRANT	IS
7	IWS_Temp	54	RID	tblCountry	WAIT	S
8	IWS_Temp	54	PAGE	tblCountry	GRANT	IS

Figure 8.2   Output showing which locks are currently held

Where possible, the resource involved has been decoded (tblCountry in the output). All the locks have been granted for session 51 (the request_status column has a value of GRANT in the output for each row that belongs to session 51).

Session 54 contains the SELECT statement; you can see that it has a request_status of WAIT. In essence, it's trying to issue a share lock (S) at the row level, but it's unable to be granted because session 51 hasn't committed its transaction. Higher objects in the database structure hierarchy for session 54 have issued share (S) and intent share (IS) locks, and these have been granted.

Sometimes, if many rows are being locked, SQL Server will escalate the many row-level locks to higher-level page-level locks. Although this can be more restrictive for other SQL queries, it uses fewer resources and improves the performance of the current SQL query. We discuss lock escalation in further detail toward the end of this chapter.

An UPDATE SQL query involves a SELECT to obtain the data and then an UPDATE to change the data. During the transition between these modes, it's possible to see a status of CONVERT in the column request_status.

Having discussed the typical output from conflicting queries, we'll now examine the specific contended resources.

8.8   Identifying the contended resources

Although it's interesting to get a complete picture of the locks taken out by transactions on different objects within the database object hierarchy, oftentimes you'll want to see just details of the specific contended resources (in much the same way that a script in an earlier chapter presented details of only which SQL queries are running, in contrast with all the details produced by sp_who2).

Seeing the details of contention should allow you to quickly target the relevant resources and SQL queries for further investigation, with a view to reducing this contention.

8.8.1   Contended resources—basic version

The script we use to find only the contended resources is shown in the following listing.

Listing 8.9   How to identify contended resources

```
SET TRANSACTION ISOLATION LEVEL READ UNCOMMITTED
SELECT
  tl1.resource_type,
  DB_NAME(tl1.resource_database_id) AS DatabaseName,
  tl1.resource_associated_entity_id,
  tl1.request_session_id,
  tl1.request_mode,
  tl1.request_status                                     Decode
  , CASE                                                 resource
      WHEN tl1.resource_type = 'OBJECT'
```

```
        THEN OBJECT_NAME(tll.resource_associated_entity_id)
     WHEN tll.resource_type IN ('KEY', 'PAGE', 'RID')
       THEN (SELECT OBJECT_NAME(OBJECT_ID)
             FROM sys.partitions s
             WHERE s.hobt_id = tll.resource_associated_entity_id)
    END AS resource_type_name
FROM sys.dm_tran_locks as tll
INNER JOIN sys.dm_tran_locks as tl2
   ON tll.resource_associated_entity_id = tl2.resource_associated_entity_id
      AND tll.request_status <> tl2.request_status
      AND (tll.resource_description = tl2.resource_description
      OR (tll.resource_description IS NULL
AND tl2.resource_description IS NULL))
ORDER BY tll.resource_associated_entity_id, tll.request_status
```

Self join of ❶
sys.dm_tran_locks

Here a single DMV, self joined ❶, is involved in identifying the resources in contention; a brief description of it is given in table 8.5.

Table 8.5 DMV used to find contended resources

DMV	Description
sys.dm_tran_locks	Contains details of locks held by transactions

In the script the DMV sys.dm_tran_locks is joined to itself ❶ based on its key columns of resource_associated_entity_id and resource_description. Because locks will exist for both the query that has the lock and the query that wants the lock, we retrieve results where the request_status isn't the same. This allows us, for example, to retrieve details of queries that have a GRANT lock and a WAIT lock on a given resource.

Figure 8.3 provides an example of the type of output for this query.

	resource_type	DatabaseName	resource_associated_entity_id	request_session_id	request_mode	request_status	resource_type_name
1	RID	IWS_Temp	72057594038779904	51	X	GRANT	tblCountry
2	RID	IWS_Temp	72057594038779904	54	S	WAIT	tblCountry

Figure 8.3 Output showing contended resources

Although knowing which resources are in contention is useful, including details of the SQL queries involved should prove useful in pinpointing the location in the SQL query of the area of contention. A script that provides this information follows next.

8.8.2 *Contended resources—enhanced version*

The script given in the following listing will provide details of both the batch of SQL included (or a stored procedure) and the Individual Query being executed (or attempting to execute).

Listing 8.10 How to identify contended resources, including SQL query details

```
SET TRANSACTION ISOLATION LEVEL READ UNCOMMITTED

SELECT
  tl1.resource_type
  , DB_NAME(tl1.resource_database_id) AS DatabaseName
  , tl1.resource_associated_entity_id
  , tl1.request_session_id
  , tl1.request_mode
  , tl1.request_status                                Decode
  , CASE                                        ◁──┘  resource
      WHEN tl1.resource_type = 'OBJECT'
        THEN OBJECT_NAME(tl1.resource_associated_entity_id)
      WHEN tl1.resource_type IN ('KEY', 'PAGE', 'RID')
        THEN (SELECT OBJECT_NAME(OBJECT_ID)
              FROM sys.partitions s
              WHERE s.hobt_id = tl1.resource_associated_entity_id)
    END AS resource_type_name
  , t.text AS [Parent Query]
  ,  SUBSTRING (t.text,(r.statement_start_offset/2) + 1,
     ((CASE WHEN r.statement_end_offset = -1            Self join of  ❶
       THEN LEN(CONVERT(NVARCHAR(MAX), t.text)) * 2   sys.dm_tran_locks
       ELSE r.statement_end_offset
       END - r.statement_start_offset)/2) + 1) AS [Individual Query]
FROM sys.dm_tran_locks as tl1                              ◁────────┘
INNER JOIN sys.dm_tran_locks as tl2
   ON tl1.resource_associated_entity_id = tl2.resource_associated_entity_id
        AND tl1.request_status <> tl2.request_status
        AND (tl1.resource_description = tl2.resource_description
        OR (tl1.resource_description IS NULL
AND tl2.resource_description IS NULL))
INNER JOIN sys.dm_exec_connections c
        ON tl1.request_session_id = c.most_recent_session_id
CROSS APPLY sys.dm_exec_sql_text(c.most_recent_sql_handle) t
LEFT OUTER JOIN sys.dm_exec_requests r ON c.connection_id = r.connection_id
ORDER BY tl1.resource_associated_entity_id, tl1.request_status
```

In the listing, three DMVs and a single DMF are involved in identifying the resources and queries involved in contention. A brief description of them is given in table 8.6.

Table 8.6 DMVs/DMF used to find contended resources and queries

DMV/DMF	Description
sys.dm_tran_locks	Contains details of locks held by transactions
sys.dm_exec_connections	Contains details of connections to SQL Server
sys.dm_exec_requests	Contains details of requests executing on SQL Server
sys.dm_exec_sql_text	DMF that returns the SQL text identified by a given sql_handle

In the script the DMV sys.dm_tran_locks is joined to itself ❶ based on its key columns of resource_associated_entity_id and resource_description. Because locks will exist for both the query that has the lock and the query that wants the lock, we retrieve results where the request_status isn't the same. This allows us, for example, to retrieve details of queries that have a GRANT lock and a WAIT lock on a given resource.

An INNER JOIN is used to link the self join output with the sys.dm_exec_ connections DMV, on the key column of session_id. A CROSS APPLY with the DMF sys.dm_exec_sql_text allows the Parent Query to be extracted. A LEFT OUTER JOIN with the sys.dm_exec_requests DMV allows details of any executing individual queries to be extracted.

An example of the type of output for this query is shown in figure 8.4.

	resource_type	DatabaseName	resource_associated_entity_id	request_session_id	request_mode	request_status	resource_type_name	Parent Query	Individual Query
1	RID	IWS_Temp	72057594038779904	51	X	GRANT	tblCountry	USE IWS_TEMP B...	NULL
2	RID	IWS_Temp	72057594038779904	53	S	WAIT	tblCountry	USE IWS_TEMP S...	SELECT * FROM [...

Figure 8.4   Output showing contended resources and SQL queries

The output shows both the contended resource (tblCountry) and the SQL queries involved. For both sessions, the Parent Query is present. Because there's no active request for the session that begins a transaction but doesn't commit or roll back, its Individual Query column value is set to NULL. For the request that's waiting, its Individual Query value has been calculated and displayed.

Knowing the Individual Queries (or just one query in this example), it's possible to examine why the blocking is occurring and take steps toward a resolution. Knowing the SQL query involved, you can use the scripts in chapter 4 to obtain the cached plans for the queries. Examining these will illustrate at a more granular level how the queries are being fulfilled and should provide further input on how the blocking can be reduced.

Having looked at how we can target only those contended resources, we'll now look at idle transactions. These can have a dramatic impact on performance via locking and blocking if left unchecked.

8.9   *Identifying inactive sessions with open transactions*

Transactions increase the scope of locks, typically across multiple SQL queries, providing more opportunity for any potential blocking and a subsequent decrease in concurrency and performance.

An idle session with an open transaction is a session that has no request currently running, is not active, but contains uncommitted work. Such transactions can increase the possibility of blocking and performance degradation. Identifying these open transactions will enable you to resolve some blocking problems and prevent others from occurring.

8.9.1 *How idle sessions with open transactions arise*

Sometimes during your testing, you might want to start a transaction, do some work, and then based on the inspection of the results, either commit or roll back the transaction. This is a common pattern used by DBAs/developers. But it's easy to get distracted by something else and leave the transaction open (yes, I'm guilty of doing this too). An example of an open transaction is given earlier in this chapter, for illustrating locks, in the simple case study section.

This is easily corrected with a little forethought. If you know the information you'll need to commit or roll back the transaction, you can include this in your open transaction (perhaps with a NOLOCK hint on the SELECT statements) and use this to commit or roll back the transaction programmatically.

Another perhaps more serious version of this problem can occur when a SQL query errors and because of inadequate error handling leaves the transaction open. Using the script given in this section should identify the SQL query that contains this type of error and allow you to correct it.

8.9.2 *How to find an idle session with an open transaction*

Open transactions can result in poor concurrency and reduced performance, owing to the locks being held. Running the SQL script given in the next listing will identify any idle sessions that have open transactions.

Listing 8.11 How to find an idle session with an open transaction

```
SET TRANSACTION ISOLATION LEVEL READ UNCOMMITTED

SELECT es.session_id, es.login_name, es.host_name, est.text
 , cn.last_read, cn.last_write, es.program_name
FROM sys.dm_exec_sessions es
INNER JOIN sys.dm_tran_session_transactions st
        ON es.session_id = st.session_id
INNER JOIN sys.dm_exec_connections cn
        ON es.session_id = cn.session_id
CROSS APPLY sys.dm_exec_sql_text(cn.most_recent_sql_handle) est
LEFT OUTER JOIN sys.dm_exec_requests er
        ON st.session_id = er.session_id        Identify idle
            AND er.session_id IS NULL    <-|    sessions
```

Four DMVs and one DMF are involved in finding idle sessions that have open transactions; a brief description of each is given in table 8.7.

Table 8.7 DMVs/DMF used to find idle sessions with open transactions

DMV/DMF	Description
sys.dm_exec_sessions	Contains details of sessions on SQL Server
sys.dm_tran_session_transactions	Returns correlation information for transactions/sessions

Table 8.7   DMVs/DMF used to find idle sessions with open transactions (*continued*)

DMV/DMF	Description
sys.dm_exec_connections	Contains details of connections to SQL Server
sys.dm_exec_sql_text	DMF that returns the SQL text identified by a given sql_handle
sys.dm_exec_requests	Contains details of requests executing on SQL Server

The joining of the DMVs and the DMF provides you with enough information to identify any idle sessions that have open transactions, across all the databases on the server. The DMVs sys.dm_exec_sessions, sys.dm_tran_session_transactions, and sys.dm_exec_connections are joined on their common key column session_id. The connection contains the column most_recent_sql_handle, which is passed to the DMF sys.dm_exec_sql_text to retrieve the text of the SQL query. A LEFT OUTER JOIN is then performed on the DMV sys.dm_exec_requests. Any requests with a NULL session_id are identified as sessions with idle transactions.

An example of the type of output for this query is shown in figure 8.5.

Figure 8.5   Output showing idle sessions with open transactions

The output shows that there are two idle sessions (with session ids of 51 and 54) with open transactions. For each transaction, you can see the login name of the user who owns the transaction, the machine the query is running from (host_name), the SQL query that contains the open transaction, the time of the last read and write to the database, and the name of the program that's running the query. This information should be enough to identify who has the open transaction, where it's running from, what SQL is causing the problem, and how long it's been since there was any activity.

Having identified which idle sessions have open transactions, our next logical step would be to ask what's being blocked by these open transactions.

8.10   *Waiting due to transaction locks*

SQL queries can wait for many reasons; all result in a perceived decrease in performance. Identifying these queries and transactions will allow you to investigate how different queries and transactions interact and whether their performance can be improved. The following scripts will examine what's waiting (being blocked) by transactions that have idle sessions, non-idle sessions, and both idle and non-idle sessions.

8.10.1 *Waiting because of an idle session with an open transaction*

We can enhance the script presented in the previous section to obtain details of which queries are being blocked by open transactions. This could be useful in informing these users that their queries are being processed slowly. Similarly, we could inform the perpetrator that their query is preventing other users from doing work. Note that this still applies to idle sessions with open transactions.

The script we use to find what queries are being blocked by idle sessions with open transactions is shown here.

Listing 8.12 What's being blocked by idle sessions with open transactions

```
SET TRANSACTION ISOLATION LEVEL READ UNCOMMITTED
SELECT
  Waits.wait_duration_ms / 1000 AS WaitInSeconds
  , Blocking.session_id as BlockingSessionId
  , DB_NAME(Blocked.database_id) AS DatabaseName
  , Sess.login_name AS BlockingUser
  , Sess.host_name AS BlockingLocation
  , BlockingSQL.text AS BlockingSQL
  , Blocked.session_id AS BlockedSessionId
  , BlockedSess.login_name AS BlockedUser
  , BlockedSess.host_name AS BlockedLocation
  , BlockedSQL.text AS BlockedSQL
  , SUBSTRING (BlockedSQL.text, (BlockedReq.statement_start_offset/2) + 1,
    ((CASE WHEN BlockedReq.statement_end_offset = -1
      THEN LEN(CONVERT(NVARCHAR(MAX), BlockedSQL.text)) * 2
      ELSE BlockedReq.statement_end_offset
      END - BlockedReq.statement_start_offset)/2) + 1)
                  AS [Blocked Individual Query]
  , Waits.wait_type                                              ⟵┐ Blocker
FROM sys.dm_exec_connections AS Blocking                          ┘ joins
INNER JOIN sys.dm_exec_requests AS Blocked
        ON Blocking.session_id = Blocked.blocking_session_id
INNER JOIN sys.dm_exec_sessions Sess
        ON Blocking.session_id = sess.session_id
INNER JOIN sys.dm_tran_session_transactions st
        ON Blocking.session_id = st.session_id
LEFT OUTER JOIN sys.dm_exec_requests er
        ON st.session_id = er.session_id
            AND er.session_id IS NULL
INNER JOIN sys.dm_os_waiting_tasks AS Waits
        ON Blocked.session_id = Waits.session_id
CROSS APPLY sys.dm_exec_sql_text(Blocking.most_recent_sql_handle)
                        AS BlockingSQL
INNER JOIN sys.dm_exec_requests AS BlockedReq                    ⟵┐ Blocked
        ON Waits.session_id = BlockedReq.session_id               ┘ joins
INNER JOIN sys.dm_exec_sessions AS BlockedSess
        ON Waits.session_id = BlockedSess.session_id
CROSS APPLY sys.dm_exec_sql_text(Blocked.sql_handle) AS BlockedSQL
ORDER BY WaitInSeconds
```

In the listing, five DMVs and one DMF are involved in finding idle sessions that have open transactions. A brief description of each is given in table 8.8.

Table 8.8   DMVs/DMF used to find idle sessions with open transactions

DMV/DMF	Description
sys.dm_exec_sessions	Contains details of sessions on SQL Server
sys.dm_tran_session_transactions	Returns correlation information for transactions/sessions
sys.dm_exec_connections	Contains details of connections to SQL Server
sys.dm_exec_sql_text	DMF that returns the SQL text identified by a given sql_handle
sys.dm_exec_requests	Contains details of requests executing on SQL Server
sys.dm_os_waiting_tasks	Contains details of wait queues of tasks that are waiting on a resource

The joining of the DMVs and the DMF provides you with enough information to identify what's being blocked by idle sessions that have open transactions, across all the databases on the server. The DMVs sys.dm_exec_sessions, sys.dm_tran_session_transactions, and sys.dm_exec_connections are joined on their common key column session_id. The connection contains the column most_recent_sql_handle, which is passed to the DMF sys.dm_exec_sql_text to retrieve the text of the SQL query. A LEFT OUTER JOIN is then performed on the DMV sys.dm_exec_requests. Any requests with a NULL session_id are identified as sessions with idle transactions. An INNER JOIN on both sys.dm_exec_requests and sys.dm_exec_sessions for the waiting query, using the DMV sys.dm_os_waiting_tasks, allows you to obtain details of the waiting query.

Note that because transactions can go across batches of SQL (for example, a .NET client may begin a transaction and then call two or more batches or stored procedures), you might not be able to discern the cause of the blocking from the queries shown. But inspecting the call stack should give you some insight into when the transaction started.

An example of the type of output for this query is shown in figure 8.6.

In the output, you can see details of the SQL queries, the users, and the location where the queries are running from, for both the blocking and the blocked queries. This is useful in determining who/what/where the blocking process is and who it's affecting.

Figure 8.6   Output showing what's waiting because of idle sessions with open transactions

If the blocked user is running a SELECT query, it may be possible to bypass the waiting by preceding the SELECT statement with SET TRANSACTION ISOLATION LEVEL READ UNCOMMITTED. This typically won't take out locks or honor any locks.

8.10.2 *Waiting because of active session transactions only*

Although it can be useful to identify what's being blocked by idle sessions with open transactions, this is a relatively rare situation. A more common situation occurs when queries are being blocked by other queries in a transaction.

The script we use to find what queries are being blocked by active sessions with open transactions is shown in the following listing.

Listing 8.13 What's blocked by active sessions with open transactions

```
SET TRANSACTION ISOLATION LEVEL READ UNCOMMITTED

SELECT
  Waits.wait_duration_ms / 1000 AS WaitInSeconds
  , Blocking.session_id as BlockingSessionId
  , DB_NAME(Blocked.database_id) AS DatabaseName
  , Sess.login_name AS BlockingUser
  , Sess.host_name AS BlockingLocation
  , BlockingSQL.text AS BlockingSQL
  , Blocked.session_id AS BlockedSessionId
  , BlockedSess.login_name AS BlockedUser
  , BlockedSess.host_name AS BlockedLocation
  , BlockedSQL.text AS BlockedSQL
  , SUBSTRING (BlockedSQL.text, (BlockedReq.statement_start_offset/2) + 1,
    ((CASE WHEN BlockedReq.statement_end_offset = -1
      THEN LEN(CONVERT(NVARCHAR(MAX), BlockedSQL.text)) * 2
      ELSE BlockedReq.statement_end_offset
      END - BlockedReq.statement_start_offset)/2) + 1)
                              AS [Blocked Individual Query]
  , Waits.wait_type                                                      Blocker
FROM sys.dm_exec_connections AS Blocking                          ◁───   joins
INNER JOIN sys.dm_exec_requests AS Blocked
        ON Blocking.session_id = Blocked.blocking_session_id
INNER JOIN sys.dm_exec_sessions Sess
        ON Blocking.session_id = sess.session_id
INNER JOIN sys.dm_tran_session_transactions st
        ON Blocking.session_id = st.session_id
INNER JOIN sys.dm_exec_requests er
        ON st.session_id = er.session_id
INNER JOIN sys.dm_os_waiting_tasks AS Waits
        ON Blocked.session_id = Waits.session_id
CROSS APPLY sys.dm_exec_sql_text(Blocking.most_recent_sql_handle)
                        AS BlockingSQL
INNER JOIN sys.dm_exec_requests AS BlockedReq                     ◁───   Blocked
        ON Waits.session_id = BlockedReq.session_id                      joins
INNER JOIN sys.dm_exec_sessions AS BlockedSess
        ON Waits.session_id = BlockedSess.session_id
CROSS APPLY sys.dm_exec_sql_text(Blocked.sql_handle) AS BlockedSQL
ORDER BY WaitInSeconds
```

The DMVs/DMFs and joins involved in this script are largely the same as those in the previous script. Please see that script for greater detail. Where the current script does differ is that the LEFT OUTER JOIN is replaced with an INNER JOIN, and NULL session_ids are filtered out, resulting in including transactions with active sessions only.

Again, knowing the SQL queries involved should be the starting point of examining and resolving any conflicts.

8.10.3 *Waiting because of both active and idle session transactions*

Concentrating individually on idle sessions and active sessions can provide useful information for subsequent analysis. But sometimes a combined approach might provide more insight into any blocking problems.

The script we use to find which queries are being blocked by both active and idle sessions with open transactions is given here.

Listing 8.14 What's blocked—active and idle sessions with open transactions

```
SET TRANSACTION ISOLATION LEVEL READ UNCOMMITTED

SELECT
  Waits.wait_duration_ms / 1000 AS WaitInSeconds
  , Blocking.session_id as BlockingSessionId
  , DB_NAME(Blocked.database_id) AS DatabaseName
  , Sess.login_name AS BlockingUser
  , Sess.host_name AS BlockingLocation
  , BlockingSQL.text AS BlockingSQL
  , Blocked.session_id AS BlockedSessionId
  , BlockedSess.login_name AS BlockedUser
  , BlockedSess.host_name AS BlockedLocation
  , BlockedSQL.text AS BlockedSQL
  , SUBSTRING (BlockedSQL.text, (BlockedReq.statement_start_offset/2) + 1,
    ((CASE WHEN BlockedReq.statement_end_offset = -1
      THEN LEN(CONVERT(NVARCHAR(MAX), BlockedSQL.text)) * 2
      ELSE BlockedReq.statement_end_offset
      END - BlockedReq.statement_start_offset)/2) + 1)
                          AS [Blocked Individual Query]
  , Waits.wait_type
FROM sys.dm_exec_connections AS Blocking
INNER JOIN sys.dm_exec_requests AS Blocked
        ON Blocking.session_id = Blocked.blocking_session_id
INNER JOIN sys.dm_exec_sessions Sess
        ON Blocking.session_id = sess.session_id
INNER JOIN sys.dm_tran_session_transactions st
        ON Blocking.session_id = st.session_id
LEFT OUTER JOIN sys.dm_exec_requests er
        ON st.session_id = er.session_id
INNER JOIN sys.dm_os_waiting_tasks AS Waits
        ON Blocked.session_id = Waits.session_id
CROSS APPLY sys.dm_exec_sql_text(Blocking.most_recent_sql_handle)
                          AS BlockingSQL
INNER JOIN sys.dm_exec_requests AS BlockedReq
        ON Waits.session_id = BlockedReq.session_id
```

Blocker joins ⬅

Blocked joins ⬅

```
INNER JOIN sys.dm_exec_sessions AS BlockedSess
        ON Waits.session_id = BlockedSess.session_id
CROSS APPLY sys.dm_exec_sql_text(Blocked.sql_handle) AS BlockedSQL
ORDER BY WaitInSeconds
```

The DMVs/DMFs and joins involved in this script are largely the same as in the previous script, relating to waiting because of idle sessions with open transactions. Please see that script for greater detail. This script differs in that the filter based on AND er.session_id IS NULL has been removed, resulting in the inclusion of transactions with both active and idle sessions.

Again, knowing the SQL queries involved should be the starting point of examining and resolving any conflicts.

8.11 Queries waiting for more than 30 seconds

Queries that are blocked for a short time are probably of little concern, because this tends to be the normal pattern of usage with SQL Server. Perhaps of more concern are the queries that have been waiting for a longer time. Investigating them will allow you to determine why they're waiting and the cause of the blocking and will also provide you with clues as to how to reduce the waiting and increase throughput.

The script we use to find which queries are being blocked for more than 30 seconds by idle sessions with open transactions is shown here.

> **Listing 8.15   What has been blocked for more than 30 seconds**

```
SET TRANSACTION ISOLATION LEVEL READ UNCOMMITTED
SELECT
  Waits.wait_duration_ms / 1000 AS WaitInSeconds
  , Blocking.session_id as BlockingSessionId
  , Sess.login_name AS BlockingUser
  , Sess.host_name AS BlockingLocation
  , BlockingSQL.text AS BlockingSQL
  , Blocked.session_id AS BlockedSessionId
  , BlockedSess.login_name AS BlockedUser
  , BlockedSess.host_name AS BlockedLocation
  , BlockedSQL.text AS BlockedSQL
  , DB_NAME(Blocked.database_id) AS DatabaseName          ◁─┐ Blocker
FROM sys.dm_exec_connections AS Blocking                     │ joins
INNER JOIN sys.dm_exec_requests AS Blocked
        ON Blocking.session_id = Blocked.blocking_session_id
INNER JOIN sys.dm_exec_sessions Sess
        ON Blocking.session_id = sess.session_id
INNER JOIN sys.dm_tran_session_transactions st
        ON Blocking.session_id = st.session_id
LEFT OUTER JOIN sys.dm_exec_requests er
        ON st.session_id = er.session_id
            AND er.session_id IS NULL
INNER JOIN sys.dm_os_waiting_tasks AS Waits
        ON Blocked.session_id = Waits.session_id
CROSS APPLY sys.dm_exec_sql_text(Blocking.most_recent_sql_handle)
                                AS BlockingSQL
```

```
INNER JOIN sys.dm_exec_requests AS BlockedReq
        ON Waits.session_id = BlockedReq.session_id
INNER JOIN sys.dm_exec_sessions AS BlockedSess
        ON Waits.session_id = BlockedSess.session_id
CROSS APPLY sys.dm_exec_sql_text(Blocked.sql_handle) AS BlockedSQL
WHERE Waits.wait_duration_ms > 30000
ORDER BY WaitInSeconds
```

Blocked joins

This script is essentially the same as the previous one, in that it determines what's being blocked by open transactions, with an additional filter based on the waiting for a given time interval. Please see the previous script for more detail of the DMVs/DMFs and joins involved.

The script determines which queries have been blocked, for an interval of 30 seconds or more, by any open transactions. The results are sorted by the time spent waiting. It's possible to amend this time interval to include or exclude shorter or longer periods of waiting.

Having identified the query causing the most waiting, together with the queries being blocked, you can examine the SQL query to determine why the blocking is occurring. It's also possible to use the scripts in chapter 4 to obtain the cached plans for the queries; this again should help illustrate why blocking is occurring. Later, at the end of this chapter, I'll provide some tips on how blocking/waiting can be reduced.

Depending on what you're looking for (for example, open transactions with idle sessions), you could incorporate each of the scripts given in this section into the generic monitor job given in chapter 1.

Figure 8.7 shows an example of the type of output for this query.

	WaitInSeconds	BlockingSessionId	BlockingUser	BlockingSQL	BlockedSessionId	BlockedUser	BlockedSQL	DatabaseName
1	2307	51	MAI	-- 4. Start transaction,...	54	dbo	-- Change to working d...	IWS_Temp

Figure 8.7   Output showing what's waiting for more than 30 seconds

Having looked at various scripts pertaining to transactions and blocking, we'll next take a brief look at lock escalation and how it influences the range of locks within the database structure hierarchy.

8.12 *Lock escalation*

Locks are taken on data to ensure consistency of data. As the amount of data involved in a transaction increases, so does the number of locks. Because locks take up resources and require coordination, when the number of locks increases above a certain threshold (typically 5,000 objects), SQL Server will often escalate the low-level locks (for example, on rows) to fewer locks on higher-level objects (for example, page or table locks).

Locking higher-level objects typically provides greater performance for the running query but reduced concurrency for other queries that would like to run. You might argue that SQL Server isn't always correct in escalating the low-level locks to high-level locks because it can significantly reduce concurrency.

Lock escalation can be responsible for increased occurrence of blocking and deadlocks. With this in mind, it may be desirable to reduce the occurrence of lock escalation. Details on how to do this follow.

In SQL Server 2008 it's possible to prevent this automatic lock escalation on a table-by-table basis. The syntax is as follows:

```
ALTER TABLE SchemaName.TableName SET (LOCK_ESCALATION = DISABLE)
```

It's also possible to prevent lock escalation in SQL Server 2005, using more tortuous methods. Two such methods follow; either of these scripts could be added as a startup stored procedure:

```
BEGIN TRAN
SELECT *
FROM dbo.tblCountry WITH (UPDLOCK, HOLDLOCK)
WHERE 1=2
```

or

```
BEGIN TRAN
DELETE FROM dbo.tblCountry
WHERE 1=2
```

It's also possible to set trace flag 1211 to disable lock escalation for all tables or set trace flag 1224 to disable lock escalation only when there are memory pressures.

Remember that automatic lock escalation exists for a reason—that reason being to optimize the use and coordination of resources that locks acquire—so you should change the default implementation only after due consideration and testing.

8.13 *How to reduce blocking*

Blocking in SQL Server is normal and to be expected. But excessive blocking, with its resultant decrease in performance, scalability, and concurrency, is not. In essence, you should aim to run SQL queries with the minimum of blocking but still maintain the integrity and consistency of the underlying data.

With this in mind, I'll provide a number of methods that you can use to reduce the amount of blocking. As in much of life, there are conflicting interests that need to be balanced. For example, adding columns as an INCLUDE to an index may be great for a given SELECT query but may increase the time taken for INSERTs (and thus extend the interval locks/transactions are held).

Look at the many scripts given in this book, over the many different areas; most of them aim to improve the performance of your database, which in itself should help reduce the amount of blocking.

A brief description of some of the methods that can be used to reduce blocking is given in table 8.9.

Table 8.9 Methods to reduce blocking

Method	Description
Process the required rows quickly.	To process the required rows quickly, you'll often need to implement indexes. Remember that indexes are great for quickly selecting data but often have an overhead when modifying data (DELETE, INSERT/UPDATE). That said, modification queries often have a WHERE clause, so they may use an index themselves.
	The clustered index should be used for the most important range-based queries, where you want most of the row's data and in the order specified by the index. For example, if the most important query is the production of month-end invoices, you might consider a clustered index on the invoice date.
	Checking the output from the various scripts in chapter 3 will allow you to determine whether you should consider implementing any missing indexes.
	Because indexes can be detrimental to the performance of modification queries, you can use the scripts in chapter 3 to identify, and possibly remove, indexes that aren't used or have a high maintenance cost.
	If you know which indexes are being used (from the cached plan or from the script in chapter 3, section 3.7), you can ensure that they are optimal. Again, you can use the scripts in chapter 3 to ensure that the index's statistics are up to date with an optimal sample size, that fragmentation is minimal, and that the fill factor has an appropriate setting (full for relatively static data but having space if there are updates).
	You can check the cached plans to ensure the number of key lookups is minimal (or perhaps INCLUDE the lookup column as part of the index). You should examine table scans and index scans to determine if they're appropriate.
	Where possible, you should place tempdb and any important indexes on different disks, each with its own disk controller; this should help improve query performance. You might also want to place tables that are commonly joined together on their own separate disks.
	Databases typically hold data for a large time period, often many months or years. Because you're often interested in only the last few days or months of data, it makes sense (if you have SQL Server 2008 or higher) to take advantage of filtered indexes and their associated filtered statistics. It may be possible to produce a version of the database that reflects only a few days' or months' worth of data.
	Again, if you have SQL Server 2008 or higher, you might want to use compression. Compression allows more data to be held on a page. There's a cost to uncompressing the data, but typically this is compensated for by the improved I/O (most database systems I've seen tend to be limited by I/O and not CPU). Typically, compression has the biggest impact on queries that extract data based on a range.
	It's also possible to partition large tables; this in essence splits the table horizontally, typically by month. Any locks are typically restricted to a given partition rather than the whole table, leading to reduced locking and better concurrency.

Table 8.9   Methods to reduce blocking *(continued)*

Method	Description
Process only the data you need.	The smaller the number of rows you need to select or modify, the smaller the number of locks held. Supplying a WHERE clause to your queries will help with this. Processing only the columns you require will also reduce the size of the dataset. Too often additional columns are retrieved in the hope they might be useful. If you need to process a large number of rows, you could consider breaking up the rows into smaller processing units. For example, if you need to update many accounts, you might want to execute them in units that are split by the first letter of the account name or by account numbers within a certain range.
Schedule the job when nothing else is running.	There may be times when your system is processing little data. It may be possible to reschedule some jobs to run when nothing else is happening in the system, thus reducing the opportunity for blocking.
Take advantage of asynchronous processing.	If the updates aren't immediately required, it may be possible to use asynchronous processing to limit the number of blocks. For example, you could use Service Broker to store intermediate results until they're ready to be processed further. This has the additional benefit of control over the order of resource usage, which can be beneficial in reducing both blocking and deadlocks.
Use a lower isolation level.	Often SELECTs can be blocked by modification queries (and the reverse). If the data being queried is sufficiently distinct from the data being modified, setting the transaction isolation level of a batch of SELECT queries to READ UNCOMMITTED will ignore any locks, and the amount of blocking will be reduced. It's possible to produce a similar effect by using the NOLOCK hint on the tables in the SELECT statements. Regarding the distinctness of the modification and select queries, often in a business the people who run SELECTs on the data are aware of and responsible for any updates on their underlying data. Knowing this should give credence to this solution.

Set the LOCK_TIMEOUT value.	It's possible to limit the amount of time a query waits for a lock to be released (that is, the time it spends waiting) by setting the LOCK_TIMEOUT property within a batch of SQL. For example, the following code ensures the SELECT statement will wait 5 seconds (5000 milliseconds) for any locks to be released. If the locks are still present after 5 seconds, an error (error number 1222) is raised.
	
	`SET LOCK_TIMEOUT 5000`
	`SELECT * FROM [dbo].[tblCountry]`
	
	It's possible to handle this error in your SQL code, in a manner similar to how deadlocks can be handled (for example, wait a given period and retry the query a given number of times, in the hope that the locking will pass). To return LOCK_TIMEOUT to its default setting (wait forever) set it to -1.

Set the TIMEOUT value on clients.	For certain clients, for example, .NET web applications, it's possible to specify how long a query is allowed to run before it should time out. Any timed-out queries can be resubmitted using the same pattern as for deadlock retries given earlier. This can be used to reduce the amount of blocking and prevent runaway queries on SQL Server.

8.14 *How to reduce deadlocks*

Many of the suggestions given to reduce blocking apply equally to reducing deadlocks, which result from circular blocking. If you can reduce the time it takes to process data, then locks are held less, and the incidence of blocking and deadlocks should be reduced.

Sometimes deadlocks occur when two queries start to escalate their locks; again it may be possible to prevent or reduce this lock escalation (see the previous section). A brief description of some of the methods that can be used to reduce deadlocks is given in table 8.10.

Table 8.10 Methods to reduce deadlocks

Method	Description
Process resources in the same order.	If different routines access resources (for example, tables) in the same order, they'll typically acquire and release locks in the same order. This should help prevent the primary cause of deadlocks, where each routine holds the resource the other routine requires.
Automatically retry after getting a deadlock.	A script presented in an earlier deadlock section provides template code for handling deadlocks. In essence, when a deadlock occurs, the client can wait awhile (hoping that the other query will finish or free up its locks) and then retry a given number of times.
Hold an update lock on relevant SELECTs.	As stated earlier, deadlocks occur because two queries each hold a resource and then want the resource that the other query owns. If you apply an UPDATE lock hint to the SELECT statement, this will ensure that any other query will wait for the associated update to finish before obtaining the data, reducing the incidence of deadlocks.
	An example of this is shown in the following script:
	```\nBEGIN TRAN\nDECLARE @key INT\nSELECT @key = KeyId\nFROM dbo.SomeTable\nWHERE SomeField = 99\nIF @key IS NOT NULL\nBEGIN\n UPDATE dbo.SomeTable\n SET SomeOtherField = 1\nEND\nCOMMIT\n```
	In the script, some information (KeyId) is obtained from the table named dbo.SomeTable. This information is used subsequently to decide whether to update the table. There could be another query running similar code (but it selects the record that's currently requires updating and wants to update the record that has currently been selected); this would result in a deadlock. Adding an update lock hint to the SELECT will ensure the lock on the SELECT is held until the record is committed or rolled back. The SELECT statement needs to change to the following:
	```\nSELECT @key = KeyId\nFROM dbo.SomeTable WITH (UPDLOCK)\nWHERE SomeField = 99\n```

Table 8.10   Methods to reduce deadlocks *(continued)*

Method	Description
Add another index.	Microsoft support has estimated that 50% of deadlocks that occur in production systems can be eliminated by applying an appropriate index. The premise is that getting data from the index instead of the underlying table obviates locking.
	Looking at the deadlock information given in the SQL Server error log should identify the SQL queries involved in the deadlocks. Examining the SQL code along with its cached plans should help identify the area of conflict and its potential solution.
Keep transactions short.	Keeping processing times short helps ensure that there's less opportunity for blocking or deadlocks. It may be possible to offload some of the query's work to asynchronous processing. Service Broker can be an ideal tool for this. Candidates for asynchronous processing include email confirmation and job completion confirmation.

8.15   Summary

Congratulations on making it to the end of the chapter! I hope you now have a better understanding of locks, blocks, deadlocks, and transactions. Although the small case study provided was quite simple, hopefully it allowed adequate discussion of the underlying concepts provided by the scripts.

I provided several template scripts, for example, deadlock handling, as a base for your own developments. The core scripts will allow you to investigate blocking, identifying the SQL queries involved, the blocked resources, and the id of the user/machine causing the blocking.

We discussed various methods of reducing both blocking and deadlocking. Following these guidelines should lead to queries that have better performance, greater concurrency, and less blocking.

Next we'll look at the varied group of database-related DMVs. We'll look at topics including memory problems and indexes with hotspots, with a view to investigating and fixing problems they highlight.

Database-level DMVs

This chapter covers a miscellany of functionality that collectively belongs to the database DMVs. We'll examine and discuss the importance of tempdb, how its space is used by different objects, how much space is used by individual sessions and running tasks, and why it's important to monitor. If tempdb has problems, it can affect all the databases on SQL Server. Typically tempdb problems are reported in the SQL Server error log. We'll examine how to check tempdb for potential problems and how to fix them, as we'll look at a list of tempdb best practices.

We'll investigate various aspects of index contention and explore solutions. Topics include indexes under locking pressure, lock escalations, indexes with page splits, and metrics about how tables and indexes are specifically used. All these scripts will provide opportunities to identify problem areas and optimize the performance of your tables and indexes.

First, let's look at why tempdb is such an important database, what it's used for, and how it's used.

9.1 Space usage in tempdb

Here we'll examine and discuss the importance of tempdb, see how to determine the amount of total and free space it has, and drill down into the amount of space used by the different types of objects it contains.

Tempdb is a shared resource. All the databases on a given SQL Server instance share tempdb. It typically has more activity and transactions than all the other databases put together. If tempdb has problems, it can impact all the other databases on the server, thus highlighting the importance of keeping tempdb problem free.

When you query the DMVs that relate to tempdb space usages, they report values based on the number of pages of data. Each page represents 8 KB of data, so if you multiply the page count values by 8.0, you get the amount of data as kilobytes. Alternatively, you can multiply the page count by 8.0 and then divide by 1024 to get the amount of data as megabytes (MB). Where possible, I'll convert the metrics to this more familiar unit.

9.1.1 What is tempdb?

Tempdb is a database. There's only one per SQL Server instance, and it's used by all the other databases on the server. When SQL queries running on your databases need to work with transient data, for example, sorting data, this takes place in tempdb. SQL Server itself also makes extensive use of tempdb. Tempdb holds temporary data, and when the server is restarted, tempdb is rebuilt using a definition from the model database.

Tempdb holds information relating to user objects, internal objects, and version store data. A list of some of the more common objects associated with each type is shown in table 9.1.

Table 9.1 Objects in tempdb

DMV/Object	Description
User objects	Local temporary tables and indexes
	Global temporary tables and indexes
	Table variables
	User-defined tables and indexes
Internal objects	Sort results
	Hash joins
	XML variables
	Work tables for cursors

Table 9.1   Objects in tempdb *(continued)*

DMV/Object	Description
Version store objects	Temporary large object (LOB) storage
	Spool operations that store intermediate results
	Snapshot isolation
	Triggers
	Multiple active result sets (MARS)
	Online index build

When a server experiences problems, tempdb is a typical area to check. Checking its free space will either eliminate it from your concerns or require you to investigate further, perhaps drilling down on the individual sessions and tasks using it. You can determine how much space tempdb has free by using the DMV sys.dm_db_space_usage. We'll investigate this next.

9.1.2   *Total, free, and used space in tempdb*

As part of the normal housekeeping tasks, it makes sense to regularly check tempdb for space usage. Recording this over a period of time will allow you to plan for future space usage before it becomes an urgent problem that needs to be fixed.

The script I use to find the amount of space (total, used, and free) in tempdb is shown in this listing.

Listing 9.1   Amount of space (total, used, and free) in tempdb

```
SET TRANSACTION ISOLATION LEVEL READ UNCOMMITTED

SELECT SUM(user_object_reserved_page_count
        + internal_object_reserved_page_count
        + version_store_reserved_page_count
        + mixed_extent_page_count
        + unallocated_extent_page_count) * (8.0/1024.0)
                    AS [TotalSizeOfTempDB(MB)]
    , SUM(user_object_reserved_page_count
        + internal_object_reserved_page_count
        + version_store_reserved_page_count
        + mixed_extent_page_count) * (8.0/1024.0)
                    AS [UsedSpace (MB)]
    , SUM(unallocated_extent_page_count * (8.0/1024.0))
AS [FreeSpace (MB)]
FROM sys.dm_db_file_space_usage
```

The script calculates the total size of the tempdb database space by summing the value of the following columns, across all the files that make up tempdb:

- user_object_reserved_page_count
- internal_object_reserved_page_count
- version_store_reserved_page_count
- mixed_extent_page_count
- unallocated_extent_page_count

The amount of used space is calculated by summing the value of the following columns, across all the files that make up tempdb:

- user_object_reserved_page_count
- internal_object_reserved_page_count
- version_store_reserved_page_count
- mixed_extent_page_count

Finally, the amount of free space is calculated by summing the value of the column unallocated_extent_page_count, across all the files that make up tempdb.

In all cases, because the column values relate to the number of database pages, I've multiplied the value by 8 (one page is 8 KB in size) and divided the result by 1024 to calculate the sizes as megabytes. Mixed extents are pages that contain a mixture of different object types.

An example of the type of output for this query is shown in figure 9.1.

The output in this example shows that the total size of tempdb is about 98 gigabytes (100857.5 / 1024), of which about 1 gigabyte is currently being used, and 97 gigabytes are unused.

Monitoring this output over time will allow you to determine the pattern of tempdb usage, perhaps identifying periods when it's nearing its size limit. In this case, it makes sense to preempt the file growth and expand tempdb before an increase is needed. I've experienced several occasions where the client code (for example, a .NET client) has terminated with a timeout error because the database has been busy growing its files.

You could use the metrics relating to the amount of free space to determine at runtime if a routine that uses a lot of tempdb space should be run now or be rescheduled to run when more space is available.

It's also possible to obtain details of the size of all the files that make up the database, not just tempdb, by querying the sys.dm_os_performance_counters DMV. The output includes the total size of the data file, the log file, and the amount of the log file that has been used.

The script we use to find the total amount of space (data, log, and log used) in each of the databases on the server is shown in the following listing.

	TotalSizeOfTempDB(MB)	UsedSpace (MB)	FreeSpace (MB)
1	100857.544704	1057.744800	99799.799904

Figure 9.1
Output showing space (total, used, and free) in tempdb

Listing 9.2   Total amount of space (data, log, and log used) by database

```
SET TRANSACTION ISOLATION LEVEL READ UNCOMMITTED
SELECT instance_name
, counter_name
, cntr_value / 1024.0 AS [Size(MB)]
FROM sys.dm_os_performance_counters
WHERE object_name = 'SQLServer:Databases'
AND counter_name IN (
'Data File(s) Size (KB)'
, 'Log File(s) Size (KB)'
, 'Log File(s) Used Size (KB)')
ORDER BY instance_name, counter_name
```

This script queries the sys.dm_os_performance_counters DMV for information relating to database file sizes. It does this by selecting counters where the object name is equal to 'SQLServer: Databases' and the counter name is one of the following: 'Data File(s) Size (KB)', 'Log File(s) Size (KB)', or 'Log File(s) Used Size (KB)'. The output is sorted by database name (instance_name) and counter_name (type of data file).

Sample output for this query is shown in figure 9.2.

Although it's interesting to know how much total space is used or free, you can get more detailed information about both by drilling further into the sys.dm_db_space_usage DMV. We'll discuss this next.

	instanc...	counter_name	Size(MB)
18	mssqls...	Log File(s) Used Size (KB)	0.273437
19	Paris	Data File(s) Size (KB)	2836965.000000
20	Paris	Log File(s) Size (KB)	308223.929687
21	Paris	Log File(s) Used Size (KB)	170.159179
22	Paris_...	Data File(s) Size (KB)	606115.000000
23	Paris_...	Log File(s) Size (KB)	66815.929687
24	Paris_...	Log File(s) Used Size (KB)	214.800781
25	Sys_S...	Data File(s) Size (KB)	3.000000
26	Sys_S...	Log File(s) Size (KB)	0.992187
27	Sys_S...	Log File(s) Used Size (KB)	0.514648
28	tempdb	Data File(s) Size (KB)	106752.000000
29	tempdb	Log File(s) Size (KB)	45055.992187
30	tempdb	Log File(s) Used Size (KB)	28809.623046

Figure 9.2   Output showing space usage (data and log) by database

9.1.3   *Tempdb total space usage by object type*

In the previous section you saw that tempdb can contain various types of objects, namely, user-defined, internal, and version store objects. Examining the amount of space used by each area (and how it changes over a given time interval) can be useful in preempting and highlighting the cause of space problems.

The script we use to find the total amount of tempdb space used by object type is shown here.

Listing 9.3   Tempdb total space usage by object type

```
SET TRANSACTION ISOLATION LEVEL READ UNCOMMITTED
SELECT
    SUM (user_object_reserved_page_count) * (8.0/1024.0)
        AS [User Objects (MB)],
```

```
    SUM (internal_object_reserved_page_count) * (8.0/1024.0)
            AS [Internal Objects (MB)],
    SUM (version_store_reserved_page_count) * (8.0/1024.0)
          AS [Version Store (MB)],
    SUM (mixed_extent_page_count)* (8.0/1024.0)
            AS [Mixed Extent (MB)],
    SUM (unallocated_extent_page_count)* (8.0/1024.0)
            AS [Unallocated (MB)]
FROM sys.dm_db_file_space_usage
```

This script queries the sys.dm_db_file_space_usage DMV, summing up for each of the tempdb files the total space used by user objects, internal objects, and version store objects.

Again, monitoring this output over time will allow you to determine the pattern of usage, as determined by the various component areas of the tempdb database. If too much space is being used, it may be possible to reschedule some SQL queries to run at another time, when the server is less busy.

An example of the type of output for this query is shown in figure 9.3.

	User Objects (MB)	Internal Objects (MB)	Version Store (MB)	Mixed Extent (MB)	Unallocated (MB)
1	742.764960	180.300960	1.062432	39.434976	99893.981376

Figure 9.3   Output showing tempdb space usage by object type

The output shows that 743 MB of tempdb is used by user objects, 180 MB by internal objects, 1 MB by version store, and 39 MB by mixed extents.

Now we've identified the types of object and the space they're consuming, it would be worthwhile to drill down on the sessions that have used this space. This would allow us to identify specific sessions (users/connections) that might be causing space usage problems.

9.2   Session usage in tempdb

In addition to looking at how much space is used by each of the object types within tempdb, you can also see how much space each session has used. This can be useful for identifying the job or person that's using most of tempdb or is displaying a pattern of usage that could be causing space problems now or in the future.

Here we'll look at how much tempdb space is used by sessions and how much of it has been released back to SQL Server to be reused. Sessions that make excessive use of tempdb space can lead to problems with other sessions that use tempdb and might necessitate the rescheduling of certain SQL queries.

The core DMV used is sys.dm_db_session_space_usage. This contains, for each session, details of the number of pages allocated (and de-allocated) for both user objects and internal objects, for completed batches of SQL queries.

9.2.1   *Session usage of tempdb space*

This script shows you how much space each session has used in tempdb. It shows both allocated page counts and de-allocated (reclaimed) page counts, for a batch of SQL queries that have completed. Ideally, any allocated storage would be reclaimed relatively quickly. If this is not being done, it perhaps indicates some coordination problems within SQL Server itself.

The script used to find the space usage by session is shown in the following listing.

Listing 9.4   Space usage by session

```
SET TRANSACTION ISOLATION LEVEL READ UNCOMMITTED

SELECT es.session_id
  , ec.connection_id
  , es.login_name
  , es.host_name
  , st.text
  , su.user_objects_alloc_page_count
  , su.user_objects_dealloc_page_count
  , su.internal_objects_alloc_page_count
  , su.internal_objects_dealloc_page_count
  , ec.last_read
  , ec.last_write
  , es.program_name
FROM sys.dm_db_session_space_usage su
INNER JOIN sys.dm_exec_sessions es
        ON su.session_id = es.session_id
LEFT OUTER JOIN sys.dm_exec_connections ec
        ON su.session_id = ec.most_recent_session_id
OUTER APPLY sys.dm_exec_sql_text(ec.most_recent_sql_handle) st
WHERE su.session_id > 50
```

You can see that three DMVs and one DMF are involved in finding the space used by sessions of completed batches. A brief description of each is given shown in table 9.2.

Table 9.2   DMVs/DMF that show the tempdb space used by sessions for completed batches

DMV/DMF	Description
sys.dm_db_session_space_usage	Contains details of space used by user and internal objects for each session
sys.dm_exec_sessions	Contains details of sessions on SQL Server
sys.dm_exec_connections	Contains details of connections to SQL Server
sys.dm_exec_sql_text	DMF that returns the SQL text identified by a given sql_handle or plan_handle

The joining of the DMVs and the DMF provides us with enough information to identify the tempdb space used by each session, for completed batches, across all the databases on the server. The DMVs sys.dm_db_session_space_usage, sys.dm_exec_sessions,

Figure 9.4   Output showing tempdb space usage by session, for completed batches

and sys.dm_exec_connections are joined on their common key column session_id. The connection contains the column most_recent_sql_handle, which is passed to the DMF sys.dm_exec_sql_text to retrieve the text of the SQL query. A LEFT OUTER JOIN is used to join sys.dm_exec_sessions and sys.dm_exec_connections because a session can have multiple connections. We filter out any system sessions that have a session_id of 50 or less. An example of the type of output for this query is shown in figure 9.4.

The output shows the relevant space columns together with details of the session and connection that allow you to report on where the query is running from (host_name), who is running the SQL query (login_name), together with the text of the last-completed SQL query. If space usage is a problem (as reported in the SQL Server error log), you can use this output to determine which session/user/SQL query is consuming the most space and how that space is composed (user object or internal objects), with a view to taking corrective action. Such action includes rescheduling the queries to run at a time when more resources are available or rewriting the relevant query to use less tempdb space, for example, replacing a hash join with a nested loop join.

9.2.2   Space used and not reclaimed in tempdb by session

This script shows you how much space is still being used by the completed batches of SQL queries. Usually, any allocated space is reclaimed. This script is useful in showing which sessions still have tempdb space associated with them.

Listing 9.5   Space used and reclaimed in tempdb for completed batches

```
SET TRANSACTION ISOLATION LEVEL READ UNCOMMITTED

SELECT  CAST(SUM(su.user_objects_alloc_page_count
        + su.internal_objects_alloc_page_count) * (8.0/1024.0)
                    AS DECIMAL(20,3)) AS [SpaceUsed(MB)]
      , CAST(SUM(su.user_objects_alloc_page_count
          - su.user_objects_dealloc_page_count
          + su.internal_objects_alloc_page_count
          -  su.internal_objects_dealloc_page_count)
          * (8.0/1024.0) AS DECIMAL(20,3)) AS [SpaceStillUsed(MB)]
      , su.session_id
      , ec.connection_id
      , es.login_name
```

```
        , es.host_name
        , st.text AS [LastQuery]
        , ec.last_read
        , ec.last_write
        , es.program_name
FROM sys.dm_db_session_space_usage su
INNER JOIN sys.dm_exec_sessions es ON su.session_id = es.session_id
LEFT OUTER JOIN sys.dm_exec_connections ec
        ON su.session_id = ec.most_recent_session_id
OUTER APPLY sys.dm_exec_sql_text(ec.most_recent_sql_handle) st
WHERE su.session_id > 50
GROUP BY su.session_id, ec.connection_id, es.login_name, es.host_name
        , st.text, ec.last_read, ec.last_write, es.program_name
ORDER BY [SpaceStillUsed(MB)] DESC
```

This script uses three DMVs and one DMF to find the space used and not reclaimed by sessions; a brief description of each is given in table 9.3.

Table 9.3 DMVs/DMF that reveal tempdb space used and not reclaimed by sessions for completed batches

DMV/DMF	Description
sys.dm_db_session_space_usage	Contains details of space used by user and internal objects for each session. Specifically, contains the number of pages allocated and de-allocated by each session.
sys.dm_exec_sessions	Contains details of sessions on SQL Server.
sys.dm_exec_connections	Contains details of connections to SQL Server.
sys.dm_exec_sql_text	DMF that returns the SQL text identified by a given sql_handle or plan_handle.

Joining the DMVs and the DMF gives us enough information to identify the tempdb space used and not reclaimed by each session, across all the databases on the server. The DMVs sys.dm_db_session_space_usage, sys.dm_exec_sessions, and sys.dm_exec_connections are joined on their common key column session_id. The connection contains the column most_recent_sql_handle, which is passed to the DMF sys.dm_exec_sql_text to retrieve the text of the SQL query. A LEFT OUTER JOIN is used to join sys.dm_exec_sessions and sys.dm_exec_connections because a session can have multiple connections.

Any system sessions that have a session_id of 50 or less are filtered out. The amount of space used by a session is calculated by summing user_objects_alloc_page_count and internal_objects_alloc_page_count. Similarly, the amount of space not reclaimed is calculated as the difference between user_objects_alloc_page_count and user_objects_dealloc_page_count added to the difference between internal_objects_alloc_page_count and internal_objects_dealloc_page_count. The results are sorted by the amount of space each session still owns. An example of the type of output for this query is shown in figure 9.5.

Figure 9.5 Output showing tempdb space used and reclaimed by session

The output shows, for completed batches, the amount of space in tempdb that each session still has associated with it, along with details of the session and connection that allow you to report on where the query is running from (host_name), who is running the SQL query (login_name), and the text of the last-completed SQL query. If space usage is a problem (as reported in the SQL Server error log), you can use the output to determine which session/user/SQL query is using the most space, with a view to taking corrective action. Such action includes rescheduling the queries to run at a time when more resources are available or rewriting the relevant query to use less tempdb space, for example, replacing a hash join with a nested loop join.

Having looked at how space is used in tempdb by the different object types and completed sessions, we'll now look at how active batches of SQL (sometimes called *tasks*) make use of tempdb space.

9.3 Task usage in tempdb

Tasks are batches of SQL queries that are currently running. Analyzing these can be useful when you're debugging space issues on production databases in real time.

Here we'll look at how much tempdb space is used by tasks and how much of it has been released by SQL Server to be reused. Tasks that make excessive use of tempdb space can lead to problems for other SQL queries that use tempdb and might necessitate the rescheduling of certain SQL queries.

The core DMV used is sys.dm_db_task_space_usage, which contains, for each session, details of the number of pages allocated (and de-allocated) for both user objects and internal objects, for currently active batches of SQL queries.

9.3.1 Space used by running SQL queries

This script shows you how much space each session is using in tempdb. It shows both allocated page counts and de-allocated (reclaimed) page counts, for a batch of SQL queries that are currently active. Ideally, any allocated storage would be reclaimed relatively quickly. If this isn't the case, it perhaps indicates some coordination problems within SQL Server itself.

The script used to find the space usage by task is given in the following listing.

Listing 9.6   Space usage by task

```
SET TRANSACTION ISOLATION LEVEL READ UNCOMMITTED

SELECT es.session_id
  , ec.connection_id
  , es.login_name
  , es.host_name
  , st.text
  , tu.user_objects_alloc_page_count
  , tu.user_objects_dealloc_page_count
  , tu.internal_objects_alloc_page_count
  , tu.internal_objects_dealloc_page_count
  , ec.last_read
  , ec.last_write
  , es.program_name
FROM sys.dm_db_task_space_usage tu
INNER JOIN sys.dm_exec_sessions es ON tu.session_id = es.session_id
LEFT OUTER JOIN sys.dm_exec_connections ec
        ON tu.session_id = ec.most_recent_session_id
OUTER APPLY sys.dm_exec_sql_text(ec.most_recent_sql_handle) st
WHERE tu.session_id > 50
```

In the listing, you can see that three DMVs and one DMF are involved in finding the space used by sessions of currently active batches. Table 9.4 provides a brief description of each.

Table 9.4   DMVs/DMF used to show tempdb space used by sessions for active batches

DMV/DMF	Description
sys.dm_db_task_space_usage	Contains details of space used by user and internal objects for each session, for active SQL queries
sys.dm_exec_sessions	Contains details of sessions on SQL Server
sys.dm_exec_connections	Contains details of connections to SQL Server
sys.dm_exec_sql_text	DMF that returns the SQL text identified by a given sql_handle

By joining the DMVs and the DMF, we obtain enough information to identify the tempdb space used by each session, for active batches, across all the databases on the server. The DMVs sys.dm_db_task_space_usage, sys.dm_exec_sessions, and sys.dm_exec_connections are joined on their common key column session_id. The connection contains the column most_recent_sql_handle, which is passed to the DMF sys.dm_exec_sql_text to retrieve the text of the SQL query. A LEFT OUTER JOIN is used to join sys.dm_exec_sessions and sys.dm_exec_connections because a session can have multiple connections. We filter out any system sessions that have a session_id of 50 or less. An example of the type of output for this query is shown in figure 9.6.

The output shows the relevant space columns together with details of the session and connection that allow us to report on where the query is running from

Figure 9.6 Output showing tempdb space usage by object type, for active batches

(host_name), who is running the SQL query (login_name), and the text of the last-completed SQL query. If space usage is a problem (as reported in the SQL Server error log), you can use the output to determine which session/user/SQL query is using the most space and how that space is composed (user object or internal objects), with a view to taking corrective action. Such action includes rescheduling the queries to run at a time when more resources are available or rewriting the relevant query to use less tempdb space, for example, replacing a hash join with a nested loop join.

9.3.2 Space used and not reclaimed by active SQL queries

This script shows you how much space is still being used by the active batches of SQL queries. Usually, any allocated space is reclaimed. This script is useful in showing which sessions still have tempdb space associated with them.

Listing 9.7 Space used and not reclaimed in tempdb for active batches

```
SET TRANSACTION ISOLATION LEVEL READ UNCOMMITTED

SELECT   SUM(ts.user_objects_alloc_page_count
             + ts.internal_objects_alloc_page_count)
           * (8.0/1024.0) AS [SpaceUsed(MB)]
         , SUM(ts.user_objects_alloc_page_count
             - ts.user_objects_dealloc_page_count
             + ts.internal_objects_alloc_page_count
             - ts.internal_objects_dealloc_page_count)
                     * (8.0/1024.0) AS [SpaceStillUsed(MB)]
         , ts.session_id
         , ec.connection_id
         , es.login_name
         , es.host_name
         , st.text AS [Parent Query]
         , SUBSTRING (st.text,(er.statement_start_offset/2) + 1,
           ((CASE WHEN er.statement_end_offset = -1
           THEN LEN(CONVERT(NVARCHAR(MAX), st.text)) * 2
           ELSE er.statement_end_offset
           END - er.statement_start_offset)/2) + 1) AS [Current Query]
         , ec.last_read
         , ec.last_write
         , es.program_name
```

```
FROM sys.dm_db_task_space_usage ts
INNER JOIN sys.dm_exec_sessions es ON ts.session_id = es.session_id
LEFT OUTER JOIN sys.dm_exec_connections ec
        ON ts.session_id = ec.most_recent_session_id
OUTER APPLY sys.dm_exec_sql_text(ec.most_recent_sql_handle) st
LEFT OUTER JOIN sys.dm_exec_requests er ON ts.session_id = er.session_id
WHERE ts.session_id > 50
GROUP BY ts.session_id, ec.connection_id, es.login_name, es.host_name
        , st.text, ec.last_read, ec.last_write, es.program_name
        , SUBSTRING (st.text,(er.statement_start_offset/2) + 1,
          ((CASE WHEN er.statement_end_offset = -1
            THEN LEN(CONVERT(NVARCHAR(MAX), st.text)) * 2
            ELSE er.statement_end_offset
            END - er.statement_start_offset)/2) + 1)
ORDER BY [SpaceStillUsed(MB)] DESC
```

As you can see, three DMVs and one DMF are involved in finding the space used and not reclaimed by sessions; a brief description of each is shown in table 9.5.

Table 9.5   DMVs/DMF that reveal tempdb space used and not reclaimed by sessions for active batches

DMV/DMF	Description
sys.dm_db_task_space_usage	Contains details of space used by user and internal objects for each session, for active SQL queries
sys.dm_exec_sessions	Contains details of sessions on SQL Server
sys.dm_exec_connections	Contains details of connections to SQL Server
sys.dm_exec_sql_text	DMF that returns the SQL text identified by a given sql_handle

The joining of the DMVs and the DMF produces enough information to identify the tempdb space used and not reclaimed by each session, across all the databases on the server. The DMVs sys.dm_db_task_space_usage, sys.dm_exec_sessions, and sys.dm_exec_connections are joined on their common key column session_id. The connection contains the column most_recent_sql_handle, which is passed to the DMF sys.dm_exec_sql_text to retrieve the text of the SQL query. A LEFT OUTER JOIN is used to join sys.dm_exec_sessions and sys.dm_exec_connections because a session can have multiple connections.

Any system sessions that have a session_id of 50 or less are filtered out. The amount of space used by a task is calculated by summing user_objects_alloc_page_count and internal_objects_alloc_page_count. Similarly, the amount of space not reclaimed is calculated as the sum of the difference between user_objects_alloc_page_count and user_objects_dealloc_page_count and the difference between internal_objects_alloc_page_count and internal_objects_dealloc_page_count. The results are sorted by the amount of space each session still owns. Sample output for this query is shown in figure 9.7.

Figure 9.7   Output showing tempdb space usage by object type

The output shows, for active batches, the amount of space in tempdb that each session still has associated with it, together with details of the session and connection that allow you to report on where the query is running from (host_name), who is running the SQL query (login_name), and the text of the last-completed SQL query. If space usage is a problem (as reported in the SQL Server error log), you can use the output to determine which session/user/SQL query is using the most space, with a view to taking corrective action. Such action includes rescheduling the queries to run at a time when more resources are available or rewriting the relevant query to use less tempdb space, for example, replacing a hash join with a nested loop join.

Having looked at how objects, sessions, and tasks make use of tempdb and the potential problems that can arise, I'll now provide some recommendations that should improve the usage of tempdb.

9.4   *Tempdb recommendations*

Tempdb is a shared resource, used by all the other databases on the server instance. Problems in tempdb can result in problems in any other database on SQL Server. You can use the recommendations given in table 9.6 to help optimize it.

Table 9.6   Tempdb recommendations

Recommendation	Description
Put tempdb on its own disk.	If tempdb has its own disk and controller, it doesn't contend with other databases for this resource, thus improving concurrency and performance.
Set tempdb's initial size appropriately.	When the server is rebooted, tempdb is created from the definition of the model database. Typically, the default values (8 MB data file and 1 MB transaction) are insufficient. If you monitor tempdb's size regularly, you'll know what value to set its initial size to.
Pre-grow tempdb.	Growing the size of database files can take time. I've seen cases where some client applications have terminated with timeout errors due to file growth happening. If you know the expected pattern of file growth, it makes sense to pre-grow the files. This applies to all databases files, not just tempdb. I would recommend you investigate Instant File Initialization (IFI), because it can dramatically speed up the growing of files. In addition, to minimize any impact on performance, any pre-growth should be done during quiet periods of activity.

Table 9.6   Tempdb recommendations (continued)

Recommendation	Description
Don't drop temporary tables explicitly.	I've seen the performance of some routines improve dramatically by not explicitly dropping temporary tables. The temp tables will automatically fall out of scope and the space will be reclaimed when SQL Server has time. In many ways, this is similar to how the garbage collector in .NET reclaims storage, when it is able to.
Monitor tempdb space usage regularly.	This can be daily or weekly or even monthly, depending on your system usage. The point I want to make is that monitoring should remove any upcoming surprises (make sure you actually read the output from the monitoring!).
Use multiple data files for tempdb.	Spreading tempdb over several files helps prevent the inherent contention problems that come with the shared usage of tempdb. One area of contention is around the pages that contain details of what is where on tempdb and its usage, for example, Page Free Space (PFS) and Shared Global Allocation Map (SGAM) pages. As a starting point, the number of files should equal the number of processor cores. These different files should be the same size because this allows SQL Server's round-robin algorithm to spread the load more easily.

Having looked at tempdb and its space usage, we'll now look at another group of database-related DMVs that relate to index contention.

9.5   *Index contention*

The DMV sys.dm_db_index_operational_stats can be used to extract lots of valuable information concerning indexes. This information includes identifying indexes under locking pressure, escalated locks on indexes, and the occurrence of page splits. I'll explain each of these in the relevant section.

The sys.dm_db_index_operational_stats DMV takes four parameters:

- *Database_id*—Id of the database
- *Object_id*—Object id of the table or view the index is on
- *Index_id*—Id of the index
- *Partition_number*—Partition number of the object

In our case, we're typically interested in all the objects/indexes/partitions, so when we use the DMV, we supply the database_id as the id of the database the script is running in. All the other parameters are NULL, ensuring all information for the current database is reported.

In the scripts, the DMV is joined to various system views (sys.objects, sys.indexes, and sys.schemas) to allow descriptive information about the index to be reported on. In most of the listings, you'll see that one DMV and three system views are used. A brief description of each is given in table 9.7.

Table 9.7 DMV/system views used for investigating index contention

DMV/system view	Description
sys.dm_db_index_operational_stats	Contains details of low-level I/O, locking, latching for each index in the given database
sys.objects	Contains details of objects in the database
sys.indexes	Contains details of indexes in the database
sys.schemas	Contains details of schemas in the database

Often I see scripts that report on the number of times an event has occurred, for example, the number of times that index-locking pressure has occurred. Because users would typically experience problems in terms of waiting, I feel it's more appropriate to report on the time involved rather than the count values, even though there's probably a degree of correlation.

Within the results, instead of concentrating on specific indexes, it might make more sense to look for groups of indexes that have the same underlying table. This might indicate a fundamental problem with the underlying table, for example, the table may be over-indexed or incorrectly normalized.

In all the scripts in this section, you should run the script in the database about which you're recording the results. When I talk about data being *updated* or *modified*, I'm referring to data that is inserted, updated, or deleted, unless otherwise stated.

9.5.1 *Indexes under row-locking pressure*

When data in a table is being modified (that is, updated, inserted, or deleted), locks are taken on the associated indexes. If many queries are doing similar things, this locking may cause some queries to wait, increasing their duration and resulting in a decrease in their performance. Examining the indexes that are under the most locking pressure will allow you to investigate the cause of the excess pressure, with a view to reducing it, allowing better concurrency and performance.

The script we use to find the indexes under the most row-locking pressure is shown next.

Listing 9.8 Indexes under the most row-locking pressure

```
SET TRANSACTION ISOLATION LEVEL READ UNCOMMITTED
SELECT TOP 20
  x.name AS SchemaName
  , OBJECT_NAME(s.object_id) AS TableName
  , i.name AS IndexName
  , s.row_lock_wait_in_ms
  , s.row_lock_wait_count
FROM sys.dm_db_index_operational_stats(db_ID(), NULL, NULL, NULL) s
INNER JOIN sys.objects o ON s.object_id = o.object_id
```

```
INNER JOIN sys.indexes i ON s.index_id = i.index_id
                        AND i.object_id = o.object_id
INNER JOIN sys.schemas x ON x.schema_id = o.schema_id
WHERE s.row_lock_wait_in_ms > 0
  AND o.is_ms_shipped = 0
ORDER BY s.row_lock_wait_in_ms DESC
```

The DMV sys.dm_db_index_operational_stats is linked to the sys.object view via their common object_id key. Similarly, the DMV is linked to the sys.indexes view via their shared index_id key. The sys.objects view is linked to the sys.schemas view via their common schema_id key.

The script reports on the TOP 20 indexes that have the most locking pressure as shown by the row_lock_wait_in_ms column. The results are sorted by row_lock_wait_in_ms in descending order, so the most important ones are reported first. An example of the type of output for this query is shown in figure 9.8.

The output identifies the name of the schema, table, and index of the indexes that are under the most row-locking pressure. It shows the amount of time involved in waiting for the lock to clear (in milliseconds) and the number of times this locking occurred.

Examining the indexes that are under the most locking pressure will allow you to investigate why the locking is occurring. You could create a snapshot delta (see chapter 2 for details of this) to obtain details of the locking pressure along with which queries are running. An example of this is given toward the end of this chapter in the section titled "Indexes under row-locking pressure—snapshot version." You could then examine the relationship between these, allowing you to identify the queries causing the delay due to locking. In addition, searching the cached plans (chapter 4) will identify where these specific indexes are used. Knowing the problematic indexes and where they're used, you can aim to reduce the index contention.

Such methods that could reduce index contention include running the contended queries at different times, perhaps lowering the transaction isolation level, and creating new indexes allowing other access paths to reduce the contention.

The previous script looked at indexes under row-level locking pressure. It's possible to look at locking pressure at the page level by replacing the column row_lock_wait_in_ms with page_lock_wait_in_ms.

	SchemaName	TableName	IndexName	row_lock_wait_in_ms	row_lock_wait_count
1	dbo	Request	IX_Request_C...	681362	8
2	dbo	Deal	IX_Deal_2	154609	89
3	dbo	StagingReq...	PK__StagingR...	110734	31
4	dbo	Request	PK_Request	32768	28
5	dbo	PositionGrid...	IX_PositionGri...	25767	17

Figure 9.8   Output showing indexes under row-locking pressure

The high values reported might be indicative of too many conflicting and related queries running at the same time; better scheduling might alleviate the problem. I recommend that you revisit the section concerning recommendations for decreasing blocking in chapter 8 to review methods of decreasing contention.

9.5.2 *Escalated indexes*

SQL Server typically chooses an appropriate locking strategy for SQL queries; this is usually a row or page-level lock. But if more than a given number of objects (for example, 5,000 rows) need to be locked, SQL Server will often escalate (or promote) the lock to a higher level in the database object hierarchy (see chapter 8 for greater detail about this). The typical threshold for escalating locks is 5,000 objects. A query that has its locks escalated typically runs faster because less time is spent in the management of lower-level resources. Also, because the higher-level locks are taken, it should spend less time being blocked. Conversely, other related queries running at the same time as the escalated-locks query will typically run slower because they may experience blocking.

The script we use to find the indexes with most lock escalations follows.

Listing 9.9 Indexes with the most lock escalations

```
SET TRANSACTION ISOLATION LEVEL READ UNCOMMITTED

SELECT TOP 20
  x.name AS SchemaName
  , OBJECT_NAME (s.object_id) AS TableName
  , i.name AS IndexName
  , s.index_lock_promotion_count
FROM sys.dm_db_index_operational_stats(db_ID(), NULL, NULL, NULL) s
INNER JOIN sys.objects o ON s.object_id = o.object_id
INNER JOIN sys.indexes i ON s.index_id = i.index_id
                        AND i.object_id = o.object_id
INNER JOIN sys.schemas x ON x.schema_id = o.schema_id
WHERE s.index_lock_promotion_count > 0
  AND o.is_ms_shipped = 0
ORDER BY s.index_lock_promotion_count DESC
```

The script uses the same joins as the script in listing 9.8 (indexes under locking pressure) but reports on the column index_lock_promotion_count. The results are sorted by index_lock_promotion_count in descending order, so the most important ones are reported first. An example of the type of output for this query is shown in figure 9.9.

The output identifies the name of the schema, table, and index of the indexes that have had the most index-lock escalations.

Examining the indexes that have had the most index-lock escalations will allow you to investigate why the escalation is occurring. You could create a snapshot delta (see chapter 2 for details of this) to obtain details of the lock escalations, together

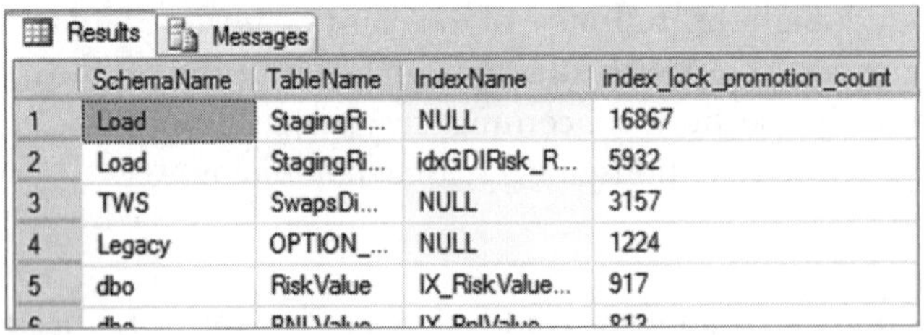

Figure 9.9
Output showing index-lock
promotion counts

with which queries are running. It should be possible to examine the relationship between these, allowing you to identify the queries causing the lock escalation. An example of this is given toward the end of this chapter in the section titled "Indexes under row-locking pressure—snapshot version." You could also search the cached plans (discussed in chapter 4) for details of where these indexes are used. Knowing the problematic indexes and where they're used, you can try to reduce the lock promotions.

High-value lock escalations might also indicate out-of-date statistics. The statistics contain details of the distribution and density of data values; this is used when creating a plan containing instruction on how the underlying data and indexes are used.

In addition, high values might be indicative of too many conflicting and related queries running at the same time. Better scheduling or providing another index (giving a different access path to the underlying data) might alleviate the problem. If you want the query to automatically acquire the higher locking level (to increase its performance), it's possible to achieve this using table hints.

9.5.3 *Unsuccessful index-lock promotions*

Not all lock promotions are successful. It may not be possible for the query to acquire the higher-level locks because of other SQL queries holding locks on related data. In this case, after every further 1,250 objects locked (above the aforementioned 5,000-objects threshold), escalation of the locks will be attempted again. Each time the escalation is attempted, the appropriate DMV columns are updated.

The script we use to find the indexes with the most unsuccessful lock escalations is shown in the following listing.

Listing 9.10 Indexes with the most unsuccessful lock escalations

```
SET TRANSACTION ISOLATION LEVEL READ UNCOMMITTED

SELECT TOP 20
    x.name AS SchemaName
  , OBJECT_NAME (s.object_id) AS TableName
  , i.name AS IndexName
```

```
      , s.index_lock_promotion_attempt_count - s.index_lock_promotion_count
                          AS UnsuccessfulIndexLockPromotions
FROM sys.dm_db_index_operational_stats(db_ID(), NULL, NULL, NULL) s
INNER JOIN sys.objects o ON s.object_id = o.object_id
INNER JOIN sys.indexes i ON s.index_id = i.index_id
                          AND i.object_id = o.object_id
INNER JOIN sys.schemas x ON x.schema_id = o.schema_id
WHERE (s.index_lock_promotion_attempt_count - index_lock_promotion_count)>0
  AND o.is_ms_shipped = 0
ORDER BY UnsuccessfulIndexLockPromotions DESC
```

The script uses the same joins as the script in listing 9.8 (indexes under locking pressure) but calculates the number of unsuccessful lock promotions as the difference between index_lock_promotion_count and index_lock_promotion_attempt_count. The results are sorted by the number of unsuccessful lock promotions, in descending order, so the most important ones are reported first. Sample output for this query is shown in figure 9.10.

The output identifies the name of the schema, table, and index of the indexes that have had the highest number of unsuccessful index-lock promotions. Again, creating a snapshot delta containing details of the SQL queries running at the time of the unsuccessful lock promotions will enable you to determine the cause of the lack of lock promotions. It may be that too many related jobs are running at the same time; scheduling should help with this.

If you want the query to automatically acquire the higher locking level to increase its performance, it's possible to achieve this using table hints. I recommend you revisit the section concerning recommendations for decreasing blocking in chapter 8 to review methods of decreasing contention.

9.5.4 Indexes with the most page splits

Page splits occur when data is updated or inserted and there's insufficient space on the page to hold the data. Page splits result in additional time being required to access the data. Identifying these should allow you to take corrective action on the most important ones and thus improve performance. The script used to find the indexes with the most page splits is shown here.

	SchemaName	TableName	IndexName	UnsuccessfulIndexLockPromotions
1	dbo	StagingRequ...	PK__StagingRequest...	510728
2	dbo	Org	PK_Org	285363
3	dbo	OrgNetwork	PK_OrgHierarchy	263887
4	dbo	OrgNetwork	IX_OrgHierarchy_Par...	219260
5	Load	StagingRisk	NULL	190593

Figure 9.10   Output showing unsuccessful index-lock promotions

Listing 9.11　Indexes with the most page splits

```
SET TRANSACTION ISOLATION LEVEL READ UNCOMMITTED

SELECT TOP 20
  x.name AS SchemaName
  , object_name(s.object_id) AS TableName
  , i.name AS IndexName
  , s.leaf_allocation_count
  , s.nonleaf_allocation_count
FROM sys.dm_db_index_operational_stats(DB_ID(), NULL, NULL, NULL) s
INNER JOIN sys.objects o ON s.object_id = o.object_id
INNER JOIN sys.indexes i ON s.index_id = i.index_id
                          AND i.object_id = o.object_id
INNER JOIN sys.schemas x ON x.schema_id = o.schema_id
WHERE s.leaf_allocation_count > 0
  AND o.is_ms_shipped = 0
ORDER BY s.leaf_allocation_count DESC
```

The script uses the same joins as the script in listing 9.8 (indexes under locking pressure) but reports on the column leaf_allocation_count; this corresponds to the number of page splits. The results are sorted by leaf_allocation_count in descending order, so the most important ones are reported first. An example of the type of output for this query is shown in figure 9.11.

One possible solution to reduce the number of page splits is to use a low fill factor when creating the index. That, however, can have a detrimental effect on reads. Because there's less data on a page, more data needs to be read, resulting in more I/O and CPU usage and decreased performance. A balanced solution between reads and writes is needed. You can examine your indexes to identify which ones are used mostly for reads rather than for modification and alter the fill factor accordingly.

A word of warning

Be careful if your clustered index is on an identity column that's used as the primary key. New rows will be added to the last page. If many queries are running and trying to insert data at the same time, it can result in a high number of page splits. This can also result in page latch waits.

	SchemaName	TableName	IndexName	leaf_allocation_count	nonleaf_allocation_count
1	Load	StagingR...	NULL	6558529	0
2	Load	StagingR...	NULL	4496387	0
3	dbo	RiskValue	IX_RiskValue	3320336	14758
4	dbo	RiskValue	IX_RiskValue_Compone...	3228767	24013
5	TWS	SwapsDi...	NULL	1104306	0

Figure 9.11　Output showing indexes with the most page splits

Over time, the free space on the index page gets used up. Rebuilding your indexes allows the fill factor's free space to be reset to its original value, resulting in more space being made available for any changes. Rebuilding your indexes more often should also help reduce the number of page splits.

Next up, we'll look at page latch waits.

9.5.5 Indexes with most latch contention

Latches are used by SQL Server as short-term synchronization objects. In many ways they're similar to locks but relate to internal SQL Server structures. Like locks, they have an associated duration, and a high latch wait is generally a bad thing, typically resulting in decreased performance and decreased concurrency.

The script we use to find the indexes with most latch contention follows.

Listing 9.12 Indexes with the most latch contention

```
SET TRANSACTION ISOLATION LEVEL READ UNCOMMITTED

SELECT TOP 20
  x.name AS SchemaName
  , OBJECT_NAME(s.object_id) AS TableName
  , i.name AS IndexName
  , s.page_latch_wait_in_ms
  , s.page_latch_wait_count
FROM sys.dm_db_index_operational_stats(db_ID(), NULL, NULL, NULL) s
INNER JOIN sys.objects o ON s.object_id = o.object_id
INNER JOIN sys.indexes i ON s.index_id = i.index_id
                        AND i.object_id = o.object_id
INNER JOIN sys.schemas x ON x.schema_id = o.schema_id
WHERE s.page_latch_wait_in_ms > 0
  AND o.is_ms_shipped = 0
ORDER BY s.page_latch_wait_in_ms DESC
```

The script uses the same joins as the script in listing 9.8 (indexes under locking pressure) but reports on the column page_latch_wait_in_ms. The results are sorted by page_latch_wait_in_ms in descending order, so the most important ones are reported first. Figure 9.12 shows an example of the type of output for this query.

	SchemaName	TableName	IndexName	page_latch_wait_in_ms	page_latch_wait_count
1	dbo	Deal	IX_Deal_2	4458970	5678189
2	dbo	PNLValue	IX_PnlValue_Po...	1904261	514829
3	Load	StagingR...	NULL	1323292	4339188
4	Legacy	StagingPnl	NULL	100409	55713
5	Legacy	StagingR...	NULL	58881	35056

Figure 9.12 Output showing indexes with most latch contention

The output identifies the name of the schema, table, and index of the indexes that have had the most page latch waits.

A common cause of page latches is a poorly performing I/O subsystem. Checking the various disk-related performance counters (as discussed in chapter 6) should help you identify whether this is the problem here. Another common cause can be contention on internal system tables. We discussed this previously in this chapter in relation to tempdb, but it applies equally to other databases. Certain pages within each database file contain allocation information (for example, see the PFS and SGAM pages, as discussed in the tempdb recommendations section of this chapter); these can be sources of contention if many queries access them concurrently. Creating more files should help alleviate this problem.

Latches can also be caused by the combination of clustered index/primary key/ identity column usage. In essence, new rows are added to the last page, and if many queries are running, this creates contention, resulting in page latch waits. This can have the additional detrimental effect of creating page splits. A potential solution is to reorder the columns in the index; however, you'll need to ensure that this doesn't have a subsequent detrimental effect on query performance.

Examining the indexes that have had the most page latch waits will allow you to investigate why the waiting is occurring. You could create a snapshot delta (see chapter 2 for details of this) to obtain details of the page waits as well as which queries are running. It should be possible to examine the relationship between these, allowing you to identify the queries causing the page waits. An example of this is given toward the end of this chapter in the section titled "Indexes under row-locking pressure— snapshot version." You could also search the cached plans (discussed in chapter 4) for details of where these indexes are used. Knowing the problematic indexes and where they're used can help you reduce the page waits.

Also, high values might be indicative of too many conflicting and related queries running at the same time. Better scheduling or providing another index might alleviate the problem. I recommend that you revisit the section concerning decreasing blocking in chapter 8 to review methods of decreasing contention.

9.5.6 *Indexes with most page I/O-latch contention*

Page I/O latches are similar to page latches, but where the I/O has yet to complete. It relates to the physical I/O used to bring the index or heap data into the buffer pool (SQL Server's memory). High time values can indicate problems with the I/O subsystem or concurrency contention problems, both of which can decrease performance.

The script we use to find the indexes with most page I/O-latch contention is shown in the following listing.

Listing 9.13   Indexes with the most page I/O-latch contention

```
SET TRANSACTION ISOLATION LEVEL READ UNCOMMITTED

SELECT TOP 20
  x.name AS SchemaName
  , OBJECT_NAME(s.object_id) AS TableName
  , i.name AS IndexName
  , s.page_io_latch_wait_count
  , s.page_io_latch_wait_in_ms
FROM sys.dm_db_index_operational_stats(db_ID(), NULL, NULL, NULL) s
INNER JOIN sys.objects o ON s.object_id = o.object_id
INNER JOIN sys.indexes i ON s.index_id = i.index_id
                        AND i.object_id = o.object_id
INNER JOIN sys.schemas x ON x.schema_id = o.schema_id
WHERE s.page_io_latch_wait_in_ms > 0
  AND o.is_ms_shipped = 0
ORDER BY s.page_io_latch_wait_in_ms DESC
```

This script uses the same joins as the script in listing 9.8 (indexes under locking pressure) but reports on the column page_io_latch_wait_in_ms. The results are sorted by page_io_latch_wait_in_ms in descending order, so the most important ones are reported first. Sample output for this query is shown in figure 9.13.

The output identifies the name of the schema, table, and index of the indexes that have had the most page I/O-latch waits. The cause of these page I/O-latches and a possible solution are discussed in the previous section relating to page latches.

9.5.7   *Indexes under row-locking pressure—snapshot version*

Previously in this section, we looked at the values of the various DMV counters accumulated since the server was last rebooted. Sometimes it's more prudent to take a snapshot of the DMVs within a given time interval or while running a given batch or SQL query. This will allow you to associate the changes in the DMVs with the known queries. In this example, the time period is 60 minutes, but you may want to alter this time interval to suit your needs.

The script we use to find the indexes under the most row-locking pressure (snapshot version) is shown here.

	SchemaName	TableName	IndexName	page_io_latch_wait_count	page_io_latch_wait_in_ms
1	dbo	PNLValue	IX_PNLValue_R...	3163666	72495143
2	dbo	RiskValue	IX_RiskValue	8942389	64673318
3	dbo	PNLValue	IX_PnlValue_Pos...	3912542	27547817
4	dbo	RiskValue	IX_RiskValue_C...	2168447	18261329
5	dbo	PositionG...	PK_PositionGrid...	1221762	6877044

Figure 9.13   Output showing indexes with most page I/O-latch contention

Listing 9.14   Indexes under the most row-locking pressure—snapshot version

```
SET TRANSACTION ISOLATION LEVEL READ UNCOMMITTED                    ❶ Get pre-work
                                                                      index counters
SELECT x.name AS SchemaName
  , OBJECT_NAME (s.object_id) AS TableName
  , i.name AS IndexName
  , s.row_lock_wait_in_ms
INTO #PreWorkIndexCount
FROM sys.dm_db_index_operational_stats(DB_ID(), NULL, NULL, NULL) s
INNER JOIN sys.objects o ON s.object_id = o.object_id
INNER JOIN sys.indexes i ON s.index_id = i.index_id
                        AND i.object_id = o.object_id
INNER JOIN sys.schemas x ON x.schema_id = o.schema_id
WHERE s.row_lock_wait_in_ms > 0
  AND o.is_ms_shipped = 0

SELECT sql_handle, plan_handle, total_elapsed_time, total_worker_time
  , total_logical_reads, total_logical_writes, total_clr_time
  , execution_count, statement_start_offset, statement_end_offset
INTO #PreWorkQuerySnapShot
FROM sys.dm_exec_query_stats
                                                    ❷ Do something here,
                                                      (query/time interval)
WAITFOR DELAY '01:00:00'

SELECT x.name AS SchemaName                         ❸ Get post-work
  , OBJECT_NAME (s.object_id) AS TableName              index counters
  , i.name AS IndexName
  , s.row_lock_wait_in_ms
INTO #PostWorkIndexCount
FROM sys.dm_db_index_operational_stats(DB_ID(), NULL, NULL, NULL) s
INNER JOIN sys.objects o ON s.object_id = o.object_id
INNER JOIN sys.indexes i ON s.index_id = i.index_id
                        AND i.object_id = o.object_id
INNER JOIN sys.schemas x ON x.schema_id = o.schema_id
WHERE s.row_lock_wait_in_ms > 0
  AND o.is_ms_shipped = 0

SELECT sql_handle, plan_handle, total_elapsed_time, total_worker_time
  , total_logical_reads, total_logical_writes, total_clr_time
  , execution_count, statement_start_offset, statement_end_offset
INTO #PostWorkQuerySnapShot
FROM sys.dm_exec_query_stats
                                                    ❹ Calculate changes
SELECT                                                 in index counters
  p2.SchemaName
  , p2.TableName
  , p2.IndexName
  , p2.row_lock_wait_in_ms - ISNULL(p1.row_lock_wait_in_ms, 0)
                                        AS RowLockWaitTimeDelta_ms
FROM #PreWorkIndexCount p1
RIGHT OUTER JOIN
#PostWorkIndexCount p2 ON p2.SchemaName =
                ISNULL(p1.SchemaName, p2.SchemaName)
        AND   p2.TableName = ISNULL(p1.TableName, p2.TableName)
        AND   p2.IndexName = ISNULL(p1.IndexName, p2.IndexName)
```

```
WHERE p2.row_lock_wait_in_ms - ISNULL(p1.row_lock_wait_in_ms, 0) > 0
ORDER BY RowLockWaitTimeDelta_ms DESC                      ←┐ Sort by time
                                                            │ spent locked
SELECT
  p2.total_elapsed_time - ISNULL(p1.total_elapsed_time, 0) AS [Duration]
  , p2.total_worker_time - ISNULL(p1.total_worker_time, 0) AS [Time on CPU]
  , (p2.total_elapsed_time - ISNULL(p1.total_elapsed_time, 0)) -
       (p2.total_worker_time - ISNULL(p1.total_worker_time, 0))
                                                      AS [Time blocked]
  , p2.total_logical_reads - ISNULL(p1.total_logical_reads, 0) AS [Reads]
  , p2.total_logical_writes - ISNULL(p1.total_logical_writes, 0)
                                                          AS [Writes]
  , p2.total_clr_time - ISNULL(p1.total_clr_time, 0) AS [CLR time]
  , p2.execution_count - ISNULL(p1.execution_count, 0) AS [Executions]
  , SUBSTRING (qt.text,p2.statement_start_offset/2 + 1,
    ((CASE WHEN p2.statement_end_offset = -1
      THEN LEN(CONVERT(NVARCHAR(MAX), qt.text)) * 2
      ELSE p2.statement_end_offset
      END - p2.statement_start_offset)/2) + 1) AS [Individual Query]
  , qt.text AS [Parent Query]
  , DB_NAME(qt.dbid) AS DatabaseName
FROM #PreWorkQuerySnapShot p1
RIGHT OUTER JOIN
#PostWorkQuerySnapShot p2 ON p2.sql_handle =
     ISNULL(p1.sql_handle, p2.sql_handle)
  AND p2.plan_handle = ISNULL(p1.plan_handle, p2.plan_handle)
  AND p2.statement_start_offset =
     ISNULL(p1.statement_start_offset, p2.statement_start_offset)
  AND p2.statement_end_offset =
     ISNULL(p1.statement_end_offset, p2.statement_end_offset)
CROSS APPLY sys.dm_exec_sql_text(p2.sql_handle) as qt
WHERE p2.execution_count != ISNULL(p1.execution_count, 0)
  AND qt.text NOT LIKE '--ThisRoutineIdentifier%'            │ Sort by time
ORDER BY [Duration] DESC                                    ←┘ duration

DROP TABLE #PreWorkIndexCount
DROP TABLE #PostWorkIndexCount
DROP TABLE #PreWorkQuerySnapShot
DROP TABLE #PostWorkQuerySnapShot
```

The listing follows the approach outlined in chapter 2, where metrics of the relevant DMV/system views are recorded ❶. The script then waits until a given time interval has passed ❷. The metrics are then taken again ❸, and finally the change in the DMV counters is calculated ❹. We do this for both the DMV counter that we're investigating (row_lock_wait_in_ms in this case) and the queries that are running. We use a RIGHT OUTER JOIN because there may be indexes that might not have been used before, so they wouldn't be present in the pre-work snapshot. An example of the type of output for this query is shown in figure 9.14.

The output identifies the name of the schema, table, and index of the indexes that have had the most row-lock wait times, together with details of the queries that have run over the time interval examined.

	SchemaName	TableName	IndexName	RowLockWaitTimeDelta_ms
1	dbo	Request	PK_Request	235
2	dbo	RequestDealCom...	PK__RequestDe...	16
3	dbo	RequestPNLXML...	PK__RequestPN...	16
4	dbo	RequestPNLXML...	idxBatchNbr_RP...	15

	Duration	Time on CPU	Time blocked	Reads	Writes	CLR time	Executions	Individual Query	Parent Query	DatabaseName
96	11210939	2449221	8761718	366803	0	0	2254	UPDATE t SET t....	CREATE procedure [dbo...	Paris
97	10645509	2763672	7881837	366707	0	0	2254	UPDATE t SET t....	CREATE procedure [dbo...	Paris
98	10594727	4583008	6011719	444989	7	0	66	INSERT INTO @Pr...	/*------------------------...	Paris
99	10560547	4373047	6187500	1509417	2	0	2	select dealcode, dealv...	select dealcode, dealversi...	NULL
100	10422850	2474610	7948240	265654	0	0	2254	UPDATE t SET t....	CREATE procedure [dbo...	Paris
101	10369144	2825199	7543945	366803	0	0	2254	UPDATE t SET t....	CREATE procedure [dbo...	Paris

Figure 9.14   Output showing indexes under row-locking pressure (snapshot version)

It's possible to replace the time interval with a batch of SQL queries. In either case the queries that run in the given time interval or by explicitly including a batch of SQL queries can be associated with the recorded results. A caveat regarding this method is that it records details of all the queries that are currently running on your database. In the case of contention, this may not be a problem (indeed it may be exactly what you want to record). You can filter out queries that aren't running in the current database.

It's possible to combine this script with other snapshot-related queries (for example, those in chapter 5) to display what other DMV changes are also occurring. This includes which SQL queries are running and missing indexes.

It would be interesting to examine which indexes were deemed missing, because this might be the reason for the excessive pressure on the indexes examined here.

The snapshot script given here, while useful, is for illustrative purposes. You can replace the DMV columns examined (row_lock_wait_in_ms) with any (or all) of the DMV columns discussed in this section to get a better understanding of what happens when your queries run.

9.5.8 *How many rows are being inserted/deleted/updated/selected?*

In chapter 3 we looked at various aspects of index usage, including the number of modifications (updates, inserts, and deletes) that occur during a given time interval or when a given batch of SQL queries is run. The DMV sys.dm_db_index_usage_stats records this information at the batch level. For example, if a SQL query updates 20 rows, it would record this as 1 in the relevant DMV column rather than 20. Luckily, the DMV we're currently examining (sys.dm_db_index_operational_stats) enables us to discover how each index is changed by recording the number of rows affected by updates, deletes, inserts, scans, and lookups.

If the index has an entry for every row in its underlying table, then the index indirectly records the activity on its underlying table. This can be useful in determining the range (type of modification) and depth (number of rows affected) of a batch of SQL queries or an overnight batch. It can also be useful for baselining, monitoring, capacity planning, defragging, and updating statistics. In this example, the time period is 60 minutes; you can change this value to suit your needs.

The script we use to find how many rows are inserted/deleted/updated/selected is shown in the following listing.

Listing 9.15 Determining how many rows are inserted/deleted/updated/selected

```
SET TRANSACTION ISOLATION LEVEL READ UNCOMMITTED             ❶ Get pre-work
                                                               index counters
SELECT
  sql_handle, plan_handle, total_elapsed_time, total_worker_time
  , total_logical_reads, total_logical_writes, total_clr_time
  , execution_count, statement_start_offset, statement_end_offset
INTO #PreWorkQuerySnapShot
FROM sys.dm_exec_query_stats

SELECT x.name AS SchemaName
  , OBJECT_NAME (s.object_id) AS TableName
  , i.name AS IndexName
  , s.leaf_delete_count
  , s.leaf_ghost_count
  , s.leaf_insert_count
  , s.leaf_update_count
  , s.range_scan_count
  , s.singleton_lookup_count
INTO #PreWorkIndexCount
FROM sys.dm_db_index_operational_stats(DB_ID(), NULL, NULL, NULL) s
INNER JOIN sys.objects o ON s.object_id = o.object_id
INNER JOIN sys.indexes i ON s.index_id = i.index_id
                        AND i.object_id = o.object_id
INNER JOIN sys.schemas x ON x.schema_id = o.schema_id    ❷ Do something here,
WHERE o.is_ms_shipped = 0                                   (query/time interval)

WAITFOR DELAY '01:00:00'                                  ❸ Get post-work
                                                            index counters
SELECT
  sql_handle, plan_handle, total_elapsed_time, total_worker_time
  , total_logical_reads, total_logical_writes, total_clr_time
  , execution_count, statement_start_offset, statement_end_offset
INTO #PostWorkQuerySnapShot
FROM sys.dm_exec_query_stats

SELECT x.name AS SchemaName
  , OBJECT_NAME (s.object_id) AS TableName
  , i.name AS IndexName
  , s.leaf_delete_count
  , s.leaf_ghost_count
  , s.leaf_insert_count
  , s.leaf_update_count
  , s.range_scan_count
  , s.singleton_lookup_count
INTO #PostWorkIndexCount
FROM sys.dm_db_index_operational_stats(DB_ID(), NULL, NULL, NULL) s
INNER JOIN sys.objects o ON s.object_id = o.object_id
INNER JOIN sys.indexes i ON s.index_id = i.index_id
                        AND i.object_id = o.object_id
INNER JOIN sys.schemas x ON x.schema_id = o.schema_id
WHERE o.is_ms_shipped = 0
```

```
SELECT
  p2.SchemaName
, p2.TableName
, p2.IndexName
, p2.leaf_delete_count - ISNULL(p1.leaf_delete_count, 0)
                                AS leaf_delete_countDelta
, p2.leaf_ghost_count - ISNULL(p1.leaf_ghost_count, 0)
                                AS leaf_ghost_countDelta
, p2.leaf_insert_count - ISNULL(p1.leaf_insert_count, 0)
                                AS leaf_insert_countDelta
, p2.leaf_update_count - ISNULL(p1.leaf_update_count, 0)
                                AS leaf_update_countDelta
, p2.range_scan_count - ISNULL(p1.range_scan_count, 0)
                                AS range_scan_countDelta
, p2.singleton_lookup_count - ISNULL(p1.singleton_lookup_count, 0)
                                AS singleton_lookup_countDelta
FROM #PreWorkIndexCount p1
RIGHT OUTER JOIN
#PostWorkIndexCount p2 ON p2.SchemaName =
                ISNULL(p1.SchemaName, p2.SchemaName)
      AND  p2.TableName = ISNULL(p1.TableName, p2.TableName)
      AND  p2.IndexName = ISNULL(p1.IndexName, p2.IndexName)
WHERE p2.leaf_delete_count - ISNULL(p1.leaf_delete_count, 0) > 0
  OR p2.leaf_ghost_count - ISNULL(p1.leaf_ghost_count, 0) > 0
  OR p2.leaf_insert_count - ISNULL(p1.leaf_insert_count, 0) > 0
  OR p2.leaf_update_count - ISNULL(p1.leaf_update_count, 0) > 0
  OR p2.range_scan_count - ISNULL(p1.range_scan_count, 0) > 0
  OR p2.singleton_lookup_count - ISNULL(p1.singleton_lookup_count, 0) > 0
ORDER BY leaf_delete_countDelta DESC

SELECT
  p2.total_elapsed_time - ISNULL(p1.total_elapsed_time, 0) AS [Duration]
, p2.total_worker_time - ISNULL(p1.total_worker_time, 0) AS [Time on CPU]
, (p2.total_elapsed_time - ISNULL(p1.total_elapsed_time, 0)) -
        (p2.total_worker_time - ISNULL(p1.total_worker_time, 0))
                                AS [Time blocked]
, p2.total_logical_reads - ISNULL(p1.total_logical_reads, 0) AS [Reads]
, p2.total_logical_writes - ISNULL(p1.total_logical_writes, 0)
                                AS [Writes]
, p2.total_clr_time - ISNULL(p1.total_clr_time, 0) AS [CLR time]
, p2.execution_count - ISNULL(p1.execution_count, 0) AS [Executions]
, SUBSTRING (qt.text,p2.statement_start_offset/2 + 1,
  ((CASE WHEN p2.statement_end_offset = -1
    THEN LEN(CONVERT(NVARCHAR(MAX), qt.text)) * 2
    ELSE p2.statement_end_offset
    END - p2.statement_start_offset)/2) + 1) AS [Individual Query]
, qt.text AS [Parent Query]
, DB_NAME(qt.dbid) AS DatabaseName
FROM #PreWorkQuerySnapShot p1
RIGHT OUTER JOIN
  #PostWorkQuerySnapShot p2 ON p2.sql_handle =
      ISNULL(p1.sql_handle, p2.sql_handle)
  AND p2.plan_handle = ISNULL(p1.plan_handle, p2.plan_handle)
  AND p2.statement_start_offset =
      ISNULL(p1.statement_start_offset, p2.statement_start_offset)
```

**Calculate changes
in index counters** ④

```
  AND p2.statement_end_offset =
      ISNULL(p1.statement_end_offset, p2.statement_end_offset)
CROSS APPLY sys.dm_exec_sql_text(p2.sql_handle) as qt
WHERE p2.execution_count != ISNULL(p1.execution_count, 0)
ORDER BY [Duration] DESC

DROP TABLE #PreWorkIndexCount
DROP TABLE #PostWorkIndexCount
DROP TABLE #PreWorkQuerySnapShot
DROP TABLE #PostWorkQuerySnapShot
```

The listing follows the familiar approach outlined in chapter 2, where metrics of the relevant DMV/system views are recorded ❶. The script then waits until a given time interval has passed ❷. The metrics are then taken again ❸, and finally the change in the DMV counters is calculated ❹. We do this for both the DMV counters we're investigating (counters that relate to the number of rows, in this case) and the queries that are running. We use a RIGHT OUTER JOIN because there may be indexes that might not have been used before, so they wouldn't be present in the pre-work snapshot. The time interval can be replaced with a given SQL query or batch of SQL queries.

An overview of the columns in the script is given in table 9.8.

Table 9.8 Columns used in the row index usage script

Column	Description
leaf_delete_count	Count of the number of rows deleted
leaf_ghost_count	Count of the number of rows marked as deleted that have yet to be removed, examined together with the column leaf_delete_count
leaf_insert_count	Count of the number of rows inserted
leaf_update_count	Count of the number of rows updated
range_scan_count	Count of the number of scans started on this index
singleton_lookup_count	Count of the number of single rows looked up

Figure 9.15 shows an example of the type of output for this query.

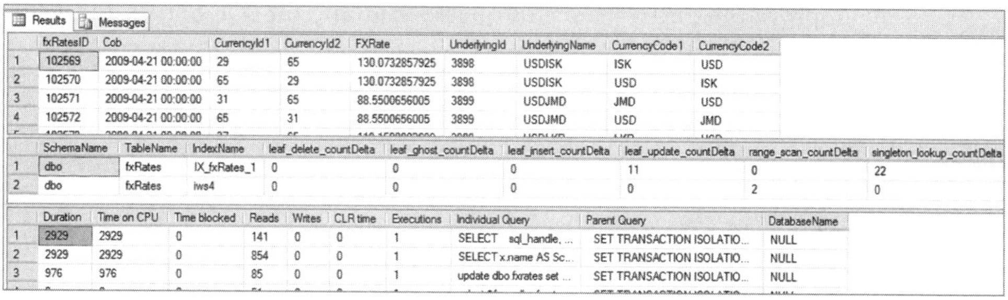

	fxRatesID	Cob	CurrencyId1	CurrencyId2	FXRate	UnderlyingId	UnderlyingName	CurrencyCode1	CurrencyCode2
1	102569	2009-04-21 00:00:00	29	65	130.0732857925	3898	USDISK	ISK	USD
2	102570	2009-04-21 00:00:00	65	29	130.0732857925	3898	USDISK	USD	ISK
3	102571	2009-04-21 00:00:00	31	65	88.5500656005	3899	USDJMD	JMD	USD
4	102572	2009-04-21 00:00:00	65	31	88.5500656005	3899	USDJMD	USD	JMD

	SchemaName	TableName	IndexName	leaf_delete_countDelta	leaf_ghost_countDelta	leaf_insert_countDelta	leaf_update_countDelta	range_scan_countDelta	singleton_lookup_countDelta
1	dbo	fxRates	IX_fxRates_1	0	0	0	11	0	22
2	dbo	fxRates	iws4	0	0	0	0	2	0

	Duration	Time on CPU	Time blocked	Reads	Writes	CLR time	Executions	Individual Query	Parent Query	DatabaseName
1	2929	2929	0	141	0	0	1	SELECT sql_handle, ...	SET TRANSACTION ISOLATIO...	NULL
2	2929	2929	0	854	0	0	1	SELECT x.name AS Sc...	SET TRANSACTION ISOLATIO...	NULL
3	976	976	0	85	0	0	1	update dbo.fxrates set ...	SET TRANSACTION ISOLATIO...	NULL

Figure 9.15 Output showing index column usage

The results show how the indexes are used by the SQL queries. The figure shows three grids. The first grid is the output from running a given SQL query (note that for this output, a query was run in place of the WAITFOR command). The second grid shows the number of rows modified in the named index. The third grid shows which SQL queries were running during the period this script was run.

9.6   *Summary*

This chapter has been a rather mixed bag of functionality, falling under the name of database-level DMVs. In reality, we've taken an in-depth look at tempdb, examining how its space is used by its different object types (user, internal, and version store). I showed you scripts to determine the amount of free space, which can be useful in preventing space problems and capacity planning.

We also examined how much space has been used by given sessions, with a view to identifying sessions that might be using too much and are a possible area of concern. We then looked at the space used by currently active SQL queries; this can prove useful when debugging an active space problem on a server. Finally, I provided some helpful performance recommendations concerning tempdb.

The next major area covered was index contention. This allowed us to create and discuss scripts that relate to

- Row-lock pressure
- Escalated indexes
- Unsuccessful lock promotions
- Latch contention

We also discussed a DMV snapshot script showing how row-lock pressure changes over a given time period. While useful, this was provided for illustrative purposes, but you can modify or extend it to incorporate escalated indexes, unsuccessful lock promotions, and latch contention.

I provided a script to determine how queries affect the number of rows in indexes. This can be useful for baselining, monitoring, capacity planning, defragging, and updating statistics.

Next we'll look at how it might be possible to implement scripts that will automatically improve the performance of queries running on SQL Server and lead to a self-healing database.

The self-healing database 10

This chapter covers

- The self-healing database and automation
- Automatically recompiling slow routines
- Automatically performing index and statistics maintenance
- Automatically disabling or dropping unused indexes
- Automatically creating the most-important missing indexes

The concept of a self-healing database relates to the ability of SQL Server to self-correct problems and potential problems before they become noticeable to users. You can implement this by creating a series of SQL Server agent jobs that run periodically. This chapter covers a miscellany of functionality that collectively can automatically improve the performance of your database queries.

The scripts contained in this chapter will improve the performance of your slow-running SQL queries. They accomplish this by recompiling routines that have become slow, improving the retrieval of data from your indexes, intelligently updating index statistics upon which your optimal query plans will be based, and creating or removing indexes as necessary.

All the scripts build up dynamic SQL, which is subsequently executed via the system stored procedure sp_executesql. The dynamic nature of the creation of the SQL to execute allows you to apply further filtering conditions, for example, limiting the SQL to a given database. Each script contains an EXECUTE command to run the SQL and a PRINT command to show what's being executed.

Because some of these scripts can have wide-reaching and potentially detrimental effects if used inappropriately, it makes sense to first test them in a nonproduction environment. Additionally, it might be prudent to comment out the line in the script that executes the dynamic SQL and instead use the output from the associated PRINT command to inspect the SQL created to determine if it's what is required. You can then manipulate and apply this separately.

10.1   Self-healing database

SQL Server has many useful automated features, for example, automatically updating statistics when the underlying data changes significantly and automatically growing database files when required. This automation helps ensure that the system is tuned and requires little maintenance input. But there are times when finer tuning is needed for better performance.

The underlying concept of this chapter is to present a series of scripts that will help further improve the automatic and self-correcting nature of SQL Server, ensuring that it's finely tuned and helping fix problems before they become noticeable to users.

Hopefully, you can use the approach and patterns discussed, for example, to implement missing indexes, as a template to implement other features as you deem necessary.

Having looked at the concept of the self-healing database, let's get straight into our first example, recompiling slow-running routines.

Automatically running the scripts

Each of the scripts given in this chapter should be implemented as an individual SQL Server agent job. SQL Server agent allows you to create jobs that can be scheduled to run automatically at regular intervals. In addition, you can communicate details of the success or failure of the job to the relevant people via email, pager, and the net send command.

How often these automated jobs should run will vary depending on the nature of the database, namely, transactional or reporting, how often the data is updated, and the data volumes involved. As an example, I could imagine the intelligently update statistics job running as often as hourly, whereas the rebuild/reorganize index script could run weekly or even monthly. It's best to experiment on a test system to determine an optimal frequency for your particular system.

10.2   Recompiling slow routines

Sometimes you can have a query that runs in a timely manner and then suddenly runs slowly. Typically, this is the result of parameter sniffing, where the query plan is created based on the parameter values passed to it when it's first run. Although this may be good for its first run, it can prove disastrous for subsequent runs, especially if the underlying data has changed significantly or the parameters first used were atypical.

We fully discussed the reason for slow-running queries and how to detect them in chapter 5, section 5.5, "Slower-than-normal queries."

Here we'll discuss how you can extend this script to automatically recompile these slow-running routines. The identified routines will be marked for recompilation, such that when they're next used, their query plan will be re-created based on the parameters used. Hopefully this will result in a better-performing query.

10.2.1   Recompiling routines that are running slower than usual

The script "Finding queries that are running slower than normal," discussed in section 5.5 of chapter 5, outputs the name of the routine that's running slower than normal. To automate the routine's recompilation, we'll put the output into a temporary table that can be queried to extract the routine name. These routine names can then be wrapped in relevant SQL statements, so that when this script is executed, the identified routines will be marked to be recompiled on their next usage.

Extracting the name of the routine from the output of the script proved a little troublesome, owing to the variability in the format of the routine's name and the limits of SQL Server's string function-parsing capabilities, so I decided to write a CLR function to do it. You should deploy this function to your databases if you want to implement this example. Details of how to create and deploy a CLR function are discussed fully in chapter 7, section 7.2. You should follow that example but use the code given in listing 10.1 as the example CLR function.

Here's the script we use to extract the name of the routine from the SQL text.

Listing 10.1   CLR function to extract the routine name

```
using System;
using Microsoft.SqlServer.Server;

public partial class UserDefinedFunctions               ❶ Extract SQL
{                                                           routine name

    [SqlFunction(IsDeterministic = true, DataAccess = DataAccessKind.None)]
    public static String ExtractSQLRoutineName(String sSource)
    {

        int _routineStartOffset;
        int _firstSpaceOffset;
        int _endOfRoutineNameOffset;                    ❷ Check data
                                                            present
        if (String.IsNullOrEmpty(sSource) == true)
        {
```

```
            return null;
        }                                                    ❸ Look for
                                                                PROC
    _routineStartOffset = sSource.IndexOf("CREATE PROC",    ◁┘
                    StringComparison.CurrentCultureIgnoreCase);

    if (_routineStartOffset == -1)                           ◁┐ If not found,
    {                                                           look for
        _routineStartOffset = sSource.IndexOf("CREATE FUNC", ❹ FUNCTION
                    StringComparison.CurrentCultureIgnoreCase);
    }

    if (_routineStartOffset == -1)              ◁┐ If not found,
    {                                           ❺ return NULL
        return null;                                           Find space ❻
    }                                                          before name
    _routineStartOffset = _routineStartOffset + "CREATE FUNC".Length;

    _firstSpaceOffset = sSource.IndexOf(" ", _routineStartOffset);  ◁┘

    for (int i = _firstSpaceOffset; i < (sSource.Length - 1); i++)  ◁┐
    {                                           Find space
        if (sSource.Substring(i, 1) != " ")     after name ❼
        {
            _firstSpaceOffset = i;
            break;
        }                                          Find end of ❽
    }                                              routine name
    _endOfRoutineNameOffset = sSource.IndexOfAny(new char[] { ' ',  ◁┘
                    '(', '\t', '\r', '\n' }, _firstSpaceOffset + 1);

    if (_endOfRoutineNameOffset > _routineStartOffset)  ◁┐ Extract
    {                                                   ❾ routine name
        return sSource.Substring(_firstSpaceOffset,
                    (_endOfRoutineNameOffset - _firstSpaceOffset));
    }
    else
        return null;
    }
};
```

The CLR function contains one function named ExtractSQLRoutineName ❶, which extracts the SQL routine name from the passed string variable named sSource. The function checks that the sSource variable is not NULL or empty ❷. If it is, then a NULL value is returned to the caller. The function then looks for the position of the text "CREATE PROC" ❸ or "CREATE FUNC" ❹, ignoring the case, within the variable sSource. If the text isn't found, a NULL value is returned to the caller ❺. If the text is found, we look for the start of the routine's name ❻ and the end of the routine's name ❼ (this can be a space, bracket, tab, return, or newline ❽). Knowing these start and end locations, we can extract the routine's name ❾, which is returned to the caller.

Now that we've discussed the CLR function that's used to extract the name of the routine from the passed text, the next step is to amend the routine that identifies queries that are running slower than normal. This script is essentially the same as the one discussed in chapter 5, section 5.5, except the output has been placed into a temporary table. The name of the routine to recompile is extracted from this temporary table, using the CLR function we just discussed. The routine name is wrapped in SQL statements, which when executed will recompile the routines that are running slower than normal.

The script we use to automatically recompile routines that are running slower than normal is shown here.

Listing 10.2 Recompile routines that are running slower than normal

```
SET TRANSACTION ISOLATION LEVEL READ UNCOMMITTED

SELECT TOP 100                                              ◁――  ❶ Get raw
  qs.execution_count AS [Runs]                                      values
  , (qs.total_worker_time - qs.last_worker_time) /
                  (qs.execution_count - 1) AS [Avg time]
  , qs.last_worker_time AS [Last time]
  , (qs.last_worker_time - ((qs.total_worker_time - qs.last_worker_time)
                  / (qs.execution_count - 1))) AS [Time Deviation]
  , CASE WHEN qs.last_worker_time = 0
            THEN 100
    ELSE (qs.last_worker_time - ((qs.total_worker_time -
            qs.last_worker_time) / (qs.execution_count - 1))) * 100
    END
        / (((qs.total_worker_time - qs.last_worker_time)
        / (qs.execution_count - 1))) AS [% Time Deviation]
  , qs.last_logical_reads + qs.last_logical_writes
        + qs.last_physical_reads AS [Last IO]
  , ((qs.total_logical_reads + qs.total_logical_writes +
                  qs.total_physical_reads) - (qs.last_logical_reads +
                  qs.last_logical_writes + qs.last_physical_reads))
                        / (qs.execution_count - 1) AS [Avg IO]
  , SUBSTRING (qt.text,(qs.statement_start_offset/2) + 1,
    ((CASE WHEN qs.statement_end_offset = -1
      THEN LEN(CONVERT(NVARCHAR(MAX), qt.text)) * 2
      ELSE qs.statement_end_offset
      END - qs.statement_start_offset)/2) + 1) AS [Individual Query]
  , qt.text AS [Parent Query]
  , DB_NAME(qt.dbid) AS [DatabaseName]
INTO #SlowQueries
FROM sys.dm_exec_query_stats qs
CROSS APPLY sys.dm_exec_sql_text(qs.plan_handle) qt
WHERE qs.execution_count > 1
  AND qs.total_worker_time != qs.last_worker_time
ORDER BY [% Time Deviation] DESC

SELECT TOP 100 [Runs]                              ◁――  **Calculate IO Deviation**
    , [Avg time]                                     ❷  **and % IO Deviation**
    , [Last time]
    , [Time Deviation]
    , [% Time Deviation]
    , [Last IO]
```

```
        , [Avg IO]
        , [Last IO] - [Avg IO] AS [IO Deviation]
        , CASE WHEN [Avg IO] = 0
                THEN 0
            ELSE ([Last IO]- [Avg IO]) * 100 / [Avg IO]
          END AS [% IO Deviation]
        , [Individual Query]
        , [Parent Query]
        , [DatabaseName]
INTO #SlowQueriesByIO
FROM #SlowQueries
ORDER BY [% Time Deviation] DESC
```

❸ **Calculate Impedance**

```
SELECT TOP 100
    [Runs]
    , [Avg time]
    , [Last time]
    , [Time Deviation]
    , [% Time Deviation]
    , [Last IO]
    , [Avg IO]
    , [IO Deviation]
    , [% IO Deviation]
    , [Impedance] = [% Time Deviation] - [% IO Deviation]
    , [Individual Query]
    , [Parent Query]
    , [DatabaseName]
INTO #QueriesRunningSlowerThanNormal
FROM #SlowQueriesByIO
WHERE [% Time Deviation] - [% IO Deviation] > 20
ORDER BY [Impedance] DESC
```

❹ **Build recompilation SQL**

```
SELECT DISTINCT
    ' EXEC sp_recompile ' + '''' + '[' + [DatabaseName] + '].'
        + dbo.ExtractSQLRoutineName([Parent Query]) + ''''
                                AS recompileRoutineSQL

INTO #RecompileQuery
FROM #QueriesRunningSlowerThanNormal
WHERE [DatabaseName] NOT IN ('master', 'msdb', '')
```

❺ **Amalgamate recompilation SQL**

```
DECLARE @RecompilationSQL NVARCHAR(MAX)
SET @RecompilationSQL = ''

SELECT @RecompilationSQL = @RecompilationSQL
                    + recompileRoutineSQL + CHAR(10)
FROM #RecompileQuery
WHERE recompileRoutineSQL IS NOT NULL

DECLARE @StartOffset INT
DECLARE @Length INT
SET @StartOffset = 0
SET @Length = 4000
```

❻ **Debug**

```
WHILE (@StartOffset < LEN(@RecompilationSQL))
BEGIN
    PRINT SUBSTRING(@RecompilationSQL, @StartOffset, @Length)
    SET @StartOffset = @StartOffset + @Length
END
```

```
PRINT SUBSTRING(@RecompilationSQL, @StartOffset, @Length)

EXECUTE sp_executesql @RecompilationSQL

DROP TABLE #SlowQueries
DROP TABLE #SlowQueriesByIO
DROP TABLE #QueriesRunningSlowerThanNormal
DROP TABLE #RecompileQuery
```

❼ **Run**

In this script, we look only at queries that are slower than normal based on the
_worker_time columns ❶. To determine whether a query is running slower than normal, we need to calculate the average duration of the query and compare it to its last
run value, adjusted for the amount of data it has processed ❷. The data is sorted to
show the TOP 100 queries running slower than normal, by Impedance; this is a reflection of Time Deviation taking into account IO Deviation ❸.

The routines that are running slower than normal are stored in the temporary table named #QueriesRunningSlowerThanNormal. The name of the routines
to recompile is extracted by calling the CLR function dbo.ExtractSQLRoutineName, passing it the Parent Query as input. The routine name is prepended with
the text "EXEC sp_recompile" ❹. All the wrapped-up routine names are concatenated, and the result is stored in the variable @RecompilationSQL ❺. The content of the variable @RecompilationSQL is also displayed for debugging purposes,
via the PRINT command ❻. This variable is then used as input to the system
stored procedure sp_executesql. Running this executes the text and marks any
routines that are running slower than normal to be recompiled when they are
next run ❼.

The script ignores any routines that are in the master or msdb system database or
queries implemented as native SQL (resulting in a blank database name). It's possible
to amend the script to include only those databases that you're interested in, by
changing the line

```
WHERE [DatabaseName] NOT IN ('master', 'msdb', '')
```

to

```
WHERE [DatabaseName] IN ('ReplaceWithTheNameOfYourDatabaseHere')
```

> **Recompilation note**
> You should note that recompilation can cause a spike in CPU usage and create
> compilation locks. But you should balance this against the advantages recompilation will give, because the routines identified here are targeted based on their
> known recent poor performance.

If many of the queries to be recompiled have a large impedance value, but their absolute time using the CPU is relatively small, it might be sensible to include only queries
that have a duration above a certain threshold. You can achieve this by adding a filter

to the WHERE clause of the first query in listing 10.2, for example, to include queries where their last run exceeded five seconds on the CPU:

```
AND qs.last_worker_time > 5000000
```

Having looked at how you can automatically recompile routines that are running slower than normal, let's now examine another script to automatically improve query performance, by removing the fragmentation from indexes.

10.3   *Automatically rebuild and reorganize indexes*

Fragmentation relates to index entries that are out of sequence. So for queries that access data sequentially, typically index scans, you'll need to do additional work to retrieve the index's data. This additional work can reflect itself in longer-running queries, with potentially more blocking and client timeouts. Where possible, remove any fragmentation, so that you don't perform any unnecessary work.

> ### Determining the degree of fragmentation can take a long time
> Please be aware the DMV used to obtain the fragmentation details (sys.dm_db_ index_physical_stats) can take a long time to run. You should balance this time against the time it would take just to rebuild or organize the indexes without inspecting them for their degree of fragmentation. On an Enterprise-level system with 600 indexes, some containing billions of rows, querying the DMV can take several hours to complete.

We discussed fragmentation fully in chapter 3, in section 3.6, "Fragmented indexes." A script was presented to identify the most-fragmented indexes.

Let's discuss how this script can be extended to automatically remove or reduce the impact of this fragmentation, resulting in better-performing queries, especially range-based ones.

10.3.1   *Rebuilding and reorganizing fragmented indexes*

The script I use to automatically rebuild or reorganize indexes is shown in the following listing. This script is an extension of the one given in chapter 3, in section 3.6, which identified the most-fragmented indexes.

Listing 10.3   Rebuild/reorganize for a given database

```
SET TRANSACTION ISOLATION LEVEL READ UNCOMMITTED          ❶ Create
                                                              table
CREATE TABLE #FragmentedIndexes(
    DatabaseName        SYSNAME
    , SchemaName        SYSNAME
    , TableName         SYSNAME
    , IndexName         SYSNAME
    , [Fragmentation%]    FLOAT)
```

```
INSERT INTO #FragmentedIndexes
SELECT
    DB_NAME(DB_ID()) AS DatabaseName
    , ss.name AS SchemaName
    , OBJECT_NAME (s.object_id) AS TableName
    , i.name AS IndexName
    , s.avg_fragmentation_in_percent AS [Fragmentation%]
FROM sys.dm_db_index_physical_stats(db_id(),NULL, NULL, NULL, 'SAMPLED') s
INNER JOIN sys.indexes i ON s.[object_id] = i.[object_id]
                        AND s.index_id = i.index_id
INNER JOIN sys.objects o ON s.object_id = o.object_id
INNER JOIN sys.schemas ss ON ss.[schema_id] = o.[schema_id]
WHERE s.database_id = DB_ID()                        ❷  Ignore heaps
    AND i.index_id != 0
    AND s.record_count > 0                              Only indexes
    AND o.is_ms_shipped = 0                          ❸  with data
DECLARE @RebuildIndexesSQL NVARCHAR(MAX)             ❹  User tables only
SET @RebuildIndexesSQL = ''

SELECT                                                  Build rebuild/
@RebuildIndexesSQL = @RebuildIndexesSQL +           ❺  reorg SQL
CASE
    WHEN [Fragmentation%] > 30
        THEN CHAR(10) + 'ALTER INDEX ' + QUOTENAME(IndexName) + ' ON '
            + QUOTENAME(SchemaName) + '.'
            + QUOTENAME(TableName) + ' REBUILD;'
    WHEN [Fragmentation%] > 10
        THEN CHAR(10) + 'ALTER INDEX ' + QUOTENAME(IndexName) + ' ON '
            + QUOTENAME(SchemaName) + '.'
            + QUOTENAME(TableName) + ' REORGANIZE;'
    END
FROM  #FragmentedIndexes
WHERE [Fragmentation%] > 10

DECLARE @StartOffset INT
DECLARE @Length INT
SET @StartOffset = 0
SET @Length = 4000
                                                    ❻  Debug
WHILE (@StartOffset < LEN(@RebuildIndexesSQL))
BEGIN
    PRINT SUBSTRING(@RebuildIndexesSQL, @StartOffset, @Length)
    SET @StartOffset = @StartOffset + @Length
END

PRINT SUBSTRING(@RebuildIndexesSQL, @StartOffset, @Length)

EXECUTE sp_executesql @RebuildIndexesSQL

DROP TABLE #FragmentedIndexes                       ❼  Execute SQL
```

In the listing we create a temporary table named #FragmentedIndexes to hold the details of the fragmented indexes ❶. The DMV sys.dm_db_index_physical_stats is queried to determine the degree of fragmentation. We ignore heaps ❷ and include indexes that have at least one row of data ❸. In addition, we're interested only in indexes that relate to user tables ❹.

The rebuild or reorganize SQL commands are created from a combination of index name, schema name, and table name; all these details are given in the temporary table. The name of the index to rebuild or reorganize is prepended with the appropriate ALTER INDEX keywords and appended with a REBUILD or REORGANIZE keyword, depending on the degree of fragmentation ❺.

> **NOTE** Only indexes where the degree of fragmentation is greater than 10% are included for further processing. Indexes that are fragmented by more than 30% will be rebuilt, whereas indexes that are fragmented by between 10% and 30% will be reorganized.

All the wrapped-up ALTER INDEX statements are concatenated and the result stored in the variable @RebuildIndexesSQL. The content of the variable @RebuildIndexesSQL is also displayed for debugging purposes, via the PRINT command ❻. This variable is then used as input to the system stored procedure sp_executesql ❼; running this executes the text and rebuilds or reorganizes the indexes.

It's also possible to have a script that performs this rebuilding/reorganization on each database on the server. This script is given in the following listing.

Listing 10.4   Rebuild/reorganize for all databases on a given server

```
SET TRANSACTION ISOLATION LEVEL READ UNCOMMITTED          ❶ Create
                                                            table
CREATE TABLE #FragmentedIndexes(
    DatabaseName          SYSNAME
    , SchemaName          SYSNAME
    , TableName           SYSNAME
    , IndexName           SYSNAME
    , [Fragmentation%]    FLOAT)
                                              ❷ Loop around
EXEC sp_MSForEachDB      'USE [?];              all databases

INSERT INTO #FragmentedIndexes
SELECT
    DB_NAME(DB_ID()) AS DatabaseName
    , ss.name AS SchemaName
    , OBJECT_NAME (s.object_id) AS TableName
    , i.name AS IndexName
    , s.avg_fragmentation_in_percent AS [Fragmentation%]
FROM sys.dm_db_index_physical_stats(db_id(),NULL, NULL, NULL,
                                    ''SAMPLED'') s
INNER JOIN sys.indexes i ON s.[object_id] = i.[object_id]
    AND s.index_id = i.index_id
INNER JOIN sys.objects o ON s.object_id = o.object_id
INNER JOIN sys.schemas ss ON ss.[schema_id] = o.[schema_id]
WHERE s.database_id = DB_ID()                      ❸ Ignore
    AND i.index_id != 0                              heaps
    AND s.record_count > 0                          ❹ Only indexes
    AND o.is_ms_shipped = 0                            with data
; '
                                          ❺ User tables
DECLARE @RebuildIndexesSQL NVARCHAR(MAX)    only
SET @RebuildIndexesSQL = ''
```

```
SELECT
@RebuildIndexesSQL = @RebuildIndexesSQL +
CASE
WHEN [Fragmentation%] > 30
        THEN CHAR(10) + 'ALTER INDEX ' +  QUOTENAME(IndexName) + ' ON '
        + QUOTENAME(DatabaseName) + '.'+ QUOTENAME(SchemaName) + '.'
        + QUOTENAME(TableName) + ' REBUILD;'
WHEN [Fragmentation%] > 10
        THEN CHAR(10) + 'ALTER INDEX ' +  QUOTENAME(IndexName) + ' ON '
        + QUOTENAME(DatabaseName) + '.'+ QUOTENAME(SchemaName) + '.'
        + QUOTENAME(TableName) + ' REORGANIZE;'
END
FROM  #FragmentedIndexes
WHERE [Fragmentation%] > 10

DECLARE @StartOffset INT
DECLARE @Length INT
SET @StartOffset = 0
SET @Length = 4000

WHILE (@StartOffset < LEN(@RebuildIndexesSQL))
BEGIN
    PRINT SUBSTRING(@RebuildIndexesSQL, @StartOffset, @Length)
    SET @StartOffset = @StartOffset + @Length
END

PRINT SUBSTRING(@RebuildIndexesSQL, @StartOffset, @Length)

EXECUTE sp_executesql @RebuildIndexesSQL

DROP TABLE #FragmentedIndexes
```

6 Build rebuild/reorg SQL

7 Debug

8 Execute SQL

This script is essentially the same as that given in listing 10.3, but it queries all the databases on the server. In the listing a temporary table named #FragmentedIndexes is created to hold the details of the fragmented indexes ❶. The system stored procedure sp_MSForEachDB ❷ is executed, which allows you to run the contained script on each of the databases in the server in turn. In the contained script we use the DMV sys.dm_db_index_physical_stats to determine the degree of fragmentation. In the script we ignore heaps ❸ and include indexes that have at least one row of data ❹. Also, we're interested only in indexes that relate to user tables ❺.

The rebuild or reorganize SQL commands are created from a combination of index name, schema name, and table name; all these details are given in the temporary table. The name of the index to rebuild or reorganize is prepended with the appropriate ALTER INDEX keywords and appended with a REBUILD or REORGANIZE keyword, depending on the degree of fragmentation ❻. The content of the variable @RebuildIndexesSQL is also displayed for debugging purposes, via the PRINT command ❼. This variable is then used as input to the system stored procedure sp_executesql ❽; running this executes the text and rebuilds or reorganizes the indexes.

It's possible to amend the script to include only the databases, schemas, or indexes that you're interested in by adding a WHERE clause to the query that dynamically builds up the rebuild/reorganization SQL. Alternatively you could provide relevant parameters to the sys.dm_db_index_physical_stats DMV.

It should be possible to extend this script to examine the degree of page splits, fragmentation, and fill factor (using your knowledge of the profile of any index modifications) to produce a more appropriate fill factor for the index, resulting in fewer page splits and less fragmentation.

One of the benefits of performing a rebuild is that because the whole index is rebuilt, it results in the statistics for the index being optimal, because it has a 100% sample. Be sure not to run an UPDATE STATISTICS command on any indexes immediately after an index rebuild; otherwise you might reduce the effectiveness of the index's statistics. This leads nicely to our next script, concerning the intelligent updating of an index's statistics.

10.4　*Intelligently update statistics*

As discussed in chapter 3, section 3.10, "Your statistics," maintaining up-to-date statistics is of vital importance if you want your queries to run optimally. Having up-to-date statistics allows SQL Server to create a query plan with an optimal data access mechanism, for example, using an index appropriately.

The statistics relate to indexes, but because a table can have many indexes, it's common to talk about the statistics relating to the table. Often the UPDATE STATISTICS command is run against a given table, updating all the indexes on the table, even if data in the index hasn't changed. The script given in listing 10.5 works more efficiently because it identifies and updates the statistics of only those indexes that have changed. This is a more targeted and intelligent approach.

> **NOTE**　The scripts given here don't use DMVs, but they do use related system tables. Owing to the importance of statistics for the selection of an optimal access mechanism needed to create a query plan, I decided to include these scripts in this chapter.

Typically, SQL Server will update statistics when 20% of the underlying data changes. Usually this data relates to an index. If the statistics change, any cached plan that uses the statistics (for example, via an index) is recompiled to take advantage of the new statistics, which in turn may lead to a more optimal method of data access and a faster query.

For very large tables in particular, waiting for the underlying data to change by 20% might take too long. For example, if 1% of the data changes each day, it might take a month before the statistics are automatically updated, resulting in suboptimal execution plans being used and slower-performing queries. I've experienced a great many queries that have been running slowly because of out-of-date statistics, some of which have run for an hour or more, but these run in seconds when the statistics are updated. With this in mind, it makes sense to consider updating the statistics on a more regular basis.

10.4.1 *Simple intelligent statistics update*

Statistics contain information about the distribution and density of data values. For larger tables in particular, it can take a long time to obtain detailed statistics, so a sample of data is typically used to create the statistics rather than an examination of all the data.

Typically, the default update statistics, which occur when 20% of the underlying data changes, use the sampling percentage when update statistics was last run. In our script, we can be more intelligent, creating a sampling algorithm based on the number of rows in the underlying index.

The script we use to automatically update the statistics intelligently is shown here.

> **Listing 10.5 Intelligently update statistics—simple version**

```
SET TRANSACTION ISOLATION LEVEL READ UNCOMMITTED

SELECT                                                    ◁  ❶ Select indexes
    ss.name AS SchemaName                                       to update
    , st.name AS TableName
    , si.name AS IndexName
    , si.type_desc AS IndexType
    , STATS_DATE(si.object_id,si.index_id) AS StatsLastTaken
    , ssi.rowcnt
    , ssi.rowmodctr
INTO #IndexUsage
FROM sys.indexes si
INNER JOIN sys.sysindexes ssi ON si.object_id = ssi.id
                              AND si.name = ssi.name
INNER JOIN sys.tables st ON st.[object_id] = si.[object_id]   ❷ User
INNER JOIN sys.schemas ss ON ss.[schema_id] = st.[schema_id]     indexes
WHERE st.is_ms_shipped = 0                                       only
  AND si.index_id != 0                                   ◁    ❸ Ignore
  AND ssi.rowcnt > 100                                   ◁      heaps
  AND ssi.rowmodctr > 0
                                              Indexes   Indexes with 100
DECLARE @UpdateStatisticsSQL NVARCHAR(MAX)    with some  ❹ or more rows
SET @UpdateStatisticsSQL = ''                 changed
                                           ❺ data
SELECT                                                   ◁    Build SQL to
    @UpdateStatisticsSQL = @UpdateStatisticsSQL            ❻ update statistics
    + CHAR(10) + 'UPDATE STATISTICS '
    + QUOTENAME(SchemaName) + '.' + QUOTENAME(TableName)
    + ' ' + QUOTENAME(IndexName) + ' WITH SAMPLE '
    + CASE
        WHEN rowcnt <     500000 THEN '100 PERCENT'
        WHEN rowcnt <    1000000 THEN '50 PERCENT'
        WHEN rowcnt <    5000000 THEN '25 PERCENT'
        WHEN rowcnt <   10000000 THEN '10 PERCENT'
        WHEN rowcnt <   50000000 THEN '2 PERCENT'
        WHEN rowcnt <  100000000 THEN '1 PERCENT'
        ELSE '3000000 ROWS '
    END
    + '-- ' + CAST(rowcnt AS VARCHAR(22)) + ' rows'
FROM #IndexUsage
```

```
DECLARE @StartOffset INT
DECLARE @Length INT
SET @StartOffset = 0
SET @Length = 4000
                                                                    ❼  Debug
WHILE (@StartOffset < LEN(@UpdateStatisticsSQL))
BEGIN
    PRINT SUBSTRING(@UpdateStatisticsSQL, @StartOffset, @Length)
    SET @StartOffset = @StartOffset + @Length
END

PRINT SUBSTRING(@UpdateStatisticsSQL, @StartOffset, @Length)

EXECUTE sp_executesql @UpdateStatisticsSQL                          Execute
                                                                ❽  SQL
DROP TABLE #IndexUsage
```

In the listing, four system tables are involved in intelligently updating statistics. A brief description of each is given in table 10.1.

Table 10.1 Tables used for intelligently updating statistics

Tables	Description
sys.indexes	Contains details for each index, for example, name
sys.sysindexes	Contains details for each index and table, for example, row count, number of row changes since statistics last updated
sys.tables	Contains table information, for example, name
sys.schemas	Contains details of schema objects, for example, name

The script joins the sys.indexes system view with the sys.sysindexes system view based on their common name and id columns. Joins to the sys.table and sys.schema system tables are provided to obtain the name of the schema and table the index's statistics relate to. This is required when you want to update the relevant statistics.

We capture the name of the schema, table, and index ❶ into a temporary table named #IndexUsage. We also record the number of rows in the index together with the number of modifications since update statistics was last applied (this date itself is also recorded in the column StatsLastTaken). This information could prove useful in any subsequent debugging, analysis, or further filtering.

We filter on the joined system views based on various criteria; specifically, we're concerned only with indexes that relate to user tables ❷ as opposed to system tables. Additionally, we're concerned only with clustered and nonclustered indexes, ignoring heaps ❸. We want only indexes that have at least 100 rows ❹, and finally, we're concerned only with indexes whose data has changed since the last time update statistics was run on the index ❺. It's possible to amend this section of the script so that we update only the statistics of indexes that have changed by a given number or percentage of rows.

The name of the index that we want to update the statistics on is prepended with the name of the schema and table, together with the keywords UPDATE STATISTICS. The resultant commands are concatenated, and the result is stored in the variable @UpdateStatisticsSQL ❻. The content of the variable @UpdateStatisticsSQL is displayed for debugging purposes, via the PRINT command ❼. This variable is then used as input to the system stored procedure sp_executesql; running this executes the text and updates the statistics on the relevant indexes ❽.

The algorithm used to determine the percentage of rows to sample is given in table 10.2.

Table 10.2   Sampling strategy used for intelligently updating statistics

Rows in index	Sampling percentage/row count
Up to 500,000	100 percent (up to 500,000 rows sampled)
Up to 1,000,000	50 percent (up to 500,000 rows sampled)
Up to 5,000,000	25 percent (up to 1,250,000 rows sampled)
Up to 10,000,000	10 percent (up to 1,000,000 rows sampled)
Up to 50,000,000	2 percent (up to 1,000,000 rows sampled)
Up to 100,000,000	1 percent (up to 1,000,000 rows sampled)
Over 100,000,000	3,000,000 rows

The algorithm is weighted such that smaller indexes have a higher sampling percentage. This seems appropriate because you're more likely to miss an important data value if you have a lower sampling percentage in a small index. Similarly, you're more likely to repeat a data value if you have a high sampling percentage on a large index.

You can alter this algorithm to suit your needs. These values have proved helpful on some of the systems I've used (that have 600 indexes, some with row counts in excess of 11 billion). Ultimately, the sampling percentages should reflect the variability in the underlying column data values.

It's possible to limit the number of indexes that will have their statistics updated by filtering, out or in, by adding a WHERE condition. It's also possible to filter out or in by database name, schema name, table name, index name, the date when the statistics were last updated, or the number of rows changed.

Ideally, you should be able to run as many statistics updates as possible, weighted by the row counts for the different indexes, within a given time period. This is the idea behind the next script.

10.4.2   *Time-based intelligent statistics update*

Updating an index's statistics takes time. Having provided an algorithm to obtain a sampling of rows, it makes sense to provide a script that adjusts the sampling to fit a given time frame; for example, update as many statistics as possible in 30 minutes. The script we use to automatically update the statistics intelligently, using a time-based approach, is shown next.

Listing 10.6   Intelligently update statistics—time-based version

```
SET TRANSACTION ISOLATION LEVEL READ UNCOMMITTED           ❶  Do stats need
                                                               updating
IF EXISTS
    (SELECT 1
    FROM sys.indexes si
    INNER JOIN sys.sysindexes ssi ON si.object_id = ssi.id
            AND si.name = ssi.name
    INNER JOIN sys.tables st ON st.[object_id] = si.[object_id]
    INNER JOIN sys.schemas ss ON ss.[schema_id] = st.[schema_id]
    WHERE st.is_ms_shipped = 0
            AND si.index_id != 0
            AND ssi.rowcnt > 100
            AND ssi.rowmodctr > 0)
BEGIN

DECLARE @StatsMarker          NVARCHAR(2000)
DECLARE @SamplingComplete      BIT
DECLARE @RowsToBenchMark       BIGINT
SET @RowsToBenchMark = 500
SET @SamplingComplete = 0

DECLARE @TotalStatsTime        BIGINT
DECLARE @StartTime             DATETIME
DECLARE @TimePerRow            FLOAT                  ❷  How long to
                                                         update one row
WHILE (@SamplingComplete = 0)
BEGIN
    SELECT TOP 1 @StatsMarker = 'UPDATE STATISTICS '
        + QUOTENAME(ss.name) + '.' + QUOTENAME(st.name)
        + ' ' + QUOTENAME(si.name) + ' WITH SAMPLE '
        + CAST(@RowsToBenchMark AS VARCHAR(22)) + ' ROWS'
    FROM sys.indexes si
    INNER JOIN sys.sysindexes ssi ON si.object_id = ssi.id
            AND si.name = ssi.name
    INNER JOIN sys.tables st ON st.[object_id] = si.[object_id]
    INNER JOIN sys.schemas ss ON ss.[schema_id] = st.[schema_id]
    WHERE st.is_ms_shipped = 0        -- User tables only
      AND si.index_id != 0              -- ignore heaps
      AND ssi.rowcnt > @RowsToBenchMark
    ORDER BY ssi.rowcnt

    IF @@ROWCOUNT > 0
    BEGIN
        PRINT 'Testing sampling time with: ' + @StatsMarker

        SET @StartTime = GETDATE()
```

```
        EXECUTE sp_executesql @StatsMarker

        SET @TotalStatsTime = DATEDIFF(SECOND, @StartTime, GETDATE())
        PRINT '@TotalStatsTime: ' + CAST(@TotalStatsTime AS VARCHAR(22))

        IF (@TotalStatsTime > 5)
        BEGIN
            SET @TimePerRow = @TotalStatsTime /
                              (@RowsToBenchMark * 1.0)

            PRINT @TimePerRow

            SET @SamplingComplete = 1
        END
        ELSE
            SET @RowsToBenchMark = @RowsToBenchMark * 10
    END
    ELSE
    BEGIN
        DECLARE @ErrorMsg VARCHAR(200)
        SET @ErrorMsg = 'No indexes found with @RowsToBenchMark > '
                        + CAST(@RowsToBenchMark AS VARCHAR(22))
        RAISERROR(@ErrorMsg, 16, 1)
        RETURN
    END
END

DECLARE @RowsToSample BIGINT
SET @RowsToSample = 0

SELECT
    ss.name AS SchemaName
    , st.name AS TableName
    , si.name AS IndexName
    , si.type_desc AS IndexType
    , STATS_DATE(si.object_id,si.index_id) AS StatsLastTaken
    , ssi.rowcnt
    , ssi.rowmodctr
    , @RowsToSample AS RowsToSample
INTO #IndexUsage
FROM sys.indexes si
INNER JOIN sys.sysindexes ssi ON si.object_id = ssi.id
           AND si.name = ssi.name
INNER JOIN sys.tables st ON st.[object_id] = si.[object_id]
INNER JOIN sys.schemas ss ON ss.[schema_id] = st.[schema_id]
WHERE st.is_ms_shipped = 0
           AND si.index_id != 0
           AND ssi.rowcnt > 100
           AND ssi.rowmodctr > 0

DECLARE @MaxSamplingTimeInSeconds INT
SET @MaxSamplingTimeInSeconds = 600 -- 10 mins
DECLARE @WorkIsWithinTimeLimit BIT
SET @WorkIsWithinTimeLimit = 0
DECLARE @TotalTimeForAllStats  INT
DECLARE @ReduceFraction FLOAT
SET @ReduceFraction = 1.0
DECLARE @ReduceFractionSmall FLOAT
SET @ReduceFractionSmall = 1.0
```

❸ **Want at least 5 sec of statistics**

❹ **Calculate stats time per row**

❺ **Get a bigger sample**

❻ **Not enough rows to sample, exit**

❼ **Get indexes with stats to update**

```
UPDATE #IndexUsage
SET RowsToSample =
    CASE
        WHEN rowcnt < 100000000 THEN rowcnt
        ELSE 3000000
    END

WHILE (@WorkIsWithinTimeLimit = 0)
BEGIN

    UPDATE #IndexUsage
    SET RowsToSample =
        CASE
        WHEN rowcnt <    500000 THEN rowcnt * @ReduceFractionSmall
        WHEN rowcnt <   1000000 THEN rowcnt / 2 * @ReduceFractionSmall
        WHEN rowcnt <   5000000 THEN rowcnt / 4 * @ReduceFractionSmall
        WHEN rowcnt <  10000000 THEN rowcnt / 10 * @ReduceFraction
        WHEN rowcnt <  50000000 THEN rowcnt / 50 * @ReduceFraction
        WHEN rowcnt < 100000000 THEN rowcnt / 100 * @ReduceFraction
        ELSE 3000000 * @ReduceFraction
        END

    SELECT @TotalTimeForAllStats = SUM(RowsToSample) * @TimePerRow
    FROM #IndexUsage

    PRINT '@TotalTimeForAllStats: '
            + CAST(@TotalTimeForAllStats AS VARCHAR(22))

    IF (@TotalTimeForAllStats < @MaxSamplingTimeInSeconds)
        SET @WorkIsWithinTimeLimit = 1
    ELSE
    BEGIN
        SET @ReduceFraction = @ReduceFraction - 0.01
        SET @ReduceFractionSmall = @ReduceFractionSmall - 0.001
    END
END

DECLARE @UpdateStatisticsSQL NVARCHAR(MAX)
SET @UpdateStatisticsSQL = ''

SELECT
  @UpdateStatisticsSQL = @UpdateStatisticsSQL
  + CHAR(10) + 'UPDATE STATISTICS ' + QUOTENAME(SchemaName)
  + '.' + QUOTENAME(TableName)
  + ' ' + QUOTENAME(IndexName) + ' WITH SAMPLE '
  + CAST(RowsToSample AS VARCHAR(22)) + ' ROWS '
FROM #IndexUsage

DECLARE @StartOffset INT
DECLARE @Length INT
SET @StartOffset = 0
SET @Length = 4000

WHILE (@StartOffset < LEN(@UpdateStatisticsSQL))
BEGIN
    PRINT SUBSTRING(@UpdateStatisticsSQL, @StartOffset, @Length)
    SET @StartOffset = @StartOffset + @Length
END
```

8 Apply weighting factor

9 Calc total time for stats update

10 Sampling time exceeded

11 Decrease rows to sample

12 Build SQL to update statistics

13 Debug

```
PRINT SUBSTRING(@UpdateStatisticsSQL, @StartOffset, @Length)

EXECUTE sp_executesql @UpdateStatisticsSQL

DROP TABLE #IndexUsage

END
```

⟵┐ **Execute**
⑭ **SQL**

This script uses the same tables and initial sample weighted algorithm as the previous intelligently update statistics script. The big difference is that this script will adjust the number of rows sampled to complete within a given time interval.

The script first determines if there are any indexes that need to have their statistics updated ❶; if rows exist, it proceeds. This ensures you don't do any unnecessary processing.

The script next calculates how long it takes to update the statistics for a known number of rows ❷. We want statistics that take at least five seconds to calculate for our subsequent calculations to be meaningful ❸. If our sample completes within five seconds, we increase the sample size ❺ and inspect an index that has more rows to sample. If we can't find an index of sufficient size, an error message is set, a RAISERROR is issued ❻, and the routine is exited.

If we can obtain a statistics sample that takes at least five seconds to calculate, we then calculate how long it takes to update the statistics for a given row ❹. This is important in determining how long it will take to update all the rows on the indexes that need to have their statistics updated.

We next get the indexes that need to have their statistics updated ❼ and apply the intelligent sampling weighting based on the number of rows the index contains ❽. From this we can determine how long updating the statistics should take ❾. If it exceeds the time we have available ❿, we reduce the sampling size, again with an intelligent sampling weighting based on the number of rows the index contains ⓫, and we again estimate how long updating the statistics of this reduced number of rows will take. This process is repeated until the rows can be sampled within the time period allowed.

In the last part of the script, the names of the indexes that you want to update the statistics on are prepended with the name of the schema and table, together with the keywords UPDATE STATISTICS ⓬. The resultant commands are concatenated and the result stored in the variable @UpdateStatisticsSQL. The content of the variable @UpdateStatisticsSQL is also displayed for debugging purposes, via the PRINT command ⓭. This variable is then used as input to the system stored procedure sp_executesql; running this executes the text and updates the statistics on the relevant indexes ⓮.

> **NOTE** This method assumes the performance of the system is the same when the updates are done as when the sample was taken. If the system is busier when the index's statistics are updated, then this will result in a longer time interval than has been estimated.

The smaller indexes have a smaller reduction factor; this is to ensure that we'll have a more representative range of data values in the smaller row sets. The WHILE loop exits when the number of rows to sample can be achieved within the specified time interval.

It's possible to amend the script to include only the databases, schemas, or indexes that you're interested in by adding a WHERE clause to the query that dynamically builds up the UPDATE STATISTICS SQL.

Having discussed intelligent statistics, let's now discuss how you can automatically update the statistics used by a given routine.

10.5   *Automatically updating a routine's statistics*

If you have SQL queries that run at given times or in a certain sequence, it makes sense to ensure the statistics the queries use are up to date before the queries are run. You can schedule an update statistics job to run automatically to update a routine's statistics before the routine itself runs. This will allow the queries to take advantage of the latest data relating to the distribution and density of column values.

The following script allows you to run a given batch of SQL queries and records the indexes that are accessed. It then creates the appropriate UPDATE STATISTICS statement with a weighted sampling percentage applied. Instead of running a batch of SQL queries, it's also possible to record the indexes that are accessed during a given time period, by making use of the WAITFOR DELAY keywords. In this example, the time period is 10 minutes; you may want to modify this interval to meet your needs.

Having previously run this script to obtain details of the indexes used by a given routine, or for a given time period, you should run this dynamic SQL before the normal run of your batch. In the script it's run immediately afterward for illustrative purposes only.

The script we use to automatically update the statistics intelligently, using a time-interval approach, is shown in the following listing.

Listing 10.7   Update statistics used by a SQL routine or a time interval

```
SET TRANSACTION ISOLATION LEVEL READ UNCOMMITTED

SELECT                                                  ◁─┐  Get index usage
    SchemaName = ss.name                                   │  counter values,
    , TableName = st.name                               ❶  pre-work
    , IndexName = si.name
    , si.type_desc AS IndexType
    , user_updates = ISNULL(ius.user_updates, 0)
    , user_seeks = ISNULL(ius.user_seeks, 0)
    , user_scans = ISNULL(ius.user_scans, 0)
    , user_lookups = ISNULL(ius.user_lookups, 0)
    , ssi.rowcnt
    , ssi.rowmodctr
INTO #IndexStatsPre
FROM    sys.dm_db_index_usage_stats ius
```

```
RIGHT OUTER JOIN sys.indexes si ON   ius.[object_id] = si.[object_id]
                                AND ius.index_id = si.index_id
INNER JOIN sys.sysindexes ssi ON si.object_id = ssi.id
                            AND si.name = ssi.name
INNER JOIN sys.tables st ON st.[object_id] = si.[object_id]
INNER JOIN sys.schemas ss ON ss.[schema_id] = st.[schema_id]
WHERE ius.database_id = DB_ID()
    AND st.is_ms_shipped = 0
```

❷ Run SQL batch or wait for time interval

```
WAITFOR DELAY '00:10:00'

SELECT
```

❸ Get index usage counter values, post-work

```
    SchemaName = ss.name
    , TableName = st.name
    , IndexName = si.name
    , si.type_desc AS IndexType
    , user_updates = ISNULL(ius.user_updates, 0)
    , user_seeks = ISNULL(ius.user_seeks, 0)
    , user_scans = ISNULL(ius.user_scans, 0)
    , user_lookups = ISNULL(ius.user_lookups, 0)
    , ssi.rowcnt
    , ssi.rowmodctr
INTO #IndexStatsPost
FROM sys.dm_db_index_usage_stats ius
RIGHT OUTER JOIN sys.indexes si ON  ius.[object_id] = si.[object_id]
                 AND ius.index_id = si.index_id
INNER JOIN sys.sysindexes ssi ON si.object_id = ssi.id
                    AND si.name = ssi.name
INNER JOIN sys.tables st ON st.[object_id] = si.[object_id]
INNER JOIN sys.schemas ss ON ss.[schema_id] = st.[schema_id]
WHERE ius.database_id = DB_ID()
    AND st.is_ms_shipped = 0

SELECT
```

❹ Determine which counters have changed

```
    po.[SchemaName]
    , po.[TableName]
    , po.[IndexName]
    , po.rowcnt
    , po.[IndexType]
    , [User Updates] = po.user_updates - ISNULL(pr.user_updates, 0)
    , [User Seeks] = po.user_seeks - ISNULL(pr.user_seeks, 0)
    , [User Scans] = po.user_scans - ISNULL(pr.user_scans, 0)
    , [User Lookups] = po.user_lookups - ISNULL(pr.user_lookups, 0)
    , [Rows Inserted] = po.rowcnt - ISNULL(pr.rowcnt, 0)
    , [Updates I/U/D] = po.rowmodctr - ISNULL(pr.rowmodctr, 0)
INTO #IndexUsage
FROM #IndexStatsPost po
LEFT OUTER JOIN #IndexStatsPre pr ON pr.SchemaName = po.SchemaName
        AND pr.TableName = po.TableName
        AND pr.IndexName = po.IndexName
        AND pr.IndexType = po.IndexType
WHERE ISNULL(pr.user_updates, 0) != po.user_updates
  OR ISNULL(pr.user_seeks, 0) != po.user_seeks
  OR ISNULL(pr.user_scans, 0) != po.user_scans
  OR ISNULL(pr.user_lookups, 0) != po.user_lookups
```

```
DECLARE @UpdateStatisticsSQL NVARCHAR(MAX)
SET @UpdateStatisticsSQL = ''

SELECT
  @UpdateStatisticsSQL = @UpdateStatisticsSQL
  + CHAR(10) + 'UPDATE STATISTICS ' + QUOTENAME(SchemaName)
  + '.' + QUOTENAME(TableName)
  + ' ' + QUOTENAME(IndexName) + ' WITH SAMPLE '
  + CASE
      WHEN rowcnt <     500000 THEN '100 PERCENT'
      WHEN rowcnt <    1000000 THEN '50 PERCENT'
      WHEN rowcnt <    5000000 THEN '25 PERCENT'
      WHEN rowcnt <   10000000 THEN '10 PERCENT'
      WHEN rowcnt <   50000000 THEN '2 PERCENT'
      WHEN rowcnt <  100000000 THEN '1 PERCENT'
      ELSE '3000000 ROWS '
    END
FROM   #IndexUsage
WHERE [User Seeks] != 0 OR [User Scans] != 0  OR [User Lookups] != 0

DECLARE @StartOffset INT
DECLARE @Length INT
SET @StartOffset = 0
SET @Length = 4000

WHILE (@StartOffset < LEN(@UpdateStatisticsSQL))
BEGIN
    PRINT SUBSTRING(@UpdateStatisticsSQL, @StartOffset, @Length)
    SET @StartOffset = @StartOffset + @Length
END

PRINT SUBSTRING(@UpdateStatisticsSQL, @StartOffset, @Length)

EXECUTE sp_executesql @UpdateStatisticsSQL

DROP TABLE #IndexStatsPre
DROP TABLE #IndexStatsPost
DROP TABLE #IndexUsage
```

❺ Build UPDATE STATISTICS SQL

❻ Debug

❼ Run SQL

This script is an extension of one given in chapter 3, section 3.7, "Indexes used by a given routine."

First, we take a snapshot of the current values of the relevant index metrics and store them in a temporary table named #IndexStatsPre ❶. Then we run the query we want to obtain index details about, or, as in our script example, we wait for a given time interval to pass to determine which indexes have changed ❷. Next, we take another snapshot and store the results into a table named #IndexStatsPost ❸. We compare the two snapshots ❹ to determine which indexes have changed during the running of the query under investigation (or a time period has elapsed).

Details of the indexes that are used by a given routine, or during a given time interval, are stored in a temporary table named #IndexUsage. The UPDATE STATISTICS command is prepended to the name of the schema, the name of the table, and the name of the index. This is then appended with a sample percentage that's based on the number of rows in the index. All these statements are concatenated and the result stored in the variable @UpdateStatisticsSQL ❺. The content of the variable

@UpdateStatisticsSQL is also displayed for debugging purposes, via the PRINT command ❻. This variable is then used as input to the system stored procedure sp_executesql ❼; running this executes the text and updates the statistics on the given index with the predetermined sample size.

It's possible to amend the script to include only the databases, schemas, or indexes that you're interested in by adding a WHERE clause to the query that dynamically builds up the UPDATE STATISTICS SQL.

Having discussed the importance of ensuring an index's statistics are up to date, we'll next discuss the problem of missing indexes and how they can be automatically implemented.

10.6 *Automatically implement missing indexes*

Indexes and their associated statistics can have a dramatic effect on SQL query performance. We fully discussed missing indexes in chapter 3, section 3.2, "Costly missing indexes." We also presented a script to identify the most-costly missing indexes.

Here we'll discuss how this script can be extended to automatically create the SQL commands necessary to implement these missing indexes. Implementing these indexes could have a significant effect on query performance.

> **Should you automatically implement missing indexes?**
> The missing indexes identified via the missing-index DMVs relate to specific SQL queries that have run. Adding the missing indexes should improve the performance of these specific queries, but they may also lead to slower updates and longer transactions. Also, no attempt is made to amalgamate any related indexes. It might be advantageous to implement the most important missing indexes automatically, especially on data warehouse databases, but I'd advise you to review fully all such indexes before automatically implementing them.

10.6.1 *Implementing missing indexes*

The script we use to automatically implement missing indexes is shown in the following listing. This script is an extension of the one given in chapter 3, section 3.2, which identified the most-important missing indexes.

Listing 10.8 Automatically create any missing indexes

```
SET TRANSACTION ISOLATION LEVEL READ UNCOMMITTED          ❶ Build SQL for most-important
                                                              missing indexes
SELECT TOP 20
    'CREATE NONCLUSTERED INDEX '
    + QUOTENAME('IX_AutoGenerated_'
    + REPLACE(REPLACE(CONVERT(VARCHAR(25), GETDATE(), 113)
                        , ' ', '_'), ':', '_')
    + '_' + CAST(d.index_handle AS VARCHAR(22))
            )
    + ' ON ' + d.[statement] + '('
```

```
        + CASE
            WHEN d.equality_columns IS NULL THEN d.inequality_columns
            WHEN d.inequality_columns IS NULL THEN d.equality_columns
            ELSE d.equality_columns + ',' + d.inequality_columns
        END
        + ')'
        + CASE
            WHEN d.included_columns IS NOT NULL THEN
                ' INCLUDE ( ' +  d.included_columns +  ')'
            ELSE ''
            END          AS MissingIndexSQL
    , ROUND(s.avg_total_user_cost * s.avg_user_impact
        * (s.user_seeks + s.user_scans),0) AS [Total Cost]
    , d.[statement] AS [Table Name]
    , d.equality_columns
    , d.inequality_columns
    , d.included_columns
INTO #MissingIndexes
FROM sys.dm_db_missing_index_groups g
INNER JOIN sys.dm_db_missing_index_group_stats s
        ON s.group_handle = g.index_group_handle
INNER JOIN sys.dm_db_missing_index_details d
        ON d.index_handle = g.index_handle
ORDER BY [Total Cost] DESC

DECLARE @MissingIndexesSQL NVARCHAR(MAX)
SET @MissingIndexesSQL = ''

SELECT
  @MissingIndexesSQL = @MissingIndexesSQL + MissingIndexSQL + CHAR(10)
FROM #MissingIndexes

DECLARE @StartOffset INT
DECLARE @Length INT
SET @StartOffset = 0
SET @Length = 4000

WHILE (@StartOffset < LEN(@MissingIndexesSQL))
BEGIN
    PRINT SUBSTRING(@MissingIndexesSQL, @StartOffset, @Length)
    SET @StartOffset = @StartOffset + @Length
END

PRINT SUBSTRING(@MissingIndexesSQL, @StartOffset, @Length)

EXECUTE sp_executesql @MissingIndexesSQL

DROP TABLE #MissingIndexes
```

❷ **Amalgamate missing indexes SQL**

❸ **Debug**

❹ **Execute SQL**

This script was largely discussed in chapter 3. We'll discuss here only the changes that allow the creation of the automation of the missing-indexes script.

The first part of the script identifies the 20 most-important missing indexes. These missing indexes are wrapped with SQL keywords that create a nonclustered index ❶. The unique name of the index is created from a combination of a static piece of text (IX_Autogenerated_), the date the script was run, and the index_handle of the missing index.

The structure of the indexes is created from the columns identified by the equality_columns and/or inequality_columns, together with any columns given by the included_columns column. The results are stored in the temporary table named #MissingIndexes.

All the wrapped-up CREATE NONCLUSTERED INDEX statements are concatenated, and the result is stored in the variable @MissingIndexesSQL ❷. The content of the variable @MissingIndexesSQL is displayed for debugging purposes, via the PRINT command ❸. This variable is then used as input to the system stored procedure sp_executesql; running this executes the text and creates the missing indexes ❹.

It's possible to amend the script to include only the databases, schemas, or indexes that you're interested in by adding a WHERE clause to the query that dynamically builds the missing-indexes SQL.

Having looked at implementing missing indexes, we'll next discuss the diametrically opposite functionality—automatic disabling or dropping of unused indexes.

10.7　*Automatically disable or drop unused indexes*

Perhaps the most important message from this section is that you should drop an index only if you're *certain* that it's never used.

Should you automatically disable or drop indexes?

I was unsure whether to include this script because of the uncertainty in determining whether an index is used or not. The DMVs record data accumulated since the last reboot; if a query that uses a given index hasn't been run yet, it will be reported as unused and could be removed. But to ease my fears, the default option in the script is to disable the index. This will remove the index and its data but keep its definition tied to the underlying table, allowing it to be reinstated if it's required. Ensure that you test this functionality on your test systems. Only if you're certain that an index isn't used should you drop it.

Indexes are often of paramount importance for the performance of SQL queries, allowing the relevant data to be retrieved much quicker than scanning the underlying table. But indexes can have a detrimental effect on updates (via UPDATE, DELETE, or INSERT), because the index data may also need to be updated. This will add to the query duration, length of transaction, and locks, leading to blocking and potential timeouts for clients.

Unused indexes force SQL Server to do unnecessary work. In addition to queries taking longer to execute, administrative functions like backups and restores will take longer to complete, and there's also an additional cost associated with the storage of unnecessary data. Where possible, you should remove any unused indexes.

Costly unused indexes were discussed fully in chapter 3, section 3.3, "Unused indexes." A script was presented to identify the most-costly unused indexes.

Here we'll discuss how you can extend this script to automatically create the SQL commands to disable or drop these unused indexes. Disabling or removing these indexes could have a significant effect on query performance.

10.7.1 *Disabling or dropping unused indexes*

The script we use to automatically disable or drop unused indexes is shown in the following listing. This script is an extension of the one given in chapter 3, section 3.3, which identified the most-costly unused indexes.

Listing 10.9   Automatically disable or drop unused indexes

```
SET TRANSACTION ISOLATION LEVEL READ UNCOMMITTED
SELECT
    DB_NAME() AS DatabaseName
    , SCHEMA_NAME(o.Schema_ID) AS SchemaName
    , OBJECT_NAME(s.[object_id]) AS TableName
    , i.name AS IndexName
    , s.user_updates
    , s.system_seeks + s.system_scans + s.system_lookups
                                    AS [System usage]
INTO #TempUnusedIndexes
FROM   sys.dm_db_index_usage_stats s
INNER JOIN sys.indexes i ON s.[object_id] = i.[object_id]
    AND s.index_id = i.index_id
INNER JOIN sys.objects o ON i.object_id = O.object_id
WHERE 1=2

EXEC sp_MSForEachDB 'USE [?];
INSERT INTO #TempUnusedIndexes
SELECT TOP 20
    DB_NAME() AS DatabaseName
    , SCHEMA_NAME(o.Schema_ID) AS SchemaName
    , OBJECT_NAME(s.[object_id]) AS TableName
    , i.name AS IndexName
    , s.user_updates
    , s.system_seeks + s.system_scans + s.system_lookups
                                    AS [System usage]
FROM   sys.dm_db_index_usage_stats s
INNER JOIN sys.indexes i ON s.[object_id] = i.[object_id]
    AND s.index_id = i.index_id
INNER JOIN sys.objects o ON i.object_id = O.object_id
WHERE s.database_id = DB_ID()
  AND OBJECTPROPERTY(s.[object_id], ''IsMsShipped'') = 0
  AND user_seeks = 0
  AND user_scans = 0
  AND user_lookups = 0
  AND i.name IS NOT NULL
ORDER BY user_updates DESC'

DECLARE @DisableOrDrop INT
SET @DisableOrDrop = 1

DECLARE @DisableIndexesSQL NVARCHAR(MAX)
SET @DisableIndexesSQL = ''
```

❶ Identify most-important unused indexes

```
SELECT
    @DisableIndexesSQL = @DisableIndexesSQL +
    CASE
    WHEN @DisableOrDrop = 1
        THEN CHAR(10) + 'ALTER INDEX ' +  QUOTENAME(IndexName) + ' ON '
            + QUOTENAME(DatabaseName) + '.'+ QUOTENAME(SchemaName) + '.'
            + QUOTENAME(TableName) + ' DISABLE;'
    ELSE CHAR(10) + 'DROP INDEX ' +  QUOTENAME(IndexName) + ' ON '
            + QUOTENAME(DatabaseName) + '.'+ QUOTENAME(SchemaName) + '.'
            + QUOTENAME(TableName)
    END
FROM  #TempUnusedIndexes

DECLARE @StartOffset INT
DECLARE @Length INT
SET @StartOffset = 0
SET @Length = 4000

WHILE (@StartOffset < LEN(@DisableIndexesSQL))
BEGIN
    PRINT SUBSTRING(@DisableIndexesSQL, @StartOffset, @Length)
    SET @StartOffset = @StartOffset + @Length
END

PRINT SUBSTRING(@DisableIndexesSQL, @StartOffset, @Length)

EXECUTE sp_executesql @DisableIndexesSQL

DROP TABLE #TempUnusedIndexes
```

❷ Amalgamate unused indexes SQL

❸ Build the disable or drop index SQL

❹ Debug

❺ Execute SQL

This script was largely discussed in chapter 3. We'll discuss here only the changes that allow the automation of disabling or dropping of the unused indexes script.

The first part of the script identifies the 20 most-important unused indexes, across all the databases on the server ❶. Details of these unused indexes are stored in the temporary table named #TempUnusedIndexes. These unused indexes are concatenated ❷ and wrapped with SQL keywords that will disable or drop the indexes ❸. The contents of the variable @DisableOrDrop determine whether the indexes should be disabled or dropped. By default the indexes will be disabled. If you change the value of the variable @DisableOrDrop to a value other than 1, it will cause SQL to be built to drop the indexes.

The wrapped-up INDEX statements are concatenated and the result stored in the variable @DisableIndexesSQL. The content of the variable @DisableIndcxesSQL is also displayed for debugging purposes, via the PRINT command ❹. This variable is then used as input to the system stored procedure sp_executesql; running this executes the text and disables or drops the unused indexes ❺.

It's possible to amend the script to include only the databases, schemas, or indexes that you're interested in by adding a WHERE clause to the query that dynamically builds up the disable or drop indexes SQL.

As discussed already, you should drop an index only if you're *certain* that it's never used. As a side note, you could use this script that disables/drops indexes and the previous script that creates missing indexes together to automatically create required indexes and remove undesirable indexes.

10.8 *Summary*

This chapter introduced the concept of a self-healing database that enhances the automated features provided out of the box for SQL Server maintenance. I took several of the scripts discussed in previous chapters and extended them so they could be run periodically, as jobs, via the SQL agent to perform various self-healing functions.

I described how to identify queries that are running slower than normal and mark them for recompilation, so that the next time they're used, a new query plan would be created, hopefully with a better data access mechanism.

I addressed the perennial problem of retrieving fragmented data via a script that determines the degree of fragmentation and either performs an index rebuild or index reorganization.

I provided a script to intelligently update the statistics of those indexes whose data content has changed. The weighted algorithm provided allowed sufficient sampling to be undertaken irrespective of the index's size. A related time-limiting sampling algorithm was also provided.

For systems with regular SQL batches or batches with known sequencing, I provided a script that allows updating of the relevant statistics immediately prior to running the SQL batches. This should improve the performance of these queries.

Two related but diametrical scripts were provided to implement missing indexes and to disable or drop any unused indexes. The potential danger of automating this particular functionality was highlighted.

Having discussed several features to automate the optimization of your SQL Server systems, we've almost come to end of the book. The final chapter will discuss a gallimaufry of scripts that I think you'll find both interesting and useful.

Useful scripts

Gallimaufry refers to "odds and ends," and that nicely sums up the content of this chapter. It contains a hodgepodge of scripts that can reveal some interesting and useful information. The scripts given in this chapter wouldn't sit comfortably within the other chapters of the book.

The content of this chapter is wide ranging, covering such diverse areas as finding which SQL queries everyone last ran, getting Windows system information within SQL Server, determining where your queries really spend their time (as opposed to the cached plan estimate), and a lightweight SQL tracing utility. We'll begin by looking at how you can view everyone's last-run query.

11.1 Viewing everyone's last-run SQL query

Viewing details of everyone's last-run SQL queries can be useful in understanding how your users use the database. It can also be useful in checking users when they say, "the only SQL I ran was...." Often there's a difference between what users say they've done and what they've really done. The script provided here should help clear up this discrepancy.

11.1.1 Find the last-run queries

It can be both useful and informative to look at the SQL queries that users of your servers have been running. This can help you examine the level of understanding of your users (do they use stored procedures or inline SQL?). Running the SQL script given in our first listing will identify everyone's last-run query.

Listing 11.1   Finding everyone's last-run query

```
SET TRANSACTION ISOLATION LEVEL READ UNCOMMITTED
SELECT c.session_id, s.host_name, s.login_name, s.status
        , st.text, s.login_time, s.program_name, *
FROM sys.dm_exec_connections c
INNER JOIN sys.dm_exec_sessions s ON c.session_id = s.session_id
CROSS APPLY sys.dm_exec_sql_text(most_recent_sql_handle) AS st
ORDER BY c.session_id
```

The listing shows that two DMVs and one DMF are involved in finding everyone's last-run SQL query. Table 11.1 provides a brief description of each.

Table 11.1   DMVs/DMF used to find everyone's last-run SQL query

DMV/DMF	Description
sys.dm_exec_connections	Contains details of connections to SQL Server
sys.dm_exec_sessions	Contains details of sessions on SQL Server
sys.dm_exec_sql_text	DMF that returns the SQL text identified by a given sql_handle

The joining of the DMVs and DMF provides us with enough information to discover everyone's last-run SQL query, across all the databases on the server. The DMVs sys.dm_exec_connections and sys.dm_exec_sessions are joined on their common key column session_id. The connection's most_recent_sql_handle is passed to the DMF sys.dm_exec_sql_text to retrieve the text of the SQL query.

> **NOTE**   Because we're not joining to any actively running SQL queries (via the DMV sys.dm_exec_requests), this script enables us to see everyone's last-run SQL query, even if they're not actively running anything.

An example of the type of output for this query is shown in figure 11.1.

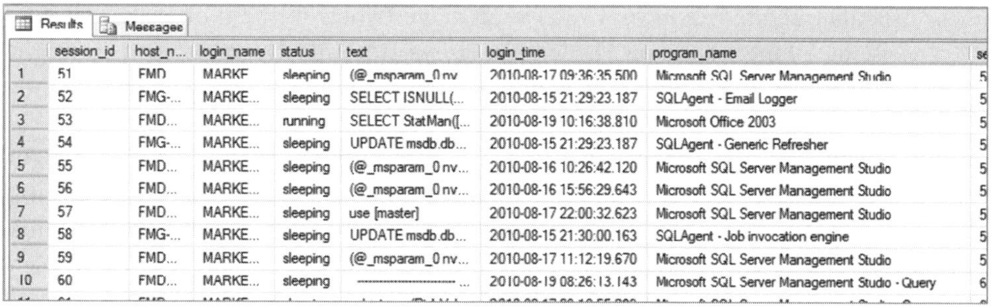

	session_id	host_n...	login_name	status	text	login_time	program_name	se
1	51	FMD	MARKE	sleeping	(@_msparam_0 nv	2010-08-17 09:36:35.500	Microsoft SQL Server Management Studio	5
2	52	FMG-...	MARKE...	sleeping	SELECT ISNULL(...	2010-08-15 21:29:23.187	SQLAgent - Email Logger	5
3	53	FMD...	MARKE...	running	SELECT StatMan([...	2010-08-19 10:16:38.810	Microsoft Office 2003	5
4	54	FMG-...	MARKE...	sleeping	UPDATE msdb.db...	2010-08-15 21:29:23.187	SQLAgent - Generic Refresher	5
5	55	FMD...	MARKE...	sleeping	(@_msparam_0 nv...	2010-08-16 10:26:42.120	Microsoft SQL Server Management Studio	5
6	56	FMD...	MARKE...	sleeping	(@_msparam_0 nv...	2010-08-16 15:56:29.643	Microsoft SQL Server Management Studio	5
7	57	FMD...	MARKE...	sleeping	use [master]	2010-08-17 22:00:32.623	Microsoft SQL Server Management Studio	5
8	58	FMG-...	MARKE...	sleeping	UPDATE msdb.db...	2010-08-15 21:30:00.163	SQLAgent - Job invocation engine	5
9	59	FMD...	MARKE...	sleeping	(@_msparam_0 nv...	2010-08-17 11:12:19.670	Microsoft SQL Server Management Studio	5
10	60	FMD...	MARKE...	sleeping	------------------------ ...	2010-08-19 08:26:13.143	Microsoft SQL Server Management Studio - Query	6

Figure 11.1 Output showing details of everyone's last-run SQL queries

Figure 11.1 shows the result of running the "finding everyone's last-run query" script. The columns that are output show where the SQL query was run from, the name of the user who ran the query, the name of the program that issued the query, and the text of the SQL query.

Now that you've seen the details of how you can view everyone's last-run query, I'll show you a script that can be used to test the performance of your code.

11.2 A generic performance test harness

Often it can be difficult to determine whether any improvements have been made when you change your SQL queries. Sometimes the time differences seem too small to measure, or they involve the cumbersome task of instrumenting your queries to output timings and other debug information. In addition to time differences, changes could also be reflecting a fewer number of reads or writes occurring; having these details might also determine whether a prospective change is good or not.

The test harness described here allows you to record performance details relating to your queries, for example, total duration, number of reads, and number of writes. Its purpose is to obtain these performance metrics first when the unchanged SQL query is run and then again when you change the query to incorporate a potential improvement. For example, you might change the algorithm the SQL query uses or add an index that you think might be useful. Finally, you compare the two outputs and determine whether the change is an improvement.

The script given in this section will enable you to test the changes in your queries within a generic test framework. The script will output, for each SQL query run within a given batch or stored procedure, the total duration of the query, the time it spent using the CPU, the time it spent waiting (or being blocked), the number of reads, the number of writes, the number of times each line of SQL within the query was executed, the text of the individual SQL query, the text of the parent SQL query, and the database the query ran on.

As always, there's the caveat that the DMVs will record details of all the queries that are running on the server. It's possible to extract your particular queries from the output or limit the output to a given database. If you really need to determine the standalone metrics of your queries, I suggest you run them on a standalone server or else at a time when you know little else is running. On occasion you might actually want details of all the other running queries to see how your query runs when interacting with other queries.

This script can prove quite useful in determining which of a series of algorithms to use, rather than guess or follow conventional wisdom, where a given approach is assumed to be correct. For example, when is it better to replace the contents of an IN clause with an INNER JOIN to a temporary table containing the IN clause's details? Using this script will provide metrics to support your decisions.

11.2.1 Using the generic performance test harness

Using a generic test harness to conduct your performance measurements provides a repeatable method of testing. Running the SQL script given in the following listing shows how the generic performance test harness is used.

Listing 11.2   Generic performance test harness

```
SET TRANSACTION ISOLATION LEVEL READ UNCOMMITTED                    ➊ Get pre-work query
SELECT                                                                 DMV counters
    sql_handle, plan_handle, total_elapsed_time, total_worker_time
    , total_logical_reads, total_logical_writes, total_clr_time
    , execution_count, statement_start_offset, statement_end_offset
INTO #PreWorkQuerySnapShot                            ➋ Run your test
FROM sys.dm_exec_query_stats                             query here
                                                              ➌ Get post-
EXEC PutYourQueryHere                                            work query
                                                                DMV counters
SELECT
    sql_handle, plan_handle, total_elapsed_time, total_worker_time
    , total_logical_reads, total_logical_writes, total_clr_time
    , execution_count, statement_start_offset, statement_end_offset
INTO #PostWorkQuerySnapShot
FROM sys.dm_exec_query_stats                          ➍ Calculate
                                                        metrics for
SELECT                                                  your query
    p2.total_elapsed_time - ISNULL(p1.total_elapsed_time, 0) AS [Duration]
    , p2.total_worker_time - ISNULL(p1.total_worker_time, 0) AS [Time on CPU]
    , (p2.total_elapsed_time - ISNULL(p1.total_elapsed_time, 0)) -
                (p2.total_worker_time - ISNULL(p1.total_worker_time, 0))
                                                    AS [Time blocked]
    , p2.total_logical_reads - ISNULL(p1.total_logical_reads, 0) AS [Reads]
    , p2.total_logical_writes - ISNULL(p1.total_logical_writes, 0)
                                                    AS [Writes]
    , p2.total_clr_time - ISNULL(p1.total_clr_time, 0) AS [CLR time]
    , p2.execution_count - ISNULL(p1.execution_count, 0) AS [Executions]
    , SUBSTRING (qt.text,p2.statement_start_offset/2 + 1,
    ((CASE WHEN p2.statement_end_offset = -1
       THEN LEN(CONVERT(NVARCHAR(MAX), qt.text)) * 2
       ELSE p2.statement_end_offset
       END - p2.statement_start_offset)/2) + 1) AS [Individual Query]
    , qt.text AS [Parent Query]
    , DB_NAME(qt.dbid) AS DatabaseName
```

```
FROM #PreWorkQuerySnapShot p1
RIGHT OUTER JOIN
#PostWorkQuerySnapShot p2 ON p2.sql_handle =
        ISNULL(p1.sql_handle, p2.sql_handle)
  AND p2.plan_handle = ISNULL(p1.plan_handle, p2.plan_handle)
  AND p2.statement_start_offset =
        ISNULL(p1.statement_start_offset, p2.statement_start_offset)
  AND p2.statement_end_offset =
        ISNULL(p1.statement_end_offset, p2.statement_end_offset)
CROSS APPLY sys.dm_exec_sql_text(p2.sql_handle) as qt
WHERE p2.execution_count != ISNULL(p1.execution_count, 0)
ORDER BY qt.text, p2.statement_start_offset

DROP TABLE #PreWorkQuerySnapShot
DROP TABLE #PostWorkQuerySnapShot
```

The listing shows that one DMV and one DMF are involved in running the generic performance test harness. A brief description of each is given in table 11.2.

Table 11.2   DMV/DMF to provide a generic performance test harness

DMV/DMF	Description
sys.dm_exec_query_stats	Contains aggregated performance statistics for cached query plans
sys.dm_exec_sql_text	DMF that returns the SQL text identified by a given plan_handle or sql_handle

The script works by first taking a snapshot of the relevant columns of the DMV sys.dm_exec_query_stats ❶. The next step is to run the query you want to obtain metrics about ❷. The script then takes another snapshot of the relevant columns of the DMV sys.dm_exec_query_stats ❸ and compares the two snapshots to determine which metrics have changed ❹. The sql_handle column is decoded to obtain the Parent Query; this is further manipulated to extract the Individual Query, which the individual metrics apply to.

We use a RIGHT OUTER JOIN because there may be queries that aren't in the first snapshot but are present in the second snapshot, and we want the details of these queries. Similarly, we use ISNULL on the various DMV metric columns to catch any queries that aren't in the first snapshot.

The results are sorted by the text of the query and then by the offset of the Individual Query. This allows us to see the order of execution of the SQL statements within any batch of SQL statements. We could also use this to determine which SQL statements have (or have not) been executed for this run.

An example of the type of output for this query is shown in figure 11.2.

Figure 11.2 shows the result of running the "generic performance test harness" script. The columns in the output show the accumulated metrics for the total duration of the Individual Query, the time it spent on the CPU, the time it spent waiting (or being blocked), the number of reads and writes it performed, the number of times

	Duration	Time on CPU	Time blocked	Reads	Writes	CLR time	Executions	Individual Query	Parent Query	Database Name
1	976	976	0	2	0	0	1	select @MappingTypeI...	-- use of alter going forwar...	ParisDev
2	104492	70312	34180	4309	0	0	1	select m.FromValue ,s...	-- use of alter going forwar...	ParisDev
3	0	0	0	2	0	0	1	select @MappingTypeI...	-- use of alter going forwar...	ParisDev
4	241211	114258	126953	4308	0	0	1	select m.FromValue ,s...	-- use of alter going forwar...	ParisDev
5	0	0	0	2	0	0	1	select @MappingTypeI...	CREATE PROCEDURE [...	ParisDev
6	0	0	0	2	0	0	1	set @ParisSourceId = d...	CREATE PROCEDURE [...	ParisDev

Figure 11.2   Output showing details of running SQL queries within the generic performance test harness

the Individual Query was executed, and the text of the Individual Query and the Parent Query.

Having discussed a generic test harness, I'd now like to extend this into a more practical example, such as one used for determining the impact of a system upgrade.

11.3   *Determining the impact of a system upgrade*

When you implement a system upgrade, such as a new version of SQL Server or a service pack, it can be difficult to quantify its value—or indeed if it will degrade performance! If you run this script before the upgrade is made and subsequent to any upgrade, it will allow you to determine the effect of the upgrade on performance. I've used this script to determine the impact on query performance of upgrading from SQL Server 2005 to SQL Server 2008.

11.3.1   *Quantifying system upgrade impact*

Determining the impact of a system upgrade can influence whether the upgrade should be implemented. Running the SQL script given here provides a method for recording metrics at the database, Parent Query, and Individual Query levels.

Listing 11.3   Determining the performance impact of a system upgrade

```
SET TRANSACTION ISOLATION LEVEL READ UNCOMMITTED            ❶ Get pre-work
                                                              counters
SELECT
    total_elapsed_time, total_worker_time, total_logical_reads
    , total_logical_writes, total_clr_time, execution_count
    , statement_start_offset, statement_end_offset, sql_handle, plan_handle
INTO #prework
FROM sys.dm_exec_query_stats                   ❷ Do something here
                                                  (query/time interval)
EXEC PutYourWorkloadHere
                                                              ❸ Get post-work
SELECT                                                           counters
    total_elapsed_time, total_worker_time, total_logical_reads
    , total_logical_writes, total_clr_time, execution_count
    , statement_start_offset, statement_end_offset, sql_handle, plan_handle
INTO #postwork
FROM sys.dm_exec_query_stats
                                                              ❹ Get totals by
SELECT                                                           database
    SUM(p2.total_elapsed_time - ISNULL(p1.total_elapsed_time, 0))
                                        AS [TotalDuration]
```

```
        , SUM(p2.total_worker_time - ISNULL(p1.total_worker_time, 0))
                                        AS [Total Time on CPU]
        , SUM((p2.total_elapsed_time - ISNULL(p1.total_elapsed_time, 0)) -
            (p2.total_worker_time - ISNULL(p1.total_worker_time, 0)))
                                        AS [Total Time Waiting]
        , SUM(p2.total_logical_reads - ISNULL(p1.total_logical_reads, 0))
                                        AS [TotalReads]
        , SUM(p2.total_logical_writes - ISNULL(p1.total_logical_writes, 0))
                                        AS [TotalWrites]
        , SUM(p2.total_clr_time - ISNULL(p1.total_clr_time, 0))
                                        AS [Total CLR time]
        , SUM(p2.execution_count - ISNULL(p1.execution_count, 0))
                                        AS [Total Executions]
        , DB_NAME(qt.dbid) AS DatabaseName
FROM #prework p1
RIGHT OUTER JOIN
    #postwork p2 ON p2.sql_handle = ISNULL(p1.sql_handle, p2.sql_handle)
    AND p2.plan_handle = ISNULL(p1.plan_handle, p2.plan_handle)
    AND p2.statement_start_offset =
        ISNULL(p1.statement_start_offset, p2.statement_start_offset)
    AND p2.statement_end_offset =
        ISNULL(p1.statement_end_offset, p2.statement_end_offset)
CROSS APPLY sys.dm_exec_sql_text(p2.sql_handle) as qt
WHERE p2.execution_count != ISNULL(p1.execution_count, 0)
GROUP BY DB_NAME(qt.dbid)
```

⑤ Get totals by Parent Query

```
SELECT
    SUM(p2.total_elapsed_time - ISNULL(p1.total_elapsed_time, 0))
                                        AS [TotalDuration]
    , SUM(p2.total_worker_time - ISNULL(p1.total_worker_time, 0))
                                        AS [Total Time on CPU]
    , SUM((p2.total_elapsed_time - ISNULL(p1.total_elapsed_time, 0))
        - (p2.total_worker_time - ISNULL(p1.total_worker_time, 0)))
                                        AS [Total Time Waiting]
    , SUM(p2.total_logical_reads - ISNULL(p1.total_logical_reads, 0))
                                        AS [TotalReads]
    , SUM(p2.total_logical_writes - ISNULL(p1.total_logical_writes, 0))
                                        AS [TotalWrites]
    , SUM(p2.total_clr_time - ISNULL(p1.total_clr_time, 0))
                                        AS [Total CLR time]
    , SUM(p2.execution_count - ISNULL(p1.execution_count, 0))
                                        AS [Total Executions]
    , DB_NAME(qt.dbid) AS DatabaseName
    , qt.text AS [Parent Query]
FROM #prework p1
RIGHT OUTER JOIN
    #postwork p2 ON p2.sql_handle = ISNULL(p1.sql_handle, p2.sql_handle)
    AND p2.plan_handle = ISNULL(p1.plan_handle, p2.plan_handle)
    AND p2.statement_start_offset =
        ISNULL(p1.statement_start_offset, p2.statement_start_offset)
    AND p2.statement_end_offset =
        ISNULL(p1.statement_end_offset, p2.statement_end_offset)
CROSS APPLY sys.dm_exec_sql_text(p2.sql_handle) as qt
WHERE p2.execution_count != ISNULL(p1.execution_count, 0)
GROUP BY DB_NAME(qt.dbid), qt.text
ORDER BY [TotalDuration] DESC
```

```
SELECT                                        ◁─❻ Get totals by Individual Query
  p2.total_elapsed_time - ISNULL(p1.total_elapsed_time, 0)
                                               AS [TotalDuration]
  , p2.total_worker_time - ISNULL(p1.total_worker_time, 0)
                                               AS [Total Time on CPU]
  , (p2.total_elapsed_time - ISNULL(p1.total_elapsed_time, 0))
       - (p2.total_worker_time - ISNULL(p1.total_worker_time, 0))
                                               AS [Total Time Waiting]
  , p2.total_logical_reads - ISNULL(p1.total_logical_reads, 0)
                                               AS [TotalReads]
  , p2.total_logical_writes - ISNULL(p1.total_logical_writes, 0)
                                               AS [TotalWrites]
  , p2.total_clr_time - ISNULL(p1.total_clr_time, 0) AS [Total CLR time]
  , p2.execution_count - ISNULL(p1.execution_count, 0)
                                               AS [Total Executions]
  , SUBSTRING (qt.text,p2.statement_start_offset/2 + 1,
    ((CASE WHEN p2.statement_end_offset = -1
      THEN LEN(CONVERT(NVARCHAR(MAX), qt.text)) * 2
      ELSE p2.statement_end_offset
      END - p2.statement_start_offset)/2) + 1) AS [Individual Query]
  , qt.text AS [Parent Query]
  , DB_NAME(qt.dbid) AS DatabaseName
FROM #prework p1
RIGHT OUTER JOIN
  #postwork p2 ON p2.sql_handle = ISNULL(p1.sql_handle, p2.sql_handle)
    AND p2.plan_handle = ISNULL(p1.plan_handle, p2.plan_handle)
    AND p2.statement_start_offset =
        ISNULL(p1.statement_start_offset, p2.statement_start_offset)
    AND p2.statement_end_offset =
        ISNULL(p1.statement_end_offset, p2.statement_end_offset)
CROSS APPLY sys.dm_exec_sql_text(p2.sql_handle) as qt
WHERE p2.execution_count != ISNULL(p1.execution_count, 0)
ORDER BY [TotalDuration] DESC

DROP TABLE #prework
DROP TABLE #postwork
```

This script extends the previous "generic performance test harness" script. First, you take a snapshot of the current DMV sys.dm_exec_query_stats performance metrics ❶. Next, you should run your normal processing or overnight batch of SQL queries ❷. Then you take another snapshot of the latest sys.dm_exec_query_stats performance metrics ❸.

The important part to note is that the first query snapshot is run to get base metrics; then you need to wait a given amount of time, until the batch under investigation has completed. Then you can run the rest of the script.

The three subsequent queries in the script show varying degrees of detail. The first query shows the sum total duration of all the queries ❹, the total time on the CPU, the total time waiting (or being blocked), the total number of reads and writes, the total CLR time, and the total number of executions, for each database on the server.

The next script query ❺ is similar to the previous one, but it shows the sum details broken down by Parent Query within the database. The final query ❻

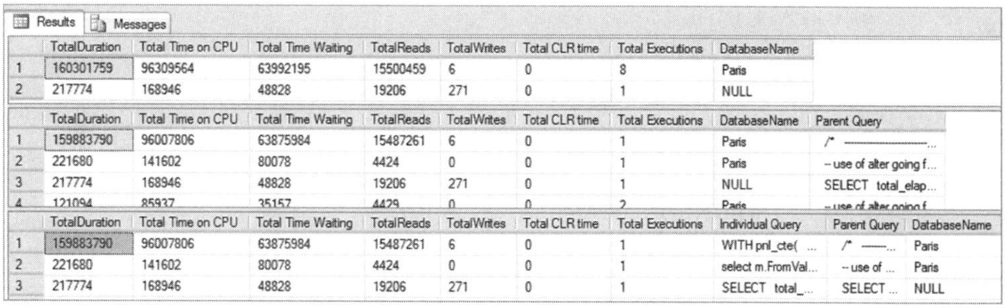

Results | Messages

	TotalDuration	Total Time on CPU	Total Time Waiting	TotalReads	TotalWrites	Total CLR time	Total Executions	DatabaseName
1	160301759	96309564	63992195	15500459	6	0	8	Paris
2	217774	168946	48828	19206	271	0	1	NULL

	TotalDuration	Total Time on CPU	Total Time Waiting	TotalReads	TotalWrites	Total CLR time	Total Executions	DatabaseName	Parent Query
1	159883790	96007806	63875984	15487261	6	0	1	Paris	/* ---------------...
2	221680	141602	80078	4424	0	0	1	Paris	-- use of alter going f...
3	217774	168946	48828	19206	271	0	1	NULL	SELECT total_elap...
4	121094	85937	35157	4429	0	0	2	Paris	-- use of alter going f

	TotalDuration	Total Time on CPU	Total Time Waiting	TotalReads	TotalWrites	Total CLR time	Total Executions	Individual Query	Parent Query	DatabaseName
1	159883790	96007806	63875984	15487261	6	0	1	WITH pnl_cte(...	/* ------...	Paris
2	221680	141602	80078	4424	0	0	1	select m.FromVal...	-- use of ...	Paris
3	217774	168946	48828	19206	271	0	1	SELECT total_...	SELECT ...	NULL

Figure 11.3 Output showing details of the impact of a system upgrade

shows the sum details broken down by Individual Query within each Parent Query within the database.

Running the script for both the original system and when the system has been upgraded allows you to compare the output from the three script-summation queries. You can import the output from these queries into Excel to allow easier comparison.

You can use the output from the first of these three script-summation queries to determine whether there's a beneficial or detrimental change. The subsequent queries allow you to drill down into specific Parent Queries or indeed Individual Queries to determine the impact of the upgrade at these levels.

Sample output for this query is shown in figure 11.3. This figure shows the result of running the "Determining the performance impact of a system upgrade" script. Three grids are output: The first contains values at the database level, for total duration, total time on the CPU, total time waiting, total reads, total writes, and total executions. The second grid contains values at the Parent Query level, within each database; it also contains the text of the Parent Query. The third grid contains values at the Individual Query level, within each Parent Query, within each database; it also contains the text of the Individual Query.

11.4 Estimating the finishing time of system jobs

For some administration tasks, such as restores, backups, and rollbacks, one of the DMVs (sys.dm_exec_requests) contains details of when the job started and how complete it is. If you know when a job started and how far it has progressed, you can perform a simple calculation to determine its expected completion time.

The relevant columns of the sys.dm_exec_requests DMV are percent_complete and start_time. According to SQL Server Books Online documentation, for sys.dm_exec_requests (available at http://msdn.microsoft.com/en-us/library/ms177648.aspx) the percent_complete column should be populated for the following commands:

- ALTER INDEX REORGANIZE
- AUTO_SHRINK option with ALTER DATABASE
- BACKUP DATABASE

- CREATE INDEX
- DBCC CHECKDB
- DBCC CHECKFILEGROUP
- DBCC CHECKTABLE
- DBCC INDEXDEFRAG
- DBCC SHRINKDATABASE
- DBCC SHRINKFILE
- KILL (Transact-SQL)
- RESTORE DATABASE
- UPDATE STATISTICS

But in my testing I discovered that the column was not updated for several of these commands, for example, UPDATE STATISTICS. For the commands that use the percent_complete column correctly, the script that follows allows you to estimate when a job will finish.

11.4.1 *Estimating when a job will end*

Estimating the finishing time of admin jobs can be useful for scheduling and informing users when the work should complete. Running the SQL script given in the following listing allows you to determine the estimated finishing time of any jobs that increment the percent_complete column of the sys.dm_exec_requests DMV.

Listing 11.4 Estimating when a job will finish

```
SET TRANSACTION ISOLATION LEVEL READ UNCOMMITTED

SELECT r.percent_complete
  , DATEDIFF(MINUTE, start_time, GETDATE()) AS Age
  , DATEADD(MINUTE, DATEDIFF(MINUTE, start_time, GETDATE()) /
    percent_complete * 100, start_time) AS EstimatedEndTime
  , t.Text AS ParentQuery
  , SUBSTRING (t.text,(r.statement_start_offset/2) + 1,
    ((CASE WHEN r.statement_end_offset = -1
      THEN LEN(CONVERT(NVARCHAR(MAX), t.text)) * 2
      ELSE r.statement_end_offset
      END - r.statement_start_offset)/2) + 1) AS IndividualQuery
  , start_time
  , DB_NAME(Database_Id) AS DatabaseName
  , Status
FROM sys.dm_exec_requests r
CROSS APPLY sys.dm_exec_sql_text(sql_handle) t
WHERE session_id > 50
    AND percent_complete > 0
ORDER BY percent_complete DESC
```

Here you can see that one DMV and one DMF are involved in estimating when a job will finish. Table 11.3 provides a brief description of each.

Table 11.3   DMV/DMF used to estimate when a job will finish

DMV/DMF	Description
sys.dm_exec_requests	Contains details of requests executing on SQL Server
sys.dm_exec_sql_text	DMF that returns the SQL text identified by a given plan_handle or sql_handle

The joining of the DMV and DMF provides you with enough information to determine when an admin job should finish. The request's sql_handle is passed to the DMF sys.dm_exec_sql_text to retrieve the text of the SQL query. Further manipulation is applied to extract the Individual Query text from the Parent Query.

The core of the calculation of the job's end time is to determine how many minutes represent 1% of the job's progress. Knowing this, you can calculate how many minutes it will take for 100% of the job's progress. You add this time to the job's start time to determine the expected end time of the job.

> **NOTE**   This calculation assumes, for the duration of this job, that the future use of the server will be the same as the past. If a resource-intensive query runs midway through the admin job's work, the estimated completion time will need to be recalculated.

An example of the type of output for this query is shown in figure 11.4.

Figure 11.4   Output showing details of when a job is expected to finish

Figure 11.4 shows the result of running the "Estimating when a job will finish" script. The columns that are output show the current level of completeness (percent_complete), how many minutes the job has been running so far (Age), the estimated end time, the text of both the Parent Query and the Individual Query, the start time, and the database.

Having discussed how you can estimate the expected end time of a system job, I'll now show you how to get system information from within SQL Server itself.

11.5   Get system information from within SQL Server

A standalone DMV named sys.dm_os_sys_info retrieves miscellaneous information about the computer that SQL Server runs on, as well as the resources available and consumed by SQL Server. This DMV can prove useful when you don't have permission to the underlying filesystem, but you have DMV access. To retrieve the system information, you just need to issue the simple SQL statement given here:

```
SELECT * FROM sys.dm_os_sys_info
```

A list of the more useful columns exposed, together with a brief description of their meaning (taken largely from SQL Server Books Online, available at http://msdn .microsoft.com/en-us/library/ms175048.aspx), is given in table 11.4.

Table 11.4 The columns of the sys.dm_os_sys_info DMV

Column	Description
ms_ticks	Number of milliseconds since the computer was started
cpu_count	Number of logical CPUs on the computer
physical_memory_in_bytes	Amount of physical memory available
virtual_memory_in_bytes	Amount of virtual memory available
sqlserver_start_time_ms_ticks	Number of milliseconds since SQL Server was last restarted (in 2008 and higher)
sqlserver_start_time	Date and time SQL Server was last started (in 2008 and higher)

You can discover the number of physical CPUs by running the following SQL snippet:

```
SELECT cpu_count AS [Logical CPUs]
,cpu_count / hyperthread_ratio AS [Physical CPUs]
FROM sys.dm_os_sys_info
```

If you're using SQL Server 2005, you can discover when the computer was restarted by running this SQL snippet:

```
SELECT DATEADD(ss, -(ms_ticks / 1000), GetDate()) AS [Start dateTime]
FROM sys.dm_os_sys_info
```

The variable ms_ticks contains the number of milliseconds since the computer was last started. To prevent an arithmetic overflow error, the value of the column ms_ticks is divided by 1000 to obtain the value in seconds, and this is subtracted from the current date (GetDate()) using the DATEADD function.

The information returned from the sys.dm_os_sys_info DMV can prove useful when making decisions within your SQL code base. For example, you might alter your code's algorithm depending on the amount of memory or the number of CPUs available (or perhaps use the output to determine whether you're running in your production or development environment). SQL Server 2008 has a column named sqlserver_start_time that contains the date and time SQL Server was started.

An example of the type of output obtained when selecting all the columns from the DMV sys.dm_os_sys_info is shown in figure 11.5. This figure shows the result of running the SQL query SELECT * FROM sys.dm_os_sys_info. The columns that are output include the number of CPUs and the amount of physical and virtual memory.

Now that you know how to obtain system information from within SQL Server itself, we'll look at how you can determine which Enterprise-level SQL Server features have been enabled.

Figure 11.5   Output showing details of SQL Server system information

11.6   *Viewing enabled Enterprise features (2008 only)*

Some SQL Server features don't exist on all editions of SQL Server. For example, the data-compression function is currently available on only the Enterprise and Developer editions of SQL Server.

A standalone DMV named sys.dm_db_persisted_sku_features retrieves details of which Enterprise-level functionality has been enabled.

It can be important to know which Enterprise features have been enabled if you want to move a copy of your database to a lesser edition of SQL Server. You might want to do this as part of your disaster recovery plans. Additionally, you might want to restore a copy of your production database to another server (on a lesser version of SQL Server) to allow you to perform a resource-intensive DBCC CHECKDB check (doing this on the nonproduction server is a common and recommended practice). It doesn't make sense to spend valuable time and resources checking the database on the production server when it can be offloaded to a nonproduction database. This also frees up the production database for other important maintenance tasks such as index defragmentation and updating statistics.

To retrieve details of which SQL Server Enterprise functions have been enabled, you just need to issue the simple SQL statement given here:

```
SELECT * FROM sys.dm_db_persisted_sku_features
```

The output from this query will show which features have been enabled. If no rows are output, then no features have been enabled. Currently, in SQL Server 2008, the features listed in table 11.5 are reported on.

Table 11.5   Enterprise-level features

Feature	Description
Compression	Indicates at least one table or index uses data compression
Partitioning	Indicates the database contains partitioned tables, indexes, schemes, or functions
Transparent DataEncryption	Indicates the database has been encrypted with transparent data encryption
ChangeCapture	Indicates the database has change data capture enabled

The information returned from the sys.dm_db_persisted_sku_features DMV can prove useful in both determining whether certain functionality has been enabled and also whether certain Enterprise-level features need to be disabled to allow you to move to a lower edition of SQL Server.

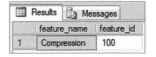

An example of the type of output for this query is shown in figure 11.6.

Figure 11.6   Output showing details of enabled Enterprise features

Figure 11.6 shows the result of running the SQL query SELECT * FROM sys.dm_db_persisted_sku_features. It contains one row for each feature that's enabled; if no features are enabled, no rows are output.

Now that we've discussed how you can determine which Enterprise-level SQL Server features have been enabled, let's look at a monitor script that can be used to determine what's been happening on your SQL Server.

11.7   Who's doing what and when?

The following script can be used to monitor who's doing what and when they're doing it. This script can be used as is as a monitor script, to identify what's happening on the server at regular intervals. Alternatively, you can use it as a template for determining how to record DMV metrics at regular intervals.

The script we use to find out who's doing what and when is shown here.

Listing 11.5   Who's doing what and when?

```
SET TRANSACTION ISOLATION LEVEL READ UNCOMMITTED

CREATE TABLE dbo.WhatsGoingOnHistory(              ❶ Create
    [Runtime] [DateTime],                             table
    [session_id] [smallint] NOT NULL,
    [login_name] [varchar](128) NOT NULL,
    [host_name] [varchar](128) NULL,
    [DBName] [varchar](128) NULL,
    [Individual Query] [varchar](max) NULL,
    [Parent Query] [varchar](200) NULL,
    [status] [varchar](30) NULL,
    [start_time] [datetime] NULL,
    [wait_type] [varchar](60) NULL,
    [program_name] [varchar](128) NULL
)
GO
                                                   ❷ Create
CREATE UNIQUE NONCLUSTERED INDEX                      index
[NONCLST_WhatsGoingOnHistory] ON [dbo].[WhatsGoingOnHistory]
([Runtime] ASC,    [session_id] ASC)
GO
                                                   ❸ Run first
INSERT INTO dbo.WhatsGoingOnHistory                  batch
SELECT
  GETDATE()
  , s.session_id
  , s.login_name
  , s.host_name
  , DB_NAME(r.database_id) AS DBName
```

```
  , SUBSTRING (t.text,(r.statement_start_offset/2) + 1,
    ((CASE WHEN r.statement_end_offset = -1
      THEN (LEN(CONVERT(NVARCHAR(MAX), t.text)) * 2
      ELSE r.statement_end_offset
      END - r.statement_start_offset)/2) + 1) AS [Individual Query]
  , SUBSTRING(text, 1, 200) AS [Parent Query]
  , r.status
  , r.start_time
  , r.wait_type
  , s.program_name
FROM sys.dm_exec_sessions s
INNER JOIN sys.dm_exec_connections c ON s.session_id = c.session_id
INNER JOIN sys.dm_exec_requests r ON c.connection_id = r.connection_id
CROSS APPLY sys.dm_exec_sql_text(r.sql_handle) t
WHERE s.session_id > 50
  AND r.session_id != @@spid

WAITFOR DELAY '00:01:00'
GO 1440     -- 60 * 24 (one day)
```

4 **Wait**

5 **Run second batch repeatedly**

This script shows that three DMVs and one DMF are involved in recording who's doing what and when. A brief description of each is given in table 11.6.

Table 11.6   DMVs/DMF to determine who's doing what and when

DMV/DMF	Description
sys.dm_exec_sessions	Contains details of sessions on SQL Server
sys.dm_exec_connections	Contains details of connections to SQL Server
sys.dm_exec_requests	Contains details of requests executing on SQL Server
sys.dm_exec_sql_text	DMF that returns the SQL text identified by a given sql_handle or plan_handle

The joining of the DMVs and the DMF provides us with enough information to record who's doing what and when, across all the databases on the server. The DMVs sys.dm_exec_sessions and sys.dm_exec_connections are joined on their common key column session_id. Similarly, the DMVs sys.dm_exec_connections and sys.dm_exec_ requests are joined on their common key column connection_id. The request contains the column sql_handle, which is passed to the DMF sys.dm_exec_sql_text to retrieve the text of the SQL query. The text of the SQL query is decoded to obtain the Individual Query within the Parent Query, which was running at the time the script was running.

We include only sessions with spids of greater than 50, because we're interested only in user queries. We also filter out details of this actual script from the results, by excluding its running spid.

The script works by creating a table to hold the results of this script **1**, together with an index on the same table **2**. The GO statement ensures that this batch runs separately **3**. The second part of the script then runs multiple times and puts its results into the created table. A delay is implemented between recording results by using the WAITFOR DELAY command ❹. In this example, the time period is one minute; you may want to alter this time interval to suit your needs.

The number of times this second batch (the DMV query and WAITFOR command) is run is determined by the number that follows the GO command ❺. Hopefully, you can use this script as a template for your own investigations.

Having discussed a monitor script that can be used to determine what's been happening on your SQL Server, we'll now look at where your query really spends its time. Sometimes this can yield quite surprising results!

11.8   Finding where your query really spends its time

The cached plan is a great tool for helping determine how SQL Server will fulfill your query's needs. It uses metadata to decide the best way to obtain data to satisfy your query. Such metadata includes the number of rows in a table, available indexes, statistics, and constraints.

The cached plan is often used to determine where your SQL query or routine is spending most of its time. For example, if a routine consists of five SQL statements, the optimizer will, based on the available metadata, assign a cost to each of the SQL statements, relative to the whole batch of statements. Often this cost is used as a starting point for optimizing the batch. The statement with the highest cost is most often targeted for improvement.

However, the optimizer knows nothing about concurrency, about what other statements are running when your SQL query is running, and the competition for resources. Competing queries can result in waiting and blocking. You can determine where your query spends its actual time by using the script given in this section.

11.8.1   Locating where your queries are spending their time

Often, where you think your queries spend their time is at odds with where they really spend their time, even with what the execution plan suggests. The only real way to determine where your queries spend their time is to wrap them in a performance harness like the one given here. Running the SQL script given in the following listing will allow you to determine where your queries really spend their time.

> **Listing 11.6   Determining where your query spends its time**

```
SET TRANSACTION ISOLATION LEVEL READ UNCOMMITTED          ❶ Store pre-work
                                                             query counters
SELECT
    sql_handle, plan_handle, total_elapsed_time, total_worker_time
    , total_logical_reads, total_logical_writes, total_clr_time
    , execution_count, statement_start_offset, statement_end_offset
INTO #PreWorkQuerySnapShot
FROM sys.dm_exec_query_stats

EXEC MO.PNLYearToDate_v01iws                              ❷ Run your query
    @pControlOrgIds = '537'                                 or batch of SQL
    , @pCOBStart = '27 may 2009'
    , @pCOBEnd = '27 may 2009'
```

```
SELECT                                                      ◄─③ Store post-work query counters
    sql_handle, plan_handle, total_elapsed_time, total_worker_time
    , total_logical_reads, total_logical_writes, total_clr_time
    , execution_count, statement_start_offset, statement_end_offset,
    last_execution_time
INTO #PostWorkQuerySnapShot
FROM sys.dm_exec_query_stats                                 ④ Calculate
                                                               statement metrics
SELECT                                                      ◄─┘
  p2.total_elapsed_time - ISNULL(p1.total_elapsed_time, 0) AS [Duration]
  , p2.total_worker_time - ISNULL(p1.total_worker_time, 0) AS [Time on CPU]
  , (p2.total_elapsed_time - ISNULL(p1.total_elapsed_time, 0)) -
      (p2.total_worker_time - ISNULL(p1.total_worker_time, 0))
                                                          AS [Time waiting]
  , p2.total_logical_reads - ISNULL(p1.total_logical_reads, 0)   AS [Reads]
  , p2.total_logical_writes - ISNULL(p1.total_logical_writes, 0)
                                                          AS [Writes]
  , p2.total_clr_time - ISNULL(p1.total_clr_time, 0) AS [CLR time]
  , p2.execution_count - ISNULL(p1.execution_count, 0) AS [Executions]
  , p2.last_execution_time
  , SUBSTRING (qt.text,p2.statement_start_offset/2 + 1,
    ((CASE WHEN p2.statement_end_offset = -1
    THEN LEN(CONVERT(NVARCHAR(MAX), qt.text)) * 2
    ELSE p2.statement_end_offset
    END - p2.statement_start_offset)/2) + 1) AS [Individual Query]
  , qt.text AS [Parent Query]
  , DB_NAME(qt.dbid) AS DatabaseName
FROM #PreWorkQuerySnapShot p1
RIGHT OUTER JOIN
#PostWorkQuerySnapShot p2
ON p2.sql_handle = ISNULL(p1.sql_handle, p2.sql_handle)
    AND p2.plan_handle = ISNULL(p1.plan_handle, p2.plan_handle)
    AND p2.statement_start_offset =
        ISNULL(p1.statement_start_offset, p2.statement_start_offset)
    AND p2.statement_end_offset =
ISNULL(p1.statement_end_offset, p2.statement_end_offset)
CROSS APPLY sys.dm_exec_sql_text(p2.sql_handle) as qt
WHERE p2.execution_count != ISNULL(p1.execution_count, 0)    ⑤ Filter in the
    AND qt.text LIKE '%PNLYearToDate_v01iws %'                 routine you want
ORDER BY [Parent Query], p2.statement_start_offset         ◄─┘
                                                            ⑥ Sort by
DROP TABLE #PreWorkQuerySnapShot                               statement offset
DROP TABLE #PostWorkQuerySnapShot
```

The listing uses one DMV and one DMF to identify where queries spend their time. Table 11.7 briefly describes each.

Table 11.7 DMV/DMF to find where queries spend their time

DMV/DMF	Description
sys.dm_exec_query_stats	Contains aggregated performance statistics for cached plans
sys.dm_exec_sql_text	DMF that returns the SQL text identified by a given sql_handle or plan_handle

In the listing, the relevant counters and identifiers from the sys.dm_exec_query_stats DMV are stored in a temporary table (#PreWorkQuerySnapShot in the example) ❶. Next, the query or stored procedure you want to investigate is run ❷. After the query is run (named 'PNLYearToDate_v01iws' in the example), the counters and identifiers are again recorded ❸. Finally, the delta between the two DMV snapshots is calculated ❹. Note that we include only those statements that relate to the query we're investigating, the text 'PNLYearToDate_v01iws' in this example ❺. We do this by filtering in those SQL statements where the Parent Query contained the name of the text we're searching for. If a batch of SQL queries has been run instead, a unique identifier associated with that batch could be used, for example, a constant piece of text like '—ThisRoutineId99'.

The pre- and post-work temporary tables are joined on their common keys (sql_handle, plan_handle, statement_start_offset, and statement_end_offset). Only those statements that have actually run and belong to the query we're investigating are included. We include a RIGHT OUTER JOIN because if the query hasn't been run previously, it won't be included in the pre-work snapshot.

The DMV's sql_handle is passed to the DMF sys.dm_exec_sql_text to retrieve the text of the SQL query. We use a common pattern to extract the Individual Query, which the timings relate to, from the Parent Query. The output is sorted by statement_start_offset ❻ in ascending order.

An example of the type of output for this query is shown in figure 11.7. This figure shows the result of running the "Determining where your query spends its time" script. The columns that are output show the duration, time on the CPU, time spent waiting (or being blocked), the number of reads and writes, the number of executions, the last time the query was executed, the text of both the Individual Query and the Parent Query, and the database name. The rows are sorted by the offset of the Individual Query within its Parent Query.

It might be worthwhile amending the script to output only the first 100 characters of the Parent Query and the Individual Query because these can take up a lot of memory. You could use the output to determine which statement should be optimized.

Because the times recorded (duration, time on CPU, time waiting) are actual times, they provide a better representation of where improvements should be targeted

	Duration	Time on CPU	Time waiting	Reads	Writes	CLR time	Executions	last_execution_time	Individual Query	Parent Query	DatabaseName
1	0	0	0	2	0	0	1	2010-03-29 15:02:34.997	SET @BaseCurre...	CREATE PROCEDURE [MO].[PN...	ParisDev
2	3907	3907	0	94	0	0	1	2010-03-29 15:02:35.003	INSERT #Domai...	CREATE PROCEDURE [MO].[PN...	ParisDev
3	977	977	0	33	0	0	1	2010-03-29 15:02:35.010	INSERT #Source...	CREATE PROCEDURE [MO].[PN...	ParisDev
4	191407	127930	63477	52763	120	0	1	2010-03-29 15:02:35.013	INSERT #Parties ...	CREATE PROCEDURE [MO].[PN...	ParisDev
5	145508	144532	976	40626	47	0	1	2010-03-29 15:02:35.243	INSERT #Orgs (...	CREATE PROCEDURE [MO].[PN...	ParisDev
6	25391	22462	2929	10460	0	0	1	2010-03-29 15:02:35.413	DELETE #Orgs F...	CREATE PROCEDURE [MO].[PN...	ParisDev
7	1954	1954	0	459	0	0	1	2010-03-29 15:02:35.440	INSERT #Produc...	CREATE PROCEDURE [MO].[PN...	ParisDev
8	977	977	0	92	0	0	1	2010-03-29 15:02:35.447	INSERT #LocalC...	CREATE PROCEDURE [MO].[PN...	ParisDev
9	1954	1954	0	370	0	0	1	2010-03-29 15:02:35.450	INSERT #Factors...	CREATE PROCEDURE [MO].[PN...	ParisDev
10	977	977	0	16	0	0	1	2010-03-29 15:02:35.453	INSERT #IsAdjus...	CREATE PROCEDURE [MO].[PN...	ParisDev

Figure 11.7 Output showing where a query spends its time

than using the cached plan alone. I had one routine that was taking five minutes to run. When I ran it inside the script included here, I could see that the last statement was taking 60% of the cost. In the cached plan, this last statement was thought to represent only 3% of the cost of the batch. If I had tried to improve this batch based on what the cached plan was suggesting to me, I would have optimized the wrong area.

Now that you know where your query really spends its time, we'll look at a useful script that determines how much memory each database is currently using.

11.9 Memory usage per database

When data is requested of SQL Server, the data is read from the underlying physical disks and brought into an area of memory called the buffer pool. If this data is subsequently required, it tends to be read from the buffer pool. When the data in the buffer pool is updated, SQL Server ensures requests for data obtain the updated data. Periodically, the changed data is written to the disks.

It's possible to determine how much memory each database is taking in the buffer pool. Sometimes, a query can run slowly owing to problems with memory, resulting in error messages being written to SQL Server's error log. As well as being a useful investigative script when memory might be a concern, the script can be used to determine whether a database is hogging the buffer pool and should perhaps be moved to its own server.

11.9.1 Determining the memory used per database

When memory problems are reported in the SQL Server error log or via SSMS, one of the first queries I run is the one given in listing 11.7. It quickly tells me which databases are using the available memory, and with the queries on tempdb memory usage (given in chapter 9) it provides a fuller picture of memory requirements. Running the SQL script given here will identify how much memory each database on the server instance is using.

Listing 11.7 Memory used per database

```
SET TRAN ISOLATION LEVEL READ UNCOMMITTED
SELECT
    ISNULL(DB_NAME(database_id), 'ResourceDb') AS DatabaseName
    , CAST(COUNT(row_count) * 8.0 / (1024.0) AS DECIMAL(28,2))
                                              AS [Size (MB)]
FROM sys.dm_os_buffer_descriptors
GROUP BY database_id
ORDER BY DatabaseName
```

Here one DMV is involved in determining how much memory is used by each database on the server instance; a brief description of it is given in table 11.8.

Table 11.8   DMV used to determine the memory used per database

DMV	Description
sys.dm_os_buffer_descriptors	Contains details of the data pages that are currently in SQL Server buffer pool

The script counts the number of pages in the buffer pool, for each database. Because a database page is 8 KB in size, you would multiply the number of pages (COUNT(row_count)), by 8.0 to get the number of kilobytes used by the database. You'd then divide this value by 1024 to obtain the value in terms of megabytes. The results are ordered by database name.

An example of the type of output for this query is shown in figure 11.8.

Figure 11.8 shows the result of running the "Memory used per database" script. The columns that are output show the amount of the memory, in megabytes, that each database is using.

Now that we've discussed how much memory each database is using, let's drill down further and look at which individual tables and indexes are using this buffer pool memory. This is important because it allows you to see how the SQL queries are using the underlying database structures, and you can use this knowledge to optimize these objects.

	DatabaseName	Size (MB)
1	ACBS	0.77
2	DMV	14.45
3	master	0.46
4	msdb	2.38
5	Paris	92904.13
6	ResourceDb	0.20
7	tempdb	2723.84

Figure 11.8   Output showing how much memory is used by each database

11.10 *Memory usage by table or index*

Having looked at how much memory in the buffer pool each database uses, the next logical step is to examine which tables/heaps and indexes make up that memory. This would give you greater insight into how the data is needed and used by the SQL queries running on your databases, providing you with an opportunity to optimize them.

In addition, if the content of the memory is recorded over a given time period, you can use this to help determine how much memory is necessary so the queries are fed from the data in RAM rather than accessing the much slower physical disks. Summing up the maximum size of all the tables, indexes, and heaps in the buffer pool over a given time interval will help you answer the question, "How much RAM do I need?"

11.10.1 *Determining the memory used by tables and indexes*

Tables, heaps, and indexes are cached into the buffer pool when SQL queries run. Having this data in the buffer pool is an optimization technique, because reading the data from memory is much more efficient than reading the data from the physical disks. This can be illustrated clearly by the fact that physical disk access is measured in milliseconds whereas buffer pool memory access is measured in nanoseconds.

Running the SQL script given in the following listing will identify how much memory specific tables, heaps, and indexes are using in the buffer pool in the current database (the database that this script runs in).

Listing 11.8 Memory used by objects in the current database

```
SET TRANSACTION ISOLATION LEVEL READ UNCOMMITTED

SELECT
    OBJECT_NAME(p.[object_id]) AS [TableName]
    , (COUNT(*) * 8) / 1024   AS [Buffer size(MB)]
    , ISNULL(i.name, '-- HEAP --') AS ObjectName
    , COUNT(*) AS NumberOf8KPages
FROM sys.allocation_units AS a
INNER JOIN sys.dm_os_buffer_descriptors AS b
    ON a.allocation_unit_id = b.allocation_unit_id
INNER JOIN sys.partitions AS p
INNER JOIN sys.indexes i ON p.index_id = i.index_id
                        AND p.[object_id] = i.[object_id]
    ON a.container_id = p.hobt_id
WHERE b.database_id = DB_ID()
  AND p.[object_id] > 100
GROUP BY p.[object_id], i.name
ORDER BY NumberOf8KPages DESC
```

The listing shows one DMV and three system tables involved in determining which tables, heaps, and indexes are using the buffer pool memory. They're briefly described in table 11.9.

Table 11.9 DMV/tables used to determine the memory used by database objects

DMV/table	Description
sys.dm_os_buffer_descriptors	Contains details of the data pages that are in SQL Server buffer pool
sys.allocation_units	Contains a row for each allocation unit in the database
sys.partitions	Contains a row for each partition of all the tables and most types of indexes in the database
sys.indexes	Contains details for each index, for example, name and type

The joining of the DMV and three system tables provides us with enough information to identify which objects are using the memory in the buffer pool. The DMV and the sys.allocation_units system table are joined on their common key column, allocation_unit_id. The system tables sys.partitions and sys.indexes are joined on the object_id and index_id key columns. In addition, the sys.indexes table joins to the sys.allocation_units and sys.partitions tables.

The script counts the number of pages in the buffer pool for each object (table, heap, or index). Because a database page is 8 KB in size, you multiply the number of pages (COUNT(*)) by 8.0 to get the number of kilobytes used by the database. You then divide this value by 1024 to obtain the value in terms of megabytes. Because some objects use little space (less than a megabyte), the script also reports on the number of pages that each object has in the buffer pool; this is reported under the column NumberOf8KPages. Indexes with a NULL value in the name column are heaps; the script decodes these to explicitly report the value '–HEAP –'. The results are ordered by the column NumberOf8KPages in descending order.

An example of the type of output for this query is shown in figure 11.9. This figure shows the result of running the "Memory used by objects in the current database" script. The columns that are output show the name of the table, the size of the memory in megabytes, the object name (table, heap, or index), and the number of 8 KB pages taken in memory.

Knowing which objects the SQL queries use allows you to optimize these identified structures. For example, in the case of indexes, you should ensure that their statistics are up to date and have a good sampling percentage. For tables, you might want to have the most-used ones on different physical disks, ensuring they can be read into memory concurrently.

You could modify this script to report periodically the usage pattern of database objects over time. A template script (for who's using the database) was given previously in section 11.7. This would provide you with a further opportunity to optimize the objects before their known usage time.

You can get a measure of how long the average page stays in the buffer pool by inspecting the DMV sys.dm_os_performance_counters, using the following query. Typically, values above 300 are viewed as good; values below this may suggest memory problems.

```
SELECT cntr_value AS [Page Life Expectancy]
FROM sys.dm_os_performance_counters
WHERE OBJECT_NAME = 'SQLServer:Buffer Manager'
    AND counter_name = 'Page life expectancy'
```

	TableName	Buffer size(MB)	ObjectName	NumberOf8KPages
1	PNLValue	77602	IX_PNLValue_RequestIdSession	9933060
2	RiskValue	7062	IX_RiskValue	904013
3	PNLAdjustment	2670	IX_PNLAdjustment	341815
4	RiskValue	1840	IX_RiskValue_RequestId	235585
5	PNLAdjustmentQueue	1422	IX_PNLAdjustmentQueue_PositionGridCellId	182111
6	Component	957	IX_Component_DealId_ComponendCode	122560
7	PNLValue	640	IX_PnlValue_PositionGridCellId	81985
8	Deal	629	IX_Deal	80533
9	MessageLog	628	– HEAP –	80505
10	PNLAdjustment	566	IX_PNLAdjustment_1	72532

Figure 11.9 Output showing how much memory is used by each object in the current database

Having discussed how much memory each object in the database is using, we'll now look at where on the server your I/O waits are occurring. This is important because I/O waits are often a neglected cause of slow SQL Server performance.

11.11 *Finding I/O waits*

SQL Server systems often have plenty of memory and processing power. Another component that influences system performance is the I/O subsystem. Perhaps because it isn't a plug-in-and-go module, or maybe because it's viewed as difficult to optimize, the I/O subsystem is often left in a suboptimal state. In my experience, the most common cause of poorly performing systems is the I/O subsystem.

You can examine, at both the database and the individual file levels, the performance of the physical disks that the data resides on using the DMV sys.dm_io_virtual_file_stats. This DMV accepts two parameters, namely, the database_id and the file_id, which limit the database and file under investigation. In our examples, we're interested in all the files on all the databases, so we supply NULL parameter values to the DMV.

The output from this DMV will allow you to concentrate on the database that has the most I/O waiting. You can drill into the underlying files in the database to examine the individual files that have the most I/O waits. If you know the disks these files reside on, you can target your investigation on improving these.

11.11.1 *I/O waits at the database level*

Waiting on I/O is a primary cause of poor server performance. Identifying the database having the most I/O waiting (stalls) is a great starting place for further investigation. The script we use to determine the amount of IO waiting by each database is shown in the following listing.

> **Listing 11.9　I/O stalls at the database level**

```
SET TRAN ISOLATION LEVEL READ UNCOMMITTED

SELECT DB_NAME(database_id) AS [DatabaseName]
  , SUM(CAST(io_stall / 1000.0 AS DECIMAL(20,2))) AS [IO stall (secs)]
  , SUM(CAST(num_of_bytes_read / 1024.0 / 1024.0 AS DECIMAL(20,2)))
                                              AS [IO read (MB)]
  , SUM(CAST(num_of_bytes_written / 1024.0 / 1024.0  AS DECIMAL(20,2)))
                                              AS [IO written (MB)]
  , SUM(CAST((num_of_bytes_read + num_of_bytes_written)
                / 1024.0 / 1024.0 AS DECIMAL(20,2))) AS [TotalIO (MB)]
FROM sys.dm_io_virtual_file_stats(NULL, NULL)
GROUP BY database_id
ORDER BY [IO stall (secs)] DESC
```

One DMV is involved in determining how much I/O waiting occurs for each database on the server instance; see table 11.10 for a brief description of it.

Table 11.10   I/O waits per database DMV

DMV	Description
sys.dm_io_virtual_file_stats	Contains details of I/O statistics for the data and log files

The script calculates the number of stalls (waits) that occur per database by summing the content of the column io_stall for each database. The value is divided by 1000 to convert the millisecond value to a value in seconds. The amount of reads, writes, and total I/O is recorded. The results are ordered by the IO stall value.

An example of the type of output for this query is shown in figure 11.10.

	Database Name	IO stall (secs)	IO read (MB)	IO written (MB)	TotalIO (MB)
1	tempdb	18853985.52	1813465.78	4279551.38	6093017.16
2	Paris	8317776.00	29420050.38	2420591.49	31840641.88
3	DMV	287431.00	573593.39	42685.20	616278.60
4	msdb	4235.98	2936.14	1293.87	4230.02
5	ACBS	3914.29	3260.89	3502.06	6762.96
6	master	67.90	114.29	60.86	175.15
7	model	8.24	24.70	0.77	25.47
8	Sys_Support	7.00	25.16	0.69	25.85

Figure 11.10
Output showing the number of I/O stalls per database

Figure 11.10 shows the result of running the "I/O stalls at the database level" script. The columns that are output show the I/O stalls, number of reads, number of writes, and total I/O, per database.

It's possible for you to drill down further into the poorly performing files on the databases; we'll look at this next.

11.11.2 I/O waits at the file level

Having identified the database with the most IO stalls, you can drill down further on the individual files in that database to get more detailed information on where the stalls are occurring. Knowing this information allows you to target your investigation and improvements to those files and underlying disks. The script to determine the amount of I/O waiting by file per database is shown here.

Listing 11.10   I/O stalls at the file level

```
SET TRAN ISOLATION LEVEL READ UNCOMMITTED

SELECT DB_NAME(database_id) AS [DatabaseName]
  , file_id
  , SUM(CAST(io_stall / 1000.0 AS DECIMAL(20,2))) AS [IO stall (secs)]
  , SUM(CAST(num_of_bytes_read / 1024.0 / 1024.0 AS DECIMAL(20,2)))
                                            AS [IO read (MB)]
  , SUM(CAST(num_of_bytes_written / 1024.0 / 1024.0  AS DECIMAL(20,2)))
                                            AS [IO written (MB)]
```

```
, SUM(CAST((num_of_bytes_read + num_of_bytes_written)
                / 1024.0 / 1024.0 AS DECIMAL(20,2))) AS [TotalIO (MB)]
FROM sys.dm_io_virtual_file_stats(NULL, NULL)
GROUP BY database_id, file_id
ORDER BY [IO stall (secs)] DESC
```

The listing shows that one DMV is involved in determining how much I/O waiting occurs for each file per database on the server instance; it's briefly described in table 11.11.

Table 11.11 DMV used to find the number of I/O waits per file, per database

DMV	Description
sys.dm_io_virtual_file_stats	Contains details of I/O statistics for the data and log files

The script calculates the number of stalls (waits) that occurs per database, by summing the content of the column io_stall for each file per database. The value is divided by 1000 to convert the millisecond value to a value in seconds. Additionally, the amount of reads, writes and total I/O is recorded. The results are ordered by IO stall value.

An example of the type of output for this query is shown in figure 11.11. This figure shows the result of running the "I/O stalls at the file level" script. The columns that are output show the I/O stalls, number of reads, number of writes, and total I/O, per database.

You can map the identified file_id to the underlying physical file, using the following SQL statement:

```
SELECT DB_NAME(DB_ID()) AS DatabaseName, file_id, name, physical_name
FROM sys.database_files
```

This SQL statement allows you to investigate the physical disks that the poorly performing I/O resides on. Investigating the type and configuration of these disks should be the starting point for improving I/O performance.

	DatabaseName	file_id	IO stall (secs)	IO read (MB)	IO written (MB)	TotalIO (MB)
1	Paris	3	2414635.36	3476473.75	708624.30	4185098.05
2	Paris	45	1429781.57	6423251.49	20140.30	6443391.79
3	tempdb	9	1175503.32	113661.00	202470.49	316131.49
4	tempdb	11	1175352.91	113422.75	202380.08	315802.83
5	tempdb	14	1175259.20	113348.13	202403.45	315751.58
6	tempdb	10	1175245.27	113488.27	202335.40	315823.66
7	tempdb	12	1175122.39	113446.88	202579.41	316026.29
8	tempdb	5	1174771.04	113725.41	202682.79	316408.20
9	tempdb	7	1174583.42	113428.99	202292.04	315721.03
10	tempdb	6	1174536.29	113836.11	202517.75	316353.86
11	tempdb	4	1174505.64	113630.00	202567.77	316197.77

Figure 11.11 Output showing the number of I/O stalls per file, per database

11.11.3 *Average read/write times per file, per database*

It's also possible to identify poorly performing files and disks by obtaining the average read and write times per file for each database on the server instance. These should be below 20 milliseconds. The script you use to determine the average read and write time (in milliseconds) by file per database is shown in the listing that follows.

Listing 11.11 Average read/write times per file, per database

```
SET TRAN ISOLATION LEVEL READ UNCOMMITTED

SELECT DB_NAME(database_id) AS DatabaseName
  , file_id
  , io_stall_read_ms / num_of_reads AS 'Average read time'
  , io_stall_write_ms / num_of_writes AS 'Average write time'
FROM sys.dm_io_virtual_file_stats(NULL, NULL)
WHERE num_of_reads > 0 and num_of_writes > 0
ORDER BY DatabaseName
```

Here one DMV is used to determine the average read and write times for each file per database on the server instance. The average read time is calculated by dividing the read stall time (io_stall_read_ms) by the number of reads (num_of_reads). Similarly, the average write time is calculated by dividing the write stall time (io_stall_write_ms) by the number of writes (num_of_writes). The results are ordered by database name.

Again, the file_id can be mapped to the underlying physical file by using the SQL statement, relating to sys.database_files, given previously.

Sample output for this query is shown in figure 11.12.

Figure 11.12 shows the result of running the "Average read/write times per file, per database" script. The columns that are output show the average read and write times per file, per database. Any values over 20 milliseconds should be investigated as a matter of priority.

	DatabaseName	file_id	Average read time	Average write time
1	ACBS	1	32	3
2	ACBS	2	6	1
3	DMV	1	23	22
4	DMV	2	7	3
5	master	1	9	3
6	master	2	7	2
7	model	1	12	3
8	model	2	8	2
9	msdb	1	51	2
10	msdb	2	7	2

Figure 11.12
Output showing the average read and write times per file, per database

Having discussed how much read/write time each database is using, we'll now look at a useful and lightweight trace utility, which might reduce your reliance on SQL Server's own Profiler tool.

11.12 A simple lightweight trace utility

In many ways, this next script is my favorite. It provides functionality similar to SQL Server's profiler but uses fewer resources, uses existing DMV data, and aggregates the results for me. The script discussed in the previous section will allow you to determine how long each of your SQL statements in the routine you're monitoring will take to run. It's a short step to create a simple, lightweight SQL trace utility.

If you typically use the inbuilt Profiler utility to identify which statements take a long time, then I think you'll find that the DMV equivalent included here is superior in terms of ease of use and resource usage.

If you replace the query you want to investigate with a WAITFOR DELAY statement and remove the filtering in of the query you're investigating, you'll monitor all the statements that are running over the time period you specify in the WAITFOR DELAY statement. In this example, the time period is one minute, but you may want to alter this time interval to suit your needs.

The script you'll use to create your simple trace utility is shown here.

Listing 11.12 Simple trace utility

```
SET TRANSACTION ISOLATION LEVEL READ UNCOMMITTED                    ❶ Store pre-work
                                                                      query counters
SELECT
    sql_handle, plan_handle, total_elapsed_time, total_worker_time
  , total_logical_reads, total_logical_writes, total_clr_time
  , execution_count, statement_start_offset, statement_end_offset
INTO #PreWorkQuerySnapShot
FROM sys.dm_exec_query_stats
                                          ❷ Record what happen
WAITFOR DELAY '00:01:00'                     in I minute
                                                          ❸ Store post-work
SELECT                                                      query counters
    sql_handle, plan_handle, total_elapsed_time, total_worker_time
  , total_logical_reads, total_logical_writes, total_clr_time
  , execution_count, statement_start_offset
  , statement_end_offset, last_execution_time
INTO #PostWorkQuerySnapShot
FROM sys.dm_exec_query_stats
                                                  ❹ Calculate metrics
SELECT
    p2.total_elapsed_time - ISNULL(p1.total_elapsed_time, 0) AS [Duration]
  , p2.total_worker_time - ISNULL(p1.total_worker_time, 0) AS [Time on CPU]
  , (p2.total_elapsed_time - ISNULL(p1.total_elapsed_time, 0))
       - (p2.total_worker_time - ISNULL(p1.total_worker_time, 0))
                                                         AS [Time waiting]
  , p2.total_logical_reads - ISNULL(p1.total_logical_reads, 0) AS [Reads]
  , p2.total_logical_writes - ISNULL(p1.total_logical_writes, 0)
                                                         AS [Writes]
```

```
      , p2.total_clr_time - ISNULL(p1.total_clr_time, 0) AS [CLR time]
      , p2.execution_count - ISNULL(p1.execution_count, 0) AS [Executions]
      , p2.last_execution_time
      , SUBSTRING (qt.text,p2.statement_start_offset/2 + 1,
        ((CASE WHEN p2.statement_end_offset = -1
        THEN LEN(CONVERT(NVARCHAR(MAX), qt.text)) * 2
        ELSE p2.statement_end_offset
        END - p2.statement_start_offset)/2) + 1) AS [Individual Query]
      , qt.text AS [Parent Query]
      , DB_NAME(qt.dbid) AS DatabaseName
FROM #PreWorkQuerySnapShot p1
RIGHT OUTER JOIN
#PostWorkQuerySnapShot p2
  ON p2.sql_handle = ISNULL(p1.sql_handle, p2.sql_handle)
    AND p2.plan_handle = ISNULL(p1.plan_handle, p2.plan_handle)
    AND p2.statement_start_offset =
          ISNULL(p1.statement_start_offset, p2.statement_start_offset)
    AND p2.statement_end_offset =
          ISNULL(p1.statement_end_offset, p2.statement_end_offset)
CROSS APPLY sys.dm_exec_sql_text(p2.sql_handle) as qt
WHERE p2.execution_count != ISNULL(p1.execution_count, 0)
ORDER BY DatabaseName, [Parent Query]
      , p2.statement_start_offset
```

⑤ Sort by statement offset

```
DROP TABLE #PreWorkQuerySnapShot
DROP TABLE #PostWorkQuerySnapShot
```

First you take a snapshot of the current DMV sys.dm_exec_query_stats performance metrics ❶, and next you wait for a given time interval (one minute in this example) ❷. Then you take another snapshot of the latest sys.dm_exec_query_stats performance metrics ❸. The differences between the two DMV snapshots are calculated ❹. Finally, the output is sorted by the Individual Query's offset within the Parent Query, for a given database ❺.

An example of the type of output for this query is shown in figure 11.13.

Figure 11.13 shows the result of running the "Simple trace utility" script. The columns that are output show the duration, time on the CPU, time spent waiting (or being blocked), the number of reads and writes, the number of executions, the last time the query was executed, the text of both the Individual Query and the Parent Query, and the database name. The rows are sorted by the offset of the Individual

	Duration	Time on CPU	Time waiting	Reads	Writes	CLR time	Executions	last_execution_time	Individual Query	Parent Query	DatabaseName
1	0	0	0	2	0	0	1	2010-03-29 15:23:36.587	set @DomainId = dbo.D...	-- use of alter going forward allows us ...	ParisDev
2	0	0	0	2	0	0	1	2010-03-29 15:23:36.587	set @SourceId = dbo.So...	-- use of alter going forward allows us ...	ParisDev
3	0	0	0	2	0	0	1	2010-03-29 15:23:36.587	SELECT @RowCount ...	-- use of alter going forward allows us ...	ParisDev
4	117188	116211	977	282	0	0	1	2010-03-29 15:23:51.530	select suser_sname(ubu...	-- use of alter going forward allows us ...	ParisDev
5	0	0	0	5	0	0	1	2010-03-29 15:23:50.090	SELECT dbo.AppCOB()	/* ...	ParisDev
6	0	0	0	5	0	0	1	2010-03-29 15:23:50.090	SELECT @Result = cob ...	CREATE FUNCTION [dbo].[AppCOB]...	ParisDev
7	0	0	0	15	0	0	3	2010-03-29 15:23:11.510	SELECT @Result = cob ...	CREATE FUNCTION [dbo].[AppCOB]...	ParisMini
8	0	0	0	6	0	0	3	2010-03-29 15:23:11.510	select @BusinessRegion...	CREATE FUNCTION [dbo].[Business...	ParisMini
9	0	0	0	2	0	0	1	2010-03-29 15:23:50.090	select @BusinessRegion...	CREATE FUNCTION [dbo].[Business...	ParisDev
10	0	0	0	2	0	0	1	2010-03-29 15:23:36.587	select @DomainId = Do...	CREATE FUNCTION [dbo].[DomainId...	ParisDev
11	53711	53711	0	5092	0	0	2546	2010-03-29 15:23:53.807	SET @ReturnOrgNam...	CREATE FUNCTION [dbo].[OrgName...	ParisDev
12	465820	466796	-976	112020	0	0	28005	2010-03-29 15:23:53.807	IF @pRequiredLevel > I...	CREATE FUNCTION [dbo].[OrgName...	ParisDev

Figure 11.13 Output showing which queries run over a given time interval

Query within its Parent Query, within the database (because the same query might run on different databases during the period under investigation).

This utility has several advantages over the trace utility that comes with SQL Server. It uses fewer resources, because the DMV information is already being recorded. This makes it more amenable to being run in a production environment. Additionally, owing to the accumulative nature of DMVs, it automatically calculates the cumulative cost of any of the queries that run during the period being monitored. Finally, although you might not have permission to run a trace in a production environment, owing to its innocuous nature it should be possible to run this lightweight trace utility.

We'll now discuss some SQL Server best practices I've come across in recent times.

11.13 Some best practices

There are many articles relating to performance tuning. Rather than repeat some of the more common ones, I'd like to add some that I think are often overlooked. Some of the more common best practices can be seen in the Microsoft checklist given here: http://msdn.microsoft.com/en-us/library/ff647681.aspx.

As always, you should test any changes you make (perhaps using the test harness provided previously in this chapter). Often we assume something should behave in a given manner, but testing shows it doesn't.

A brief description of some of these neglected SQL best practices is shown in table 11.12.

Table 11.12 Some best practices

Best practice	Description
Cache function values.	Functions are great for providing modularity and reusability. For small amounts of data, their use in SELECT lists or WHERE or JOIN clauses may be okay. But when the amount of data increases, they typically cause the query's performance to degrade. Even if the same parameters are passed to the function, it's called for each row in the result set.
	To get around this problem, where possible, the results of the function calls should be cached and the cached values used in any SELECT list or WHERE or JOIN clause.
Use temporary tables instead of table variables for large data volumes.	Table variables and temporary tables both use the tempdb database. Typically, table variables perform faster for small amounts of data. But when the amount of data increases, temporary tables often result in faster queries. One of the reasons for this is they produce statistics that often result in a better query plan, used by subsequent queries.
Consider replacing your IN clause.	Often it's easy to write a query using an IN clause. But when the number of values in the IN clause increases, it seems to degrade the performance of the query. I've seen this happen even when the number of entries in the IN clause increases from two to four entries.
	When this occurs, I'd suggest you cache the results of the IN clause into a temporary table that can be INNER JOINed to the main SQL query.

Table 11.12   Some best practices *(continued)*

Best practice	Description
Make your SQL simpler.	The optimizer typically has a limited amount of time to produce a good query plan. The more SQL statements you have in a batch, the less time it seems to use in determining this optimal plan. I've seen many queries run faster, with a better query plan, because of simplifying the SQL query.
If you have large tables, consider using partitions.	If you have the Enterprise version of SQL Server, you might want to consider using partitions. Here, a table can be divided logically, perhaps by some datetime column. Typically, only the latest data is queried often. If this latest data has its own partition, it can have its own indexes, which can be optimized independent of the rest of the large table. Other advantages include quicker defragmentation, potentially less contention/blocking, and sometimes quicker backups and restores.
If you have large tables, consider using data compression (in 2008 and higher).	If you have the Enterprise version of SQL Server, you might want to consider using data compression. Most database problems seem to relate to I/O problems. With data compression, more data can be stored on a page; this means more data can be obtained for each read. Because reads are typically much more prevalent than writes (even on OLAP systems), data compression typically, on balance, improves database performance.
	Additional benefits include faster backups and restores, together with the associated advantages of space and cost savings.
If all else fails, rewrite your queries.	Sometimes, it seems nearly impossible to improve the performance of some SQL queries. Even following all the generally accepted approaches doesn't seem to give the desired results. When this occurs, it makes sense to rewrite the query. This seems to give the optimizer new paths and opportunities to optimize the query.

Hopefully you'll find these best practices useful in your day-to-day work. Best practices can change as the systems and releases themselves change. Be sure to test any best practices, perhaps using the "Generic performance test harness" script provided in this chapter.

11.14 *Where to start with performance problems*

It can be difficult to know where to start when you're presented with a server, database, or query that you're told isn't performing well. In this section I'll walk you through a few approaches that should take the guesswork out of the investigation and have proven successful for me. Also, remember that all the scripts in this book should provide a great starting point for identifying and providing solutions to your SQL Server problems.

11.14.1 *Starting with a slow server or database*

Sometimes you're informed that a given server or database isn't performing well. Although this isn't much information to go on, you can use it as a starting point to determine why queries are running slowly.

First, you can obtain a list of wait states for the server instance (for details of how to do this, see chapter 6). This will show you, collectively for all the queries run on the server instance since the last reboot or restart, why the SQL queries have been unable to run quickly.

Use the wait states that have high values to determine what to do next. Ideally, you should inspect the performance (PerfMon) counters that relate to the wait states that have high values (for details of how to do this, see chapter 6). This allows you to correlate and corroborate these results.

For example, if the wait states give high values for I/O type waits, you can look at the corresponding I/O PerfMon counters. Having cross-checked the wait states with the PerfMon counters, you can then get a list of the queries that have the most I/O. How these queries are used subsequently is discussed in the next subsection ("Starting with slow queries").

Because results are typically provided for the server instance level, with the name of the database identified as a column in the output, the results can also be used to identify the troublesome database on the server instance. This database will be targeted for further investigation.

Both the wait states and performance counters are cumulative, so it might be advantageous to obtain a DMV snapshot delta over a given time period of typical database activity or for the query under investigation to provide an up-to-date illustration of any problems. You could use the results of this snapshot delta to determine what you should drill down into to further investigate the problem (see chapter 2 for details of how to calculate a DMV snapshot delta).

As you can see from this example, the output of the wait states drives the path you use to drill down further into the queries. Having discussed how to identify the high-level cause of poor performance at the server instance or database level, we'll now drill down into the specific queries.

11.14.2 Starting with slow queries

When you're told a query or batch is performing slowly, or you've identified the poorly performing queries as a result of wait states analysis, you should determine, at as low a level as is feasible, how the query performs its work. This typically means inspecting its cached plan for details of what it's doing. For example, is the query using a lot of I/O because it's performing table or index scans as opposed to seeks and lookups? Or maybe indexes are missing?

Because the cached plan may not show a true picture of why a query is performing slowly (because when the plan is created it doesn't know about the impact of other concurrent queries), it makes sense to profile the query using the DMV trace utility described earlier in this chapter. This will allow you to focus on the part of the query or batch that's having the most impact on poor performance.

Most of this book is concerned with how you can identify queries that are, for various reasons, running suboptimally. This book also contains details on how to improve the query performance.

Ideally, the query under investigation should form part of the various DMV snapshot deltas, allowing you to determine the effect of this query on the various DMVs and how it interacts with other running queries. Most of the scripts in this book can be used to produce these DMV snapshot deltas; indeed, several examples have been provided. Inspecting the output, in the context of the scripts provided in this book, should help you decide what path to follow next to improve the query's performance.

The example given here has been for queries that have high I/O values, which was reflected in the high values for I/O in the wait states script. You could use the wait states script similarly as the starting point for other troublesome queries that result in a poorly performing server or database.

11.15 *Summary*

This chapter has been a mixed bag of scripts. Hopefully it has shown you what's possible with the scope and depth of DMV data that's available.

We investigated how to see what everyone's last-run query was, which could prove useful in resolving conflicts. A generic performance test harness was provided. This should be useful in quickly determining if a proposed performance improvement is actually useful.

For administrators, I provided a useful little script for estimating when backups or restores should finish. In addition, there's a script to determine the amount of memory and the number of CPUs on a given SQL Server.

To help with debugging, I provided a script that shows where the time is spent within a batch of SQL queries. This was contrasted with what is provided by the query plan. The simple and lightweight trace utility should prove useful in helping to quickly and easily identify performance problems and program flow.

Congratulations, you've reached the end of the book! I hope you agree that the scripts included in this book allow you to identify problem areas quickly, easily, and cheaply, and that you've found many possible solutions to these problems.

index

RELATED MANNING TITLES

SQL Server MVP Deep Dives
Contributions from 53 SQL Server MVPs

Edited by Paul Nielsen, Kalen Delaney,
   Greg Low, Adam Machanic, Paul S. Ran-
   dal, and Kimberly L. Tripp

   ISBN: 978-1-935182-04-7
   848 pages
   $59.99
   November 2009

*SQL Server 2008 Administration
in Action*
by Rod Colledge

   ISBN: 978-1-933988-72-6
   464 pages, $44.99
   August 2009

For ordering information go to www.manning.com